COSMOS, SELF, AND HISTORY IN BANIWA RELIGION

T0369700

COSMOS, SELF, AND HISTORY IN BANIWA RELIGION
For Those Unborn

Robin M. Wright

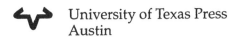

University of Texas Press
Austin

First edition, 1998

Requests for permission to reproduce material from this work
should be sent to Permissions, University of Texas Press, Box 7819,
Austin, TX 78713-7819.

♾The paper used in this publication meets the minimum
requirements of American National Standard for Information
Sciences—Permanence of Paper for Printed Library Materials,
ANSI Z39.48-1984.

Library of Congress Cataloging-in-Publication Data

Wright, Robin.
    Cosmos, self, and history in Baniwa religion : for those unborn /
    Robin M. Wright. — 1st ed.
        p.   cm.
    Includes bibliographical references and index.
    ISBN: 978-0-292-72379-5
    1. Baniwa Indians—Religion.   2. Baniwa philosophy.   3. Baniwa
Indians—Social life and customs.   4. Shamanism—Amazon River
Valley.   5. Nativistic movements—Amazon River Valley.
6. Christianity and culture—Amazon River Valley.   7. Amazon River
Valley—Social life and customs.   I. Title
F2520.1.B35W75   1998
299'.8839—dc21   97-45307

For My Family and Children

Contents

Illustrations

Preface

Walimanai ihriu, in Baniwa, an indigenous language of the Northwest Amazon, means "for those unborn" or "for our others who will be born." It is a phrase frequently spoken at the end of myth narratives when primordial beings, having created or established conditions, institutions, or practices, give them to humanity for all future times saying "thus it will be for our others who will be born." The phrase most clearly expresses the temporal continuity between these primordial beings, the first people and ancestors of humanity, and their descendants. These first people lived and made things in such and such a way for all those who would come after them.

The ways of the ancestors are known by all those who have passed through initiation, this being the principal event when the hiatus that normally separates the primordial world from humanity of the present is overcome. In curing rites, shamans must likewise traverse the barrier between these two worlds and undertake a cure in the Other World first before performing a cure on people in This World. The primordial shamans, again, legitimate the power of the shamans to do the same "for our others" of This World.

What was made in primordial times—death, initiation, birth, the alternation of day and night, and so on—was done for all times, or as narrators say, "until another end of the world." Indeed, the very possibility of "another end of the world" was also made in the beginning; it is, as it were, foretold from old. Cosmic history, as remembered in the myths, tells of various catastrophic destructions and regenerations of the world. Given the links between the primordial world and the present world, such a vision has far-reaching implications for Baniwa understanding and interpretations of human history and the construction of identity in history. The first objective of this book is to explore this, what I shall call "millenarian consciousness," through extended interpretations of cosmology, shamanism, eschatology, and their relations to social action and history.

Now, my use of the term *millenarian consciousness* requires some definition at the outset in order to distinguish it from messianism and prophetism. In the Judeo-Christian tradition, messianism refers to the belief in a messiah who is the anointed one of God and who will come in some future time at the beginning of the Messianic Age; millenarianism, to the belief in a future one-thousand-year period of Christ's rule on earth; and prophetism, to the belief that God communicates to certain chosen individuals through prophetic inspiration (Hinnells 1984). When used to refer to native South American religious experience, these terms have been given a wide range of meanings. In the case of the Baniwa, prophetism is a feature of their culture and has been common in their history. Messianism and messianic movements have been recorded among the Baniwa from the latter half of the nineteenth century to the beginning of the twentieth (see my doctoral dissertation, 1981b, and other published articles in the bibliography). Millenarianism, strictly speaking, should be restricted to certain movements of the mid-nineteenth century and to the conversion movement to Protestant evangelicalism in the 1950s. Millenarian consciousness, in the sense I will be using throughout this book, is implicit in the phrase "for those unborn," for the first ancestors gave their ways for all times, or "until another end of the world."

In the late 1940s to early 1950s, the Indians of various tributaries of the upper Rio Negro and Orinoco—border of Brazil, Venezuela, and Colombia—engaged in conversion movements of pantribal proportions that changed dramatically their ways of living. The peoples involved included the Curripaco, Baniwa, Cubeo, Guayabero, Piapoco, Guahibo, Cuiva, and Saliva—many of them Arawak-speaking peoples interconnected through ancient traditions of trade, warfare, and alliance. In large part, this movement was produced by an extraordinary individual, Sophie Muller, a native of New York, who came to the region with the Worldwide Evangelization Crusade. What occurred was a sort of "chain reaction" of conversions in which she and the new converts took the message of the Gospel to "unreached tribes" and convinced them essentially to abandon the ways of their ancestors and transform their lives into "believers," or *crentes*.

Why and how did so many people—reportedly thousands of converts scattered across the plains and jungles of southeastern Colombia and northwestern Brazil—suddenly decide to cast their lot essentially with a stranger, a white woman who simply ordered them to stop doing what had been familiar to them for generations, centuries? Certainly, whatever answer we might give would have to take into account the sociocultural situation of each of the peoples involved. They all shared a common historical situation defined by the exploitation of their labor by rubber merchants and the violence of interethnic relations on the frontier. No doubt, each of these peoples understood in a different manner the evangelical message that Sophie Muller taught, according to their specific historical and sociocultural configurations. A second main objective of this book is to explore this question in relation to the Baniwa of the Içana and its tributaries.

All ethnographers of the Baniwa since the 1950s have noted that their conversion to evangelicalism was consistent with their long tradition of millenarian and messianic movements (E. Galvão 1959; de Oliveira 1979; Wright 1981a, 1981b; Journet 1995). The movements on record, however, were all led by powerful shamans who sought to forge new religious identities grounded in mythology and ritual and the selective use of Christian symbols. Sophie Muller's adventism in contrast negated the central icons of Baniwa religion.

In the early 1950s, Eduardo Galvão, one of the most perceptive observers of the Baniwa's culture, suggested as an explanation for their conversion to Protestantism that it was

> less due to the exceptional activities of missionaries than to the righteous sense of the evangelical texts which, translated and transmitted in the native language or "geral," insist on the salvation of the weak and oppressed with which the Baniwa, traumatized by their experiences with patrons, identify. Another favorable factor is the greater emotional satisfaction derived from active participation in the rituals, the simplicity of which allows the Indians themselves to direct them. (1959, 55)[1]

While there may be some truth to this, it should be remembered that the missionaries themselves taught that what oppressed the Baniwa was their own culture, for which reason they and the new converts waged campaigns against tobacco, manioc beer, shamanism, and the sacred flutes used in initiation rituals. How the Indians understood "salvation" is also a question to be explored and not assumed. Thus, this book seeks to focus on the larger question of conversion to Christianity, its relation to indigenous religions, and especially those that have strong millenarian traditions. What is the relation between millenarian consciousness, its potential for generating religious movements, and mass conversion to evangelical Christianity?

This study begins by introducing the reader to some of the key theoretical questions and issues raised by anthropological studies of millenarian, messianic, and prophetic movements in Amazonia—questions and issues that have engaged my attention over the past twenty years, ever since I began research in the Northwest Amazon, and with which I have sought to dialogue in my publications on the Baniwa movements since then. In the introduction, I clarify my particular approach and, I hope, contribution to the study of these movements, which is grounded in ethnohistory, the history of religions, and anthropological approaches to the study of narrative forms.

Next, I introduce the reader to the Baniwa in Brazil, about whom no book-length monograph has been published until now, although there are a large number of articles on diverse topics of anthropological and historical interest. Then, I present to the reader, through my own eyes, the Baniwa of the Aiary River, and the situation that I experienced in the late 1970s, the circumstances of my research, how my research was received by them, and the questions and dilemmas I faced in the field.

Although the bulk of the research on which this book is based was conducted in the late 1970s, I have maintained contact directly or indirectly with the Baniwa over the past twenty years. In 1997, I initiated a project, in collaboration with the Association of Indigenous Communities of the Aiary River (ACIRA) and the Instituto Socioambiental in São Paulo, to publish collections of Baniwa myths and curing chants. In July of the same year, I had the opportunity to visit the Baniwa and go over the conclusions of the present monograph.

This book is divided into four parts comprising two chapters each. Part I presents various views of cosmogony and cosmology, and their relations to shamanism. Cosmogony, I shall show, presents the terms through which millenarian consciousness is formulated, especially as a series of struggles between what I shall call catastrophic and utopic visions of primordial time. Creation is represented as the transcendence of utopic visions of the cosmos over the catastrophic, the transcendence of creative knowledge over destructive demiurges. Shamanic knowledge and power are the living representations of creative transcendence in a cosmos flawed by the vestiges of primordial evil and misfortune. Shamans are thus the guardians of the cosmos whose salvific powers ensure its continued growth and well-being against the imminence of cosmic collapse.

Primordial time, mythic time, and human history are connected through the powerful, all-encompassing figure of Kuwai, the child of the Sun-creator and transformer, Iaperikuli, who teaches humanity the institution of initiation—how humanity is to reproduce the order created in the beginning and for all times. This knowledge of Kuwai creates the world order not as an eternally repeated cycle but as a constantly expanding and globalizing socialization of otherness within its domain. Part II thus focuses on the complementarity of mythic and historic consciousness in the creation of self and otherness. Consistent with the catastrophic and utopic visions that characterize millenarian consciousness, Kuwai is presented in many narratives as a "White Man"—owner of a powerful, external knowledge which is, in the course of the myth, internalized into processes of social reproduction, while the destructive aspects of his being are put at a distance. Both mythic and historic narratives go beyond explanations, however, in the sense that they may provide the terms for political strategies which have characterized millenarian and messianic movements.

At the event of death, catastrophe erupts into the ideal order which the Baniwa seek to create and sustain; for the actions of sorcerers and witches and the existence of poison in This World threaten the ideal, vertical dimension of creation with total collapse. The primordials, by their impulsiveness, prevented their own immortality and left humans with death by poison. Part III explores various modes of death in Baniwa culture—irreversible death by poison or sorcery, and reversible soul-loss and recovery—presented in myths and orations, and notions of temporality contained in these discursive forms.

Finally, Part IV outlines the recent history, from the turn of the century to the 1970s, of the Baniwa, as a way into understanding their mass conversion to evangelical Protestantism—a conversion that, at least in its initial moments in the 1950s, was in all respects millenarian. History, through written sources and oral testimony, reveals that Baniwa life trajectories were characterized by periods of dispersion and concentration—the former largely having to do with labor migration and flight from persecution by merchants and military; the latter, with a historic and millenarian tradition of return to the homeland, considered a *sanctuary* against external threats. Precisely in the periods of return and concentration, prophetic figures have arisen who affirm, through their messages, the transcendence of the creative sources of life over external destruction. In this context, we may understand the dynamics of the conversion movement to Christianity.

In each of the parts, I develop the arguments through the use of several forms of narrative discourse and non-narrative activities. One of the methodological principles that guided the construction of each part is that no one form of narrative discourse should be understood as more privileged than another; it is not by starting with myth that we will understand history. Rather, I try to show how similar themes are worked and reworked across various forms of narrative discourse: cosmogonic myth, shamans' songs, initiation chants, oral histories of contact, formulas and orations, and life histories. In each instance, I examine the speech form in its internal aspects (i.e., ethnopoetics) and external aspects (its social function as belief, knowledge, or truth).

Parts II, III, and IV extend the interpretations to their translations into historical patterns of action. I shall show that historical processes approximate patterns of action found in narrative and non-narrative speech activity. Had I started my interpretation with a historical reconstruction of social processes, in short, I would have eventually been led to narrative forms of discourse.

History reconstructed from the written sources is thus an indispensable complement to my interpretation of narrative forms—among other reasons, because it provides one of the *contexts* through which we may understand powerful mythic images and their significance for, for example, catastrophic visions of cosmic history; for another reason, because it clarifies discourses produced by actors deeply involved in conversion movements. Both together demonstrate more clearly exactly what sort of utopian vision actors sought to realize and the problems they confronted.

Acknowledgments

The research on which a greater part of this book is based was under-taken in the late 1970s for my doctoral dissertation (1981b) and was funded by the National Science Foundation. After the thesis was ap-proved, I initiated my work as an anthropologist through positions in several non-governmental organizations in the United States (the An-thropology Resource Center, Cultural Survival) and Brazil (Comissão pela Criação do Parque Yanomami, Centro Ecumênico de Documen-tação e Informação, or CEDI). In 1985, at the invitation of Dr. Manuela Carneiro da Cunha, professor of anthropology at the Universidade de São Paulo, I returned to Brazil on a Fulbright Visiting Scholar Fellow-ship to teach for one semester in the Department of Anthropology at the Universidade Estadual de Campinas (UNICAMP).

As it turned out, the department asked me to continue on as visiting professor and, simultaneously, Carlos Alberto Ricardo, coordinator of the "Indigenous People in Brazil" Program of the CEDI in São Paulo, invited me to coordinate the production of a volume of its Levanta-mento (Survey) series, on the indigenous peoples of the Northwest Amazon. Both jobs led me down long trails which, in multiple ways, were instrumental to the writing of this book.

In the second semester of 1985, the Fulbright-Hayes Commission gave me a small field research grant through which I was able to re-turn briefly to the Northwest Amazon, after nearly a decade since my doctoral research, to observe and document the "situation" which was then in turmoil caused by invasions of indigenous territories by gold panners and mining companies.

A small research grant from the Wenner-Gren Foundation for An-thropological Research and a fellowship from the Latin America and the Caribbean Program of the Social Science Research Council in 1987–1988 enabled me to organize and produce a book-length manu-script on the "Ethnohistory of the Northwest Amazon." Various parts of this study were incorporated into the present book. In 1990, as a researcher affiliated with the Núcleo de História Indígena e do Indigenismo in São Paulo, one of the first research centers in Brazil to focus on indigenous history, I continued historical research in the public archives of Manaus, with the support of the Fundação de Amparo à Pesquisa do Estado de São Paulo (FAPESP). This research brought to light important documents concerning mid-nineteenth-century messianic movements in the Northwest Amazon (see Wright 1992c).

One of the critical questions that has guided my research from the time of my initial fieldwork is the relation of Protestant and Catholic missions to the Baniwa and their religious institutions and beliefs. As I shall describe in the pages of this book, Baniwa conversion to evangelical Protestantism represented certainly one of the great transformations of their culture of the last half-century. Today, the majority of the Baniwa population in Brazil, Colombia, and Venezuela are "believers"; yet, like various other native churches in lowland South America (e.g., the Hallelujah among Carib-speaking peoples of the Brazil-Guyana border), Baniwa evangelicalism has been shaped to its present-day form by native pastors and community rituals.

In 1993–1994, the Research Enablement Program, a grant program for mission scholarship supported by the Pew Charitable Trusts (Philadelphia, Pa.) and administered by the Overseas Ministries Study Center (OMSC, New Haven, Conn.), awarded me a postdoctoral fellowship to study the relations among indigenous religions and forms of Christianity, on a comparative basis, in various regions of Brazil. Besides enabling my organizing and editing of a major collection of articles by Brazilian ethnologists on the question, the fellowship supported a period of research and writing which produced Part IV of this book. In the course of this research, Dr. Adélia de Oliveira, head of the Department of Anthropology of the Museu Goeldi in Belém do Pará, kindly allowed me to consult the collection of Eduardo Galvão's fieldnotes in the museum's library. The staff of the archives of the First Brazilian Border Commission, also in Belém, were enormously helpful in locating material relevant to the recent history of the Northwest Amazon.

Numerous individuals have been supportive of my work over the years, generously offering encouragement, comments, and criticism that have been essential to the development of ideas and approaches contained in each chapter. Jonathan Hill, my friend and colleague for more than a decade, and coauthor in two publications, has shared with me the intellectual challenges of understanding and interpreting Baniwa and Wakuenai culture and history. His perspective on the same people from a different side of the river has enriched my understanding immensely. In the same way, I thank Nicolas Journet, whose

anthropological research among the Curripaco of Colombia complemented in all respects the research undertaken by Hill and myself in
Venezuela and Brazil, respectively. Márcio Meira, my student and
friend, has shared with me the difficulties of doing anthropological
field research in the Northwest Amazon of Brazil. He has been my
teacher as much as I his, and I like to think that, through his commit-
ment to the current political movement of indigenous peoples in the
region and his work as director of the Public Archives in Belém do
Pará, he is able to continue the work that I am unable to do because of
other commitments. In a similar way, Geraldo Andrello of the Instituto Socioambiental (ISA, formerly CEDI) in São Paulo has recently
taken a major interest in undertaking field research with the Baniwa
of the Içana, particularly on ecology, and through his contacts with
indigenous political associations in the area, I have found not only a
channel for keeping up with recent events but also a source of information on questions to which I had no access at the time of my fieldwork. Together, and in collaboration with the Baniwa, we are now organizing a book of Baniwa myths. I am grateful to Carlos Alberto
Ricardo, director of the ISA, for his support and interest in my work
over the years.

Even before my first fieldwork experience, Dr. Terence Turner of the
University of Chicago was very helpful and encouraging, particularly
in relation to analyzing the mythology of the Northwest Amazon. In
a different way, Dr. Lawrence Sullivan, director of the Center for the
Study of World Religions, Harvard University, has been one of those
mentors whose influence, particularly through his published works, I
have felt profoundly in my thinking about Baniwa religion. Whether
or not I follow the hermeneutical approach to meaning in South
American religions developed in *Icanchu's Drum*, I have benefited
greatly from his insights and perceptions, often brilliant, on Baniwa
religion. I am deeply grateful for his support, in many ways, which
helped see this book to completion.

During the past eight years, many of the topics and issues contained
in this book were developed in publications and papers. Many people
gave their comments and criticisms. Bruce Albert and Alcida Ramos
were quite helpful in revising the first version of sections of Part II
which, in greatly different form, are included in their edited volume
Pacificando o Branco (Pacifying the white man [in press]). Lawrence
Sullivan and the editors of *History of Religions* (University of Chicago)
were instrumental in publishing a considerable portion of Part I—
again, in very different form—as a two-part study in that journal. A
slightly revised and translated version of the same material was published in *Xamanismo no Brasil* (Shamanism in Brazil, 1996), edited by

E. Jean Langdon. I am grateful to Jean for her friendship, constant encouragement, suggestions, and criticisms. I am also grateful to the Examining Board for my promotion to the position of Livre Docente, consisting of Professors Carlos Rodrigues Brandão, Alcida Ramos, Guilherme Rubin, Julio César Melatti, and E. Jean Langdon, for their enormously valuable comments on the Portuguese version of this manuscript. I have incorporated their suggestions for revisions into the present text. Finally, I am grateful to Theresa May and the anonymous reviewers and editors of the University of Texas Press for their comments and suggestions for revision, which I have likewise incorporated into the final version.

Other people who have helped shape this book through their perspectives include Gerald Taylor, Pierre-Yves Jacopin, Jean Jackson, Aparecida Vilaça, Stephen Hugh-Jones, and Alícia Barabas. Wanda Caldeira Brant and Beatriz Perrone-Moisés translated various parts of the manuscript into Portuguese.

This book owes its existence to the Baniwa of the Aiary River, where I conducted the bulk of my field research. The shamans, chanters, and elders who took me under their wing and taught me a little of what they knew are the raison d'être of this book: Keruaminali, José Felipe, Mandu, Laureano, Keramunhe, Luis Manuel, Marcos, Inocêncio, and so many others. Much has changed since I did extended fieldwork on the Aiary River in the late 1970s, yet external change has been a constant aspect of the Indians' lives for many generations. It is testimony to their courage that the Baniwa have never failed to affirm what is most essential to their continuity as a people.

COSMOS, SELF, AND HISTORY IN BANIWA RELIGION

Introduction

Here I seek to present my approaches to the subject of this book: my dialogue over the past fifteen years or so with various theoretical approaches to millenarian, messianic, and prophetic movements among native peoples of lowland South America; and the circumstances of my fieldwork among the Baniwa of the Northwest Amazon.

Anthropological Literature on Religious Movements among Indigenous Peoples of the Amazon

The ethnological literature on prophetic, millenarian, and messianic movements among indigenous peoples of Amazonia is quite extensive. It is also not a new theme in Latin American ethnology and continues to arouse interest. The two collections recently organized by Alícia Barabas (1989, 1994) on socioreligious movements in Latin America amply demonstrate that the theme continues to be quite present in anthropology and rightfully so: from the highlands of Chiapas, Mexico, to the rain forests of the upper Amazon, indigenous peoples affirm utopian ideals—whether in resistance movements or in mass conversion to Christianity—that seek radical changes in their historical situations.

The challenge to ethnology presented by such phenomena lies in the search for an adequate approach to understanding them, not only in their sociohistoric or politico-economic aspects, nor through analyses of their relations to myth and ritual, but also in relation to their "spiritualities"—that is, as specifically religious phenomena. The anthropological literature is replete with functionalist, structuralist, and Marxist analyses that focus on "explanations" of the "external causes," "logical structures," or even "struggles for power" of these movements. With rare exceptions, however, these studies leave aside the question of the meaning of the end of time and the regeneration of a new order as distinctly religious experiences.

To define better the approach that I shall take in this monograph, it is appropriate here to review some of the principal anthropological lines with which I have worked and dialogued, or which have exercised an influence on my reflections on messianism, prophetism, and millenarianism in Amazonia. In this discussion, I do not seek merely to recite a litany of authors and ideas but to reconstruct a theoretical dialogue undertaken over the last fifteen years, since my doctoral thesis, through which I have attempted to approximate my ethnography to the spirituality of Baniwa millenarianism.

In his article on messianism in South America, Egon Schaden (1976) characterizes the mid-nineteenth-century movements in the Northwest Amazon as a "revolt against oppression" (1086) and suggests that they were based in traditional mythology, although he laments the lack of more detailed information that could clarify the links between mythology and the messianic movements. In my doctoral thesis and in various later publications (1983, 1987–1989), I agreed with his evaluation of the movements as forms of "resistance against oppression," and my analysis of Baniwa mythology pointed to various themes related to messianic ideology.

The dialogue between French anthropology—especially structuralist—and scholars of indigenous lowland South American societies produced in the 1970s and 1980s several fundamental works in the study of messianism. Probably the first was the article by Manuela Carneiro da Cunha, "Logique du mythe et de l'action" (1973), in which she defends a structural approach to the symbolism of prophetic movements among the Canela Indians of Maranhão in the 1960s, systematically analyzing the relations among myth, ritual, and historical events. According to her analysis, the movements referred dialectically to the Canela myth of the origin of the White Man. The Canela evaluated their historical situation in terms of the explanations provided in the myth with the expectation that those meanings would prevail, that the new order instituted by the movement would conform to the structure of the creation myths, and that the future would be a development on their sacred history of creation.

Another important advance was made in the complementary studies by Hélène Clastres (1978) and Pierre Clastres (1987) on the Guarani, in which the authors defend the argument that the prophetic movements of the Tupi-Guarani—the so-called "search for the Land without Evil"—represented a radical negation of the principles of society in its normal state. The movements had, as their basis, the rejection of a possible state formation among the Tupi-Guarani and the affirmation of a utopia that only the prophets, divinely inspired and leading mass migrations, were capable of attaining.

The studies by the Clastres stimulated a series of ethnological and historical reflections on Tupi-Guarani prophetism and the possible existence of long-term political and religious cycles in indigenous history. Central categories, having to do with hierarchy and equality, are, they suggested, involved in the long-term dynamics of which messianic, millenarian, and prophetic movements are special instances.

It is not necessary to repeat here the criticisms raised against the Clastres' hypotheses by various specialists in Guarani ethnology and history (see especially, Meliá 1986). The brilliant study by Viveiros de Castro and Carneiro da Cunha (1985) explicitly argued against the Clastres' central hypotheses. According to these authors, the prophetic discourse of the Tupinamba was "fundamentalist," giving exclusive attention "to that which is fundamental to society—vengeance and warfare."

> What is transmitted from one generation to the next by the Tupinamba? What is inherited is a promise, a virtual place, that is filled by the death of the enemy. . . . It is the construction of an identity that is made in time, produced by time, and that does not refer to the beginning of time but to its end. There is an immortality promised by cannibalism. (201)

The authors suggest a contrast with the vision of the Gê-speaking peoples (such as the Krahó, for which see J. C. Melatti 1972 and Carneiro da Cunha 1978) where "everything refers to place, and this unchangeable place exorcizes time, in which relations with enemies are something that demand a conclusion." While the Gê utopia is marked by "spatial repetition" (e.g., in tightly structured village plans), according to the authors, the vision elaborated by Indians of the Northwest Amazon (Tukanoan, principally) is marked by "temporal repetition" (i.e., the negation of the "temporal hiatus" separating the present from the mythic beginning). Cosmology and ritual provide evidence of a "struggle against entropy"

> in the formation of an identity forever put at risk, with a past to be recovered. . . . Yo-yo societies . . . never let go of their beginnings. . . . In these societies, the sense of memory is much closer to the Greek *aletheia*: memory is return, retrospection, reproduction. (Ibid.)

I will have various opportunities to comment on these observations. I only wish to observe here that, while the dimensions of space and time are fundamental to cosmology, ritual, and up to a certain point, religious movements, the politico-spiritual projects of the messianic leaders went beyond a simple "temporal retrospection" or "return of the same." An inevitable risk in any mytho-praxis is that it opens itself to transformation on the way to the new order. Memory, moreover, is not mere "retrospection," for it provides the basis for political strategies in specific historical situations.

In an article that I coauthored with Jonathan Hill (Wright and Hill 1986), we sought to demonstrate that the messiahs and prophets of the mid-nineteenth-century Northwest Amazon utilized mythic concepts, ritual practices, and shamanism in their struggles against political and economic oppression. The millenarianism of the most important leader, Venancio Kamiko, a Baniwa Indian, analogically linked selected Christian symbols with basic metaphors of indigenous religion: the Christian cross with whips used in initiation rites, as symbols of ritual suffering; ceremonies of exchange, with Saint John's Day (the day prophesied by Kamiko of a world conflagration) as symbols of purification by fire; Christ, with powerful figures of Baniwa mythology and shamanism, as symbols of salvation and immortality. Mythology and shamanism clarify the selection of Christian symbols in Kamiko's movement and in narratives about the messiah.

The movements, we argued, were not merely a reenactment of mythic realities, but a historically situated praxis in which key symbols were used strategically to resist the external imposition of non-indigenous political and economic systems. The linking of powerful shamans to mythical heroes illustrates a creative process in the mediation of social and historical transitions of the mid-nineteenth century and early twentieth, through the direct incorporation of these transitions in symbolic forms in narratives about the messiah. In these narratives, Kamiko incorporates Christian elements but rejects political, economic, and social relations with the whites and thus reestablishes the spiritual integrity and political autonomy of the Baniwa.

The critical question around which the movements focused was the type of transformation the Baniwa would undergo: either be dominated by the whites, or take control of their destiny, transforming the historic moment and thereby regaining their autonomy. Narratives about Kamiko pose this problem as a choice: either remain united in opposition to the whites or be assimilated, which would mean cultural death. The specific cultural forms in which this choice is framed are derived from mythology, the rites of initiation, and shamanism. Mythology has as its central concern the mediation of processes external and internal to society. In Kamiko's movement, these same processes are the principal means through which his millenarian ideology mediated between an external order of domination and the disorganizing effects of that order on internal social processes. Hence, we concluded,

Figure 1. Statues of Venancio Kamiko, Baniwa Prophet and Messiah of the
Mid-Nineteenth Century
(lithograph courtesy of National Museum Archives, Rio de Janeiro)

Venancio Kamiko sought to redirect social, political, and economic relations between the Baniwa and the whites, a reorientation in which "the refusal to cooperate with the whites was elevated to a sacred postulate."

In an article published in *Ethnohistory* in 1991, Michael Brown criticized our interpretation of millenarian movements as expressions of resistance to colonial/neocolonial domination, and identified aspects of what he terms "utopian renewal" that reflect long-term, internal political processes and contradictions independent of, and "predating," the "encounters" of native peoples and Europeans. Such processes are dialectical, having to do with the ways in which native peoples define themselves in relation to other societies, indigenous or nonindigenous.

Among the more important of these processes, Brown, citing the arguments of the Clastres, refers to the existence of a "tension between hierarchical and egalitarian tendencies in Amazonian societies." These tendencies may "play themselves out in *longue durée* cycles of political consolidation, punctuated by self-limiting episodes of millenarian and messianic enthusiasm." Brown attributes special importance to the "outsider" status of the prophet and to the "paradoxical manner in which the prophet uses the rhetoric of egalitarianism to establish a hierarchy, greater than what otherwise existed." "Episodes" of "utopian renewal" are not so much events as instances of cyclic processes internal to Amazonian societies.

From his survey of various Amazonian movements, Brown summarizes the most important of their features. First, they may be seen as native responses to the ideological challenge of Christianity. The cases Brown surveys show how "native peoples have struggled to gain control over Christianity while reformulating it to satisfy their spiritual needs." This struggle he attributes to an "ancient tendency" to acquire, share, or exchange ritual knowledge which at once recognizes the power of its authors and the limitations of native models of explanation and ritual action. The outsider status of leaders or messianic prophets enabled them to overcome the political limitations of social units and achieve a higher level of social integration.

Second, the movements focus on the direction of interethnic relations, especially in the sense of conceptualizing the future place of the non-Indian in the postmillennial world. The ideologies of Amazonian movements have less to do with a concern for acquiring the whites' goods, merchandise, or material wealth—as in cargo cults—than with the more fundamental question of how to end the exploitative relations that "force the Indians to work so hard to gain so little of the goods that the whites have in abundance."

Third, the movements generally include programs for the hierarchical reorganization of the societies in question. According to Brown, they represent "flirtations" with chiefly politics; thus, there often occurs an intensification of organizing principles in hierarchical terms.

Brown's criticism of the notion of "resistance" provides a useful counterbalance to the liberal sentiments implied in Western understandings of this term, yet his hypotheses suffer from a series of imprecisions that survey studies of complex phenomena usually risk. In the first place, I question his reading of history in several of the cases to which he refers. For example, in referring to the movements instigated by the Baniwa prophet Kamiko in the mid-nineteenth century, Brown claims that Kamiko's power "waned by late 1858" and that his movement "seemed to have passed into relative obscurity" (1991, 395). To the contrary, I have shown (1987–1989, 1992c) that Kamiko's influence spanned a period of nearly forty years, during which time he instituted a new form of belief, called the "song of the cross" among Arawak- and Tukanoan-speaking peoples, and that, years after his death, Baniwa communities continued to follow his message of autonomy from the whites.

Second, Brown's argument of *longue durée* cycles—inverting the hypotheses of the Clastres—while suggestive, glosses over spatial and temporal dimensions of different utopian visions. By interpreting millenarian "enthusiasm" as "self-limiting experiments," Brown in effect collapses the spiritualities of such movements into a hypothetical "flirtation" with chiefly politics.

Third, while it is true that various movements "struggled to gain control over Christianity," it is also true that others represented outright and bitter rejections of Christian theology even where leaders took on Biblical names, or the name of Christ. I shall return to these points in the conclusion of this book.

In a series of articles published in 1992, I examined from various points of view the millenarian movements and ideologies in the history of Arawakan and Tukanoan societies of the Northwest Amazon. In one of these studies, I show how the movements among the Tukanoans of the Uaupés River differed in fundamental respects from Arawakan peoples (the Baniwa and Warekena). While all movements were concerned with inequalities of power in interethnic relations, the Baniwa messiah Kamiko oriented his followers to reject the external politico-economic system as a necessary step to attaining salvation. Tukanoan messiahs, by contrast, actively sought to usurp the power of the whites. Kamiko's influence remained strong for several generations; Tukanoan messiahs, however, suffered problems from the beginning, especially doubts among followers and internal dissension (1992c).

These differences, I suggest, are related, on the one hand to pre-existing cultural patterns—the dynamics of power for shamans and political leaders, eschatologies—and on the other, to the historical experiences of contact—the ambiguities of antagonism and alliance, autonomy and interdependence that have characterized the relations between Tukanoan communities and agents of contact. Such differences also influenced the ways in which Christian symbols were incorporated into the ideologies of the movements.

The argument of preexisting cultural patterns derives in part from a paper by Stephen Hugh-Jones (1989), who defines two types of shamans characteristic of Northwest Amazon societies: "vertical" and "horizontal" based on a systematic differentiation of their powers, attributes, social status, and training. Hugh-Jones suggests that the relations between the two specialists "contain the potential for rivalry and tension" which becomes evident when the "horizontal" shamans "begin to assume more prominent leadership roles." Contact with the whites, the author suggests, "exacerbated" this tension, which would explain the internal dissension characteristic of the Tukanoan movements. "Vertical" shamans have more often been associated with prophetic roles; "horizontal" shamans, with the more recent and "democratic," evangelical pastors. In my view, messianic movements among Arawakan societies were not as plagued by internal dissension because hierarchies among Arawakan shamans permit the concentration of both categories in single figures, and not their rivalry.

In Part I of this book, I argue that the salvific power of Baniwa shamans—be it in the cure of individuals afflicted by serious ailments or in the protection of This World from destruction—is essential to prophetism. Through their exclusive access to the highest levels of creation, prophets incorporate the virtues of the creator/transformer Iaperikuli, who, in primordial times, saved the world from chaos and destruction. As L. Sullivan points out, in reference to the Baniwa, the power of the prophet

> opens a new creative episode in cosmic history in which the faithful are privileged to play the role of supernatural or immortal beings. The fact that the prophet-hero is still alive among the faithful is a sure sign that they are living a fully mythic reality. (1988, 565)

Several other cases that have received attention in the recent literature, and that illustrate further aspects of native utopian visions, are the Ticuna and Cocama of the upper Solimões and the Taurepang and Kapon of the north of Roraima, border of Brazil and the Guianas.

In his monograph on the Ticuna (1988), de Oliveira Filho justly challenges previous characterizations of Ticuna millenarian movements as "cargo cults." Based on his consideration of the Ticuna's myths of world destruction, of their sense of historic time as a continuous cycle of the fall of humanity from a state of grace and prosperity and its periodic purification or salvation by the culture heroes and immortals, and of the traditional institution of youthful prophets (who bear the title of "those who desire to be enchanted"), de Oliveira Filho convincingly demonstrates that the movements—far from being "acculturative"—had more to do with traditional values and expectations transmitted in religion and myth but conjugated with specific situations of contact and Ticuna interpretations of contact agents.

De Oliveira Filho represents Ticuna conceptions of cosmic history in terms of a "cycle of fall and salvation":

> The Ticuna imagine historic time in terms of a growing distance between mortal humans and the world of marvelous natural resources where necessities can be satisfied without suffering. In continuing this separation, the world of mortals would finally be consumed by imperfection and by divisions produced by individual interests, culminating in a natural cataclysm in which all would perish. This does not happen because from time to time there occurs a new re-enchantment of daily life, the immortals come closer to human beings who seek to hear the message of the just and to prepare themselves for the orders contained therein. It is at these points of inflection in historical time when the process of the fall is reversed, producing the great changes that will permit the continuity and survival of the Ticuna. (1988, 272–273)

Utopia here is temporal, remarkably similar to the "struggle against entropy" (Viveiros de Castro and Carneiro da Cunha 1985) of Northwest Amazon societies, for the process of "re-enchantment of daily life" involves the "temporary overcoming of the hiatus between mortals and immortals" (de Oliveira Filho 1988, 271), which sets the stage for utopian movements (mass mobilization, migrations, centralized authority figures, the establishment of new ways). In de Oliveira Filho's judgment, such an interpretation would account for the series of movements recorded since the late nineteenth century, as well as more recent transformations through Baptist conversions and the Brotherhood of the Holy Cross movement.

In a similar fashion, Oscar Agüero interprets the "millennium among the Tupi-Cocama" (1992), neighbors of the Ticuna, in terms of a "religious ethno-dynamics"—that is, how symbolic representations of sociohistorical experiences in myth, ritual, and historical narrative are used to modify the objective conditions of Cocama relations with Peruvian national society. Based on his outline of the Tupi-Cocama's "traditional" religion, and their history of contact, the author concludes that one of the motives for their strong adherence to the Brotherhood of the Holy Cross movements was the continuity of Cocama millenarian beliefs through which they reformulated Christian millenarianism thereby innovating an effective strategy for modifying the objective conditions of the colonial situation.

In contrast, the approach adopted by Ari Oro (1989) seeks to explain the acceptance of the Brotherhood of the Holy Cross among the Ticuna and regional peasant population in terms of "structural" (economic infrastructure) and "cultural" causes. The movement had as its principal goal:

> to obtain better conditions for social integration—that is, through the Brotherhood of the Holy Cross, both the Ticuna and the Whites struggled to overcome their condition of being "objects" of civilization, subject to the politico-economic interests of the dominant local elites, in order to become subjects of their own integration and masters of their fate, they themselves setting the limits on their integration. (1989, 39)

Oro's monograph provides important information on José da Cruz, the wandering prophet from the interior of Minas Gerais in Brazil who founded the Brotherhood, and the internal organization of his movement. Yet his interpretation glosses over fundamental elements of Ticuna cosmogony and historical consciousness that differentiate them from the regional population. The three aforementioned studies nevertheless complement each other (see also Regan 1993) in providing a broad understanding of the articulations among indigenous religions and the sociohistoric contexts of the movements.

Studies of prophetic movements among Carib-speaking peoples of the Brazil-Guianas border region owe a great deal to the works of Audrey Butt Colson, who provided the first anthropological interpretation of the prophetic Hallelujah religion among the Macuxi and Akawaio Indians. On the basis of her analysis, she concluded that this movement is "at the same time a Christian religion in its physical details and an indigenous conceptual system . . . which began as

an enthusiastic movement and turned into an indigenous church"
([1960] 1967).

Consistent with this perspective, Geraldo Andrello in his master's
thesis (1992) defends the idea that for the Taurepang,

> prophetism presents itself not as a response to an adverse situa-
> tion derived from contact but as a solution to a dilemma internal
> to Taurepang society, that is, the impossibility of locating a "good
> place," an *upatá*, amongst the diverse domains of the terrestrial
> plane. (5)

Taurepang prophetism would have been produced by a "latent ne-
cessity for separation from the condition in which society finds itself."
The central notion of a "good place" is present in native discourse
about the past and in the dynamics of historic migrations by whole
communities along the border, in such a way that, in Andrello's view,
prophetic movements preceded continuous contact and, to a certain
extent, determined its direction.

The hypothesis that Taurepang prophetism of the nineteenth century had little to do with the contact situation seems to me difficult to
sustain, since the first reports of the movements occur during or following intense contact. In a way, a hypothesis that seeks to explain
primarily in terms of internal processes leads the author to diminish
the relevance of history prior to the first manifestations of prophetism
and consequently falls short of a more in-depth analysis of interethnic
relations. The merit of the study lies in its effort to trace the conti-
nuities and transformations in prophetic movements among the Taurepang over time and to anchor their conversion to Seventh-Day Adventism in the symbolism of prophetic traditions.

Complementing Andrello's study, the master's thesis by Stela de
Abreu (1995)—also from UNICAMP—concentrates on the ritual symbolism of Hallelujah among the Ingarikó. Abreu suggests that the
movement from its beginning in the late nineteenth century incorporated important themes of indigenous mythology, cosmology, and
shamanism, such as the quest for immortality, shamanic benches as
symbols of transcendence over death, the ritual efficacy of songs and
foreign words in effecting transformations in the human condition.
She suggests further that native prophetism experienced a "shift" in
history:

> From the postulate of an immediate and terrestrial access to uto-
> pia, it took on a symmetric form of deferred and celestial access.

Thus, the realization of its ideals through prophetic outbursts was followed by the representation of utopia through periodic ceremonies. What prophetism put into practice was transformed into representation: the transcendence of the human condition through a skin change. (1995, 2)

Certainly a study comparing the cosmologies and ritual practices among various Carib-speaking peoples of the northern Amazon region would clarify the relations among prophetism in its various forms, traditional eschatologies, and their relations to Christianity.

The final approach I shall consider derives from the history of religions, a hermeneutical approach to the interpretation of native South American religions developed by Lawrence Sullivan in his brilliant, synthetic work *Icanchu's Drum* (1988). As yet barely absorbed by South American ethnology (in large part due to the lack of a translation to Portuguese or Spanish), this work has implications for the study of South American millenarianism that are, in my view, far-reaching and profoundly important. In fact, the author's consideration of millenarianism is but one aspect of his interpretation of native South American religions, yet it is central, as the very title of the book—referring to a myth of world destruction and renewal—indicates.

The themes of catastrophe and regeneration are found in numerous mythologies throughout the South American continent. According to Sullivan, they refer to one of the most important events in South American mythic history: the cataclysmic destruction of the primordial world which marks the beginning of a new creative epoch (1988, Chapter 2). Countless mythic narratives affirm the existence of other worlds that preexist the present one; each is imperfect and suffers catastrophic destruction by flood, fire, other natural disasters, putrefaction, or petrifaction. From this destruction, there arose a variety of symbols representing "vehicles of salvation" through which new worlds would be created. At the same time that catastrophe dispelled the chaotic, homogeneous, and univocal existence of primordial beings, it produced periodicity, multivalent existence, and systematic relatedness among multiple orders of being. Primordial beings took on hidden, partial, or periodic forms. Ceremonial speech and instrumental music appear, rendering an ontological difference between primordial and mundane being. Human life and the forms of multiple human experience, including existence in historical time, complete the scenario. Yet creation was not a closed account: principles of divine order may occasionally intervene in human history, presenting the possibility that the status quo may be obliterated in favor of a totally new order (1988, Chapters 3, 4).

In this wider context of central religious concerns of native South American cosmogonies, Sullivan interprets the spiritualities of millenarian and messianic movements, or

> the extravagant symbolic threads and tatters that, against overpowering oppression, whipped up eschatological movements and gave people a grip on their own historical meaning, if not on the material forces shaping that history. (550)

Decrying what he sees as the imbalance resulting from too much attention accorded to political readings of reality and to the "many studies written from within the historicist mindset of the modern West carefully scrutinizing the political, economic, and military implications of native uprisings," Sullivan points to the scant attention given to the "spiritualities of the end of time themselves" (ibid.).

In terms of symbolic processes, the eschaton is most significant as it represents

> the culmination of symbolic life . . . it summons forth all the total conditions promised by the partial and symbolic appearances of this world. Most dramatically, the eschaton fulfills the total degeneration implied in partiality itself. The advent of its plethora causes symbolic life to collapse under its own concentrated weight and the appearance of the sacred in every form. (Ibid.)

Sullivan then examines the key symbolisms that define the religious profile of South American eschatologies "in order to frame a genuine understanding of the images of imminent universal destruction; the return of the gods, heroes and the dead; the assembly of believers; the impeachment of worldly powers; and the renewal of native health and power." Identifying a set of features common to millennial movements "that have erupted across the continent since the Conquest" (ibid.), he proceeds to examine a series of cases from the Lowlands and Andes in order to discern the religious forms and patterns common to belief and action.

According to Sullivan, eight themes are commonly found in South American eschatologies (607–614), as I have summarized here:

Ambivalence: That the eschaton, like death, is at once a trying condition, punctuated with dread and fascination, and the source of meaning that leads to the creation of terminologies that construe the social world and revitalize cosmic life.
Imminence: That the experience of imminence causes communities to rethink and reorient their lifestyles toward the end.

Disclosure: That the eschaton arrives when the cosmos reaches its limits at which time openness becomes a general and irreparable condition and mythic realities unseal themselves from their places of closure.

Assembly: That people assemble in ritual spaces, set apart from others in order to make world destruction a total presence once again. Gathering takes other forms as well, such as the collapsing of spatial and temporal differences, the razing of all forms of separateness to create unity.

Critical judgment: That the gathering of the saved presents a crucial difference from chaos, for their symbolic constitution offers criteria for judgment and their acts display the norms for salvation. Images of cataclysm, performed or acted out in ritual, theater, or military exercise, are wellsprings for change.

Cultural relativity: That eschatological crises occur with the merging of two distinct and irreconcilable orders, yet South American eschatologies may "force the West to discover the historical conditioning of every human existence, the plurality of histories, and consequently, the cultural relativity of all visions of reality."

The demise of Western civilization: South American eschatologies are not provincial visions but ecumenical positions. They not only predict their own end but promise the demise of Western dominance as well, and this includes "the end of modern readings of such movements" that ignore their religious foundations. Messiahs and prophets revile the signs of corruption, rejecting symbolic life as it stands, and "denounce the Western view of history in favor of a different evaluation of existence in time." They invoke the end "in order to prove history wrong by calling down the judgment of a renewed experience in time in the form of paradise, apocalypse, or neotraditional utopia."

Heroic destiny: That the new postmillennial world bears the consequences of the primordial age and of cosmic—i.e., historical—epochs. History has not been for naught; "the End transforms the nature of history and preserves, in transfigured forms, its significant achievement of having suffered change. The new mythical geography, which participates eternally in the transitional condition of immortal human beings, is the final age, a ceaseless feast, a world without end."

By his attention to the spiritualities of these movements, Sullivan opens the way for rethinking the material from various cases in Amazonia. As it will become evident in the pages of this book, I have sought to explore the symbolic dimensions of what Sullivan calls the "spirituality of the end of time" and I call "millenarian consciousness" among the Baniwa. One of the central themes, crucial to understanding this consciousness, is the multiple meanings that the Baniwa attribute to what I shall call the "vertical" and "horizontal" dimensions of the cosmos. These meanings become explicit through mythic and other forms of narrative and through ritual action. Each of the chapters of this book explores different aspects of these dimensions, as they relate to shamanism, life-cycle rituals, eschatology, and historical events. As I shall show, the predominant, but not exclusive, meanings that shamans and narrators attribute to the vertical dimension are of creation, resurrection—in short, a "utopic" vision of the cosmos— while they attribute to the horizontal dimension destruction, death— a "catastrophic" vision. I do not wish to suggest by this that these dimensions are opposed; rather, I believe they refer to two indissociable elements of a "spirituality of the end of time" through which millenarian, messianic, and prophetic movements in Baniwa history may be understood. Both visions, I suggest, are essential to understanding movement and dynamics in cosmos and history.

Ethnography of the Baniwa in Brazil

The Arawak-speaking Baniwa live on the frontier borders of Brazil, Venezuela, and Colombia. The majority live on the Brazilian side, a total of approximately forty-one hundred people distributed in ninety-three communities along the Içana River and its tributaries, the Cuiary, Aiary, and Cubate; in several communities of the upper Rio Negro; and on the lower Xié and Uaupés (Vaupés) Rivers (see Map 1—The Northwest Amazon). In Venezuela and Colombia, where they are known as Wakuenai and Curripaco, their population is approximately two thousand living in communities along the Guainía and its tributaries and the upper Içana. The name "Baniwa" also refers to another Arawak-speaking group with a distinct language located on the Guainía but has been applied, since early colonial times, to all Arawak-speakers in the region of Brazil defined above.

Horticulture and fishing are their principal subsistence activities, although a long history of contact has involved them in various forms of production for markets and extractive labor. Their society is organized into approximately a half-dozen exogamous phratries—the Hohodene, Oalipere-dakenai (Siuci, in *língua geral*), and Dzauinai being the principal ones located on the Aiary and mid-Içana Rivers. Each phratry is associated with distinct territories and consists of four or five patri-sibs ranked according to a mythic model of agnatic siblings. Traditional religious life was based largely on the mythology

ESCALA GRÁFICA

30km 0   30   60   90 120km

1986

POVOS INDÍGENAS NO BRASIL
· CEDI ·

NOROESTE AMAZÔNICO

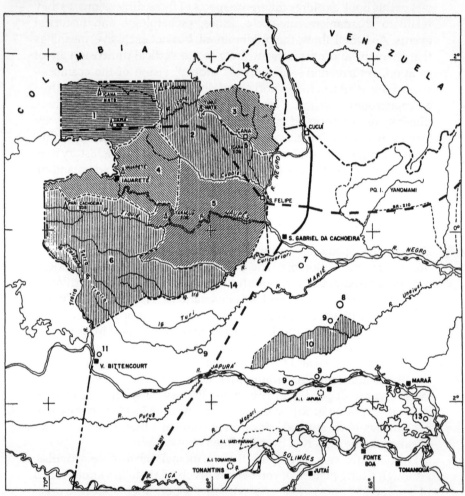

Map 1. The Northwest Amazon
(courtesy Instituto Socioambiental)

and rituals of the first ancestors, represented in the sacred flutes and trumpets called Kuwai; the importance of shamans and chanters; and a variety of complex dance festivals, *pudali*, coordinated with seasonal calendars. In the latter half of the nineteenth century, as I have mentioned above, messianic leaders instituted a new form of religious practice, called the "song of the cross" or the "religion of the cross," the memory of which is still active in several communities of the region. Since the 1950s both Catholic and Protestant missionaries have promoted the conversion of the Baniwa, adding a further dimension of complexity to their religious situation.

Beginning in the 1980s, invasions of their lands by gold panners and mining companies, and the proposed reduction of their lands by military and development projects—specifically the Northern Channel, or Calha Norte, Project—posed very grave threats to Baniwa communities in Brazil; nevertheless, indigenous political mobilization and participation in the pan-Indian Federation of Indigenous Organizations of the Rio Negro (FOIRN), founded in 1987, have guaranteed the defense of their land and resource rights. In 1996, after years of negotiation, the federal government of Brazil decreed the creation of a large and continuous land reserve for the Indians of the upper Rio Negro. In 1997, actual demarcation of the reserve was initiated through the collaborative efforts of the federation and the Instituto Socioambiental of São Paulo.

The Baniwa thus have had a relatively long history of contact with nonindigenous society dating from the first half of the eighteenth century (see Wright 1981b, 1983, 1987–1989). Yet relatively little was known of their society and culture until the beginning of the twentieth century when the German ethnologist Theodor Koch-Grünberg traveled for several months on the Içana and Aiary Rivers, leaving the first reliable ethnography on record. Before then, scientific travelers such as Alexandre Rodrigues Ferreira in the 1780s, Johann Natterer in the 1820s, and Alfred Russel Wallace in the 1850s had left a handful of notes on the Baniwa, as did various clerics and military officials. The extensive documentation that exists on the mid-nineteenth-century messianic movements (see Wright 1981b) left by government officials, military, and missionaries is extremely useful in reconstructing the situation of the time and, to a certain extent, can be read for its ethnographic content; but then, these reports are limited by the interests of the authors in controlling "disturbances" on the border.

Thus, it was Koch-Grünberg's pioneering work, which led him to stay in regions that previously had only been surveyed, that initiated a history of Baniwa ethnography. From then, at intervals of nearly every twenty-five years, ethnographers have stayed on the Içana and its tributaries, producing the records that have become vital for knowing the recent history of the Baniwa: Curt Nimuendaju in 1927 (1950), Eduardo Galvão in 1954 (1959), Adélia de Oliveira in 1971 (1979), and myself in 1976–1977 (1981b). In addition, official commissions, such as the First Brazilian Border Commission, have left valuable census information while scientific travelers and missionaries have added their accounts at various moments in time.

Besides the general ethnographies, specialized studies have included works on linguistics (Koch-Grünberg 1911; Taylor 1991, 1993), rock art (Koch-Grünberg 1907), kinship terminology (de Oliveira 1975), interethnic relations (de Oliveira 1979; Knobloch 1974), acculturation (Galvão 1959), mythology (Saake 1958a, 1958b, 1958c, 1959–1960a; Wright 1981b, 1992a, 1992b, 1993–1994), shamanism (Saake 1959–1960b; Wright 1981b, 1992a, 1992b, 1993), warfare (Wright 1990), messianic movements (Wright 1981b, 1987–1989; Wright and Hill 1986; Hill and Wright 1988), and material culture (Ribeiro 1980).

On the Venezuelan side, Jonathan Hill has published a series of studies on Wakuenai social exchange (Hill and Moran 1983; Hill 1984a), social organization (Hill 1984b, 1985a), religion (Hill 1985b), ceremonial exchange (Hill 1987a, 1987b), and a major book-length study on chant specialists ([1989] 1993). On the Curripaco of Colombia, Nicolas Journet's doctoral dissertation, published in 1995, and two published articles (1980–1981, 1993) provide excellent analyses of social, political, and economic organization and ceremonial exchange.

Circumstances of Research

For nearly a year before I first went to the Northwest Amazon, I researched a good part of the published and unpublished sources on the area and its people from the time they were first written about in the eighteenth century up to the present. From the large bibliography which this produced, I reached the conclusion that, at least on the Brazilian side, the only areas where I could expect to find anything like "traditional" institutions—e.g., shamanism, rites of passage—functioning among the Baniwa was on the Aiary River, tributary of the upper Içana. In nearly all other areas, I had read or was told, culture had changed to the point where it was probable that I would have to work more with memories. My initial impression was later confirmed by Peter Silverwood-Cope, a British anthropologist with more than eight years of field experience in the area who, in the early 1970s, was in charge of the National Indian Foundation post at Jauareté on the

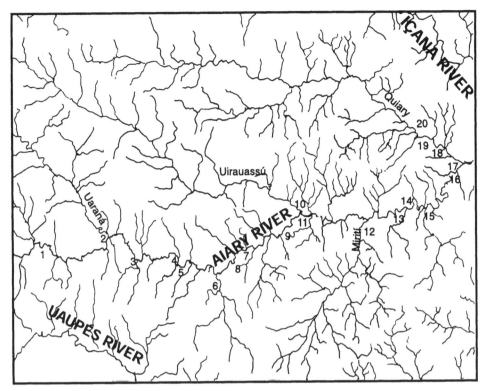

Village Name (Língua Geral or Portuguese)	Village Name (Baniwa)	Phratry
1	Iurupary (Jurupary)	Inyaipana	Cubeo
2	Ucuqui (formerly Seringa Rupitá)	Hinirípan	Hohodene and Oalipere-dakenai
3	Uapui	Hipana	Hohodene and Oalipere-dakenai
4	Santarém	Kaidawíka	Hohodene
5	Inambú	Dumali-numana	Maulieni
6	Araripira	Dupalípan	Oalipere-dakenai
7	Canadá	Kuichiali-numana	Oalipere-dakenai
8	Santa Rita	Halekuliaro	Oalipere-dakenai
9	Macedonia	Wainuma	Maulieni
10	Puraquecuara	Dakatali-kudzua	Oalipere-dakenai
11	São Joaquim	Mainiali-numana	Hohodene
12	Mirití	Itewiali-numana	Hohodene
13	Xibarú	Pidzuaro-numana	Hohodene
14	Cará	Ashiali	Hohodene
15	Camarão	Dzákapemi	Hohodene
16	Urumitu	Tchiriari	Oalipere-dakenai
17	Loiro-poço	Itána	Oalipere-dakenai
18	Sant'Ana	Kewineri-numana	Oalipere-dakenai and Kumadene
19	Nazaré	?	Oalipere-dakenai
20	América	?	Oalipere-dakenai and Hohodene

Map 2. Aiary River Communities

Uaupés River. He likewise thought the Aiary would be the most interesting place for fieldwork for, since Koch-Grünberg, no one had conducted research in that region.

In terms of physical access, the Aiary was relatively easier than, for
example, the upper Içana, since to get to the upper Içana would have
involved a two-week trip upriver by canoe while it was only a day
and a half to the Aiary by canoe up the Uaupés River from Jauareté
and an eight-hour hike through the forest by trail connecting Jandú, a
Wanano village of the upper Uaupés, with the Aiary. Setting off in the
company of two Wanano guides, I then reached the village of Uapui
Cachoeira, or Hipana in Baniwa, one of the largest villages on the
Aiary River and where, Silverwood-Cope advised me, the people
were known to be guardians of their traditions. I was initially dis-
mayed, however, by the presence of a Catholic missionary and schoolteacher in the village who, at the time, seemed to exercise a vague sort
of control over the villagers—that is, an explicit interference in their
affairs and with ideas for their future. After a few weeks of language
learning in Uapui, I decided to survey the entire river and its tributaries, gathering census and general information on the nearly thirty villages from the headwaters to the mouth. Taking into account a series
of considerations—the size of Uapui in comparison with other Aiary
villages (the average size was thirty-five people; Uapui had nearly a
hundred); the presence of various shamans and chant specialists in
Uapui; an attraction for the natural beauty of the place and its mythic
significance as "center of the world"; and access to the Uaupés—I
decided to stay in Uapui but to make visits to several other villages
(Seringa Rupitá and Ucuqui on the Uaraná stream upriver, and Santarém downriver) distant from Uapui three to five hours by canoe, to
extend my research. From then until the end of the approximately one
and one-half years of my fieldwork, I stayed for periods of up to three
months in the field, returning for two-week breaks—by trail, canoe,
and air force plane—to the capital city of Manaus.

As was to be expected from a situation where missionaries had
campaigned against traditional religious practices, my interests in
these matters were met with hesitation, if not resistance. Indeed, the
irony of my status—a North American who was not an evangelist and
who was not there to preach against native culture—was everywhere
made clear. Sophie Muller had preached in the longhouse of Uapui
in the early 1950s, an event that was still vividly remembered by the
villagers. But Uapui, in the 1970s, was a "Catholic" village, one of
the few strongholds of the Salesian missionaries on a predominantly
"evangelical" river. Suspicions no doubt arose of my being an infiltra-

tor, for my comings and goings were carefully watched by the resident Catholic lay missionary. I couldn't go to a family's garden, to see how things were done, without the missionary's being concerned about why I would ever want to venture into the forest. Subtly or not, I had stepped into a minefield—about which I knew very little at that time but where one wrong move could be disastrous.

"When in Rome . . ." seemed to me the best policy. In Uapui, I attended the Catholic masses and orations and participated as much as I cared to in mission-ordered communal activities. I conducted my interviews with shamans and chant specialists or observed curing and other rituals at a healthy distance from watchful eyes. In evangelical villages, I likewise participated in prayer meetings and other gatherings. When Catholics and Protestants confronted each other, I kept my distance.

Not always was this strategy easy to maintain, however. Once, when all the men in the village of Uapui, myself included, worked on building a new schoolhouse—a project that, like most collective work parties, was lubricated with home brew—a fight broke out in one part of the village. One man was severely clubbed and two of the most respected shamans in the village quarreled (the son of one had clubbed the younger brother of another, who had provoked and insulted him). The quarrel unexpectedly found its way into my living quarters, and I disarmed one of the shamans who threatened the other with a machete. Days after things had cooled down, I learned that the missionary had made a complaint against me to FUNAI (the National Indian Foundation), claiming that I had "caused" the disturbance by "ordering the men to drink." Indeed I had done no more than repeat what I had heard so often—like a taunting refrain—from the men: "no one can prohibit *caxiri* [manioc beer]," for the lay missionary had on a number of occasions attempted, if not to prohibit, then at least to control consumption, to the displeasure of various villagers. In any case, not only did FUNAI officials, who visited the village days after, personally question me about the incident but also, even years later, the Salesian bishop at São Gabriel accused me of being a "bad influence" on the Indians.

The shamans involved, however, turned about-face in relation to me after the incident: whereas before they treated me with caution and obliging respect, afterward they opened their doors, initiating trade, inviting me to watch their curing rites, and offering to teach me "a little" of what I wished to know. Outside of incidents such as this, my fieldwork in Uapui was in no other way compromised and, thanks to the Indians' defense of my work, the head of the mission on the Içana gave little credence to the missionary's story. My work on mythology, shamanism, chants, language, and history progressed without difficulty until nearly the end of my stay.

Uapui was in fact an ideal place to undertake the study I had contemplated. My principal informant on shamanism, Mandu, spoke Portuguese relatively well and helped me enormously in the translations of narratives and songs. He had learned his practice from two powerful shamans—Kumadeiyon, of the Dzauinai phratry on the Içana, and Kudui, a Hohodene of the Uaraná stream—both of whom had cured Mandu of a lethal sickness in his youth.

Of all the elders with whom I worked, it was Keruaminali (or José Marcelino Cornélio, his Portuguese name) who, by far, taught me the most of what I recorded of myths, chants, and history. He was then (he died in 1978) one of the most important and respected elders on the Aiary. In his late seventies, he was also a shaman, but because of his age, he was no longer able to keep up with the younger and more vigorous shamans such as Mandu. Nevertheless, he was always called on to serve as assistant in curing rites. Former chief of Uapui, he was also recognized as a narrator of myths and chanter of *kalidzamai*, the specialized chants of rites of passage. He was always sought by the villagers of Uapui and other communities to perform chants and orations. Once when he suffered an accident, the villagers were greatly disturbed and asked, "Who will perform the orations and chants for us if he dies?" His stepsons, both Dessana men, did not seem to have the same interest in following his profession, but Mandu, his nephew and a leading shaman of Uapui, made a point of learning Keruaminali's knowledge before he died.

Keruaminali spoke little Portuguese, but his stepson José Felipe served as interpreter in all interviews. Most Baniwa men speak Portuguese or Spanish, but as my understanding of the Baniwa language increased, I found I was able to conduct interviews without interpreters. Whenever I interviewed monolingual speakers, however, I would ask a close relative of the informant to help in translation. In fact, dialogic situations are the normal performative contexts for narrations.

From the beginning of my fieldwork, the Indians had forewarned me that change was about to take place on the Aiary. In conversations, they advised me that Uapui would soon become "like a city," and I, taking this to be wishful thinking, made little note of what that might mean. Then, in 1977, a dramatic visit of the Salesian bishop to Uapui— when he ordered the men to plant an enormous cross in the middle of the village plaza—confirmed what they had been saying. He announced that soon an airstrip would be built behind the village and that a small hydroelectric plant would be built on the rapids, as he said, "so that people could work at night." A few months later, air force officials and the then president of FUNAI, General Ismarth de Oliveira, visited the village and confirmed the airstrip project.

From then until I left the field, the village lived the expectation and reality of change: helicopters bringing in equipment, "peons" occupying the community house, the noise of electric generators, and all villagers—including the schoolchildren—involved in clearing and preparing the airstrip. Almost overnight, Uapui was transformed into an air base, with direct communication and transportation to the centers of outside authority in the Northwest Amazon.

Under these circumstances, I found it increasingly difficult to continue my work in Uapui. I decided to move upriver to Ucuqui (or Kuliriana) on the Uaraná stream, where the people were likewise known to have conserved their traditions well. Keruaminali spoke with Keramunhe, the aging patriarch of the Ucuqui descent group, who took me under his wing and taught me innumerable myths, songs, orations, and ritual knowledge, with admirable clarity and certainty, unequaled among the elders of the Aiary. Keramunhe's sons had learned from the elders well, which made my stay of a couple of months extremely productive and edifying. Yet one topic led to another, and I discovered that if I wanted to learn more of certain chants, I would have to go to the evangelical village of Santarém below Uapui. Indeed, I was surprised and gratified by how much and how well the *crentes* of that village knew their traditions, despite the fact they no longer participated in dance rituals nor even smoked tobacco. Brief stays in other evangelical villages and interviews with converted ex-shamans convinced me of the complexity of the religious situation on the Aiary, and that the question of belief was far from being black-and-white.

The people of Uapui were forever on my mind as I completed my work at Santarém. When I decided to return, I found that suddenly the glamorous dream of Uapui becoming "like a city" had collided head-on with the dismal reality of portable radios blaring, cheap cigarettes and *cachaça* (rotgut rum), and an alarming increase of respiratory sickness. As I got inside the helicopter to leave Uapui, Mandu asked me to take an urgent message to FUNAI to send medicine and food for the children, because the way things were going, there was no telling what the immediate future would bring. Uapui—the people and place I had come to know intensely for over a year and a half, the "center of the world" according to shamans and elders—seemed to me to be exploding at the seams.

During the years since I left the Aiary, I have followed the situation of the Baniwa at a distance—through other fieldworkers, colleagues, and students who have sent me reports; and through news of the invasions by gold panners and military development projects in the 1980s. From them I have learned, for example, that whole families have left the village of Uapui and relocated to the Rio Negro. I have also learned that the airstrip built in the 1970s behind Uapui—and which had cost so much in the way of social disruption—is no longer in use, having been abandoned by the Brazilian Air Force years ago. Telecommunications have recently arrived on the Aiary, which certainly will facilitate indigenous projects for the future. What I describe and interpret in this book, then, is in a certain sense history; yet ethnography has the task of producing such documents, and its interpretations are relative to time and context. If I succeed here in communicating what I learned from the Baniwa in the late 1970s, this book will have fulfilled its purpose.[1]

PART I
COSMOGONY, COSMOLOGY, AND SHAMANISM

Since my objective is to understand a "spirituality of the end of time," to cite Sullivan's apt phrase, or what I am calling millenarian consciousness and its imagery, a starting point is the myths of the Baniwa, fundamental expressions of their religious imagination. To what extent do narratives about the creation, primordial times, and the first beings—that is, cosmogonies[1]—contain images of catastrophe and regeneration, of prior worlds that were destroyed and re-created? How do narrators understand these myths and such images where they do occur? How do narratives of the primordial world shape people's notions of the nature of the world today and of human existence in time? In Chapter 1, these questions will help lay the foundations for an understanding of how mythic images of catastrophe and regeneration shape social action.

Based on narrators' explanations, I have ordered Baniwa cosmogonic myths into a sequence of cycles that trace what could be called cosmic history—from the beginning of time until the beginning of human history. My intention is not to present all narratives of each cycle (for which I am currently preparing a separate volume together with the Hohodene), but to illustrate each cycle with one or, at the most, two narratives.

Each narrative is, in a certain sense, a relatively fixed form of discourse about a certain phase in cosmic history. It is thus important to present each narrative, as nearly as possible (given the limitations of transforming a creative art form into a fixed and silent text) as the narrator presented it, that is, preserving its poetic form. As long ago as my doctoral dissertation (1981b), I recognized that the narrating of myths is "a form of artistic performance and interchange between teller and hearer; . . . the art is drama and through it, sacred times are created and re-created" (459). Since then, numerous studies in South American ethnology have focused on ethnopoetic aspects of mythic narratives and how these construct reality (to cite a few of the more important: Basso 1990; Graham 1995; Sherzer 1983).

Styles of narrating are part and parcel of the performance and meaning of the myth. At the same time, they present the greatest challenge to ethnographers: how to represent complex stylistic elements— e.g., music in various modalities, highly dramatic moments such as floods, conflagrations, or wars; and how to preserve the lyricism of narration that is not evident when translating from a native language into English. My presentations of the myths are *approximations* to the original, and this is as much as should be expected of them. Presented in this fashion, some of these texts may appear quite lengthy on paper, so I have tried to facilitate the reading by presenting plot summaries following each text, and/or explanatory notes in the texts.

It is in these narratives and narrators' exegeses of them—i.e., what narrators understand these myths to be about, as well as my own suggested interpretations, which seek to complement narrators' comments—that I hope to find answers to the questions raised above. Regarding the method of interpretation that I shall use, I believe that the closest I have come to a "method" is what Sullivan defines as "hermeneutics":

> the willingness to treat the attempt at interpretation as a peculiarly instructive cultural process affected by both the subject and object of understanding. In an authentic interpretation, one's method cannot stand objectively apart from one's data; it must become subject to the data in order to grasp adequately what one engages in the act of understanding. The process of interpretation must continually be re-examined in the light of one's attempts to understand. In this light, the up-front confession of one's method often appears simplistic and ill-timed for one cannot so quickly dispatch with the self-awareness that genuine understanding requires. The categories that assemble one's facts and the terms, procedures, and "conclusions" that explain them must remain problematic and subject to questions throughout the course of the inquiry. How do one's forms of knowledge reshape and reveal the meaning of another's thoughts or acts, and vice versa? Understanding is a creative process, and when it is performed well, the nature of the creativity is itself assessed in the act of interpretative culture. (1988, 16)

From this process I hope to define more concretely images and forms relevant to millenarian consciousness in the mythic narratives.

In Chapter 2, I shall present material first of all on the cosmos, that is, how religious specialists and nonspecialists understand the organization of space and time in the universe. As I hope to show, such visions are fundamentally grounded in cosmogony and constitutive of what I shall call a hierarchy of spiritualized being and power. The multitiered cosmos is like a spiritual "map"—in other words, the universe is entirely spiritualized. But it is not an essentialized, objective "thing," "out there." To the contrary, it is like a living being, and it is through their dynamic relations with this being that shamans derive and construct meaning in their curing and other activities.

According to some shamans, one of the legacies of cosmogony is that the world in which humanity lives is flawed by evil, poison, sickness and death, thus contrasting absolutely with the Other World of the creator/transformer. Like a sick person, This World is thus in constant need of healing and renovation. My second objective in Chapter 2 is to present the discourses of several shamans concerning their art, practices, and training, in which, it will become clear, they see that one of their principal tasks is to heal—or "make better"—This World. In their apprenticeship, they learn how to do this and, in this sense, they can be considered as "guardians of the cosmos." This is an important point which speaks directly to the question of how shamans interpret cosmogony in millenarian terms, act as intermediaries between humanity and the Other World, and may even embody the creative powers of the deities.

Finally, in Chapter 2, I shall consider shamans' songs—one of the principal art forms associated with healing. While many of these songs are grounded in the events of cosmogonic myths and are organized according to the space-time of the cosmos, they go beyond the conclusions of the myths. For the songs—and shamanic voyages on the songs—open a direct relation between the Other World of the deities and This World of humanity which permits new creative episodes, so to speak, to be added to the account of creation. It is in such creative acts that the shaman fully performs his salvific role.

1. Cosmogony: Perspectives on the Beginning and Its Legacy

The Bone God

The myths of the Baniwa creator/transformer Iaperikuli form a complex corpus of more than twenty stories beginning with the appearance of Iaperikuli in the primordial world and ending with his creation of the first ancestors of Baniwa phratries and withdrawal from the world. More than any other figure in the Baniwa pantheon, Iaperikuli is responsible for the way the world is in its essence and form.

The name Iaperikuli means "he-inside-of-bone," referring to his origin from inside the bone of a devoured and dismembered person, victim of voracious cannibalistic jaguars and animals who roamed the world at the beginning of time. The myth of Iaperikuli's origin, however, leaves it clear that not just one person came from inside the bone but three—Iaperikuli and his younger brothers, collectively known as the Iaperikunai, "those-inside-the-bone," or the *hekwapinai*, "universe people." Narrators sometimes compared the three brothers to the three joined bones of a finger. While the three brothers were responsible for the creation of the universe, it was Iaperikuli alone who sought vengeance against the animals that constantly threatened the world with chaos.

I shall first consider the myth of Iaperikuli's beginning. The version presented here was told to me at my request by Keruaminali of Uapui Cachoeira. In general, when Hohodene narrators told this story, one of the most widely known, either they would recount it in the manner transcribed here or, more often, they would tell the first and last "pieces" of the version presented here—or what I call episodes in the following summary—and omit the middle. Episode 1 tells of an initial state of killing in which nearly all of the Duemieni, primordial beings, were killed and devoured by tribes of predatory animals. From the bone of a devoured being, the three brothers called the Iaperikunai (literally, "those inside the bone") emerged, are nurtured and reared by an elderly "grandmother" (or "aunt" in many versions) until, after several transformations, they are fully grown up. Episode 1 also defines the nature of the Iaperikunai as the "universe people," *hekwa-pinai*, who are responsible for the making and transforming of everything there is in the universe. Episode 2 tells of the "return vengeances" of the Iaperikunai against the animals who had killed off all their kin. They encounter four animals, each engaged in some disordering action, which the brothers secretly observe. They then trick each into performing its disorderly act and, at the same time, showing where its weak and vulnerable spot is. With this admission, they succeed in killing the animals—all but one which feigned that it was mourning for the dead. In episode 3, the chief of the animals who is the "stepfather" of the Duemieni tries to kill the Iaperikunai by fire, a conflagration that scorched the earth, but they escape, emerging from the fire immortal and invulnerable.

In my transcription and translation of Keruaminali's narration, I have sought to preserve his style as closely as possible to the original—including, for example, onomatopoeia in italics—in order to give at least some sense of the poetry and drama of the myth. Lines were broken according to significant pauses in the narration. Where necessary, I include brief explanatory notes in brackets:

> In the beginning the Duemieni,
> Another people killed them.
> Long ago, long ago.
> They killed all of them, all of the Duemieni,
> Before them.
> Then this one, the stepfather of the Duemieni,
> [called] Enúmhere,
> Threw away a bone,
> *Pi'thi' . . . Taa*
> It falls in midriver below.
> Then, she was crying, their grandmother,
> She cried . . .
> On returning, Enúmhere hears her.
> He tells her, his wife [i.e., the grandmother is Enúmhere's wife],
> To go fetch the little bone.
> She gets a fishnet,
> She takes a gourd and goes,
> They [the Iaperikunai] appeared for her.
> They transformed into shrimp.
> A bone appeared for her, they made noise inside [i.e., the shrimp are inside the bone].

She catches the bone and takes it back in the gourd.
She carries it and sets it on the hearth,
Below her hammock.
Then the shrimp transform into little crickets,
Crickets.
She gets tapioca,
And she gives them to eat.
The next day, she gives them [to eat] again.
Quickly they grew up, the Iaperikunai, *quickly* they grew.
Until . . . the next day,
"*Tchiri*," they sing. "Hey," she strikes the gourd.
She opens it.
Until . . . all of the crickets sing, all of them,
That's all, then she carries them in a basket into the garden,
Into the garden.
There she opened the basket.
They ate, and ate what she gave them . . .
They ate it all . . .
"Oh that's enough," they say.
She goes back to the house and puts them down,
There in the house.
She puts them in the same place.
She gets tapioca and gives it to them,
"*Tchiritchiritchiri*" was their song.
They transformed again, into another kind of cricket.
Untiiiiil they climb up above the hearth and sing for their food,
    tchiritchiri."
Untiiiiil they grow up well,
People are beginning to appear,
Iaperikunai will appear, Iaperikunai
The Iaperikunai live!
So then—"Do not do anything, keep quiet," she tells them.
"No, we are the universe people, the Iaperikunai,"
"We can do anything whatsoever," so they say,
"We can do everything . . ."
"However it will be."
Until . . . they climb up again . . .
They transform again,
Into small woodpeckers.
Later, they transform again,
Into painted-face woodpeckers.
The woodpeckers climb up again . . .
She carries them again and they appeared as adults.

In the garden, she opens her basket and they appeared.
"Hey! You have to be quiet, don't make noise, I am watching you,
    my grandchildren."
"No, we won't go away,"
"We are the Iaperikunai, the universe people," so they say.
"Oh." They climbed up a fruit tree . . .
To the top.
"You will fall!" she says.
"We won't fall."
"We won't fall, we are the universe people."
So then,
They stay there.
Thus it will be, they first make this agouti.
They take a fruit.
"Grandmother, look . . ."
For, "an agouti it will be."
tsetsetsetsetsetse . . . gengengengengeng . . .
[i.e., they throw the fruit and it transforms into an agouti as it falls
    to the ground]
So began the agouti, she sees it coming.
Thus the agouti likes gardens.
It eats manioc bread, the agouti.
"Ohh." . . . they come back down.
"You will fall!" she says.
"No," they come back down.
They approach . . . *tatatatata*
"You will fall!"
"We won't fall, we are the universe people, Iaperikunai," so they
    say.
Until . . . they come back down,
And arrive.
"So you come." . . . "Yes, thus is our way, we the Iaperikunai." . . .
    "Oh"
Then they transform . . .
Everything! They transform, in the beginning the Iaperikunai
    made everything!!
The universe appears . . . Everything! Iaperikuli, he lives.
However he could IAPERIKULI!
IAPERIKULI *WORLD!*
The universe people
The universe people lived.
Then they transform . . .
Everything . . . they make the world ready, all of it . . .

Thus it was they made the world, the Iaperikunai.

The *IAPERIKUNAI LONG AGO!!*

Began this for us . . .

The universe began for us,

They made it long ago.

Then when they had finished everything,

Later, they asked each other,

"How will it be that we look for our return vengeance?" [i.e.,
    return vengeance against the animals who killed off all their kin]

"Now let's go back to kill in payment." "All right."

Then they leave her.

First, they meet up with the *sarapó* fish

At a lake.

The fish throws water from the lake with a gourd . . . *pa'pa'* [sound
    of throwing water]

He empties out the lake . . . *pa'pa'*

Then they came,

There, the Iaperikunai.

They watched him throw water.

"What are you doing, grandfather?"

"No, I throw water like so from the lake,"

"Out of the jaguar-people's-lake," he says. [The jaguar people are
    the Duemieni who have been finished off]

"Oh, throw it for us to see."

"All right."

He gets water, throws it, but the lake doesn't empty out.

"I heard you say . . .

'No-owner-jaguar-people's-lake' you said as you threw" . . . "Oh,
    so it was, 'no-owner-jaguar-people's-lake'" *tchiaaaaa pa!* He sees
    the water go out. [The narrator explained: If the *sarapó* did not
    speak these magic words, the lake could not empty out.]

So then . . .

They jump into the lake,

The three of them.

They defecate in the lake.

Then they take a gourd and make gas bubbles . . . *pupu*

"Oh, your anus," Iaperikuli says.

"It's not my anus,

"I don't have an anus," the *sarapó* says, "only a hole here in my
    neck."

"Oh, one of our kin has a good thing, he makes people's anuses,"
    Iaperikuli says.

They make a hole for him . . .

They take a spear and stick him through from one end out to his
   neck . . . dead,
Dead was the *sarapó* fish.
They had killed in return.
Ooooh . . . they left him.
Until . . . they meet up with,
They meet this spiny hedgehog.
He chips pieces off black brazilwood *tshiu, tshiu* . . .
"No-owner-jaguar-people's-black-brazilwood-tree," he says as he
   chips, *tshiu tshiu*
They went there, they came and heard.
They arrive: "What are you working on, grandfather?"
"I chip the black brazilwood tree."
"Chip it for us to see, then."
He chips . . .
His claws didn't go in!
"We heard you say
'No-owner-jaguar-people's-black-brazilwood-tree,' we heard you
   say."
"Oh, so it was."   "*Ha!* Chip it!"
"No-owner-jaguar-people's-black-brazilwood-tree" *tshiutshiutshiu*
   Ha!   They see him chip.
Hedgehog takes and puts on his coat of spines . . . *paaaalililili!*
"No way you can kill me," he says, "no way . . ."
"No way you can kill me," he says, "you can't . . ."
"There is only one place you can kill me, at the bridge of my nose,"
   he says.
"Hmmm? So it is," Iaperikuli says.
Then they come back to kill.
"Where is it that they made to kill you, grandfather?"   "Up here,"
   he shows with his paw.
"HERE?!"   *TAAWWHH!!*
They'd killed in return . . . dead.
Ooooh . . . They went on,
Then they met the little sloth *paapali*.
He was eating their plants, those *urucú* plants, in an old, old
   village,
"No-owner-jaguar-people's-*urucú*-plants" [*urucú*: annatto, the
   fruits of which produce a red dye].   Agh, little sloth ate.
He hears Iaperikuli coming.
Little sloth takes *urucú*
And paints his eyes.
Aahh, how red are little sloth's eyes!

Then they come, "What are you working on, grandfather?"
"I've been crying . . . I cry for my dead affines who have been
    killed," he says.
"REALLY!?"   "Yes."
"Look at my rotting eyes, so much have I cried for my affines,"
    he says.
"Hey, so it seems," they did not kill him.
They went on . . . until . . .
Then they met up with the Tapir.
They watched him kick
The *abacate* [avocado] fruit tree in their plantation.   *Taaa!*   Fruits
    fell . . .
They went, "What are you working on, grandfather?"
"I kick the *abacate*," he says.
"So, kick it for us to see," they say.
"All right."
He doesn't kick it right,
No *abacate* fell down.
"Oooohhh? We heard you say, 'no-owner-jaguar-people's-*abacate*-
    tree' we heard you say as you kicked," they say.
"Yes, so it was."   "So, kick it then."   "No-owner-jaguar-people's-
    abacate"   PA! TA! *Puululululululu* . . . fruits fell. . . . "Ah, that's it."
"Let's go see where our grandfather kicked."
They got as they went,
They put thorns, poison-darts, the stingray's tail into the hole.
They went back, "So, grandfather, kick it for us to see."
He ran and kicked hard . . . *TAAAAA!*   "*PAUUGH!!!*"
Tik'tik'tik'   Tapir ran away . . .
He went to lie down on the bank of a lake on a hill.
Once more he ran . . .
To Tucunaré Lake and lay down again.
He ran . . . Until he came out of the forest around the Quiary River.
There he died.
And so they killed everyone in return . . .
Until they had finished.
They'd finished their vengeance on all of them . . .
So then . . .
"There is nothing they can do to the Iaperikunai, the universe
    people."
"There is nothing they can do," they say.
"Hey, so it is."
They were all grown-up.
All grown-up.

Then, . . . this Enúmhere made a garden,
Then, it became a beautiful summer!
"Hey, let's go set fire to the garden," they say, "All right."
They went, to burn the new garden.
"Go over there in the middle," Enúmhere says and makes them go.
Enúmhere would kill them and runs to set fire to the garden edge
    and the fire approaches   *titititititi* . . .
He comes back and calls, "Heeeeeyyyyyyyy!"
"Heeeyyy, you will burn!"
"We will never burn, we are the Iaperikunai," they say, "we don't
    burn ever."
They carried *ambaúba* [trumpetwood] trees to the middle of the
    garden and made holes at the top.
Eeeeeee, the fire burns quickly to the middle, it approaches
    titititititi . . . it made an inferno, as they say.
They went inside the *ambaúba* and closed them off.
The fire burned! . . .
FIERCELY the fire came!!
Then one *ambaúba* burst, *PA!!*
That's all, one of the three flew out.
Quickly another, *PA!!*
Then another, *PA!!*
Three of them had come out.
Alive.
"Why does he do this to us, our stepfather?" they say,
"We are the Iaperikunai . . . this cannot be."
They come to a trail.
Then along comes a turtle crying, along comes the turtle.
They catch the turtle.
The turtle comes to the trail.
Then there was a tree with ribs on its trunk that were HUGE!
They catch the turtle,
"How will it be? They have burned, they were all grown-up, all
    grown-up . . . ," the turtle says, crying.
He comes and throws the turtle onto the tree trunk
    ribs   *fiuuuuhhhh* . . . *Taaa!!*
Thus the turtle's shell is turned inside, its rib cage, you know?
TOOOOWHH!!   Dead it is!
Iaperikuli stayed watching Enúmhere.
They got tobacco, chanted, and blew smoke over their stepfather.
They descend to the river ahead of him . . .
At the port, they bathe in the river.
Later, he came to the port crying.

"How is it?!" he says,
"You did not burn?"   "We never burn, we are the universe
    people, the Iaperikunai, you didn't leave us to burn," they say.
They bathed, "Heyy," they laughed, they had arrived.
So it was.

Interpretation

The chaotic situation of the beginning can be seen as representing, I suggest, the first catastrophe, of which there are many in Baniwa cosmic history, in the sense that it was a near total destruction of the first people, the Duemieni, who were killed and consumed by the insatiable appetites of the predatory animals. Yet, it was the prelude to a new beginning when the universe would be re-created and the disorder of the animals at least controlled. The chief of the animals and thunders, Enúmhere, throws a bone into the middle of the river, a watery grave of nothingness in which all distinct forms are dissolved. From this condition, the bone becomes a vehicle, a container for the three beings who would eventually save the world and create its form anew. The bone may thus be seen as the first symbol of the new world.

The "grandmother" (or "aunt" in some narratives) is the guardian of the container, nurturing and protecting the heroes—"educating them" as some narrators say—as they grow and transform. In other myths, she is a key figure associated in various ways with the creation of the world and the protection of humanity from death and destruction. In one myth, she is the one who closes off the earth compartment where people escape from the fires that destroy the world. In the myth of the first person who died (see Chapter 5), she keeps the life-giving remedies that counteract the lethal poison of the animals with which they attempt to kill Iaperikuli and his brothers. I shall have occasion to return to these associations and their importance for millenarian consciousness throughout this book.

One of the striking themes in the first part of this story is the distinct development of its spatial dimension, which seems to be closely connected to the growth of the Iaperikunai and the creation of a new form of the universe in the postdestruction period. Note, for example, that the first space indicated in the first part of the myth is the "midriver below" where the bone of the Iaperikunai in their prenatal state as shrimp inside the bone is fished out. From there, the bone is brought into the house and set below the grandmother's hammock where the Iaperikunai—transformed into land insects, crickets—sing and grow. Following this, there is an alternation between garden and house, spaces of domestication in which growth and transformation occur. In both spaces, the Iaperikunai ascend (the hearth and a fruit tree) as they eat-sing-grow-transform. The culmination of this process occurs when the Iaperikunai, fully grown, at the top of a fruit tree, transform a fruit into a domesticable animal—an agouti, an animal that likes to eat manioc in the garden and is sometimes reared as a household pet. In short, spatial movements—from river to house to garden—seem to represent the re-creation of form coinciding with the growth of the Iaperikunai: from the river, a place of absolutely formless space; to the house, a place of rearing and domestication; to the garden, a place of the domestication of nature.[1] Within each space, vertical movement (down-up-down) would seem to establish the heroes' "way" of ascent and descent.

In this process, the myth uses concrete forms—especially, containers—to express central ideas about growth and change: the bone from which the Iaperikunai emerged; the gourd and the basket in which the grandmother carried and kept them; and the *ambaúba* tree with a hole at the top from which the Iaperikunai emerged immortal. All are containers which express transformations; "coming out" of containers is a common expression, in Baniwa myths and rituals, for the reintegration of newly transformed beings into society. Here, I suggest that the coming-out of the bone is a transition from death into life; the coming-out of the basket, from childhood to adulthood; and the explosive coming-out of the *ambaúba* tree trunk, from mortality to immortality.

The grandmother's warnings to the Iaperikunai are, I further suggest, significant statements of the nature of the "universe people" and of what may be thought to hold the universe together: (1) "Don't do anything," she says—to which they respond, "We can do anything whatsoever." The warning pleads for the heroes to remain static and inactive, yet it is their nature—i.e., the nature of the universe—to change and transform. The heroes declare their omniscience—one narrator said, "They knew everything when they were born, no one explained to them"—and omnificence. (2) "You have to be quiet, don't make noise," she says—to which they reply, "We won't go away." Here again, the warning pleads for them to be inactive and silent, to which they affirm their permanence—they will not disappear as they transform and leave their container. (3) and (4) "You will fall!"—to which they say, "No, we won't fall," as they ascend and descend. This final warning refers, I suggest, to their power of transcendence: the vertical passage the heroes complete—upon which their power to transform and to overcome the destructive nature of the animals depends—represents the final demonstration of their having fully grown up. Completely separate now from their original condition inside a container totally dependent on the grandmother for protection, the heroes remake life, transforming a wild fruit into a tame animal, symbolic of the new world that will take shape henceforth around them. To Baniwa narrators, there is no definite sequence in which creation took place: the Iaperikunai's knowledge and power to create "everything whatsoever," "however they could," imperishable and transcendent, are the basic conditions for saving the universe from destruction. As I will show later on, this power is likewise fundamental to shamanism.

In the sequence of "return vengeances" that the Iaperikunai take on the animals, in each instance when the heroes encounter animals engaged in some disordering action, they get the animal to reveal its "magic" by repeating a formula of nonownership—indicating that the Duemieni had been killed—and showing its weak point. The scenes of vengeance killings are all comical, provoking laughter among listeners, and seem to emphasize the Iaperikunai's trickster nature. As the heroes subdue the animals, they sustain their "ownership" (i.e., ownership of the "jaguar-people") and return order to the world. The four animals, however, are minor threats when compared to the stepfather animal chief who returns in the final episode to attempt to kill the heroes by fire.

Sullivan's interpretation of cosmic conflagrations in South American mythologies is, I think, highly pertinent to understanding the meaning of the final episode of this myth:

Cosmic conflagration demonstrates the absolute spirituality of matter in the primordial world and shows that being in all its forms is susceptible to total spiritualization. (1988, 66)

Cataclysmic fire "reveals a condition of complete and unbridled consumption," indicating that "the life of the cosmos is deeply associated with food":

The catastrophe of fire "cooks" existence to render primordial reality consumable and to make this world an endless cycle of consumption in which all is food, i.e., subject to a consumptive power that manifests its presence as spirit. The conflagration spiritualized the universe. That is, reality ultimately proved itself to be transcendent, able to sustain life beyond the forms of its primordial appearance. It "creates" the spiritual world by rendering it eternal and invisible. Because they were totally consumed, the first beings have become spirits. (69)

The animal chief, whose insatiable appetite destroyed all life before, returns to destroy the universe people with the all-consuming flames of a garden fire. It is a new garden made in the dry season, the beginning of the annual agricultural cycle and, it seems reasonable to say, symbolic of the new life of the cosmos. The heroes stay in the center of the garden, the center generally being a sacred space, and as the flames reach them, they reenter containers—*ambaúba* logs, which are generally associated in Baniwa myths with spiritual passage. The conflagration, or "inferno" as the narrator said, consumes all but the miniature, closed-off containers which burst open with three loud noises, like gunshots, as the heroes narrowly escape from death. In fact, the themes of a narrow escape from death inside containers and of powerful noises that burst containers apart are common in Hohodene mythology and seem to represent birth and rebirth in the process of creation. As spiritual beings, the Iaperikunai "do not die"; that is, they are immortal, thus completing the aspects of the universe revealed throughout the myth. Finally, their passage is completed by bathing in the river, but on the way, they demonstrate the weakness and invertibility of natural forms by breaking the turtle's shell on the trunk of a huge tree. They then shamanize the animal chief, blowing tobacco smoke over him, and descend to the river to bathe. The heroes thus complete a full cycle, for bathing is a fully cultural—spiritual and purifying—use of an otherwise formless space from which, in the beginning of the myth, they were originally retrieved.

The Animals and Thunders

The struggles of the Iaperikunai—or more often Iaperikuli (the one brother who is the principal hero of the myths)—against the animals continue through a sequence of myths, the outcome of which by no means represents a clear victory for the heroes. These myths, I suggest, seem to contain an extended discourse on, among other things, the theme of the deaths of primordial beings and the end of the primordial world, which is explored from multiple points of view and, as in the myth of Iaperikuli, through a series of catastrophic images.

To take an example, in one myth that some narrators say follows the "beginning of Iaperikuli," the hero seeks to kill Ipeku, the night monkey—or as he is known here, the primordial being Dzauikuapa—the chief of both the animals, *itchirinai*, and the thunders, *eenunai* (all tree-dwelling animals, monkeys, and sloths). For some narrators, this chief is the same as Enúmhere, the stepfather of the first myth; it is as though the same personage goes by different names in various myths, expressing different qualities and attributes of an "enemy" figure.

Through his extraordinary shamanistic powers, Iaperikuli kills all the animals—in a catastrophic flood—all except for the chief who, according to the myth, began evil omens, *hinimai*, which in real life forewarn of people's deaths by poison. The Dzauikuapa was the primordial "owner of poison"; the *ipeku* today, when it appears in villages at night, is considered an evil omen for its appearance means that deaths by poison will occur.

The following narration of the myth of Dzauikuapa was told to me at my request, again by Keruaminali of Uapui, with comments by his stepson José Felipe, which I have put in brackets at the appropriate places:

> Iaperikuli went walking with those thunders, *eenunai*, those
>   animals, *itchirinai*.
> He was naming everything.
> Then he walked with the *itchirinai* to a river.
> "This river, how is it called?" they asked.
> "It's called Kaparoali [Howler Monkey River]."   "That's our
>   name," they said.
> They walked to another river.
> "How is it called?"   "Pithipithiali [Other Monkey
>   River]."   "That's us, our name."
> To another river—"It's called Wakiali [Other Monkey
>   River]."   "Our name."
> To another river—"It's Ipekuali [Night Monkey River]."   "Our
>   name."
> To another river—"Tchitchiali [*Uacari* Monkey River]."
> So they went.
> Then it began to get dark.
> Iaperikuli made it get dark.
> Then they came to a huge *karapa* [*abiú*] fruit tree.
> The monkeys ate and ate the *karapa* fruit.
> It was already getting dark.
> They climbed up the tree.
> Iaperikuli made night come on quickly. . . .
> The monkeys climbed up the tree.
> There they stayed.
> Iaperikuli made the river rise and rise and rise [José Felipe
>   explained: The river rose to just below the branch where the
>   monkeys had gathered together. All the monkeys were on the
>   branch and the river kept rising.]
> So then, Dzauikuapa,
> He always roams at night, getting fruits, cutting, eating.

Below him, there was water.
He dropped the fruit into the water.
Khuu   Te'pi   Khuu Te'   pi
It was piranha-grandfather eating the fruit that fell in the water.
"What is doing this?" Dzauikuapa got [a fruit], cut it—*Khuu*—
   "What is doing this to us? They will kill us."
He got another, came back—*khuu*—he got another, cut it, the fish
   ate it.
He got one that didn't have a seed, came back, and nothing
   happened. [i.e., the piranha eat only the seeds of the fruit]
"Now I'm going to wash this fruit that is already dried up."
He got one, made a little hole, got inside, and the fish didn't eat it.
He dropped into the river and floated away inside the fruit to the
   edge of the sky.
Then Iaperikuli made thunder and lightning which struck the tree,
PAAAA!   bobobobobobo. . . . [J. F. explained: the tree is broken in the
   middle and falls into the river.]
They ate them, the alligator and piranha ate those *eenunai*,
All of them . . . they were finished off.
So then, they killed all of them.
Only one was left, the *uacarí*,
Sitting on top of the broken tree in midriver, with his grandchild
   on his shoulders.
They couldn't get to land.
Woodpecker started to take them but got scared, turned around,
   and came back.
Vulture tried to take them but turned around and came back.
Then the alligator takes them [J. F. explained: The alligator had
   eaten a lot and was full, "I will take you, I am a good boat." The
   uacarí sat on top of the alligator. Midway, alligator broke wind.
   "Hai! how smelly!"   "Is it smelly?"   "Hai, it's very
   smelly!"   They got to the riverbank and he broke wind again—
   "Hai, is it smelly?"   "Yes, very smelly." *Uacarí* jumped off. "Hai,
   very smelly, very bad." Alligator bit off *uacarí*'s tail. That's why
   the *uacarí* has a short tail today.]
Uacarí and his grandchild survived and Iaperikuli does not kill
   them, it seems.
Two, three days later, Dzauikuapa came back singing, *"Hee hee
   hee hee oopi eenunai hee hee hee hee oopi eenunai"* [no translation
   possible—the evil omen song, remembering that the *eenunai*
   had died].
Thus the *ipeku* lived.

He didn't kill the Dzauikuapa [i.e., the night monkey, *ipeku*, is the
    living descendant of the Dzauikuapa whom Iaperikuli did not
    kill].
Then Iaperikuli made the water go down.
He sent the dove, *mulitu*, to get saw grass.
It took a piece and showed it to Iaperikuli,
"Ah, now this will be your food," he says.
Thus it is, so it is today.
That's all.

Interpretation

This myth has a special meaning for shamans since it refers to one of
the main instances when, shamans say, Iaperikuli caused "the world
to end" in the catastrophe which befalls the animals; in total obscurity,
they are devoured in the waters. Yet, just as the animal chief failed to
"consume" Iaperikuli in the conflagration, so—narrators point out—
the hero fails to have the chief devoured in the flood, and the animal
chief's song—*"hee hee hee hee oopi eenunai"*—is the beginning of evil
omens which presage people's deaths by poison, for the Dzauikuapa
is the primordial "poison owner," *manhene iminali*.

The meaning of the myth, as I have outlined above, was made clear
to me one afternoon as I was working with Mandu, a shaman, on shamanic powers. In referring to shamanic control over celestial phenomena (clouds, night, thunder, lightning), he spoke the enigmatic
phrase *"deepi karumi oopi Apakwa Hekwapi"* ("the Night End Long Ago,
the Other World"); *"deepi idzakale"* ("night village"). Only much later,
when working with Mandu on shamans' songs, did he refer again to
"the Night End Long Ago," and after performing a song to which the
phrase referred, he explained its meaning in the following terms:

> This is a song for shamans. . . . This world ended once. Night cov-
> ered the whole world. The shaman asks that Iaperikuli make the
> night pass, to let the world be the way it is now.
> For night came and stayed awhile. Iaperikuli himself did this. Later,
> he saved the world in his song. . . . [After he saved people] he
> asked, "So, you are not going to stay like animals? Eating people
> with poison?" Iaperikuli saved us.

I shall refer again to this song later in this book, but I wish to point
out here that the "Night End" song theme refers directly to the moment in the myth when Iaperikuli brings on the night, forcing the ani-

mals up the tree in order to later provoke the catastrophe of lightning which broke the tree and in which the animals were devoured in the waters. Bringing on thunder and lightning, clearing the sky of clouds, or "closing" it through darkness are all shamanic powers, according to Mandu, for shamans are *hekwapinai*, or universe people.

Now, recall that in the myth of the beginning of Iaperikuli, the heroes are called *hekwapinai*, universe people, and exhibit the shamanic powers to transform and to act as tricksters. It is evident, then, that both myths that I have cited refer to shamanism and its importance to cosmic cycles. In the myth of Dzauikuapa, Iaperikuli uses his shamanic power to cause night and so forth, in an attempt to kill the animals, specifically the animal chief Dzauikuapa. The explicit purpose of Iaperikuli's trick, stated by all narrators, is to kill the chief in order that he not make evil omens, *hinimai*; however, Iaperikuli did not succeed in doing so. Omens, today, thus presage people's deaths; the *ipeku*—the descendant of the original omen maker—is, according to Mandu, also "poison owner," and poison, *manhene*, is what the Hohodene believe makes people die.

If, today, a person hears the cry of certain animals, such as the monkey *ipeku*, which may appear at night at the edge of villages, it is an omen and sure to cause a fatal sickness, diagnosed as "poison," for it is believed to be the animals who give people poison, "eat people with poison" (a concept I hope will become clear during the course of this book; see especially, Chapter 5). Briefly, *this enigmatic phrase refers to a fundamental dynamic of exchange between humanity and the animals and spirits of nature in which, in return for the animals which humans kill to eat with pepper, the animal-spirits come back to kill and consume humans with poison.*

Various narrators also linked this myth directly to seasonal referents: Mandu told the myth, for example, immediately following his explanation of how shamans make the summer, or dry season, come. Another narrator, Nocêncio, an evangelical pastor of the village of Santarém, told the myth when talking about the *cigarra* spirits called *dzurunai*, whose cries in the forest are reminders of the early dry season time of cutting gardens. I suspect that if one were to probe more deeply into the ecological links between the animal, fruit, and fish species mentioned in this myth, the links to the dry season would become more evident.

But what is perhaps more important, at least from narrators' comments, is that the myth is one of a series of stories of Iaperikuli's struggles against the animal chief and the *eenunai*. I will have occasion to refer to other myths in Parts II and III of this book. In my understanding, this mythic discourse presents a sequence of catastrophes and regenerations all of which are related to the end of the primordial world and the new world created from the vestiges of the old.

If, for example, we compare—and note, this is *my* suggestion, for no narrator explicitly did this—the myth of the Dzauikuapa with the final episode of the beginning of Iaperikuli, when Enúmhere attempts to kill the Iaperikunai by fire, we may see how both work with images of catastrophe and regeneration. In the myth of the beginning of Iaperikuli, the animal chief Enúmhere burns a garden in the early dry season and orders the heroes to stay in the center of the garden. As the fire threatens to consume them, the heroes enter a container— an *ambaúba* tree which bursts apart from the heat—and the heroes fly out, "not dead." In the myth of the Dzauikuapa, it is Iaperikuli who, through his shamanism, forces the animals to ascend the fruit tree in midriver. As the piranha and alligators threaten to consume them, the chief enters a container—a dried-up fruit—and floats away to the "edge of the sky." Nearly all the other animals are devoured, but the chief comes back, singing as it ascends the river. Comparison between the two episodes is interesting, for whereas the first announces the triumph of the heroes over death, the second announces that the harbinger of death continues to exist—a sort of dialectical tension, or cosmic battle, between order and chaos in the world today.

This mythic discourse develops through a series of themes: different modes of death (cannibalistic feasts, catastrophic consumption, poison and poisonous drink), manners of dealing with death (avenging or "returning" deaths, outwitting the killers), and the lasting traces of death (evil omens, wild and poisonous plants, a heap of bones and the spirit of death, and the multiple species of tree animals) are central to a single story about the end of the primordial world and the new order created from its remains. The new order contains traces of the old for Iaperikuli never succeeded in totally eliminating the forces of chaos that the thunders and animals represent: poison, *manhene,* and evil omens, *hinimai,* are still seen as the persistent causes of people's deaths in the world today, despite the efforts to control them.

Catastrophic destruction of the world also remains a real possibility; for when it seems that the world has become dominated by insupportable evil—as represented in the myths by demons, predatory animals, an excess of poison—then the conditions are sufficient for destruction and renewal. The history of the cosmos attests to this pattern: Before Iaperikuli brought forth the first ancestors of humanity, he caused a great flood to wash away the demons and forest spirits to a distant mountain. Then he burned the world, forcing the remaining demons and forest spirits to flee. Once he had rid the world of these dangers, he then looked for the first ancestors.

Kuwai

The myth of Kuwai is the next major cycle on the history of the cosmos. Infinitely rich in symbolism, it is a central myth which narrators tell to explain at least four critical questions about the nature of the world: how the order and ways of life of the ancestors are transmitted to all future generations; how children are taught the nature of the world; how sicknesses and misfortune entered the world; and the nature of the relationship among humans, animals, and spirits that is the legacy of the primordial world.

The myth of Kuwai is the central focus of Chapter 4, but to summarize it briefly here, the story recounts the life of Kuwai, the child of Iaperikuli and Amaru, the first woman. Kuwai is an extraordinary being whose body consists of all worldly elements and whose humming and singing brings into being all animal species. His birth sets in motion a rapid process of growth in which the miniature and chaotic world of Iaperikuli opens up into the life-size world of forests and rivers inhabited by human beings and the various species of forest animals, birds, and fish. Kuwai teaches humanity the first rituals of initiation; yet at the end of the ritual, Iaperikuli "kills" Kuwai by pushing him into an enormous fire—an "inferno" as the narrator Keruaminali said—that scorches the earth, and the world then contracts back to its miniature size. Out of Kuwai's ashes are born poisonous plants, sickness-giving spirits (*iupinai*), and the plant materials for making the sacred flutes and trumpets with which the Baniwa initiate their children today. Amaru and the women steal these instruments from Iaperikuli, setting off a long chase in which the world opens up for a second time as the women play the instruments throughout the world. Eventually, the men regain the flutes, and with them Iaperikuli brings forth the first ancestors of humanity.

The myth, it may be seen, marks a transition from the primordial world to a more recent human past that is brought directly into the experience of living people through rituals. The first world of the animals and thunders was doomed to demise and destruction; humanity only sees its vestiges as a given condition, while the world of Kuwai connects the distant world of the beginning to the world that is constantly being created by humanity. For this reason shamans say that Kuwai is both of This World and of the Other (ancient) World of the sky and lives in "the center of the world." In their cures, shamans bring the two worlds together in order to effect a cure, that is, to regain the lost soul of an afflicted person. To shamans, Kuwai is the "owner of sickness," *idzamikaite iminali*, for his body also consists of all the sicknesses that he left for humanity in the great conflagration that marked his "death" and withdrawal from the world. It is he whom the shamans must seek in order to cure those fatally ill from *manhene* today.

Kuwai is also known by the name of Wamundana, a word which would appear to be composed of the merging of two elements, both of which point to the nature of this being: *wamu*, the black sloth; and *dana*, shadow, shade, invisible dark interior. The notion is of a spiritualized animal, another aspect of Kuwai and a particularly dangerous one for its associations with sickness, death, and catastrophe. *Wamu* is the mythic "owner of poison," as the Dzauikuapa was said to be; *wamu* is one of the forms of the chief of the animals whom Iaperikuli failed to kill; *wamu*, shamans say, is the "shadow-soul" of Kuwai, a projection of its dark interior.[2] For this reason the flutes and trumpets, also called Kuwai, are considered to be extremely dangerous and can cause a catastrophe—collective death by poison—if they are exposed outside their ritual context. Ritual fasting and abstinence from eating animals are thus seen as forms of voluntary suffering to which individuals must submit if they wish to be cured, or to become fully cultural beings through initiation.

The New Order

The world that Iaperikuli created was not only one of perilous danger for, parallel to the heroes' struggles, a series of myths also recount how Iaperikuli brings into being conditions that sustain and renew life—the fertility of gardens, the alternation of day and night and corresponding human activities, the acquisition of tobacco and cooking fire. As will become evident in the following story told by Luis, a Oalipere-dakenai elder, all of these elements and conditions are considered necessary for a "good" life. Iaperikuli obtained them in sequence from their spiritual "owners" or "masters" and later transmitted them to humanity, to the "others who will be born." In his narration, Luis presented three stories of creation in sequence which tell how Iaperikuli obtained the earth for making gardens, the container of night, and tobacco. Other narrators told each of the three separately without connecting one with the other as is done here.

When this Kuwai is born, for him our father, orphan Iaperikuli
   [*pawaada*: orphan, for Iaperikuli's kin had all been killed],
At his birth, so little, so little is his child.
Then Kuwai shits, he shits, he shits.

This earth is his shit, Kuwai's shit is this earth.
It grew a little, like so little it was, thus we saw the earth long ago,
The world began for us.
His earth, then, our orphan father: a rock, thus it was a rock,
A rock was his village.
Then he thought about this garden land—
Is there no way to get it for people, to get plants?
Then he went to get the earth with Kuwai.
Thus it was so little, the first earth,
It grew the earth. . . . He shat the earth Kuwai, . . . he saw it.
Then, the white people call him Adam, for us Baniwa we know
    him as Kaali,
He saw the earth and got it with Iaperikuli for gardens.
Then he made gardens on it.
Then he got for the gardens our food for today, it remains truly for
    us as it began.
He got plants from Kuwai . . . all of them! Potatoes, bananas, all
    plants . . .
They were his, Kuwai's.
Kaali, whom they call Adam, saw and took them for his
    plantations.
His garden things, thus they are. Thus, in the beginning the earth
    was from long ago for gardens.
Then after, truly it was, we grew on it until today.
That's all, but it was so little as I said in the beginning.
Now, the day for him, our orphan father, was always there.
The sun was forever there.
It never went away, the day, the sun was always there.
He went off to work,
Came back, arrived, and stayed,
He fixed his food,
The sun didn't set.
He went away again,
Returned and arrived,
Fixed his food,
The sun didn't set.
His wife, she his wife, the elders say, was the daughter of night.
"It's good what my father has, Iaperiko," she says to him [Iaperiko
    is a familiar term of address for Iaperikuli],
"It's good what my father has there,
"He goes off, works, comes back . . .
"He makes his food and then at dusk he says, 'We stay apart,

tomorrow it will be [a good-night farewell],'" she says to her
husband Iaperikuli.
Then Iaperikuli thinks, "Mmhmm, so it is, let's go see," and he
went.
He went to get this basket of night [i.e., a basket containing
darkness, all night animals, insects, and so on].
Night gave it to him there,
Far away there, it's called the place of night, *deepíwali*.
Night gave Iaperikuli a little basket of grass with little fruits woven
on it.
But it was very heavy!!
Iaperikuli returns and at midtrail says, "What is it that weighs so
much?" he says, for it was so little.
He opens the top a little—*tchik!*—night came out, out it came,
The sun went across the sky *liiiiiiiiiiii*. . . .
The sun then went, "Oh, it's night," Iaperikuli says,
"Oh, it's night"   "Yes, it's night"
"Now it is truly."
The sun . . . fell away.
"Ah, how will it be, my grandfathers?" he says to the animals,
All those animals and birds—the *jacu*, the *mutum*, that rooster,
the dove,
All of those animals, the big-bellied monkeys,
The black sloth *wamu* climbs up a tree and stays.
The frog *paitchi* sang *"okuekue"* because it was cold and climbed up
a tree.
The *jacu* bird went up . . . at night it stays on a tree.
"Ah, so it is for those unborn," he says.
The bird-of-the-night goes up and sings, "nnininni-night comes
out."
They began, each goes its own way as the night comes out.
The night went . . .
Untilll . . . the dawn comes out and the rooster makes its song.
This *mutum* also, that we call the "pet of *manale*," the *mutum*.
Rooster makes its song,
Then the *mutum's* song—*"hnnn hnhnhnnn"* the day it knew, *"hnn
hnnhnn"* its song.
Rooster cries out its song at dawn . . .
It goes to look, "Heeeey! It's already appearing!"
The dawn.
Mutum makes its song . . . until done. Rooster makes its song . . .
until done.

"Oooh," says this black sloth,

"The day has come," it says, *"kuku,"* it says,

"It's day," it says.

On one side, Iaperikuli sits on a treetop and watches, over there
the sun appears.

He made the sun go, turn about, and return.

The dawn Iaperikuli sees, he watches the dawn rise,

"Day it is," they say to him, "its way is made, the dawn is here."

He sees it rise, "Oooh, so it will be for those unborn," he made it so
here in the world for us today.

The sun rises . . . when it is near noon, people make their food
ready,

For us people, Iaperikuli lived long ago at Warukwa [an island on
the Uaraná stream, tributary of the upper Aiary], his village.

Thus he was coming home when he opened the container of
night—*plahh.*

The sun came out for him . . .

Iaperikuli went off to work and returned . . .

Then he made his food at night . . .

Thus it is also, it is so today truly.

Then he obtains this tobacco, Iaperikuli obtains it from Dzuli,

He obtains it from Dzuli first! In the beginning.

This dry tobacco, he knows it's good,

"Give me some, grandfather," he says.

"So it is, I will bring it,"

He gives him thus, his dry tobacco.

"No, I want the green kind, for me to plant, a basket of it," he says.

"Go back home," he says, "I myself will deliver it," he says.

Thus he would deliver it to Iaperikuli's village.

This Dzuli will meet Iaperikuli's children there.

He comes to them . . .

He meets those children, he comes to them.

He delivers tobacco to them . . .

"Where is Iaperikuli?"   "He is gone," they say.

"I bring tobacco,

"This good tobacco for him," he says to those children,

"This good tobacco for him, I leave him tobacco,

"Over there," he says.

He goes behind the house and plants it.

"I go now from you,"

That's all, he left them and returned.

Night came . . .

Iaperikuli returned, "Where is Dzuli?"   "He's already gone back."

"He left a good thing for you," they say to him.
The night passed . . .
The tobacco then grew, he went out behind the house, he went out
   to see . . .
Iaperikuli went out to see where the tobacco was,
"Oooh, thus it is, for those unborn," he says then, he left the
   knowledge for us today of all our smoke.
All of it. The tobacco the white people have . . .
There, those white people, what they have is different from us . . .
What they have, the white people, we don't know how it is.
This what I tell you, is *ours, we people!* This tobacco we have.
This what I tell you is ours, we people . . .
That's all.

Interpretation

Each piece of the narration seems to be following a similar line of story development: beginning with a primordial condition which is sterile or static (the earth is a rock, the excrement of Kuwai; it is always day, there is no alternation) or dry (tobacco), a different condition, qualified as "good," "new" is sought. This different condition is introduced from the outside (other spirit-owners have it, and Iaperikuli gets it for humanity), but in the process, a transformation occurs. Transformations are marked by strong images of passage (total darkness, for example) in which sealed, closed, or hidden containers (baskets, seeds) open or burst apart, producing a radical change. Such transformations are not necessarily catastrophic, although there is a hint of this in the case of night which covers the whole world like a flood and Iaperikuli asks, "how will it be, my grandfathers?" In each instance, however, a new order is expected and awaited: the earth is tilled; nocturnal and diurnal orders are created; strong tobacco is planted. These new orders sustain human life, defining how people can live well and prosper in This World.[3]

Rather different is the perspective that the narrator Keruaminali of Uapui had on life in This World. Far from being a "good" earth where people prosper, as Luis said, the shaman Keruaminali adamantly affirmed the "evil" and sickly nature of This World. In his version of the "Kuwai earth," Keruaminali stated the following:

Iaperikuli took the Kuwai [trumpet] and blew it—"*Heeee!*" It grew and grew—huge it became! Thus Iaperikuli made this Kuwai earth grow. The earth. The earth began, the Kuwai earth. That's all, he left it for people. Each one would have their own land. They have made it bad, this pain place, *kaiwíkwe*, this rotten place, *ekú-kwe*. It seems they wish to finish off with people. . . . Bad do we live on it, not well. Thus, it is a bad earth, *hipai maatchídali*. Another earth is good, that of Iaperikuli. When we die, we go there. Bad people who have killed do not go there. . . . The Kuwai earth is bad; Iaperikuli's earth is good. That's all."

Besides this pessimistic view of This World, Keruaminali's discourse was marked with what I would call a strongly catastrophic view of cosmogony, with various images of "infernos"—his word, which no other narrator used—great conflagrations, celestial fires, and so on. In the story of how Iaperikuli obtained tobacco, for example, the image Keruaminali used for the moment when Grandfather Tobacco brought tobacco to Iaperikuli's house was that of a great, fiery wind in the night. His view of the earth as "bad, evil," the "pain place," the "rotten place" stands in marked contrast with that of Luis, who was not a shaman and who explicitly disagreed with Keruaminali's view of the earth as *maatchíkwe*, bad place, seeing it rather as a "good" place, consistent with the images that he presented in his narratives.

A final narrative I shall cite illustrating the "new order" created in primordial times is of great importance for shamans, as it recounts how Iaperikuli and his brothers found shamanic powers, or *malikai*, i.e., thunder, shamanic vision, a jaguar-tooth collar. Like the myths presented so far, this myth also develops the theme of "food chains," which are so important to the origin of the cosmos—here, in order to talk about shamanic powers. Thus, narrators stated that this myth "follows" the myth (not cited in this book) of how manioc and garden plants were obtained from the "Great Tree of Kaali." This enormous tree, *Kaali ka thadapa*, connecting earth and sky, sprang up from the earth from the body of the hero Kaali, "master" of the earth, who sacrificed himself in a huge garden fire. The Great Tree of Kaali is the ancestral source of all cultivated plants on earth; it is from this tree, the Hohodene say, that their ancestors obtained manioc for their gardens today.

It happens that atop the Great Tree, there was a jaguar-tooth collar, a highly desired shamanic power object which Iaperikuli and his brothers seek to obtain but which the Tapir steals from them and— typical of the unbridled voraciousness of the animals that, we have seen, must be controlled—transforms into a predatory jaguar until Iaperikuli regains the power object and puts the Tapir in its rightful place in the food chain, as a harmless vegetarian. The final episode of the story recounts how the first shamans, called *wakaawenai*, ascended body and soul into the Other World. One of the points of the narrative, it seems to me, is the shaman's role as mediator in the ordering of the food chain which refers to other cosmological cycles (e.g., meteorological) as well. This has importance for understanding why, in the messianic and millenarian movements of the past, shamanic leaders were believed to have extraordinary powers over the growth of plantations.

The narrator of this myth is Keramunhe, Hohodene elder of Kuliriana and perhaps the most respected teller of myths of the upper Aiary. On the occasion, Keramunhe's son João helped with the translation, but his principal role was that of participating in the dialogic form of narration—repeating phrases, which I have indicated by asterisks in the text, and asking questions or making comments to clarify or to anticipate, which I have indicated in parentheses. To facilitate understanding of the text, since Keramunhe makes ample use of sounds and expressions only found in mythic narratives, I have again inserted brief explanatory notes where appropriate in brackets. The narrative begins with Iaperikuli's younger brother looking to make the sound of thunder, one of the shamans' powers:

Iaperikuli's younger brother,
Iaperikuli's younger brother,
Looks for *malikai* . . .
He goes and kicks the shell of a hollow tree—No? [i.e., it makes no
  sound] He kicks the shell of a hollow tree.
Then it was, he goes and sees an *ibacaba* fruit tree.
He sees it eating then,
This Kamathawa [the harpy eagle],
Jaguar Kamathawa. ["Jaguar" is here used as a title indicating
  character as fierce and solitary as the jaguar.]
He goes and looks for an animal to kill,
He goes and waits the night,
Nothing happened?
He waits the whole time,
Nothing happened?
"*Pah!* What's this?" He sits through the night . . .
Taaa . . . The middle of the night, it was,
The middle of the night . . .
He hears it coming *aaffffffff.* . . .
This, what he [Kamathawa] made then, there . . .
His *purákali* [a sort of drying-up or wasting-away sickness with
  much loss of saliva]
Tuku-Haaminawaaaahaakhhh-TIHHH! "Hey" [Kamathawa fell to
  the ground.]

Quickly he lights torchwood,
He sees nothing?
He sees nothing there?
He found nothing.
Nothing there . . .
He sits and waits,
The rest of the night.
The day was appearing, the sun was up there.
He climbed up the tree,
He climbed.
Up there, the *ibacaba* fruit tree.
He got, then, this tiny little feather,
"This must be it," he said,
He sniffs it [sniff] *TAYN! TAYYNN!!* [i.e., his vision opens]
He turns around and looks, turns around and looks.
It was lying down there below him,
A white eagle it seems, but it was a person it seems.
It seems then, he descended the tree . . . *tayn*—"Who are you?"
    "Jaguar Kamathawa, Jaguar Kamathawa."
"You were looking for me?" it said.   "Yes, I was looking for
    you."   "Ah, so it is." Then he came closer.
"So, ah, so it is." It then took its feather, (its crest feather) its crest
    feather,
Kamathawa plucked it out. "Sniff this."
He sniffed it—*TAYYNN!*
Khu'Khu'lulululululululu. . . . it was the sound of thunder!
The sun was straight above, straight above,
He went baaaaaack . . .
Iaperikuli came,
(Iaperikuli's younger brother) Iaperikuli's younger brother went to
    meet him.
"Iaperiko?" he said.
"Huh?" He didn't see him.
He didn't see his younger brother.
He had transformed, it seems.
"Now, where did you go?" he said.
"I sounded thunder. Yes, I sounded it, I found it," he said.
"Where, then?"   "Over there."
"Ah, so it seems, fine."
"Now, so it will be from now on," he gave him this, his feather.*
He sniffed it, he sniffs,* Iaperikuli sniffs [sniffs] *TAYNN! Haalaaa!*
    He sees, he was seeing as they do today—"Is it you?"   "Yes, it's

me" "Who did you meet?" "Kamathawa" "Aahh yes,
  good."
In the beginning he looked for, he first found, it seems, (first
  malikai) he found *malikai*.
So now . . .
Now, they already had it,
That's all, they remained with it.
Well! Well they had visions, before us today.
Now it will be, then, they looked for then . . .
For then, it seems, this *dzato* [i.e., *pariká*, shaman's hallucinogenic
  snuff], this *marawáthi* [another type of snuff].
Those things of theirs, and our things, ours, it seems.
This *marawáthi*, this *dzato* also. From the riverbank* [i.e., where it is
  found], from the riverbank, where they are (white sandbanks)
  white sandbanks. But what he found was this *marawáthi*.
At noon, they looked for . . . and found the *Kaali ka thadapa*, the
  Great Tree of Kaali.
Here, there weren't any people for this was in the Other World,
  Pakuma, those were Iaperikuli's people, it seems.
No, there weren't any people here.
They found the Great Tree of Kaali.
Its trunk, it seems, was of *dupa* wood, its trunk,
It was a HUGE tree!
There, at Uaracapory [on the upper Uaupés River]
On, . . . They went . . .
Those *wakaawenai** [i.e., Iaperikuli's people], *wakaawenai* went and
  he came,*
They went . . .
Heeee—suddenly—"me too, me too," said this Tapir,
He came and they went, quickly they saw him, "Let's go"
"Now you, you go kill, my grandfather," Iaperikuli said to Tapir,
  "go kill fish"
"Go catch our food before the tree falls," he said
(To Tapir) To Tapir.
"Ah, so it is."
He went to kill . . . he went on the Tapir trail,
Below Surubi Point [on the Aiary River],
He killed, he went underwater, he killed and heaped the fish
  together in the fish trap.
They killed fish . . .
"I hear it fall then," he said, for there with him was his companion.
"I do not hear it fall," his companion says, "The Great Tree of Kaali"

(Tapir?) Tapir was trapping,
He trapped for them.
Much much later, they had fished well, it was midafternoon.
So then, the *inambú* [tinamou bird] Duma sang: "*Duumaaaaa . . .* "
  They thought they heard it fall, but they heard then, (something
  else) something else.
(Tapir?) Tapir trapped fish.
He killed a *uaracú* [suckermouth] fish, a *pacú* fish,
A red *pacú* fish also—three fish he killed.
He heard—*dzeeeeellllllll*!
Now the Tapir goes underwater,* he goes underwater,
He comes back out,
"Did you hear it fall!?"
"No, no."
"Really!?" Right after, he went underwater again,
And comes back out—"Did you hear it?"   "No, no!"
Right after, he goes under again.
The Duma sings again,
"*Duumaaaaa,*" it sings:
"*Oopi Kaali ka thadapa ipoua Dumaaa*
"*Oopi Kaali ka thadapa ipoua Dumaaa*" [sung; to the effect: the Great
  Tree has already fallen], it sings, this Duma.
He heard, he heard it, it seems.
"Did you hear it?" he says.
"It's about to fall—so it will"
"Really!?" he says.
He went back under—shortly after he heard, (this Tapir) this Tapir
  heard,
"*Oopi Kaali ka thadapa ipoua Dumaaa . . .*" *tk . . .* out he came, the
  Great Tree would fall,
"Really?"
"I don't know."   "Yes it fell."
Soon after, "*Oopi Kaali ka thadapa ipoua Dumaaaa*" Oooooh—then,
  Khhhhhuuuuuu. . . . It fell.
Tapir ran then with the *uaracú*, the *pacú*, the red *pacú* also,
Tk' tsa' "ahh let's go, let's go"
Midway into the forest,
He stepped on the *uaracú tih! ap'* and killed it,
He stepped on the *pacú* fish *hat'tih,* and killed it,
He put the pieces together
The *uaracú* fish then . . . became ants
Like so the sun was, then he came running . . .
He made there,

Another kind of *sauva* ants.

Pa' They were there, he came up to Iaperikuli.

Then the swarms of bees there—so many bees there were!!! [at the top of the fallen tree]

(No way that Iaperikuli could . . .) There was no way that Iaperikuli could get the jaguar-tooth collar!!!

(Then the Tapir came) Then the Tapir came,

"Hey, how is it, grandson?" "No, grandfather" "I will go there," he says, ooooooo The Tapir . . . *kllllll* . . . He sees then, it seems,

Tapir doesn't feel anything [i.e., the bees cannot sting his thick hide],

Oooooo—he went and took it like so, so it was then,

He went, it seems, and got it there, a basketful of things

Then, inside the tree so it was then, up there, in the middle, it seems,

At the fruits of the Great Tree of Kaali fruits, it seems,

Then he took them, *hutsum*, he takes them from their owner [i.e., Iaperikuli is the rightful owner of the shamans' things], he took them.

So, then he had taken them, he sniffed "aaaahh . . . how will it be?"

(He had already taken them from Iaperikuli) He had already taken them from Iaperikuli. "*Tuupá*," Iaperikuli says, "now it's been done."

"This is not good," he says.

The *wakaawenai* came back and sat with Tapir, they came back and snuffed *pariká*, it seems, as they do today—giving snuff to one, another, another, another . . . until, many of them.

Those *wakaawenai*, many of them, it seems.

They snuffed . . .

They blew, he blew for them this *pariká* [i.e., one shaman blows the snuff through a bone into the nostrils of another]

"Patron, do it for me," Iaperikuli said to Tapir,

"I will blow for you," Tapir says, he gets it for Iaperikuli.

He blows for them *tah*—he blows for them *pariká*

All of them who snuffed,

Became drunk on it.

Drunk they were . . . *tihh!* [Tapir falls down], he runs,

Tih! Huuutsu! Thus Tapir roared,

"*Heee Heee Heeee Heeee*," he said.

"Aaah, I want to eat people," he said.

He became a jaguar, a jaguar he became, he transformed.

"No, no, this is not good," Iaperikuli said.

He blew for him.

"No, no, this is not good," he said and went to take *pariká* away
  from Tapir—*huuulu*—from the owner,

(Iaperikuli took it away from him) Iaperikuli took it away from
  him, "I do like so, grandfather," he said.

Huuulu—he came back and struck him—*taynn!*—on his snout.

On, he had already taken them [i.e., the shamans' things] from
  him, he had already taken them from Tapir.

Then—Tapir went crazy, the others went crazy,

One of them . . . ran into the forest.

The *boto* [dolphin] got up *phuaamete tih!* And fell

The otter *tih!* fell into the river.

That's all—those that went crazy, it seems.

They sat with him—Mapuiri, Makurúthuna, Weemali [i.e., the
  names of three shamans who stayed with Iaperikuli]

(Three of them) Three of them.

Iaperikuli stays among them, his younger brother, his younger
  brother, it seems,

They were, it seems, those *wakaawenai.**

For so it was that they got *malikai,** *malikai.*

It was Iaperikuli who began it.

Until, it seems, then . . .

It was ending.

Until, it seems, it remained with him. . . .

Like so, it seems . . .

"We shall see," he says

To those *wakaawenai*, about their ascent,* their ascent.

"It will be good," he says.

He left them there in the house,

He went walking.

At a certain time,

He returned,

And heard them there: "*Heee oopi ka wákawa . . . Heee oopi ka
  wákawa . . . Hee oopi wapadama linako wapadamakapi . . . Heee oopi
  ka wákawa linako wapadamakapi*" [sung; to the effect—"We have
  gone, we have transformed on it, we have gone on it, we have
  transformed"], so they sang.

They were seeing.

He stopped and heard, "Aaaah no . . ."

"*Piuka piadeta wapidzawaaa . . . Liuka karumitadieta liapidza uata . . .
  Padzu Padzuuu Dzulíferi*" [to the effect: "You come back among
  us, he comes back among them, our father, father Dzulíferi, the
  primal shaman, Iaperikuli's brother"], so they sang.

They had gone away.
He came, looked around, came out of the house,
"Where are they?" he looked for them,
He didn't find them. . . . They had gone.
They had gone, the *wakaawenai*,* the *wakaawenai* (thus it was the
   wakaawenai) thus it was the *wakaawenai* . . .
That's all, that's all.
He came back to stay, Iaperikuli *tayn*, here, in This World (already
   they'd left him) already they left him, the others.
Thus it was with *malikai*,* *malikai*.
Doctors they are, it seems,* doctors they are, those shamans.
They extract, they revive us well.
(They help us well) They help us well.
(That's truly all then?) That's truly all.

Interpretation

This myth reveals an enormous complexity of interwoven themes that
define shamans' powers, *malikai*. As Sullivan has pointed out in relation to South American shamanism:

> "The origins of shamanism account for the range of the shaman's
> responsibilities as well as for the power of his accoutrements. The
> shaman's tasks may include weather control, growth magic for
> crops, providing game animals for hunters, supplying fish, secur-
> ing names for newborns, presiding over rites of passage, curing ill-
> ness, accompanying the dead, escorting the souls of ritual offerings
> to their destinations, and many others. The shaman faces these
> tasks with confidence, sure in the knowledge that, in the very
> beginning of time, powerful beings made their accomplishments
> possible. He possesses these beings' techniques, their power items,
> their example, and their direct aid." (1988, 391)

Concretely, narrators leave it clear that two powers are explicitly
sought in this myth: the sound of thunder, *eenu*, and the jaguar-tooth
collar, *dzaui-e*, an icon of shamanic power. Yet, as I shall show, the
quests for these powers also define, along the way, the shaman's attributes, relations to food and meteorological cycles, and the transformative nature of primordial beings. Animal metaphors—particularly
the harpy and the Tapir—provide mythic models through which
proper and improper relations to shamanic powers are formulated.
Perhaps the critical transformative moment of the myth—consistent
with other myths of "the new order"—occurs at the felling of the

Great Tree of Kaali from which, despite the chaotic situation which this initially produced, a new order emerges to be reproduced for all times.

The first episode of the myth describes a process of "finding," *liwaketa*, shamanic powers, *malikai*—all the numerous elements and powers that the shaman has which, in my view, corresponds to a process of reorganizing individual perceptions and bodily forms into that of a shaman. In this, the harpy Kamathawa provides the mythic model.

According to other myths, Kamathawa is the transformed soul of Iaperikuli's younger brother who was devoured by an affinal tribe called the "Children of Grandfather Fish-poison," Kunáferi-ieni. From being an object of predation, his soul is transformed into a fierce predator who returns to avenge his own death by killing and devouring those who killed him. Kamathawa's predatory quality and solitary nature are expressed in the title "Jaguar Kamathawa," which is a title also used to refer to Iaperikuli. Kamathawa is said to be Iaperikuli's "pet," *ipira*, who dwells in the highest place of the cosmos guarding his master's house and remedies. His power resides in his piercing vision, or clairvoyance. Shamans in real life possess crystals, among their apparel, which they say are obtained from Kamathawa and which permit them to "see the whole world." The harpy's feathers are also used by shamans to "clear" the sky of clouds and to bring on the dry, summer season. The first part of this myth likewise makes reference to the beginning of the dry season, when the *ibacaba* fruit ripens, when men gather this fruit and hunt game, and when there are frequent thunderstorms in the Northwest Amazon. A time of seasonal transition, it is appropriate that it would be marked by shamanic symbolism.

The process of Iaperikuli's younger brother's transformation begins with his incapacity to make the sound of thunder and to hear and then to see the powerful harpy. After his ascent up the tree and after he sniffs the feather, which opens his vision (the first shamanic power), as *pariká* does in real life today, he is able to see the white eagle lying below him as a person, that is, the shaman's double vision. His descent of the tree and encounter with the white eagle—perhaps, the terrestrial form of the harpy—puts him in direct contact with the spirit world: "You were looking for me?" the eagle says. "Yes, I was looking for you." This process is much the same as what Reichel-Dolmatoff has stated of the Dessana shaman:

> His vision must not be blurred, his sense of hearing must be acute, he must be able to distinguish clearly the images that appear to his

mind while in a state of trance, and to understand the supernatural voices speaking to him. (1975: 77)

Sniffing the crest feather then produces the powerful roar of thunder. Having acquired this power, Iaperikuli's younger brother returns home, but is invisible to Iaperikuli—another indication of his transformation into a shamanic being.

Why is thunder considered to be such a powerful shamanic attribute, a mark of shamanic identity? It is, undoubtedly, the most powerful sound of the sky (sky and thunder are the same word, *eenu*) and one of various powerful sounds that "open the world" and that are associated with cosmic creation. In myths of the Arawakan Tariana of the middle Uaupés—kin of the Baniwa—Thunder, Enu, is one of the primordial creative powers whose shamanism gave rise to the Tariana and Baniwa peoples, as well as to "Jurupary," or Kue, the equivalent of Kuwai in Hohodene myths (S. Hugh-Jones 1979, 302–308). For the Tukanoan-speaking Dessana, the harpy eagle is considered thunder's companion and messenger (Reichel-Dolmatoff 1975, 78).

The second episode of the myth, which focuses on the felling of the Great Tree of Kaali, unmistakably develops the "ecological" cycles hinted at in the first. In fact, I consider this one of the major points of the episode and of the myth as a whole: shamanism is indispensable to the sustenance of life through the annual, natural cycles. Just as the myth of the beginning of night (see above) establishes the alternation of night and day and its correlated human activities, so the myth of Iaperikuli's search for *malikai* develops the theme of the acquisition of shamanic powers within the cycles of constellations, food chains, and control over their transformations. Hence the predominant images in this part of the myth revolve around the felling of the Great Tree of Kaali, the primordial source of all plants in the world; the ambiguous figure of the Tapir; and the acquisition of "ownership" of the jaguar-tooth collar with its transformative power. These are important symbols for shamans—even more so, considering that various messianic shamans in Baniwa history were attributed extraordinary powers over the growth of gardens.

The Great Tree of Kaali is one of the major symbols of primordial unity in Hohodene mythology—and, I would venture to say, in Baniwa religion—on a par with Iaperikuli, as the "father of all humanity," and Kuwai, as the All-Things-in-One being that gave rise to the world today. The felling of the Great Tree broke up the uniqueness of this primordial tree, so that it became the numerous cultivated plants and fruits that multiplied and filled the earth. It is said that, after the tree fell, people from all over the world came and took plants from it for their gardens.

The felling of the tree refers, as I have suggested above, to various interrelated food chains: the annual agricultural cycle synchronized with meteorological phenomena, fishing activities associated with the levels of the rivers, and the appearance of various insects. As J. Hill explains, in the short dry season,

> when the rivers begin to recede and when fishing starts to improve after the long wet season, . . . men select and cut new gardens in accordance with the mythical calendar of Kaali. (1984, 532)

and

> the general belief underlying all phases of the annual cycle of agriculture is that people can make the labor of gardening easier and safer by synchronizing their activities with the mythical calendar of Kaali and his children. (533)

Thus, in the myth under consideration, as the *wakaawenai* go to fell the Great Tree of Kaali, the Tapir is sent to fish at the large river traps. Hill's ecological analysis again helps us to understand this moment:

> The annual cycle culminates in the main planting of new manioc gardens at the end of the long dry season. This period, called Waripérinúma [the "mouth" or beginning of the Pleiades] is also the time of spectacular spawning runs of the various species of suckermouth (*uaracú*) fish: these species return each year to the same streams and appear in recently flooded areas of forest and open savannah. The mouth of the stream is blocked off with large fish traps after a wave of fish has passed into the lake upstream. (535)

This period also corresponds to the annual cycle of *pudali* exchange festivals in which affinal and kin groups drink and dance together.

The Tapir has a central importance in the second episode of the myth. Reichel-Dolmatoff's analysis of Tapir symbolism among the neighboring Tukanoan-speaking Dessana is, I think, particularly relevant to understanding the image here:

> a huge and heavy, very powerful and fast-moving, but clumsy and quite inoffensive, . . . a cunning, yet slow-witted brute. Tapirs will open trails in the dense underbrush that lead straight to the river's edge and, when frightened, will blindly rush along these tunnels

to plunge into the water. They will not hide or silently scuttle away but will noisily overcome all obstacles in their trail. (1985, 111)

In the numerous tales the Dessana tell of the Tapir, it is "described as a glutton, an egoist loth to share his property" (113). This fits with the characterization of the Tapir in the Hohodene myth under consideration. In the dry season, Dessana men organize tapir hunts for "this is the time of the year when tapirs can be found near *umarí* trees and at salt licks" (123). The Dessana believe that tapirs take human lives in retribution for their losses. In the Hohodene myth, the Tapir, in possession of shamanic powers, transforms into a voracious jaguar that desires to "eat people without end." The catastrophe that this would cause is resolved when Iaperikuli takes away the Tapir's power and replaces it with *umarí* fruits for it to eat. (Even then, one narrator said, the Tapir is later deprived of the *umarí* and left, totally harmless, to eat leaves.)

The acquisition of shamanic powers, in short, is exceedingly dangerous. The snuff and the jaguar-tooth collar are highly potent and ambivalent forces. The means by which the connection is made to the celestial realms, they are also, in the wrong hands, a source of madness. Proper ownership is necessary for the mediation between the two worlds; typically, the animals—especially the Tapir, a mediator who lives on land but is equally comfortable in water, and a selfish and greedy mediator besides—are incapable of controlling that power, producing a catastrophic situation until order is restored.

Finally, in the last part of the myth, the temporal and spatial separation between the primal shamans, the *wakaawenai*, and the human cosmos is completed with their ascension to the sky and permanent withdrawal from the world. These shamans simply "went away," transformed by their song, rising body and soul to the heavens. These primordial shamans seem to represent the idea that they never "died"—their transformation by song was a passage whole from one world to the other without the normal separation of body and soul.

I have examined cosmogony in considerable detail in this chapter, for I believe it is a fundamental basis for understanding shamanism. If I have dwelt at length on mythic discourse, it is because shamans themselves use myth as a vehicle for explaining the nature and dynamics of the universe. The special meanings they attribute to the primordial world, however, frequently go far beyond what I have presented in this chapter and refer to a hidden dimension that only they are capable of disclosing.

The images of the first world confirm, on the one hand, its catastrophic and violent nature, death-dealing and chaotic, in which the creation of order suffers the constant threat of being dismantled. The very beginning of the cosmos is a state of dismemberment, of awesome and devastating events. Such a condition was never really eliminated from possibility; humanity is constantly reminded of its presence. On the other hand, the primordial world is the source of renovation, renewal, and change. Spiritual creativity eternally transcends the destruction of matter: this is the essence of Iaperikuli's being. Spiritual creativity is the source of abundance and happiness that sustain life and create meaningful existence for the future, "for those unborn." Such images inform and shape the powers of the shamans as masters in traversing the space and time that separate the world of the present from the primordial world; as protectors of humanity and liberators of souls from entrapment; as sustainers of life and of the order created in the beginning; as creators of new life; and as messengers of the deities. In the following chapter, I shall examine more closely these images and how they and the central dramas of cosmogony are fully manifest in cosmology and the shamanic quest.

2. Guardians of the Cosmos

This chapter begins with a consideration of the diverse ways in which the Hohodene whom I interviewed—specialists and nonspecialists alike—spoke of the cosmos. My purpose is to show the special relationship that shamans have with the spirit beings of the cosmos. One of the ways shamans understand the quality of being in This World is, as I have shown in the previous chapter, in terms of the legacies of cosmogony: that This World is flawed by sickness, misfortune, and evil. In this view, This World is, like a sick person, in constant need of healing. In their apprenticeship, shamans acquire the power to "make better" and re-create This World through a total identification of their being with the creator/transformer Iaperikuli. In this sense, shamans may be considered as "guardians of the cosmos."

Another way in which shamanic knowledge of the cosmos differs from that of nonspecialists is through the extraordinary elaboration of the vertical dimension of the cosmos. Figure 2 represents the cosmos, *hekwapi*, as drawn by Mandu, a Hohodene shaman of Uapui. The drawing was made at my request and, in its overall form, is similar to the way many nonspecialists understand the universe. Differences and variations I shall consider in the section below titled "A Nonspecialist's View."

When the drawing was done, Mandu folded the two sheets of artist's paper that he used upward to make a concave shape, so that the top of the universe, where the sun is, could clearly be seen as connected with the bottom, where its reflection is—as though, Mandu said, the sun were reflected in the river that runs through the underworld. The most important shapes in the universe are drawn like the rings of a long tube and the top of the tube is closed in an arc, "like the point of a knife," people said. The rings are defined by centers and edges, or peripheries. Each ring is, in reality, a level, flat plane on which various kinds of being live. In the centers of each plane are

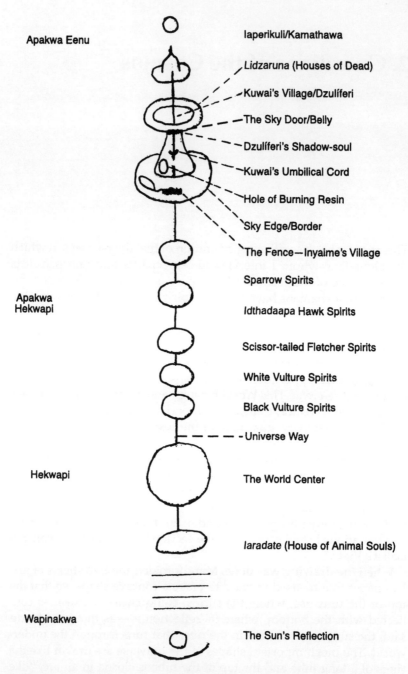

Apakwa Eenu

Apakwa
Hekwapi

Hekwapi

Wapinakwa

Iaperikuli/Kamathawa

Lidzaruna (Houses of Dead)

Kuwai's Village/Dzulíferi

The Sky Door/Belly

Dzulíferi's Shadow-soul

Kuwai's Umbilical Cord

Hole of Burning Resin

Sky Edge/Border

The Fence—Inyaime's Village

Sparrow Spirits

Idthadaapa Hawk Spirits

Scissor-tailed Fletcher Spirits

White Vulture Spirits

Black Vulture Spirits

Universe Way

The World Center

Iaradate (House of Animal Souls)

The Sun's Reflection

Figure 2. The Cosmos according to a Hohodene Shaman

villages of beings that, we might say, have the greatest immediacy. The Hohodene, for instance, say they live in the "center of This World," at Hipana, and all other groups live on the periphery around them— and are marked in other drawings as little circles inside the ellipse of the border of This World. Kuwai lives in the center of the sky, and the souls of the dead have their houses on the periphery of that plane. From the top of the universe to the bottom there are various trails and ways, all of which form one long road, *hekwapi iapoana*, "universe way," through the centers of the planes.

Basically, the universe consists of three planes: Wapinakwa, the Place of Our Bones; Hekwapi, This World; and Apakwa Hekwapi, the Other World. Shamans add that there is also Apakwa Eenu, the Other Sky, which evidently is part of the Other World. I shall briefly characterize each of these planes in terms of the beings that inhabit them and those beings' relations to shamans and human beings.

The Place of Our Bones

Wapinakwa is most directly associated with the remains of the dead and the place of various spirit beings. In the drawing, Mandu chose to represent it by four horizontal lines which are four kinds of wood (from bottom to top: *ambaúba* (trumpetwood), or *dukuli*; *umarí*, or *dumali*; *dúwiri*; and *wanada*). Each of these is a level inhabited by a different kind of spirit people: those with red bodies; those who "sleep hanging from logs," called *pawedawanai*; those with black bodies. These are treacherous, cannibalistic spirits particularly dangerous for they are predators of humans. Dukulipekwaro, a female spirit of the lowest level, is said to be a "pretty young girl," but when people look at her, she causes thunder and lightning, darkness and death. Pirimaapekwaro, another female spirit painted red (*pirimaapa* is red *urucú* vegetal dye), is said to call people, crying out for them to enter her house, where she later kills and devours them. The *pawedawanai* are, likewise, spirits associated with catastrophic death; for it is said that they are people "who never were born," but that when "people end in This World, these will come out"—strange, inverted beings who will appear at the end of the world.

A river of cold, fresh water runs through Wapinakwa. In numerous curing chants and orations, illnesses are taken from the living and cast into these waters. Shamans may also look for the souls of sick people in this dark netherworld. In short, Wapinakwa is characterized by remains—the bones of the dead and sicknesses; and predatory spirits that may bring on catastrophic death. It is curious also that, as a level, it is distinct from the rest of the cosmos by the apparent disconnectedness among its layers and to the worlds above. In contrast to the verticality above, Wapinakwa is all horizontal—as if to represent the bones of the dead lying down in permanent stasis.

This World

This World, Hekwapi, comprises two planes: in the first is the world center, *hekwapi pamudsua*; in the second, the house of animal souls, *itchiri napana*, or *iaradate*.

The world center is the place called Hipana, the principal rapids of the Aiary River. For nearly all Arawak-speaking peoples of the Northwest Amazon—Baniwa, Tariana, Puinave, and others—Hipana, or Uapui, is where the earth began and the first ancestors arose out of the holes in the rapids. It is also the sacred place of connection between the worlds above and below, where, in primordial times, Kuwai was burned and the *paxiuba* tree into which his body transformed burst out and up from the center of the sky. The large boulders of the rapids, with their numerous petroglyphs, the holes in the middle of the rapids, and the gigantic boulder in the center—all are visible evidence to the Hohodene who live at Uapui of the world in the beginning and its transformation.

In fact, the entire world beyond the center shares in its sacredness; for as the myth of Kuwai explains, when the women stole the flutes and trumpets, they played them all over the world, which then opened up to its present size. Every rapid, hill, river, and place known to the Hohodene bears the stamp of the beginning and is remembered in the *kalidzamai* chants sung at initiation rites. But just as the Kuwai myth, as I have suggested, marks a transition between the primordial world of the beginning and human existence, so geography is constantly reinterpreted and modified by historical change. A history of nearly three centuries of contact has expanded and transformed the landscape, adding new dimensions to the process of opening up the world.

Shamans, however, frequently characterize This World as *maatchíkwe*, evil place, *kaiwíkwe*, pain place, and *ekúkwe*, rotten place, contrasting it with the Other World, which is notable for its remedies against the sicknesses of This World. For This World is flawed by poison, *manhene*, and sicknesses given by sorcerers and witches in their interminable desire to inflict pain. All sicknesses and forms of pain were "begun" by Kuwai in his great conflagration and ascent to the sky at Hipana. Although initiates are severely warned against practicing sorcery, anyone can potentially do it, and shamans and chanters derive a great deal of their power from their ability to both cure and inflict illness. This World is also a "rotten place," according to shamans, because it contains so much rotting and decaying matter, such as corpses.

In one drawing of the cosmos by a nonspecialist (see below, "A Nonspecialist's View" and Figure 3), *iaradate* is a separate place connected to Wapinakwa. Here, it is the sky of the lower world, or *thiali kuma*. It is the place of the souls of all animal species on earth and of all forest spirits, or *awakarunanai* (of which there are many, but all of them characterized by some exaggeration of their physical features, e.g., enormous members). The chief of the animal and forest spirits commands a legion of the spirits of the rivers, forest, and air whom he sends to afflict humans, giving them fear, which leads to sickness. All sicknesses of This World not attributable to sorcery are inflicted by these spirits. Like the shades of deceased humans, sickness-giving animal spirits appear like a wind, encircling humans walking in the forest and leaving them with sickness. Shamans have the power to open and enter *iaradate* and request, from the chief, animals for people's food or the return of souls afflicted by the sickness-giving spirits of the forest and rivers.

The Other World

Above This World, Apakwa Hekwapi begins with five separate places—one person compared them to "compartments" or "rooms"—of the bird-spirits. These spirits are helpers of the shamans—*wapira*, our pets—in their search for lost souls and advise them of their whereabouts. They are female spirits, also known as the "daughters of Dzulíferi," the primal shaman. After a shaman has completed five or six years of his apprenticeship, he is expected to make a "marriage" with the bird-spirits, especially with the vulture-spirits, with whom he will have children who also help him in his search for lost souls. This spiritual marriage is the counterpart of the shaman's abstinence from sexual intercourse on earth. Clearly, the more spirit children a shaman has, the more powerful he will become. Each of the bird-spirits is the "owner" of a specific kind of spirit-dart that the shaman acquires in his apprenticeship and that is associated with specific kinds of sicknesses and cures.

The top of the Other World and the beginning of the Other Sky, Apakwa Eenu, is a complex place of transformation; one might say that it is pure transformation where, for example, the souls of dead kin are purified by fire and burning resin or the souls of witches and sorcerers are trapped in a place of eternal thirst and heat. It is the place where shamans must likewise "die" in order to enter the world of the primordial beings. No simple and static description could adequately convey the dynamic nature of this transformative space.

One notes that the borders of the Other Sky, *eenu tiwatakawa*, are more distinctly defined than on other planes of the cosmos. The borders separate: the souls of the deceased who have given poison, inflicted harm, or not respected the ways of life prescribed in initiation confront a "fence," *kurara*, that blocks their passage and shows a trail to another village, *inyaime dzakale*—the village of the shadows of the dead. These shadows are said to be "other Kuwai," and, inversely, *inyaime* are "the shadows of Kuwai." In other words, there is a reflexive relation between the shadows of the dead and the ancestral spirit Kuwai. Some people say that the trail to *inyaime dzakale* is "beautiful, with sweet-smelling flowers" but deceiving, for the village is "like This World" and people "work and suffer" the same things as in This World.

These images of an eternally unpurified and unchanging condition, of being permanently on the outside, contrast with the way of souls who continue the journey. These, as I shall discuss at greater length in Chapter 6, must be "washed" by passing though a hole of burning resin and fire, located in the hollowed-out open center of the sky. The burning resin separates the deceased's individual human body shape, from its "heart-soul," *ikaale*. Once purified, the soul appears a gleaming white. From there, the heart-soul follows the way to its "house"— some say, on the border of Kuwai's village; others, to Iaperikuli's village at the tip of the universe. The way is said to be "full of thorns and spirit-darts," but once there, all is clean, pure, shining white and beautiful. Souls are kept eternally occupied so that they forget their families and won't seek to return.

By contrast, the shaman's journey into the Other Sky is more complex. After passing through the hole of burning resin, his soul takes another way to the "middle sky" where the spirits Kuwai and Dzulíferi are. In order to attain this sacred center, he must pass through the sky door, *eenu ienúma* (or sky mouth, for door and mouth are the same word), which is said to be constantly opening and closing, "like a scissors," and is an extremely dangerous passage, after which he enters the sky belly, *eenu íwali*. The shaman "dies" before entering the door. Kuwai then sends down his cross-shaped "umbilical cord," *hliepuhlepi eenu*, which the shaman grasps as Kuwai pulls him up and through the door into the middle sky. There, the shaman seeks to retrieve the lost souls of the sick.

There is evident reference here to a process of reverse birth, that is, a return to the womb of the sky—which, I believe, is consistent with the generative and reproductive sense of Apakwa Hekwapi. Recall that the bird-spirits produce spiritual offspring with the shaman. The return of the shaman's soul into the womb of the cosmos brings him in touch with the source of generative life itself, Kuwai.

Before his soul passes through the sky door, he sees the shadow-soul, *idanam*, of Dzulíferi, the primordial shaman. The notion of the shadow-soul is rather complex, and appears in numerous places in the Baniwa cosmos, as we have already seen in referring to the relation between Kuwai and the shadows of the dead. I shall have occasion to discuss this notion in more detail in the section below titled "*Maliiri*, the Shamans" and in Chapter 4. The notion of "shadow soul" seems to represent what L. Sullivan, referring in general to native South American notions of the "soul" (1988, 261), called a "human heart of primordial darkness," which here is located in the center of the sky. Yet the shadow-soul refers beyond itself—it is, after all, a projection—to, again citing Sullivan, the "world of fully manifest light"—here, the world of Iaperikuli, in the highest realm of the cosmos where the eternal light of the primordial sun Heiri shines. There, is the "omniscient, omnipresent, and omnipotent mode of being that humans experience in their inner beings as a dark absence constitutive of their own soul" (ibid.)—a perfectly adequate description of the two aspects represented here in the Hohodene cosmos, the places of Kuwai and Iaperikuli.

The place of Kuwai, Apakuma, is said to contain all the kinds of lethal sicknesses that entrap human souls and which Kuwai himself sends to people. Kuwai has a plantation, it is said, with trees of poison spirit-darts. All of the primal shamans are said to inhabit this level.

Beyond the village of Kuwai, another trail leads to the level of Iaperikuli and his pet harpy Kamathawa. It is the sky tip, *eenu tsuruikwa*, closed and pointed "like a knife," where the universe ends. Very little is known of this level, for very few shamans actually attain it. Most only see it at a distance. Those who do enter are the most knowledgeable and powerful of healers. I do not know if a further transformation of the shaman's soul occurs before entering Iaperikuli's village. It is said that this level is a hidden place, *lidawanikwa*, a place of happiness, *kathimákwe*, a place of unfailing remedies and eternal light. It is the source of all knowledge, *ianheke*, that began and made the universe. In the shamans' apprenticeship (see below, "*Maliiri*, the Shamans"), they must reach a point near this level—people said, "like a room next to it"—where they, "like Iaperikuli," demonstrate their power to create, "in their thought," everything that exists in the world again, as Iaperikuli did in the myth of his beginning.

From this summary description, it becomes easy to see how cosmology, for shamans, organizes the concerns of cosmogony in the creation of what I venture to call a vertical hierarchy of spiritual being and power. In brief, what I mean by this—and what will become clearer when I consider shamans' discourse about their art and practice—is that, first of all, the highest level of the cosmos represents omniscience, the knowledge of Iaperikuli, as the "hidden" and eternal source of creative power and happiness. The next level most clearly refers to the soul, the collective soul that is Kuwai, both as the generative source of life and as the dark seat of illness and the soul's entrapment. The third level represents the temporal regeneration and reproduction of the spirit. The next level, This World, is at once made sacred by its connection to the primordial world but is also open to the creation of new meaning through individual and social histories. It is, in the shamans' views, eternally flawed, constantly threatened by the chaos of illness and the dark side of the soul, i.e., witches and sorcerers. Finally, the world below represents inverted being, horizontal stasis, yet the potentiality of new being should the world above come to an end.

A Nonspecialist's View

While Mandu's drawing highlighted the vertical dimensions of the cosmos in greater detail, as one would expect from a shaman, Mandu's younger brother Lourenço, who had never "studied" to be a shaman, produced the drawing in Figure 3, which in several respects presents important differences. Besides the evident simplification of several of the levels, there is a dislocation of two places away from the vertical axis: the way leading to *inyaime dzakale* leads down and away from the world trail; and the way to *iaradate* and its chief, Awakaruna, away from Wapinakwa. Further, Lourenço chose to elaborate This World by indicating "other groups" as circles around the periphery of the world center, where the Hohodene are located at Hipana. Such differences illustrate the point that for nonspecialists the cosmos consists of both the vertical dimensions of spiritualized being and the horizontal dimension of alterity, or other beings. Otherness is marked by degrees: "other groups" on the periphery of This World are still human, while animal spirits and the spirits of dead enemies are more distinctly "other." I will explore these aspects in greater detail in Part II. Finally, the drawing clearly shows an association between Iaperikuli and the sun—which shamans clarified by saying that the primal sun Heiri is the "body of Iaperikuli"—and between Kuwai and the moon, Keiri, which would explain the evident and rather strong associations that

Kuwai has with reproductive processes, such as menstruation, physical maturation, initiation rituals, and so on.

In general, however, I found that nonshamans elaborated their notions of the cosmos, largely on the basis of what shamans—those considered to be "true shamans" and especially the prophetic figures—advised them. Thus, when speaking about his drawing, Lourenço cited several times the shaman Kudui, a powerful Hohodene prophet of Ucuqui Cachoeira, who died in the early 1970s, but who had trained most other shamans of the Aiary River. Kudui's prophecies and miraculous cures were remembered vividly by the Hohodene of the Aiary, who considered him to be "like Iaperikuli, our salvation." (See Chapter 8 for a more complete discussion of Kudui.) To Lourenço, echoing perhaps the perspective of his uncle Keruaminali, This World is *kaiwíkwe*, place of pain, where there is poison, *manhene*, and which is "dirty," and "rotten," *ekúkwe*, contrasting absolutely with Iaperikuli's village, which is "beautiful and clean." It was also Lourenço who held the views—which no other person whom I interviewed did—that Wapinakwa was the "same as Iaperikuli's village," that "there is no *manhene* there," and that who lives there are "people who never were born," but added the somewhat enigmatic interpretation that "when This World ends, half of them will stay below and half will stay with us." Thus, while his knowledge of the cosmos was largely grounded in what shamans had informed him, he nevertheless added his own individual interpretations.

"Owners" and "Masters"

There are two main senses in which the relation of the primordial beings of the Other World to humanity may be conceptualized—as owners, *iminali*, and masters, *thayri*. I will briefly discuss these, as they will be important for understanding the following section in which I transcribe the discourse of two shamans about the art and practice of shamanism.

Iaperikuli, Dzulíferi, and Kuwai are all considered world owners, *hekwapi iminali*. Their ownership refers to their having created things, conditions, and places in the beginning and having left them for posterity. Iaperikuli made the world order and left it for humanity with instructions on how to live in it. Dzulíferi is the "owner of shaman's snuff and tobacco" and gave them to Iaperikuli, who left them to posterity, especially for shamans to "know the world" by using these substances in their cures. Kuwai is the "sickness owner" and "poison owner" who left sicknesses in This World but who also shows

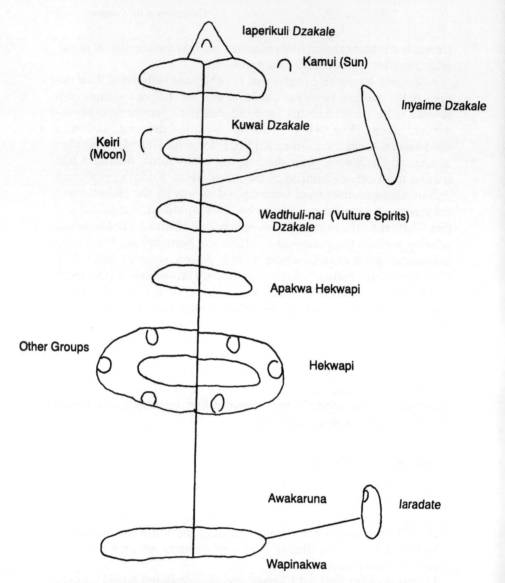

Iaperikuli *Dzakale*

Kamui (Sun)

Inyaime *Dzakale*

Kuwai *Dzakale*

Keiri
(Moon)

Wadthuli-nai (Vulture Spirits)
Dzakale

Apakwa Hekwapi

Other Groups

Hekwapi

Awakaruna

Iaradate

Wapinakwa

Figure 3. A Nonspecialist's View of the Cosmos

shamans how they may cure them. In the widest sense, Iaperikuli and Kuwai are considered our owners, *waminali*, for humanity lives, prospers, grows, and dies through the order and conditions given by them.

This relationship is far from being static. Shamans in their cures request from the owners remedies with which to cure, which may involve bargaining, for the patient must present an offering, or payment, *dawai*, which the shaman takes to Kuwai in order to bargain for the return of his soul. This payment may be refused if it is judged to be insufficient, or the sickness deemed incurable.

The relationship of masters applies to the same triad of Iaperikuli, Dzulíferi, and Kuwai—all referred to as world masters, *hekwapi thayri*. Given their association with the primordial world, they are also called eternal (or undying) masters, *midzáka thayri*. One other figure, Kaali, is called master for he instructed humanity how to make gardens. The title of "master," then, is used in the sense of one who advises or tells what to do. The world masters advise the shamans about cures, events to come, and what to do about them, and the shamans transmit these messages to people. Master is thus equivalent to chief, *thalikana*, and bears the symbols that traditionally mark chiefs (e.g., Kaali has a shield and lance) or other objects that symbolize mastery (Dzulíferi has a box of remedies).[1]

Maliiri, the Shamans

Having briefly characterized the various levels of the cosmos and the beings associated with them, I shall now present two shamans' discourses on the art and practice of shamanism which, so to speak, will give special meaning to all that has been said above.

The first is by the chief of Uapui, Mandu, who, after my innumerable questions to him about the *maliiri*, shamans, one day decided to explain to me directly his profession. The other is that of Keruaminali, ex-chief of Uapui and at that time still a practicing shaman even though in his late seventies. Both had been apprentices of the Hohodene prophet Kudui and the Dzauinai prophet Kumadeiyon; Keruaminali, however, had been trained also by his grandfather Amacio and father Marcellino. I shall transcribe both discourses here in sequence and use my translation of them as the basis for a discussion of the shaman's powers, attributes and training. When appropriate, I shall note the relation of shamanism to cosmogony and cosmology, and in particular to the millenarian themes I have discussed in Chapter 1.

Mandu's style may be at first somewhat difficult to follow (my explanatory notes are in brackets); but it is the style of a shaman explaining things of the Other World and requires some patience to understand:

Long ago Iaperikuli gave us these shamans. Then he gave us the things of sickness. For us, we people. Then we sniff this *pariká*, this world-knower. For from long ago is this *pariká*, from long ago so we have it. From long ago we have this *pariká*, this world-knower. Thus he gave us his blood, Kuwai's blood [*pariká* is considered to be the "blood of Kuwai"]. Thus is the *pariká*-owner, this Dzulíferi. Dzulíferi is this *pariká*-owner and of all sickness-things [i.e., curing]. But he gave it to us, we people, our *pariká*. They [the shamans] snuff *pariká*, then they see on it. They see this Dzulíferi, they see this Kuwai. Then they see this, our owner also, Iaperikuli. Then they see this Kamathawa also. For he also gave us, this Dzulíferi, this tobacco-owner, tobacco. But this tobacco is his plant, of this Dzulíferi. They [the shamans] look for this sickness with Dzulíferi's plant, and with this *pariká*. They see this Dzulíferi. There [in the Other World] they see him. There they see this Dzulíferi-shadow also, this Dzulíferi-shadow. After the Dzulíferi-shadow, they see the Other World, the Other World. For so he gave them this extraction of sickness by sucking out. There [in the Other World] they see this Dzulíferi and he speaks to them. "So you came, is it that you are looking for *pariká*?" says this Dzulíferi. "Yes, I want it." "Ah good. It seems then you are looking for, then, for *pariká*. Here it is, here am I the *pariká*-owner, I am. Now it will be, you will see on this . . ." Now there, Dzulíferi blows, he blows for the shamans *pariká*. There in the Other World. In the Other World he blows for them. Then, so he blows for them his *pariká*. After he blows, *pariká* shows for the shamans to see. It shows for them everything—as the world is, what Dzulíferi sings to them, this song of Dzulíferi. There, this ancient song, ancient is this other speech. [. . .] Then the shaman comes back. . . . The shamans come back and see this Kuwai. Thus they meet Kuwai on it [*pariká*]. This is the sickness-owner. There, Kuwai gives them, he gives them poison *manhene* extraction, he gives them *marudadali* [another poison] extraction, he gives them bone extraction, he gives them *umali* [poison] extraction, he gives them wood extraction, he gives them rock extraction, he gives them spirit-dart extraction, he gives them *dzauinhaita* [wood] extraction. Those extraction things. But they are Kuwai's remedies. Remedies—our remedies, we people, from the ancient times. Thus are our remedies from the beginning in This World. He gave them to us, this our owner. But they are our remedies. Then, they can

suck out sickness there in the Other World. Afterward, they come
back and cure in This World. They can tell people, they advise the
people here . . . How did the world-master tell them? Thus they
come back and tell the people. This is the way we do it, we people.
Thus it seems, what the world-master said, thus they come back
and tell it to the people. They cannot speak nonsense, what he says
to them. He tells people well, as the world-owner told them. The
world-owner tells them, so they are able to know how it is about
[the sickness], and about This World also. They are able to know
everything about this sickness also. Thus he tells what Dzulíferi
said, this *pariká*-owner, it is what he says, it seems, to them. All of
what our owner told them, thus it will be in This World. He tells
what he told them, he tells what he told them, the world-owner.
Then he comes back and tells people, what they saw that the world-
owner showed them. He tells what it showed the shamans in this
Other World, in the Other World . . . *Pariká* changes everything,
it shows everything to them whatsoever. This *pariká*. With it they
are able to know the world. *Pariká* shows for you to see not just
anything, it seems. It shows them everything. [. . .] They see this
Mawerikuli-shadow [i.e., the first person to die]. Thus, it seems, is
that evil one, Mawerikuli. This Mawerikuli-shadow also. There it
is, that one. It shows everything, whatever, it shows for them to see
this Night Village. The Night End Long Ago [see the last part of
this chapter, "Healing the World with a Song," for an explanation of this phrase]. They had, it seems, in that ancient world. But
the Night End Long Ago, it seems, it began, Iaperikuli made night
long ago, it seems he did, Iaperikuli. But this *pariká* shows for them
to see, the *pariká*-place. This *pariká* shows for the shamans to see,
however it shows them to see, this *pariká*. Then, there is Iaperikuli's
box of remedies, thus they can know everything about sickness.
Then they know everything about the world, it tells them and the
shamans come back to tell the people. They tell everything to the
people as in the beginning, before them, Iaperikuli told them. The
shamans can become as the world-master, in their thought also.
They make the world. They can in their thought, thus, imagine all
people. Everything — the shaman cannot deceive on it. They become
as Iaperikuli was, so they are. There they become, they are as Iaperikuli is. They make everything. They make the rocks, they make
the wood, they transform everything on *pariká*. They transform
into wood, they transform into the jaguar, they transform into the
caiman, they transform into the dolphin, they transform into the
vulture, all of this in their thought — they transform into people
also. Thus also, it seems, they transform into that world-master. So

they are able to know the world. For it seems this *pariká* transforms. But this is our ancient remedy, it seems, ours, we people.
For it is ours from long ago, we people, our remedies, all of our
knowing, all of our knowledge about the world. . . . There is Kuwai; Kuwai is this sickness-owner, this poison-owner, this Kuwai.
The shamans ask from Kuwai all of his sicknesses. He makes all
and whatever kind of those sicknesses. But Kuwai is the sickness-
owner. There is only one Kuwai, this sickness-owner. It seems
Kuwai shows for them to see This World. But this Kuwai also lives
in the world. The world-center is where Kuwai lives, this sickness-
owner. Thus it seems, this *pariká*, *pariká* shows the world for the
shaman to see. It shows everything for them on it, even this, our
owner, where Iaperikuli is, where Kamathawa is also. Thus this
pariká shows. [. . .] There is then the *pariká* stairs. They are able to
go to where our owner is. They are able to know Iaperikuli on it.
But we people have this Iaperikuli, this Kamathawa also. The
white people say it is the Holy Spirit but to us it is Kamathawa,
this Kamathawa, Iaperikuli's pet, this Kamathawa.

Compare now the discourse of Keruaminali, who told me the following "story of the shamans" several times, with very little variation.
In fact, the mythic quality of this version seemed to me to give a
form—in contrast to the more spontaneous style of Mandu's discourse—to the variety of shamanic experiences in apprenticeship and
cures, highlighting certain aspects which can also be detected in
Mandu's discourse but are expressed much more clearly here:

The shamans first sniff *pariká*. To start, only they do, the shamans.
They sniff *pariká*. Until their eyes transform everything. First they
see the *thiripi* [sparrow-spirits] in the Other World. They go on . . .
then they see the place of the *idthadaapa* [hawk-spirits] in the Other
World. Then they go on . . . they see the place of the scissor-tailed
fletcher-spirits, *pulimákwa*, they say. Then they go on . . . to the
place of the white vulture, *hulumana* village. Then they go up . . .
to Kamathawa, that one. It is a beautiful world where Kamathawa
lives. They see it, those shamans. We ascend to the world before
us on the *pariká* stairs. We raise the *pariká* stairs up to the world
before us. We ascend to the world before us on the *pariká* stairs.
To the entrance of the sky, on the universe stairs. They ascend
before them on the *pariká* stairs. They ascend to the end [i.e., edge]
of the Other World. They make themselves transform on it, on
pariká, the shamans say. When he blows his *pariká* . . . *tih!* he falls
down unconscious [*maliume*, which can be rendered as "dead" but

refers more to the loss of consciousness on *pariká*], as though he
was dead, he lies down. Like the dead here . . . *ta!* It's bad. They
put you to lie down as though in a grave, as it is today. Then we
see before us, we see, we shamans. We see before us our bodies,
lying dead and rotting, and we see our bones becoming white. It's
bad. Then they come out, they stay at the water mouth, the river
mouth. Then the shaman's body becomes a log. Then there is the
sky way, this other place in the sky before death. Alone, you sit
like so. You blow smoke over your kin, and say, "Oh—how sad
are they my kin" [i.e., as though the shaman's kin are mourning his
"death"], they say there. They turn around and come back in the
Other World. They turn around and come back and out in the
Other World, the Other World. A stairs is the trail—*tain, tain, tain,
tain*, they walk. A stairs is the trailway of this Other Sky. Iaperikuli
lives there—Kalah! They get to where the universe people are,
thus it is, they see then the universe people. They see Dzulíferi. He
is an old, old man! He began long ago. He blows tobacco, where
he sits, the old one. Thus, they get tobacco for the shaman. They
blow, they bring back sickness—*klale*—they don't know, they lie
there, they lie there, he lies there, they blow *pariká* [apparently
referring to the shaman's lying here in This World as his soul jour-
neys]. So well it makes him see. . . . *Taa!* Iaperikuli's shadow . . .
Tuk! They see the sky, this sky—*Peeeh!* A bright white, like silver,
a new world there, another one. *Peeeh!* Beautiful. You walk as
the world-owner. You make water, you make rocks, you make
the world—well! They make everything in their thought! Everything, like Iaperikuli. We are then, as Iaperikuli, we are then as the
universe-master. There is no more sickness, there in the sky. Then,
they enter the lake. They cast away their shaman's body. They are
cleaned well! They are purified. Then they see Kuwai, the old one,
Kuwai. Thus they get Kuwai's fur [i.e., his poison, what causes
sickness] there—poison extraction, spirit-dart extraction—they
get all the spirit-darts from him. The shaman gets all of them and
eats them. Then he transforms, that very same Kuwai. They transform into those people, those Dzulíferi *inyai* [the other shamans
of Dzulíferi] at the snuffing-place, long before us. All of them sit
there: Iumawali, Tana, Dzulíferi, Uwa, Inyaime-hmewidane—all of
them, all of them. . . . "Sit down, my grandchild, did you sniff?
Extract the sickness from me."   "What sickness do you have?"
"Poison, they say."   "You are sick with poison?"   "Yes."   "All
right." He shows him his payment, *tayn*. He sucks out, he drinks
and sucks out—*tutu*, he pulls out, he sucks out poison, *tututu*
(he pulls out) *hata*—"Pah! You are sick with poison, you are sick

with *taalikaim*" [a kind of poison, the *surubí*-poison]. *Hata*—"You are sick with *wapetha*, rheumatism," *paxiuba* darts he pulls out, and stones like so. "Now, throw water on me." Water there, in the Other World. *Pa'telelele Pa'telelele* [the shaman throws water—a form of curing]. The *walama* darts fall, all of them on the ground. They blow tobacco, they blow *hhffffffff* . . . The old one sits up, "yes, I have revived, my grandson." "You have revived?" "Yes, now you can extract for them, for those unborn *walimanai*," he says to them there. This world-master. "All right, so it seems." But they see many, many people. All seated. These Dzulíferi's people, all of them. However many, far back. All the elders. All the Iaperikunai. All the universe people. Thus it is. Then, they come back here. They come back, *ta'* To another place, another place, another place, another place. . . . [descending on the *pariká* stairs] You come to another place, you sit *tih!* You come to another place, you sit *tih!* They come back on it. At night another people see them. They come back on *pariká*. Until, you get to where you are lying, *tayn*. *Hutsu!* You sit up. "You came back?" "Yes, I came back." *Tcitcit-citci pfffff pafaaaaaaaaaa*. . . . *dzaliiiiiii*, *tih* [these are the sounds of the shaman's flight back; as one shaman said, "like a gust of wind" or "like an airplane" or "like a motorboat."] Thus they come back here, *dadadadadadadadadad tayn*. On a rock. He sits up *hutsu*. "Bad place, *maatchíkwe*, rotten place, we live like so today." *Pfffff* . . . *pariká*. He blows tobacco, the shaman. Thus, in This World here. They see all those before us. Long ago. That world before us. Thus he sees the world. They revive . . . The old ones before us. He sees them on *pariká*. Thus you see the world. They come back and sit. They think, "how do they do all this in the other world?" We think that. They cast off their body, everything. You see me, I cast off all of me, all. I have seen before me. Thus it is that *pariká* shows for them to see. Then here, they extract. *Pa'Pa'Pa'* You revive. So, that's the vision of *pariká*. They snuff here. *Pariká* in the sky. There. It's Kuwai's blood. For this *pariká* is power. When you come back, you can't look at women. You can't look at them, you can't mess with them. Nothing like that. You see women without their dress. Your eyes see everything. . . . Thus, the vision of *pariká*.

In order to discuss the specific images presented in these discourses, I shall present some complementary, contextual information on shamanic powers, practice, and training. When appropriate, I shall insert references to either or both of the discourses in order to explain them more fully.

A great deal of the power shamans have is based on an extensive knowledge and understanding of mythology and cosmology, as well as on a detailed and comprehensive knowledge of the multiple sources of sicknesses and their cures. Through the mediatory role that shamans have between the sick of This World and the spirits and primordial beings of the Other World, shamans cure, advise, and guide people, thus performing one of the most vital services to the ongoing health and well-being of the community.

Shamans are ranked by their peers and by others of the community on the extent of their knowledge, the efficacy of their cures, and the truthfulness of the advice they give. This ranking is correlated with the proven ability of a shaman to gain access to the several levels of the cosmos, each level being associated with higher and more important spirits and beings. Shamans with a "little" or "half-knowledge" have access to the lower planes of the cosmos and are called on to perform limited kinds of cures. Frequently, they are shamans who, in their apprenticeship, learned for only a few years of the usual six to eight and, for some reason, decided not to continue; or they are shamans who, like Keruaminali, were once of a higher level but "lost" their powers with age or through a fall of some kind.

Shamans who have completed their apprenticeship have experienced higher levels of the cosmos, notably where the "owner of *pariká* and tobacco," Dzulíferi, and the "owner of sickness," Kuwai, live. These "true shamans" are capable of curing all the more serious ailments and have the powers to perform a variety of tasks related to weather control, seasonal passage, obtaining food resources (making forest fruits grow; opening the "houses" of the souls of game animals for the hunt), and tasks related to human welfare (taking defensive or aggressive action against personal enemies; protecting people from the sicknesses brought on by evil omens).

True shamans also have the knowledge and powers related to eschatological concerns, and act as soul-guides in the passage of dying people's souls to the "houses" of the deceased. In Keruaminali's discourse, for example, note the part in the beginning of the shaman's voyage in which he arrives at the "river mouth" and blows tobacco smoke over the souls of the deceased, telling them that they "must leave their families behind." Mandu likewise mentioned this power of the shaman, in a separate conversation we had over his own training. He said the following:

First he goes to the mouth of the river [presumably this would be the mouth of the river of cold, fresh water in Wapinakwa, which is where the bones of the dead go]. There, there is a boat. Then comes a wind and the souls of the dead appear in the sky, the other sky.

The shaman joins together all the souls with the wind, joining them in the great boat. He joins each family of each village of the dead in the boats. The wind pushes the boats. Then, the shaman, seated alone, takes his cigar and blows above the souls of his kin and says, "You have to leave your family behind; their souls will be more content." Later, he asks them, "How is it, my family? Now the wind comes." And he blows over them with tobacco. They become beautiful and he tells them that the world will get better.

Shamans also have the power to see and communicate with the ancestors and the souls of the dead. And only they, it is said, have the power, through their vision and consultation with the primordial beings, to determine "whether This World is about to come to an end or not," as they say—as, for example, in the millenarian movements of the past.

True shamans are believed to have the power to transform (*-pada-mawa*, become other) into a variety of powerful animals (see, e.g., the list of these animals mentioned in the latter part of Mandu's discourse) but most notably the jaguar. This transformation is sometimes described as "putting on a cloak," the jaguar cloak, *dzaui maka*. They may also take on attributes, become, or "stay as" the deities themselves. In their apprenticeship, for example, they obtain features of their physiology very much like the "owner of sickness," Kuwai; for example, his "mouth," which is obviously important for the sucking-out extraction of sickness. And, most spectacularly, at the end of their apprenticeship, they are said to attain the highest level of the cosmos and become like the "universe owner," Iaperikuli. "In their thought," as both Mandu and Keruaminali stated, they make everything in the world—all elements, all people in the world. I shall return to this transformation at the end of this section.

The highest level of shamans Hill ([1989] 1993) calls *dzauinai thayri*, or "jaguar-people masters," which, I believe, refers to chiefs of the Dzauinai phratry among the Wakuenai and not to a class of shamans. I did not obtain a specific name for these figures among the Hohodene, although there was a definite recognition of the superiority of certain "true shamans" who were said to "know everything" there is to know about the cosmos, and to have truly prophetic abilities. Such historical figures as Kumadeiyon of the Dzauinai phratry, Kudui of the Hohodene phratry, and others were considered almost as of a class above the "true shamans" of the Aiary at the time of my fieldwork, although Kudui's son José was certainly on his way, so to speak, to becoming like his father.

Very few shamans attain this level; those who do often begin their learning and instruction from the time they are children of five or six and are judged by their elders to have qualities that predispose them to begin learning at an early age. Much of their lifetime, then, is devoted to a fairly continuous instruction, so that by the time they reach the age-group of elders, their knowledge far surpasses that of their companions who began instruction later. It has happened also that true shamans have gained extraordinary powers by surviving near-fatal illnesses. Such was the case of Kudui, who, during an illness in which he nearly died, was cured by Kumadeiyon; but it is said that, in his illness, Kudui had a vision of Iaperikuli, who told him that he would not die. From then on, Kudui communicated constantly with Iaperikuli in his sleep. (See Wright and Hill 1986, an article on Venancio Kamiko, the Baniwa prophet and messiah of the mid-nineteenth century whose life—both from stories and from the documents about his sickness, death, and resurrection—shows a similar pattern.)

Prophetic figures that attain the highest level in the cosmos, the place of Iaperikuli, can continuously do so even in sleeping states and are able to obtain spiritual remedies from Iaperikuli. Their powers of prescience are formidable, for they are said to know of events that occur in other villages outside of the normal means by which these events are communicated, and they know of events that will happen in the future. Thus, Kudui foretold in the late 1960s–early 1970s of the "coming of the whites" to the Aiary River, a prophecy that had great repercussions among the Hohodene. In 1977, when I was in the area, the Brazilian Air Force began construction of airstrips at strategic locations in the Northwest Amazon, one of which was at Uapui Cachoeira on the Aiary River. Many Hohodene took this and its consequences as one more proof of Kudui's prophetic capacities.

Kudui, like other prophetic figures, was reputed to know of the intentions of people who came to visit in his village before these intentions were made public. The powers of these shamans in defensive or aggressive action against enemies are considerably widened to include the ability to influence the course of events at a long distance. Their powers of advising kin extend to everything that might pose threats to health and well-being. Thus, Kudui is said to have advised his kin—at a time when sickness was apparently a major concern—that "there would be no more sicknesses," appealing to the healing powers of Dzulíferi, the primal shaman, to reinforce his message. Thus, even today, Mandu remembers Kudui, who died around 1975, as more than a saint—"like Iaperikuli, our salvation."[2]

Having spoken of shamanic power hierarchies, I will now briefly discuss apprenticeship. From the accounts of various shamans, the decision to begin apprenticeship may be due to a sickness, or the decision of the parents, who then look for a master shaman who can assume the responsibility. The apprentice will live in the house of the master for the initial period of instruction and will remain under the care of the master and his wife. Each apprentice has to furnish his own supply of *pariká* for the instruction sessions, as well as pay the master shaman for the instruction (a shotgun, for example, or a sewing machine).

The actual process of apprenticeship begins with a long period of restriction, including fasting, isolation, and celibacy, during which the apprentice begins to take *pariká* (there are two types the Hohodene use: *dzato*, the more frequent, and *marawáthi*) and to eat medicine, that is, ingest elements taken "from the sky"—such as rocks, wood slivers, hair. The master extracts these from the sky with his rattle, swallows them, vomits them up, and puts them in the apprentice's mouth, shutting them up inside with the handle of his rattle.

These elements represent all the different forms of sickness extraction, *ipútsuakaruna*, that the shaman will use in his practice—from the sickness given by forest spirits to poison given by Kuwai. In Mandu's discourse cited above, he lists all the different forms of poison extraction that Kuwai gives the shaman. Thus, at the same time the shaman is totally restricted in his external relations with This World, his interior (mouth, stomach) is literally filled up, transformed into a spiritual container that engulfs, transforms, and extrudes objects. As I have mentioned above, the shaman's mouth is said to become like "the mouth of Kuwai."

Other, more powerful spirit objects are also obtained in apprenticeship for use in higher forms of shamanic activity: for example, the crest feathers of Kamathawa, which are said to become the shaman's crest feathers and are used in the making of summer, to "open" the skies of clouds, and to "make the world better." The shaman also obtains weapons, such as spirit-darts, the darts of Kuwai and Dzulíferi, that also serve as "swords, *mapalikuita*," they say, "to cut off people's heads," recalling the ancient war practice of decapitation. For the shaman is a warrior and as he creates alliances, so must he be prepared for the possibilities of spiritual struggles against cosmic forces.

Along with these inner soul changes, the shaman acquires a series of what we might call outer coverings, extensions of his body and soul, and symbolic attire that represent his transformed nature: (1) various cloaks, *liamaka*, of Kuwai, the jaguar, red-paint *kerawidzu* that, like an outer skin, cover the shaman when he takes *pariká*; (2) various sacred

Figure 4. Shamanic Ecstasy

rocks and crystals that aid in clairvoyance, in producing thunder, and in traveling to all parts of the world (one multifaceted stone, called *miyáke*, is said to have a surface for each thing the shaman can do); (3) various weapons and clothing: shoes, belt, and guns loaded with spirit-darts—all from Dzulíferi, Maweno (the primal thunder), and the eternal master, *midzáka thayri*—with which to make lightning and thunder and to communicate with other shamans.

More than any other single object, however, his rattle *kutheruda* is the central symbol of shamanic art. It is said to be his soul, and a shaman deprived of his rattle immediately becomes vulnerable to death. Its overall shape is that of a bird's head with a long beak and crest feathers. Its handle is cut at the end in the shape of the mouth of a beak, and its globular body is incised with designs representing Dzulíferi, Kuwai, and the world trail. Four small holes are cut on each side through which, the shamans say, they see. The small seeds or stones inside are said to be alive, from the sky, from the heads of Dzulíferi and Kamathawa. As much a weapon as an instrument for extraction, the rattle is the means by which the shaman, in his cures, takes the form of sickness from the sky—for the rattle "cuts them like a knife"—and ingests them, later to extract them again from the patient. In short, it is the instrument through which the connections between the sky worlds and This World are made.

The curing of sickness is the most important concern of all shamans, and I shall now focus on that practice. They classify the major types of sicknesses into at least four groups, according to their sources: (1) "sicknesses of people"—all the more serious ailments, including those which result in death, are said to be given by sorcerers who, through fatal orations ("spells" if you will), transmit sickness to their victims; curing is done through chanting and the blowing of tobacco; (2) poison, *manhene*—substances (poisonous leaves, berries, or thorns) mixed in food and drink which are given by sorcerers but are believed to be of supernatural origin, from Kuwai; usually fatal, but depends on the poison used; curing is by extraction, sucking out pathogenic objects from the body of the victim; (3) "sicknesses of the forest"—forest spirits, *iupinai*; spirits of the rivers and air, of the ground, and so forth, transmit sicknesses to humans, many being sent by the chief of the animals, *iaradate*; curing is through both chanting and extraction; and (4) "sicknesses sent by other shamans," the symptoms of which are usually rheumatic pain; curing is by extraction. Besides these, the failure to observe food restrictions, or rules of seclusion during rites of passage, will bring on wasting-away sicknesses called *purákali* and *ifiukali*, which may cause death.

The shaman's diagnostic and curing procedure involves a snuff-induced trance, the purpose of which is to journey to the Other World and to communicate with the spirits and deities of the cosmos. A shaman's performance involves dance with rattles; songs; and especially the reading and interpretation of shapes and forms of the clouds. As both Mandu and Keruaminali clearly stated, it is *pariká* that shows the shaman everything through the visions it gives. Through *pariká* the shaman communicates with the primordial beings who dwell in the heavens and who inform, advise, and assist the shaman regarding the source, character, and treatment of the sick in This World.

In both discourses cited above, the shamans refer to encounters with the "owner of sickness," Kuwai, who gives the shaman remedies for extraction, or who actually—as the "shadow of Dzulíferi"—requests that the shaman cure him in the Other World first before curing the shaman's patient in This World afterward. Now, in real-life cures, the encounter of the shaman with Kuwai is in fact mediated by the shaman's presenting Kuwai with an offering, a payment called *dawai*. This consists of a material payment—depending on the seriousness of the illness—given to the shaman for his cure and its spiritual form which the shaman presents to Kuwai. In exchange for this, Kuwai will give the shaman the sickness from his body—in its spiritual form—with which the shaman may cure the patient in This World, and which will evidently be shown—in its material form—to the patient. Or if Kuwai has trapped the patient's soul with him, embracing him in his arms, he will let go of the victim's soul following the presentation of *dawai*. In this exchange, then, material form is given in return for spiritual form, or more precisely, the shaman in his cure restores the unity of manifest form and spirit.

But this is a process of negotiation for which a relation of exchange must be established—that is, Kuwai may refuse the payment—just as in, it would seem, the kind of social relationship characteristic of affines. Once Kuwai has accepted the payment, he then transforms into the "shadow-soul of Dzulíferi," who requests that the shaman cure him. Significantly, when this is done, Dzulíferi addresses the shaman as "my grandson" indicating the special ancestor-to-descendant social relationship so necessary for curing. The two types of relationship so represented in this encounter would seem to be critical to the realization of the cure and the regaining of the patient's soul which the shaman will later integrate with the body of his patient in This World.

The shaman's repertoire of therapeutic techniques includes: (1) blowing, *lipia*, of tobacco smoke over the patient to concentrate the soul in its central location, the heart, *ikaale*; (2) extracting, *lipútsua*, pathogenic agents—mainly in the forms of hair, wood slivers, rocks, darts, each of which has many different types—accompanied with rattle-waving over the point of extraction on the patient's body; (3) water-throwing, *liáruka*, in which consecrated bundles of leaves are mixed in a large pan of water which the shaman drinks, scoops out some of the water and leaves, and spits out in a stream of water onto the patient; the sources of sickness are then found in the vicinity of the fallen leaves; and (4) counsel and advice, *likaite*, in which the shaman informs the patient of the source of sickness, how the patient got it, whether it can be cured, and, if the cure undertaken by one shaman will be partial, what other remedies should be obtained or measures taken to alleviate the sickness.

A point worth noting in regard to shamans' cures is that, in a majority of the curing sessions that I heard of or witnessed, shamans performed their cures in groups of three or four, with one lead shaman who guided the ritual songs and actions, while the others served as respondents to the songs and procedures of curing. The number of patients varies for cures, yet in the majority of cases, more than one and up to six patients received treatment in any one session. Both facts have importance in suggesting that not only do shamans serve the needs of individual patients but also their collective concerns are directed toward the health and well-being of groups of kin and non-kin of several communities. Prophetic figures have probably been considered saviors because their messages of salvation and the efficacy of their cures extended to a wide network of communities throughout the region. Thus, Kudui's influence extended to various communities of the Uaupés.

Complementary to the shaman's extractive form of curing, elders (not necessarily shamans) know a great many "formulas" or orations, called *iapakana* or *iwapakaite*, accompanied frequently by the blowing of tobacco smoke over medicinal substances. Elderly people are asked more than anyone else to speak or chant these orations, which are employed for an enormous variety of purposes: for protecting against sickness, protecting against evil omens, healing injuries and alleviating painful conditions, reverting the attacks of witches, reverting the desire of an enemy to inflict harm, calling animals for the hunt, or fish into traps, calling the "master of the earth" to ensure the growth of gardens, and so on. The more knowledgeable elders also know the special sets of chants for naming rites, the lengthy sets of chants called *kalidzamai* sung at the end of all life-cycle rituals (postpartum, initiation, death). These chants are considered shamanizing activity, *malikai*, for their purpose is to shamanize pepper and the food of those who have undergone seclusion and fasting from eating fish and game. One

does not need to be a shaman, *maliiri*, to know them, although shamans often do.

There is no indication either from mythology or from statements by
specialists to me that chanters are more powerful or important than
shamans, as Hill has suggested ([1989] 1993) for the Wakuenai of the
upper Guainía in Venezuela. Hohodene myths leave it ambiguous, in
fact, which activity was "created" first, and in any case, both derive
from the same source. On the one hand, shamans have a great deal
more visible prestige, which can extend over wide areas due to the
efficacy of their collective cures. On the other hand, the *kalidzamai*
chanters have internal prestige in the exercise of an extremely important function in life-passage rituals, based on an esoteric knowledge
of the cosmos. Shamans have, as I have pointed out in this chapter, the
power to create and sustain the cosmos and prevent its destruction
through their journeys to the Other World and intercession on behalf
of humanity. In this, the shamans utilize an esoteric knowledge equal
to but different from that of the chanters. This is equivalent to the difference, found in many native Amazonian religions, between *canonical*
knowledge of the sacred, as in priestly functions—here, on the part of
the chanters—and experiential, *ecstatic* knowledge of the sacred—as
here, among the shamans (see Sullivan 1988, Chapter 7, for further
discussion of this difference in South American religions). As I have
suggested on various occasions (e.g., in items published in 1992), at
least some of the great Baniwa prophets of the past, such as Kudui,
were shamans who had reached the apex of shamanic hierarchy *and*
were *kalidzamai* chanters at the same time.

It will be noted that both of the shamans' discourses I have cited
above make reference to four or five aspects of the shaman's journeys
to the Other World and encounters with primordial beings: their ascent and transformation on *pariká*; guiding the souls of the dead to
their destiny in the other sky; remaking the world; curing in the Other
World first before curing in This World; and finally, descent and re-
entry into This World and transmitting messages and experiences to
people in This World. In nearly every one of these aspects, the shaman's quest is characterized in terms of the protective and beneficial:
to make the world beautiful; to make This World and people in it better and content; to not let This World fall or end; to retrieve lost souls
and make sick persons well. In fact, it is as though the specific intent
of the shaman's journey to the Other World—that is, to retrieve lost
souls—were so interconnected with the larger concern of making the
world better, keeping the world, that it is impossible to separate them.
In all phases, the beauty, goodness, unity, order, and truth of the primordial world stand in contrast with This World of multiple pain and

evil. In one sense, then, the shaman's quest would seem to be one of "beautifying" This World through the effort to sustain order and prevent chaos.

Perhaps this is most dramatically illustrated in the phase in which he becomes like Iaperikuli, the world-master, and re-creates everything in the world "in his thought." How this is done is a great mystery which defies explanation, for the shaman, as Keruaminali said in the end of his discourse, is completely devoid of form, having cast off all corporeal qualities after passing through the hole of burning resin. Having been purified of all traces of humanness, the shaman's soul is formless and, it would seem, can assume any form whatsoever, including that of the universe master. When I asked Mandu about this transformation into Iaperikuli, he answered that the shaman's soul becomes "like a log." Not just any log, however, but one called *dzaui Kamathawa ikudaita*, which is one of the spiritual medicines the shaman obtains from the harpy Kamathawa during his apprenticeship. The shaman literally becomes a medicine, then, but the special power of this wood lies in its great strength for "opening the world." Now, in the following section, I shall try to show that the act of "opening the world"—that is, the ancient and hidden world of Iaperikuli—is an act of revelation which unlocks the power to create the elements of the world and thus to restore its order.

Healing the World with a Song

In all phases of shamans' apprenticeship, songs accompany their acts of transformation and creation. Unlike orations, chants, or myths, shamans' songs seem to have no fixed form—that is, they comprise a genre of free verse, and in this the shamans derive their creativity and aesthetic style. One of the criteria that people use for evaluating or appreciating shamanic cures, in fact, is how well they sing. The songs refer to the myths and to the diverse primordial beings of the cosmos—in this sense they are like chants which, according to Hill's analysis ([1989] 1993), "musicalize mythical speech"—but they do so in such a way as to leave open a large margin of creativity for the shaman's *direct experience* of these beings in his ecstatic journeys throughout the cosmic planes.

I shall consider here two songs, both sung by Mandu and both, according to him, taken from the phase of the shaman's spiritual development when he "remakes the world." These demonstrate that, far from being simply a feat of pure technical mastery, the spiritual remaking of the world is the basis of the salvific power of the shamans. That is, his power to save the world from death and destruction, and

hence to guard the cosmos, derives from his mastery over the creation
of forms.

In the first, Mandu sings that the shaman keeps/heals the world,
pamatchiatsa hekwapi. The following is my translation of the song:

Heeeey —heeeeey
Where will it be, it comes back to stay with us,
His world,
Dzulíferi.
Where will it be, it comes back to stay with us, his hidden place
Of long ago,
My grandfather Dzulíferi,
Dzulíferi.
For now I come and open his hidden place of long ago,
My grandfather, grandfather.
I will brush away, brush away
Their tobacco
Smoke, ["brush away their tobacco smoke" = clean the sky of
    clouds]
Of the jaguar shamans.
Thus it will be I open his dwelling-place,
Father Dzulíferi, *Heeeeee*,
Thus it will be I raise his wood, Jaguar Kamathawa.
Thus it will be I raise his crest feather, Jaguar Kamathawa.
With them I will brush away their tobacco smoke,
Of the jaguar shamans, I come and open
His world.
Never do we seek him who does not want to know how
To open the ancient, hidden world, my grandfather.
Thus it will be, I open, I open his world, Jaguar Iaperikuli.
Thus it will be I look for his medicine to open his world.
Never do we seek him who does not want to know how to open
    his
World, Eternal Master,
Heeeee.
He sees that we open his ancient world,
My grandfather, grandfather, *heeee*,
Thus it will be his medicine box in the place of happiness, his
    world
Of Jaguar Iaperikuli, *heeee*.
There is his ancient, hidden place, my grandfather, my
    grandfather,
The Eternal Master.

Thus will it be I open it with him, the sun's children,
Heee—I open it, his world, the Eternal Master.
Thus I brush away and open,
With us, I open his ancient, hidden world, my grandfather,
   grandfather,
Thus will it be his medicine box, Jaguar Iaperikuli
His happiness-place, Jaguar Iaperikuli, *heee*
Thus will be his happiness-place, Jaguar Iaperikuli.
Thus I open it, he comes and opens it, *heee*.
Thus will it be he comes and opens it, his ancient, hidden world,
My grandfather, my grandfather.
For so it will be I open it with this *teko teko Maliweko-kuthe* [= "the
   medicine of Maliweko, a stone house of fruits," Mandu
   explained].
I raise it, thus will it be, his wood Jaguar Kamathawa.
Thus will I stay in his place, Dzulíferi,
His place, Dzulíferi.
Thus he comes and stays, he opens his world.
Thus he comes and opens it, his world, Dzulíferi,
His happiness-place.
Thus will be his happiness-place, the Eternal Master.
Thus will be his ancient, hidden place.
For thus will be I open it, his ancient place, my grandfather,
My grandfather.
Thus will it be never do we seek him who does not want to know
   how
To open it, his ancient, hidden place, Jaguar Iaperikuli.
Thus he comes and opens it with us, our ancestors:
Our ancestor—Eternal Master; our ancestor—Dzulíferi;
Our ancestor—Jaguar Iaperikuli.
Thus will be his world, his world, Jaguar Iaperikuli, I open it for
   us.
The other sky, the other sky, we are with Jaguar Iaperikuli.
We are with him, Jaguar Iaperikuli, we are in the other sky.
His companion, my grandfather, my grandfather—the primal sun
   Heiri.
His companion, my grandfather Heiri.
His companion—Heiri Heiri; his companion—our ancestor Jaguar
   Iaperikuli.
I open it with them.
Thus will it be his ancient, hidden world,
My grandfather, Jaguar Iaperikuli.

For so it will be, I open it with them,
The Eternal Ones,
His world,
His ancient, hidden world,
My grandfather, grandfather, Jaguar Iaperikuli.
Haaaaaaaaaw! Haaaaaaaawwwffff!

Mandu explained this song in the following manner:

He [the shaman] looks for the ancient, hidden world, *lidawanikwa oopi* of Iaperikuli. In his thought, he sits where Iaperikuli sits and seeks to open the ancient, hidden world. He uses the wood and crest feathers of Kamathawa [Iaperikuli's pet harpy eagle] to open it. He blows away the clouds to open the sky, to make a beautiful sky. He [the shaman] thinks: there are others who don't want to know, to become as in the beginning. But they cannot open the ancient, hidden world. The hidden world is the place of happiness, *kathimákwe*, the world of Jaguar Iaperikuli. When the hidden world opens for him, he ascends to it. He sits in the place of Dzulíferi and opens the world again in the sky above. He is then near Iaperikuli and sees the whole world. He can make everything, as Iaperikuli did in the beginning. He gets what Iaperikuli had in the beginning—how-Iaperikuli-saw-the-world-in-the-beginning, Iaperikuli *ikenyuakarumi likapa kuameka hekwapi*—in his thought. He can then make the world. He [the shaman] is near the sun [the primal sun] Heiri, the body of Iaperikuli. He has arisen and requests from the sun Heiri to open the ancient, hidden world of Iaperikuli. He sees that the world becomes happy, that all people become happy, as in the beginning. So he [the shaman] makes the world better, *pamatch-iatsa hekwapi*, and does not let it end. He [the shaman] knows when it will end. He advises Iaperikuli and he doesn't let it end.

Opening—that is, revealing—the "ancient, hidden" primordial world of "eternal happiness" unlocks Iaperikuli's primordial creative act—"how he saw the world in the beginning"—at the same time, preventing the end, or closing of the world. It stands to reason that the shaman has the power to heal the world, considering that the cosmos, as I have suggested, represents spiritualized being and that the healing of individuals is a drama of cosmic proportions.

The second song refers to a time when the world, as Mandu stated, *did* come to an end. It is called "The Night End Long Ago," *deepi*

karumi oopi, to which I have already referred in Chapter 1 in considering the myth of how Iaperikuli sought to kill the Dzauikuapa, chief of
the animals and "owner of poison." In a long night, Iaperikuli caused
a flood forcing the animals to ascend an *abiú* fruit tree which he later
broke with thunder and lightning and all the animals except one were
devoured in the waters by piranha, alligators, and so on.

Given the length of this song, I shall only cite Mandu's exegesis of
it, which speaks of its principal ideas:

> This is a song for shamans. When people don't know how to see
> with *pariká*, they don't know how to explain this song. The world
> ended once. Night covered the whole world. The shaman requests
> that Iaperikuli make the night pass, to leave the world as it is now.
> *Pariká* shows the shaman. It opens the world. *Pariká* makes the
> stairs on which he ascends. He rises up to the sky. Then he takes
> three kinds of tobacco and blows them on top of the people. He
> asks that the world not be left to end. He [the shaman] ascends and
> gets near to Iaperikuli. He doesn't want that the world be left to
> end. He opens the world. For night came and stayed for awhile.
> It was Iaperikuli himself who made this happen. Later, he saved
> people by his song. The shaman takes *pariká*, ascends, and raises
> people up again and they become happy. They were sad, now they
> are happy, Iaperikuli's people. Then Iaperikuli asked them, "So,
> you are not going to stay like animals? Killing and eating people
> with poison?" Iaperikuli saved us.

The acts of raising the *pariká* ladder, of opening the world, and the
shaman's request that the day return—all restore the temporal and
spatial separation of night and day, the living from the dead, happiness from sadness. The catastrophic end of the world thus signifies a
time when sadness reigns, in total obscurity, as in the world of the
shades of the dead. The shaman intercedes—it is only the shaman
who knows when, for only he knows how to see with pariká—on behalf of humanity, for the end to pass and the world to become beautiful and happy again.

The salvific power of the shamans consists, then, of at least three
processes: revealing the ancient, hidden world of eternal happiness
and assuming the place of the creator; reestablishing temporal and
spatial orders of the cosmos; shamanizing the spiritualized beings of
the cosmos. In all these endeavors, the eternal light of the sun, the
smoke of sacred tobacco, and the visionary, transformative qualities
of *pariká* are the source of the shaman's creative acts.

We are now in a better position to understand more fully the millenarian and prophetic powers of the shamans. Through cosmogonic myths, we saw that in the view of many shamans, This World is intrinsically flawed by evil, misfortune, and death—*maatchíkwe*, place of evil. Like a sick person, the world constantly needs to be healed; in other words, to be returned to a state of integrated spatial and temporal order. The "death of the world," when the world collapses into total darkness, is the equivalent of being consumed by poison and death-dealing sickness, most closely associated with the powers of the animals. The shaman's apprenticeship and constant journeys to the Other World fulfill the most vital goal of sustaining ordered life, of preventing the death of the world, and of constantly healing the world from sickness.

It follows from this that if there were no more shamans, then the world as the Baniwa know it would come to an end. For that reason, as we shall see in Chapter 8, during the 1950s and 1960s, when evangelical Protestants attacked and destroyed the shamans and the sacred flutes, converted Baniwa concluded that the end was imminent. In fact, they declared that the waters would rise and that people should tie up their canoes to the tops of their houses, that the world would become totally dark, exactly as in the myth and in the shamans' song, *deepi karumi oopi*, "The Night End Long Ago." But when a group of evangelical elders went to kill the prophet Kudui of the upper Aiary, with poison—shutting out the last light, in a sense—he, like Iaperikuli, knew of their intentions even before they had arrived and made them go back home. This explains, among other things, why the shamans of the Aiary, and many other nonspecialists, still today remember Kudui as "our salvation."

PART II
CREATION OF SELF AND OTHER
IN MYTH AND HISTORY

One of the most common themes found in native Amazonian millenarian and messianic movements is the prophesy of an imminent
transformation of the Indians into whites and vice versa. Documented
examples include native peoples of the middle Amazon in the late seventeenth century (Porro 1987–1989), Carib-speaking peoples of the
Brazil-Guyana border since the first half of the nineteenth century
(Schaden 1976; Andrello 1993; de Abreu 1995), and native peoples of
the Northwest Amazon in the second half of the nineteenth century.

A variant of this notion holds that outsiders, often white and often
religious, are perceived as "deities," "returning gods," or are assimilated to the worlds of primordial beings. Probably the first native
Amazonian messianic movement on record, among the Jurimagua
people of the upper Amazon in the seventeenth century, involved the
Jesuit priest Samuel Fritz, who was attributed powers analogous to
the native deity Guaricaya (Porro 1987–1989, 384–385). In the twentieth century, the Ticuna of the upper Solimões, according to anthropologist João Pacheco de Oliveira Filho (1988, 278), believe that among
the many forms that the creator deity Yoi can take is the White Man.
The Tukanoan Barasana of southeastern Colombia believe that their
culture hero Warimi ("He who went away") is the ancestor of all the
white people (S. Hugh-Jones 1988, 142–143).

For the Baniwa, the question of the whites likewise has been a critical element in their long history of millenarian, messianic, and prophetic movements. In some cases, prophets have urged their followers
to avoid the whites, even while incorporating Christian practices and
symbols into ritual and mythic structures. In other cases, prophets
have warned of an imminent "coming of the whites" for which their
people should prepare. One central element in the ideology of the
Baniwa's conversion to Protestant evangelicalism in the 1950s consisted in "becoming white, half-civilized."

From some of the earliest written sources on the Baniwa, we learn that their first contacts with the whites impressed them with the totally strange nature of their ways. When the famous British naturalist Alfred R. Wallace visited Baniwa communities of the Cubate River, tributary of the lower Içana, in 1853, he found them eager to learn about the world of the whites. For example, they prodded this knowledgeable man for information about:

> where iron came from, how calico was made, if paper grew in my country, if we had much manioc and plantains. They were greatly astonished to hear that all were white men there and could not imagine how white men could work, or how there could be a country without a forest. ([1853] 1969, 154)

From this statement we get an idea of the intense interest these Baniwa had in the ability of the whites to produce new and useful goods, as if magically, without the forest they thought would have been necessary. Their astonishment that white men work indicates two things: an accurate historical perception that the whites until then had only ordered others—the Indians—to work, and a notion that the whites lived in a world of abundance without work.

Over a century later, when I began my fieldwork with the Baniwa, I, like Wallace, was the object of intense observations, questioning, and daily conversations. From the beginning, I sensed that the category of "white man," *ialanawi*, was marked by a dimension that went beyond the concrete reality of the contact situation; that is, *ialanawinai* (pl.) were not like other humans. Initially, their questions sought to classify me according to the groups of white men they knew: was I with FUNAI? a trader? a missionary? As a North American, was I a Protestant pastor there to preach the Bible? Given that FUNAI authorized my fieldwork, I was put into the category of the *"governo"* (government) and therefore a *"patrão"* (boss). Despite my unwillingness to accept this label, it stuck for the duration of my fieldwork, thus determining, in many ways, my relations with the Baniwa. *"Antropólogo"*—or *"polócolo,"* as some said—meant nothing. Toward the end of my fieldwork, I was seen more as a "friend," *kitchinda,* or "younger brother," *mhereri*; however, in situations where white authorities visited, I was put back into the category of *"patrão."*

This meant that I was often in the position of an intermediary between the Baniwa and the sources of wealth and power in the capital cities. It meant that I was seen as a source of information about the white world in general—especially, its geography, industry, and technology. And it implied a set of intense attitudes and behavior ranging from fear and avoidance, to skillful manipulation, to admiration and wonder.

My interests in Baniwa history to some extent clarified these attitudes. Daily living was another set of information, for the differences between the whites and Baniwa were everywhere visible: Baniwa who worked for the whites displayed their material wealth (clothes, shoes, watches, radios, etc.), while those who did not continued to wear ragged clothes and to live as in *antigamente* (the old times). It was through the study of symbolic representations in mythic narratives and oral histories, however, that I came to have a deeper understanding of the meaning of the category. For I soon discovered that the white men were assimilated to the world of the deities. Indeed, two of the most powerful spirit beings were said to be *ialanawinai*, with the material attributes of the whites; and whenever these were mentioned in the myths, narrators would say to me, "*You* know how it is," or "They [the figures in question] are beautiful white men" ("*branquinho, bonito*"). This, to me, disturbing association demands clarification, and it is precisely the set of beliefs underlying these statements that I will explore in this part.

The recent anthropological interest in indigenous representations of whites suggests ways for approaching these questions: S. Hugh-Jones' analysis (1988) of the representations of the whites in Barasana mythology; Bidou's study (1986) of Tatuyo mythology as at once a way of explaining and of shaping historical events; Albert's analysis (1988) of symbolic representations of historical contact among the Yanomami; and my own studies together with Jonathan Hill (Wright and Hill 1986; Hill and Wright 1988) of narrative forms, ritual, and historical religious movements are all examples from the North and Northwest Amazon that serve as a basis for discussion in the following two chapters. Hill's collection *Rethinking History and Myth* (1988) and two 1993 issues of *South American Indian Studies*, one edited by Hill and the other by Turner, on interethnic contact also are fundamental guides for our theoretical considerations concerning the relations among forms of mythic and historical consciousness.

I propose to undertake this study through an intensive investigation of the construction of the categories of self and other in myth and history. By self I refer specifically to the Hohodene phratry of the Aiary, and I shall examine how the Hohodene have constructed and reconstructed their collective identity as a phratry through history, in alliance with and in opposition to diverse other groups, especially the whites. I shall further examine how the Hohodene understood collective self-identity as it is constructed in cosmogony, specifically through the myth of Kuwai. By other I understand the various categories of beings on the periphery of their society which the Hohodene include in their universe of knowledge—spirit beings, non-Hohodene, non-Indian, and the various subcategories of white people.

Chapter 3 concentrates on a discussion of the principal categories of whites with whom the Baniwa have been in contact over the past two and one-half centuries and the nature, form, and quality of these contacts, in order to give dimension to the category of whites as a historical construction. My discussion is divided into two parts: the first being a panoramic history of contact based on written sources; the second, an interpretation of Hohodene oral histories of their contacts with the whites.

History from the written sources demonstrates the critical roles of economic interest groups and the military as the groups of whites who have most drastically affected the peoples of the Northwest Amazon. Hohodene oral histories represent both groups as responsible for catastrophic changes that have occurred in their society. The decisions and actions of Hohodene ancestors in relation to the whites affirm the critical importance of processes of social reproduction as the key to survival and the regeneration of society in the face of imminent ethnic extinction.

Chapter 4 considers the question of myth as "history in the most essential sense of the word" (Turner 1988), as the process of producing society which implies, at the same time, the process of producing the other—those outside of society. The central myth which the Baniwa tell to explain processes related to the reproduction of their society is that of Kuwai, the child of the sun who teaches humanity the first initiation rites, and who left the knowledge, *ianheke*, for men to continue this process for all times. In the myth, Kuwai is identified with, among other beings, the White Man, and Kuwai's mother, Amaru, becomes the "mother of the whites." One central objective of the extended interpretation I make of this myth, and narrators' discourse about this myth, is to understand why these images are appropriate and what narrators do with them in the course of narrating. I argue that the Kuwai/White Man image represents the figure of a wandering intermediary, an outsider, whose dangerous powers are ultimately brought under control and transformed into the ancestral powers by which society is reproduced. I further argue that myth and history are complementary forms of consciousness through which the millenarian themes of catastrophe and regeneration are expressed.

3. Indians and Whites in Baniwa History

Introduction

Before proceeding, a brief discussion is fitting here to clarify the paths I have followed to arrive at indigenous conceptions of history, and their relations to myth and ritual.

In fact, my choice of the Baniwa to undertake anthropological research had as an initial concern the possibility of writing a long-range history of an Amazonian people utilizing both written and oral sources. In the case of the Baniwa, this seemed possible because I knew that there existed a relatively large collection of documents in the National Historical Archives in Rio de Janeiro on a series of historic messianic movements in the Northwest Amazon, and I imagined that the Baniwa today would have some memory of these events and their leaders. I intended to complement research in the written sources and on oral history with intensive research on mythology, shamanism, eschatology, and ritual organization. At the time I was planning this research, the paradigm of French structuralism predominated in the studies of South American mythology and ritual; while the paradigm demanded in-depth and detailed studies of native categories, it nevertheless had to be historicized in order to conceptualize the relations between religion and history.

In the field, my research project took on a new direction when, in response to my questions on their past, the Hohodene insisted on telling me a story of a war, an event of great importance to the people of the Aiary River that occurred in a determined place to which narrators would point and that involved the whites. This story seemed to have nothing to do with the messianic movements in which I was interested, however. I heard the same story various times told by different narrators and in more or less the same fashion. It seemed like an "official history" of the Hohodene phratry, and certain narrators from groups considered of high status in the hierarchy of Hohodene sibs, I was told, knew how to tell it "the most certain," and with more details. Memories of messianic movements and leaders of the past, however, did not have the same importance to narrators. To be sure, they had many stories of the recently deceased prophet Kudui, which I noted, but only en passant there emerged fragments of a story of Kamiko, the famous "Christ of the Içana," as the mid-nineteenth-century sources called him.

Years later, my colleague Jonathan Hill, who had done his research among the Dzauinai phratry of the Guainía River in Venezuela, sent me tape recordings of several detailed traditions regarding Kamiko. The narrator was a descendant of the messiah, just as narrators of the Hohodene history considered themselves direct descendants of the war chief of their history. The first conclusion that I came to regarding ethnohistory, then, was that each phratry has its own history or histories, and that various perspectives on the past are transmitted in these traditions. Later, the French anthropologist Nicolas Journet, working among Curripaco phratries in Colombia, presented in his thesis (1995) various traditions of war which confirmed this conclusion. On the other hand, even though history was local and phratry-specific, all histories seemed to have a central concern in common: forms of sociocultural reproduction of the phratry and their relations with other phratries and enemy peoples, including the whites. It was from this wider perspective that I began to comprehend ethnohistory among the Baniwa.

A word on my use of written sources: the Northwest Amazon is notable in Lowland South America for the quantity of material written on it since the eighteenth century, and of the most diverse kinds— from records of Indians enslaved in the 1740s to missionary diaries in the 1950s. With all of that, it was relatively easy to construct a chronology of contact and to demonstrate conclusively that the indigenous societies of the region, far from being "isolated," have lived within the colonial context for two and one-half centuries and have passed through periods of profound transformation. The written sources allowed me to reconstruct a history of contact focusing on political economy in the region, that is, a sequence of forms of political and economic penetration and domination and their impacts on indigenous societies. In this perspective, the indigenous peoples have utilized a series of predominantly political and religious strategies to challenge, resist, subvert, or adapt to the colonial context.

Although this perspective is perfectly acceptable as anthropological history, if the objective is to understand ethnohistory—the conception of history forged by native peoples—it is insufficient, because it suggests that the Baniwa have simply reacted to a series of transformations, as the receptors of processes that originated in the urban centers of colonial Amazonia. In other words, the *epicenter* of history is with colonial society, downriver, and not with the Baniwa, upriver. In order to relocate the perspective, it was necessary to take seriously the principle, so well put by Renato Rosaldo in *Ilongot Headhunting* (1980), that "history on the local level must break down the false dichotomy between internal studies of oral traditions and external studies of the written sources." This dichotomy ends up privileging the written sources while oral memory is somehow "less true." The epicenter must originate from within indigenous conceptual references, for only in this way do the lives and actions of the Baniwa "become intelligible when accompanied through a series of events, be these external or internal in origin" (ibid.), but which are totally *filtered* by sociocultural patterns and processes on the local level.

When, for example, Portuguese colonizers made Baniwa phratries descend from their territories to the lower Rio Negro, the impact of this action—different from what the colonizers thought—was totally filtered by Baniwa war patterns. Or when evangelical missionaries began a campaign to convert the Baniwa, the movement that this produced was entirely filtered by millenarian traditions, ritual patterns, and the political dynamics already existing among phratries—hence, the sense in which the Baniwa, even though "reacting" to outside forces, are *agents* of their history. It is on this level, which works from within Baniwa perspectives and their conceptual references, that I shall seek to interpret Hohodene oral histories presented in this chapter.

Another fundamental methodological question has to do with the temporalities of mythic and historical traditions. Recent anthropological discussions (see, for example, Turner, in Hill 1988, 252) support the idea that myth and history are complementary forms of consciousness that explain social experiences on different levels. Myth seeks to formulate the essential properties of social experience in terms of "generic" events, at a level that transcends any specific context of historical relations or events. At the same time that it provides explanatory references for historical events, it presents a model of historical action. History, in turn, is concerned basically with the level of specific relations among specific events. It can serve as much as a justification for certain situations as a strategy for sociopolitical action in the present context.

Mythic time—I think it is safe to say, for all Baniwa narrators—is *oopídali,* "ancient time," but it is important to recognize, as Lawrence Sullivan well remembers for South American religions (1988, 224), the complexity of this time, for *oopídali* may refer simultaneously to various modalities: the cosmogonic time of the creation and transformation of the cosmos (the myths of the miniature world of Iaperikuli, as discussed in Part 1); the times exhibited by each modality of supernatural being or divinity; the times manifest in the constitution of the human being; ritual time; and the eternal time of the cosmos.

Several of these modalities are cyclical. The cosmogonic time of the creation and transformation of the cosmos, for example, can be thought of as a closed cycle at the beginning of time. The history of the cosmos refers to the eternal (*midzáka*) existence of the spirit beings and divinities that "return" and "walk with" human beings today in rites of passage and shamanic curing rites. Normally, this eternal existence is separate, sealed and closed to people in the present (*pandza*). What the rites do is to open a passage between the space-time of *oopídali* and *pandza.* We may thus think of this relation between *oopídali* and *pandza* as a series of multiple, intercalated cycles, a relation in which music and powerful sounds are the principal means of intermediation. As Eduardo Viveiros de Castro and Manuela Carneiro da Cunha put it so well, societies of the Northwest Amazon are "yo-yo societies whose identity is forever put at risk." But beyond the cycles of eternal returns, there is the notion of *closure*—that is, in the same way that cosmogonic time came to its end, so the cycle of cosmic history may close, at an indeterminate point, or "another end of the world," as shamans and narrators say. It is in this sense that "catastrophe and regeneration" may be considered metaphors that define the rupture and reordering of space-time in the history of the cosmos. I shall return to this point at various moments in this book.

By contrast, the Hohodene oral history that I shall consider in this chapter took place, according to the narrator, "almost yesterday," *hwekudza deetsa.* It is, as I have said, local and phratry-specific, "microhistory" in contrast with cosmic "macrohistory." It refers not to a chronological sequence of events but to a "horizontal space-time." The episodes of this history, I shall show, can be represented in the form of three concentric circles. The largest, corresponding to the first episode of the story, represents the most distant time and coincides with the relations between the Hohodene and the spatially and socially most distant groups—the whites and enemies (*ipuunda*). The next circle represents an intermediary time coinciding with the relations between the Hohodene and other phratries, potential affines (*itenaaki*). And the last, smallest circle is the time nearest to the narrator, the time of "our grandparents," and refers to the relations among the "brothers" (*im-*

hereridam) of the same phratry. Temporality here is therefore defined by the parameters of spatial and social distance (compare the vision of the Yanomami; see Ramos 1990).

For now, I only wish to emphasize that the themes of catastrophe and regeneration are also parameters of historical temporality. It is in this sense that the two modes of temporality that I have discussed in this introduction complement each other. I shall return to this point following my interpretation of oral history.

The Category of the Whites (*Ialanawinai*)

The term for "white man," *ialanawi*, is used by all Arawak-speaking peoples of the Northwest Amazon, as well as the Carib-speaking Umaua of the upper Vaupés (Koch-Grünberg 1911) and Maquiritare of the Padamo (Hill [1989] 1993). Alexander von Humboldt, writing in the late eighteenth century, was perhaps the first to note its use among Arawak-speaking peoples of the Atabapo River in Venezuela, and gives "Sons of Musicians" as a translation (1907, 331). An alternate word for the whites, however, was noted by Koch-Grünberg among the Oalipere-dakenai and Tariana: *hielani*, which may also signify a direction, the west.

In Baniwa, specifically Hohodene and Oalipere-dakenai, classifications of being, the class of "people" or *newiki* (specifically referring to phratry but also used in the more generic sense of "people") contrasts with a variety of classes of animal beings, spirit beings, and "other" beings of This World on the periphery of Baniwa society. Each of these classes consists of a range of groups that share common, distinguishing features that define the class and contrast it with other classes. Thus, the term Maakunai is a generic designation referring to non-Arawak-speaking groups at the frontier or periphery of Baniwa society but with whom Baniwa phratries have had some historic relation, usually that of warfare. The term does not refer exclusively to the forest-dwelling hunting and foraging peoples of the interfluvial regions of the Northwest Amazon, as the term "Maku" has often been used, but to such groups as the Maquiritare, or Ye'cuana, a Carib-speaking people of the Orinoco basin; and the Tukanoan Tuyuka, or Dékai, of the upper Tiquié. One of the defining features of both groups is that they do not speak the Baniwa language; the word *maaku* means "non- [negative particle *ma-*] speech [*-aku*]" and is opposed to the word that defines a fundamental feature of Baniwa phratries—*waaku*, "our speech." According to Jonathan Hill ([1989] 1993), the term Wakuenai, or "those of our speech," is an ethnonym referring to all phratries of the upper Guainía in Venezuela.

Similarly, the term for whites includes various groups of "outsiders" with whom the Baniwa have been in contact since the eighteenth century, from the first Portuguese and Spanish colonizers (*pútchuwishi* and *kútheana*, respectively) to the variety of whites representing different nationalities and interests who are in one way or another in contact with Baniwa phratries today. It also includes "blacks," or *tapayunanai*, and mixed Indian/white *caboclos*, or descendants of indigenous groups that have historically "transformed" (-*padamawa*, "become other") into whites—such as the Baré or Baalenai of the Rio Negro, or members of Baniwa phratries who were absorbed into the peripheral, nonindigenous society of the Rio Negro. It thus becomes necessary to approach the category of whites as a historical construction in order to determine the common features of the groups it includes.

Chronologically, the Portuguese military (*tsuraranai*: *tsurara*, derived from the Portuguese "*soldado*" + -*nai*, a collective suffix) were probably the first to have important contacts with Baniwa phratries, beginning with the slave-running ransom troops (*tropas de resgate*) in the first half of the eighteenth century, followed by military reconnaissance expeditions, outposts and forts, and descents (*descimentos*)[1] to the Rio Negro in the latter half of the same century. The Baniwa have had fairly continuous contact with the military of the frontier outposts of São Gabriel, Marabitanas, and Cucuy from the nineteenth century to the present. Over the last twenty years, Baniwa communities have had an especially intense contact with the military as the result of the construction of airstrips and the Northern Channel (Calha Norte) Project—a large-scale military development and colonization project implemented in the mid-1980s.

The second group to contact the Baniwa includes various representatives of the government (*governo*) on the upper Rio Negro which, until recently, have hardly differed from the military: Directors of Indians in the late eighteenth century and again in the mid-nineteenth century; an SPI (Serviço de Proteço ao Índio, the Indian protection agency from 1910 until the 1960s) post on the Içana in the 1940s and 1950s; and more recently, FUNAI (Fundação Nacional do Índio) posts. It has only been in the last thirty years, in fact, that the municipal capital, São Gabriel da Cachoeira, has become a center of political authority in the region, replacing the more distant Barcellos and Manaus as the historical seat of government.

The third group includes all representatives of religious orders, mainly Catholic: Jesuits and Carmelites in the eighteenth century; Capuchins and Franciscans in the nineteenth; and Salesians from 1950 on. Evangelical Protestants have been among the Baniwa from the late

1940s to the present. Until the 1950s, however, missionaries from all orders only occasionally visited the Baniwa to administer sacraments, but they did not establish any permanent missions on the Içana or its tributaries. Far more influential on Baniwa religion has been the popular Catholicism of the region, with its calendar of saint's days, folk healers, and mixture of indigenous and *caboclo* beliefs since the late eighteenth century.

A fourth category comprises all representatives of economic interests, extractive and commercial, but most especially those for whom the Baniwa have worked, or *patrões*, bosses. Merchants and traders began to have a significant presence on the upper Rio Negro in the early to mid-nineteenth century, but assumed major importance during the rubber boom throughout the latter half of the nineteenth century and into the twentieth. After the collapse of rubber, Baniwa work for rubber *patrões* diminished but never stopped altogether, renewing in intensity from the Second World War to the 1960s, frequently involving migration to Venezuela and Colombia. Besides rubber, the Baniwa have worked for *patrões* in the extraction of chicle, *sorva*, *piaçaba*, and *castanha* on the Rio Negro. In the 1970s, most Baniwa manufactured artwork (principally baskets) for sale to Colombian traders. In the 1980s, many worked in gold-panning, selling what they extracted to merchants in São Gabriel or to companies such as GOLDMAZON. In short, the Baniwa have had a long and continuous history of working for *patrões* with experiences ranging from extreme exploitation and slavery to enrichment from the trade goods they earned.

Of the groups of the whites, the *patrão* is thus the most significant in terms of its meaning for Baniwa livelihood. On the other hand, the term *patrão*, like *ialanawi*, has become an epithet used in a generic way and is not limited to traders or economic interest groups. The missionaries, military, and the government are all considered *patrões* in utilizing Baniwa labor in return for goods and services. Thus, *patrão*, like *ialanawi*, means a white man for whom the Baniwa work, or "who orders the Baniwa to work."

A History of Contact: Evidence from Written Sources

In the first half of the eighteenth century, the Portuguese and Spanish slave trade had penetrated well into the upper Rio Negro region, resulting in severe depopulation of nearly all peoples of the area (Sweet 1974; Wright 1981b). Probably the first documentary reference to the Baniwa, in the early 1700s, mentions their alliance with the Caverre, a Piapoco phratry on the Guaviare River, in defense against Carib war parties engaged in taking slaves for the Spaniards. The Baniwa are also mentioned in early eighteenth century Portuguese sources as having been brought down the Rio Negro as slaves, probably by the Manao people[2] of the middle Rio Negro, to the Fort of Barra, distant ancestor of the capital city of Manaus.

The Baniwa appear to have escaped the most violent entries of the slave troops, however, and it is possible that they absorbed renegades from other peoples during the wars for the capture of slaves. Numerous survivors of the Portuguese wars against the Manao and Mayapena peoples of the middle Rio Negro in the 1720s and 1730s, for example, sought refuge on the region's northern tributaries (Sweet 1974, 594) and, by the 1760s, were found in Spanish settlements of the upper Rio Negro.

Those who were taken were shipped off to distant cities and towns; if they survived the journey, they were forced to accommodate their lives to their permanent status as slaves. Those who remained in the region saw various neighboring peoples—kin, allies, and enemies alike—decline drastically in number and suffer the catastrophic effects of the slave trade, which continued to be felt years after its official abolition in 1755.

With the intensification of colonization on the Rio Negro in the latter half of the eighteenth century, exogenous diseases began to take a toll on Baniwa lives. Although it is impossible to estimate numbers, the records mention several epidemics of smallpox and measles in the 1780s. Facing the overall deterioration of living conditions and, on the other hand, the offer of a reliable source of trade goods, many Baniwa were persuaded to descend from their homelands and settle in newly formed colonial towns on the lower Rio Negro where they were expected to work either in agriculture, in the Royal Service, or in the gathering of forest products. If persuasion failed, the Portuguese military—often in alliance with other Arawak peoples such as the Baré—resorted to force, and there are several instances on record of descents in the 1780s consisting of armed attacks on Baniwa settlements, which the Indians resisted and for which they gained the reputation of "warlike."

The Indians' stays in colonial towns were more often than not temporary, as many saw what they had gotten into and quickly withdrew. Colonial towns of the late eighteenth century were chronically plagued by diseases and suffered from depopulation and frequent desertions of Indians who had descended from the upper regions. The Baniwa, who never seemed to have been settled anywhere else than on the lower Rio Negro, were among those who often deserted. Those who stayed were assimilated into the white, or *caboclo*, population.

By the end of the eighteenth century, the Portuguese and Spanish colonies had fallen into a period of disorganization which enabled native peoples to recover, in part, from the losses they had suffered and to reorganize. The Baniwa were barely surviving by the turn of the eighteenth century, but with the disorganization of the colonies, they returned to their homelands on the Içana and sought to rebuild their society.

By the 1830s, traders and merchants began to work permanently on the upper Rio Negro. Many of these were *caboclos* who lived for long periods of time in Indian villages and served as useful allies to the military at the forts of São Gabriel and Marabitanas, corralling Indian laborers to work in the Royal Service, commercial and extractive industries, or as domestic servants in elite family households of Manaus. Whatever business the military needed done, traders could be engaged to do it for them in return for protection of their trade. Numerous cases may be found in the records of military officials who conducted their own trade or became full-time traders once they had left military service. Wallace, for example, mentions cases of former soldiers turned merchants on the Içana who continued to receive the sponsorship and protection of the military commander at Marabitanas to take Baniwa Indians to work for him in gathering sarsaparilla ([1853] 1969, 215–216).

Through their skillful manipulation of the threat of force, distribution of trade goods and *cachaça*, and manipulation of local chiefs, the merchants and military maintained an oppressive system of labor exploitation in operation for years, doing what they could to increase production and revenues and, at the same time, their own wealth. Indigenist policy of the state government in Manaus in the early 1850s seemed to grant legitimacy to this system, for the records amply testify to the unchecked abuses of authority by local officials on the upper Rio Negro (for more thorough discussions of indigenist policy at this time, see Wright 1981b; Wright and Hill 1986).

The Baniwa bore a great deal of the brunt of this system although, where they could, they kept their distance from the whites. Growing popular resistance to white domination among Indians of the upper Rio Negro culminated in a series of millenarian movements among the Baniwa, Tukano, and Warekena from 1857 on. Some messianic leaders prophesied a cataclysmic destruction of the world by fire; others, an overturning of the dominant socioeconomic order in which the whites would become subservient to the Indians. Oral narratives referring to this time leave no doubt that Baniwa messiahs pitted their spiritual power against the political and economic oppression of the whites and that the key to Baniwa survival was autonomy from the corrupting and debilitating influence of contact. The movement led by

Venancio Kamiko, the most famous of the mid-nineteenth-century prophets, for example, demanded a rigorous observance of ritual fasting and prayer as well as strict avoidance of social and economic relations with the military as the means to attain salvation in the promised Paradise (Wright 1981b; Wright and Hill 1986; Hill and Wright 1987; Wright 1992c).[3]

With the military repression of these movements, the messiahs and their followers had no choice but to retreat into inaccessible areas of refuge; many refused to obey the military's orders to return to riverine settlements, or only did so with reluctance. The messiahs, however, continued to have great influence throughout the latter half of the nineteenth century, practicing their cures and providing counsel to the Indians who came to visit them from throughout the region (Wright 1992c).

By the 1870s, the rubber boom had reached the upper Rio Negro, introducing a more intense system of labor exploitation than the Baniwa had known before. Local bosses working for large export firms gained control over the lands and resources of vast areas of the region, which they exploited with their armies of rubber-gatherers. The Içana and its tributaries came under the control of a Spanish-born merchant, Germano Garrido y Otero, who with his brothers and sons literally controlled the region for more than fifty years (see Chapter 7 for a more complete history of this period). Garrido set up a sort of feudal system in the region, with hundreds of Baniwa at his service. With considerable skill, he placed his sons and allies as "Delegates of the Indians" in strategic villages, manipulated social relations of *compadrio* and marriage with the Indians, maintained a regular supply of goods and controlled commerce on the Içana, and held in permanent debt a sufficient number of Indians to serve as examples to others (Koch-Grünberg [1909] 1967; MacReigh, 1926).

While the Baniwa remember Garrido as the most influential *patrão* of this time, they also remember the terror and persecution from the troops at the Fort of Cucuy who, at the turn of the century, hunted the Indians of the Içana and Uaupés to serve as rowers, invaded longhouses, stole commercial products from the Indians, cheated Indian laborers, and conducted trade in contraband as well. Like the Colombian *patrões* of the Uaupés at this time, the military were feared, as evidenced by reports of whole villages seeking refuge in inaccessible areas, or taking to immediate flight at the appearance of whites.

While the creation of SPI posts from 1919 on, and Salesian missions from 1914 on, helped control the situation in the region, they had minimal effects, at least initially, on the Içana. Testimony of Baniwa experiences with *patrões* from the 1930s on (see de Oliveira 1979) confirms that the extractivist regime continued in operation, intensifying during the Second World War, and that life histories in large measure were defined by work for *patrões*.

In the late 1940s, the North American evangelist Sophie Muller, of the New Tribes Mission, began her work of missionizing the Curripaco of Colombia, extending this to the Içana in 1949–1950. Initially at least, Baniwa conversion to evangelicalism had all the makings of a millenarian movement—many Baniwa considered Muller a messiah and flocked to hear her message and convert to the new faith. At about the same time, Salesian priests began working on the Içana, producing a division between evangelical, or *crente*, and Catholic communities which has lasted until the present day (Chapters 7 and 8 are dedicated to the history of this conversion movement and its consequences).

Over the last two decades, Baniwa communities have confronted a new level of white penetration, representing the interests of national security and corporate mining. Beginning with the announcement in the 1970s that the Northern Perimeter highway would cut through their lands, followed soon after by the building of airstrips and, since 1986, the implantation of the Northern Channel Project, top-level government commissions from Brasília have visited the area with frequency, introducing a qualitatively different dimension of government interest in, and control over, the Baniwa's future. Official indigenist policy of assimilation, supported at least initially by the Salesians and until the present day by the military, has also put a new strain on the Baniwa's defense of their territory and culture. Since the early 1980s, gold panners, followed by mining companies, often with the protection of the Federal Police (Wright n.d.), have invaded Baniwa territory, causing disruption and various instances of violence.

In the face of these recent invasions, the Baniwa initially reaffirmed their historical stance of autonomy from the whites, seeking control over their mineral resources and the removal of all gold panners from their lands. The constant pressure exercised by mining companies, such as Paranapanema and GOLDMAZON, supported by repression from Federal Police agents, produced grave internal divisions among Baniwa communities: some took the side of the companies, others against. At the same time, the Northern Channel Project threatened to diminish drastically both the size of Baniwa territory and their capacity to impede the invasions.

In view of these circumstances, various leaders emerged to organize resistance in a more effective way. The active participation of these leaders in the Federation of Indigenous Organizations of the upper Rio Negro (FOIRN)—a panindigenous political organization founded in 1987—and in party politics, as well as the recent creation of various

local associations of Baniwa communities, represent a new configura-
tion of political articulations that is still in the making, but that will
certainly define more clearly the concrete and specific demands of
Baniwa communities.

In this brief panorama of contact history, it is clear that of the main
groups of whites, the military and merchants (or commercial interest
groups) have had the most direct and long-lasting impact on Baniwa
communities. The missionaries had a relatively unimportant role until
the evangelical campaigns and conflicts with the Catholics in the 1950s
and 1960s. Until recently, the government has acted as a distant force,
issuing documents (*cartas de patente*, letters of patent, for example, recognizing chiefs, or *capitãos*) and passing legislation, but only occasionally has sent visitors to the Baniwa or directly interfered in their
lives. For the most part, the military has represented the government's
interests in the area—through the descents of the 1700s, the "public
service" and "civilization" programs of the 1800s, or direct interference in the messianic movements of the late 1800s. In this capacity,
military officials have served as the intermediaries of the dominant,
colonial system and its distant centers (or seats) of wealth and power
in Barcellos, Barra, or Manaus, or Brasília. These have consistently
demonstrated their interest in absorbing the Baniwa into the white
population of the Rio Negro.

On numerous occasions, the military have demonstrated the excesses of their power through the use of violence and terror not only
to enforce order but also to exploit Baniwa labor to serve their own
personal interests. From the eighteenth century to the present, a long-
standing alliance between the military and traders, or economic interest groups, has served to corral labor, control the supply of trade
goods into the region, and control outlets of production. For the most
part, commerce has depended on military approval; rarely have merchants defied the military.

To understand how the Indians have perceived these relations and
their strategies for dealing with them, I turn now to Hohodene histories of contact.

Hohodene Views of History

The Hohodene of the Aiary River recount the history of their phratry's
contacts with the whites primarily through the life and deeds of their
ancestor-chief, Keruaminali. The following version, which agrees in its
overall content with other versions, was told to me by the ex-chief of
Uapui, also named Keruaminali. I shall present the story first, as it was
spoken, transcribed and translated from the tape, seeking to repro-

duce as nearly as possible its narrative form. On the occasion, the narrator's stepson helped with the translation and I have included his comments in parentheses. In brackets, I have included word-translations and explanations when necessary. When the narrator makes some sound referring to an action in the story, I have put this in italics. All names of people and places in Baniwa have also been italicized. Following the narration, I present a summary of the story, divided into episodes, with explanatory notes, highlighting aspects of the narration that appear on tape but that are evidently lost in the transcription.

Then it was . . .
They came back here
Then they make a war,
Those Tariana,
Everyone.
With them those Baalenai.
They return the war.
At Mukuali's house [Mukuali is the name of a Mulé-dakenai chief,
    phratry brother to the Hohodene],
Inyaipana [on the upper Aiary River].
At Uanalimam,
They drank and danced.
Then our ancestor Keruaminali went to call the warriors . . .
"Warriors are coming, they'll come," they say.
They went [to the Uaupés] but they didn't kill.
"What is it with you, they said war?"
[Translator explains: Mukuali says, "my arrow is very beautiful."
    Mukuali took a child for his own. Mukuali says, "I am going
    around thus," you said, 'let's kill people,' you said to me."
    Mukuali turned around, looked at a child, and shot it. Then
    everyone shot their arrows and went back home. The child was
    the son of a Cadete.]
"Oh? Oh, white people"
All of the people went together.
Everyone descended,
They go downriver to Uacariquara [on the Uaraná stream, upper
    Aiary],
It was summer,
White people are there.
There, she is thinking, this one of the Mulé-dakenai mothers,
"Hey, hey, why does he stay so far away, my elder brother?" says
    she the mother.
Then as they spoke, another of the Wadzulinai overheard

[Wadzulinai: Buzzard-people, a phratry of the Içana, allies of the whites],
"Why does he stay away?" she says.
"What is his name?" the Wadzulinai man asks.
"Mukuali"—"aaah, that is who we are looking for," they say.
He told everyone where Mukuali was—"aaah, let's go, let's go."
They go back again . . .
Theeeeere! Above Seringa Point [off the upper Uaraná stream]
The trail, they go on the trail . . . Theeere! To Kuherimádan
    [midtrail]
They light torchwood . . .
They go at night . . .
Theeere! At the Painted-Face-Stream headwaters. They kill
They throw out everyone.
Then the elder Mukuali,
Went out to hide at the edge of his plantation.
Then his grandson, Mukuethe by name,
Tuk! They catch him,
Like a little child he was.
As the torchwood lights in the house,
He jumps out, runs and falls.
He fell next to his grandfather—"My grandson?"   "Huh?"
"So you ran and fell?"
Then they take and tie them up [i.e., all the people inside the
    longhouse—both Hohodene and Mulé-dakenai],
They killed . . . *Toowhh!* [gunshots] "Oooh, that one" . . . *Toowhh!*
    "Oooh, that one" *Toowhh!*
"Everyone! Not a single one among them is saved!" says the old man,
    "That's all we are, so many among them, even to the littlest
    girl . . ."
Then they are ready to burn the house.
When done, they beat the drum—*tuuutuuutuuu.* They return.
They return with our ancestor, to Uacariquara [on the Uaraná
    stream] . . .
They go again. . . . At São Miguel they stayed [near São Gabriel
    da Cachoeira, on the Rio Negro].
They took with them those *arara*-feather crowns,
Feather crowns, quartz pendants, collars, aaah . . .
Jaguar-teeth collars. They tied together a box and an earth-pot.
At São Miguel, they stay there,
They stay and danced.
So, there they threw away everything, they put it all together in the
    pot . . . *puk! puk!*

They throw away everything there, there it is they took it all below,
Below, they took everything
Then they go . . . There! They stay below Carma, on the Cauabory
    River.
They danced with rattles.
Hardly long they stayed, then they go . . . To Barcellos.
Heeyy, they danced with rattles there.
There they wrote on paper [i.e., they began to "study" in Barcellos,
    in schools].
He went with them there,
The Tunui-chief, of the Kadapolithana [a sib of the Dzauinai
    phratry of the Içana],
Balento by name.
A year he stayed, this one our ancestor,
Then he fled and returned,
From Barcellos: "Let's go, we return.
"There is no Hohodene chief now at our village, there is none."
With them the Hawadzulunai chief [a sib of the Oalipere-dakenai
    phratry of the Içana],
He tried to flee with his son but his son had an infection in his leg
    and could not run, so the whites captured him and he stayed
    there.
Then soon they see them come in war and in fear, they flee.
The Hawadzulunai chief, our ancestor,
They return. . . . THERE! Below [on the Içana]
He looks at their villages . . .
Then he goes to live at Puatalimam [on the Uaraná stream]
He lives . . .
ALONE LIKE SO!!!
He returns with them, it seems,
He lives with them awhile, with Dthamaatanai, their chief,
The Hawadzulunai chief, that one.
On . . .
After awhile,
Keruaminali made war [i.e., Keruaminali was a warrior and made
    war for other people, to take prisoners].
He captured prisoners,
He killed people.
He ate them at his place.
Another time he captured, wherever he went he killed.
He ate people!
Only he did!
With a happy heart he was finishing off with people!

PUUUUUHHHH!!

Over there was another Dzauialípe chief [affines of the Hohodene,
    another "tribe" of people],

At the headwaters of the Aiary,

Uaaro his name.

Then Keruaminali returned,

He retuuu—rned . . . ,

They heard about him, those Oalipere-dakenai

"He is single, our *uetenaaki*" [= potential affine, ally]

"Let's go, let's offer him a wife," they say about him.

(They heard of his fame) They heard of his fame.

They were abandoning war.

They returned—she the woman, her father, her mother, she,

There! To Puatalimam.

They called out to our ancestor at the settlement—"HEEEEYY!
    HEEEYY!"

He didn't take away the fence of wood around, the fence of poison-
    darts,

The poison-dart fence.

"Hey, here am I. Hey, you lie, you come to kill me. Go away!"
    Keruaminali says.

"You come to kill me, the only Hohodene chief" he says.

"No," the Oalipere-dakenai says,

"Don't shoot me, Keruamina, don't kill me with that venom!"

He called and approached . . .

Until almost noon!

He calls out . . .

Then she called out to him, the Oalipere-dakenai's wife,

She calls out.

"I come to bring my daughter for you . . ."

"I come to bring her."

Her daughter and she approach . . . Until they are close by—"Here
    am I," she says, "I want to stay with you," she says, "You see she
    has her hammock and all, you see me," she says,

"Here I am to stay, you stay with me, you live well with me,"
    she says,

"Here is my daughter"—but he doesn't receive them.

"We are your friends, we do not come to kill, no-one will kill!!"

"FAAUUGH!"

"You lie, you come to kill me!!" Keruaminali says and opens the
    house-door—

Tsulahh!

Fiuuhh! He shoots a poison-dart!

"Put away those darts!! Don't shoot me!!" he says, "Don't kill me!!"
  says this Oalipere-dakenai.
"Nooo, do not kill," she says, "where is your sleeping quarters?"
  she says.
She goes in and sits, "Here is my daughter," she says.
She gets the hammock, she ties up the hammock, "Good I am!"
She gets some drink and gives it to him . . .
So . . .
They talk about it, the chiefs,
That's all, they talk about it . . .
Then . . . They prepare cane beer in a pot, they say, of that time,
  thurua pot (*thurua*) *thurua*.
So sweet it was!
They got food, *pacú* fish,
So . . .
With her father,
Thus all day long they speak [i.e., negotiate the marriage alliance].
She is his wife, thus that day she became his wife.
They go and sit to talk on it,
He comes back a bit drunk,
But with strength he comes back! He didn't sleep!
Until morning . . . !
"Thus it is," he says, "I don't want to kill anyone."
One moon he stays, he says.
He is not an old man,
NOT an old man! A YOUTH he is!!
Not an old man.
Five of his children stayed and became other below,
Into soldiers there, below.
Then this Balento, this Kadapolithana,
Went to Barcellos.
Soldiers began there, those his children.
These days, now, soldiers live there.
"Hooo—already they have become other," they say, "they have
  become those soldiers."
Then they went, all of them, below, all of them.
Of us, we Hohodene thus it is they became white people below
  today, all of them today,
Only one remained of us!
Keruaminali—His Descendants!!
WE ARE!!!
Our kin have all changed below!!
Thus it is,

Thus it is, I know.
Then . . .
He lived on . . .
Then it seems,
His *uetenaaki*, childless,
Went . . . THERE to Dzateam [Tucano Point, at the headwaters of
   the Quiary stream, where the Oalipere-dakenai live], he went to
   invite him,
"So it is," he called his affine,
"Let's have a *pudali*" [festival of dance and exchange].
They would make a *pudali*, he would show her, his wife.
Two of them, two women went, his wife and her mother.
THERE!! To Dzateam.
Heey! He went with *ambaúba* dance tubes, there will be many
   affines.
He went as dance leader, his affine was dance leader also.
They made *pudali*. They made ready the ornaments, as our ances-
   tors danced.
They drank and danced, and others came.
He was ready to call,
His affine with the dance tubes.
When he gives his affine the roasted fish, they danced.
They danced the Kuwaipan dance.
The dance tubes are ready!
He calls them to dance with them.
The dance leader gave drink to his affine and spoke.
Then he brings in the cane beer, and gave it to Keruaminali.
SO STRONG IT WAS!!
They take up the tubes, they do round-dancing with the tubes,
   Hoooh they come back with the tubes . . .
Her sister's husband says,
"Keruamina! How is it? Can you stand it?" he says,
"You are the only one," he says,
"Hey hey!" he says, "we shall see," he says, "we will see who of us
   can stand it," he says.
They drank . . .
They took up the dance tubes, all of them . . .
He danced . . . alll night long. He didn't sleep!
Then the others are all drunk!
So then,
He goes home again.
Thus he lived,
They return.

Then they go to make another *pudali*, those Oalipere-dakenai.

There at Puatalimam, a return *pudali*, in exchange.

They made *pudali* . . .

There they asked for land,

They the Oalipere-dakenai, thus they lived the Oalipere-dakenai, as far as their land, there was none! There was no land for the Oalipere-dakenai!

We Hohodene, we had another land. All of our land was that from the headwaters of the Quiary, to the headwaters of the Uirauassú stream, to Pupulípan on the Uaraná stream.

They asked for our land, we the Hohodene.

Thus it is, it's our land it is.

Thus our land, the earth it is.

We, the river-owners,

We, Hohodene, Hohodene villages.

"So it is,

"Here is the land," Keruaminali says,

To this Oalipere-dakenai,

"Here is the land henceforth,

"They just cannot live," he says,

"Soon it will be, people will be finished off," he says, "You live on the riverbanks above, affines, we divide it up, we live in our settlements until they've finished off everything, all their plantations, everything.

"You live on the riverbanks above, you,

"No, we cannot live."

Then Keruaminali moves,

From Puatalimam, he goes to live . . . There, at the Quiary headwaters, Putudzekan, to bring up his children.

There they grow up. Well! His children grow up.

They live on . . . Until his death.

Until they move downriver . . . There, at Keradaliapi.

They move downriver again . . . There, they come out at the Quiary headwaters.

They live on and move downriver again . . . To the same place.

Then he was killed, the elder Keruaminali died at Vulture village plaza.

Mainhakali, a Oalipere-dakenai, gave him poison.

Keruaminali they killed.

They went back and lived on, those his children. . . . For a long time. . . .

Then, this Baalenai [Baré] goes to live at Pithiriwali, on the Quiary,

He stays there.
With them, the Oalipere-dakenai.
They stay . . .
So . . .
The Baalenai made a house there.
(Baalenai?) Baalenai, what was his name?
From the Caiary [Uaupés], it seems.
"Oh, you are sad here, it is so poor here," he says,
"Let's go," he tells them to throw away their war instruments.
"So sad it is here, let's go, there is nothing here, nothing."
They make farinha,
He joins together everyone and then he goes on to São Gabriel
    below.
"All of you come," he says. "All right," they answer.
They descend from the Quiary headwaters . . . to the Quiary
    mouth.
They tie their canoes up there.
Puu' With farinha.
They accompany the white man *k'hu* . . . There to Dakadakale, the
    beach where they stopped.
Malianali is there, their elder brother.
They want their children to eat there.
He calls them—"Hey, younger brother, younger brother, let's
    drink *patchiaka!*" [farinha and water]
He calls one who arrives,
He calls another who arrives,
Their canoes are approaching . . .
"Are we going to go?" he says, "Thus it was in the same way with
    our ancestors . . .
"They wanted to kill and throw out our ancestors, we lost every-
    one, there is no more Hohodene chief . . .
"How are your hearts?" he says.
"Mmmm—yes," one says, "I truly have much work to do I tell
    you,
"I am putting up my house, I tell you, I work on my garden, all
    my plants also, everything I am working on, so much work do
    I have,
"I don't want to go."
"How then?" asks another.
"You go alone, so much work I have . . .
"So good is my garden that I am making."
"So it seems," he says,

"We go our separate ways," he says, "You younger brothers,"
   he says,
"You younger brothers, we go our separate ways."
"I am truly going," says this, Raimundo's grandfather . . .
To the Mirití stream.
"I am truly going," says another and went . . . To Santarém.
"I am truly going," says another but he could not . . .
There he goes, to Kurukuruali-numana, on the lower Aiary.
Three of them stayed,
And made longhouses.
The others already went below.
The Baalenai went below.
Thus our division, thus we began long ago.
They lived on the Quiary again . . .
They killed people again . . .
Until a long time later.
Today everyone!
Not a single one is left on the Quiary, only one Mário, a Hohodene
   chief.
Our story . . . of the Hohodene.
Sooooooooo. . . . that's it, it's finished. The story of our people.

Story Summary

Part 1

The Tariana and Baré made war against the Mulé-dakenai at Jurupary
Cachoeira or Inyaipana, on the upper Aiary. Keruaminali and his warriors went with Mukuali, chief of the Mulé-dakenai, to the Uaupés to
make war but the Hohodene did not kill anyone. Mukuali then shot a
child, the son of a white man, a soldier. The Tariana went downriver
to São Gabriel to complain to the whites. The Wadzulinai, enemies of
the Hohodene from the Içana, led a police force of Baré and others
to Mukuali's longhouse in the middle of the woods above Jurupary
Cachoeira on the upper Uaraná, off the upper Aiary, in Colombia.
They killed nearly everyone, many of them, burned the longhouse,
and took the Hohodene chief Keruaminali and his sons prisoner.

   They went back down the Rio Negro and stayed in São Miguel.
There the Hohodene chief took all the phratry's ornaments, put them
in an earthen pot, and threw them away in the river. Later, they went
down the Rio Negro again and stopped at Carma on the Cauabory,
where they drank and danced. A short while later, they descended

again, to Barcellos, and drank again. A Kadapolithana chief from the Içana, named Balento, went with them.

Then, after a while, Keruaminali fled from Barcellos, for there were no more Hohodene in their villages. His son attempted to flee but, due to an infection in his leg, was taken prisoner and remained on the lower Rio Negro. Keruaminali fled with the chief of the Hawadzulunai, sib of the Içana, the long way back up to the Içana, where they lived for some time. Only one Hohodene, Keruaminali, returned, and he lived alone. Nevertheless, the warrior Keruaminali continued to participate in war expeditions to take prisoners to be eaten.

Part 2

The Oalipere-dakenai had heard of Keruaminali and went to offer him a daughter in marriage, as Keruaminali was without a wife. They were abandoning war. They went to Keruaminali's village, but the Hohodene refused to receive them, thinking they had come in war. After a long wait, the Hohodene chief opened his door and the Oalipere entered, persuading him that they had come in peace. The chiefs talked over the alliance, and they drank strong *ialaki* (fermented drink) all night long. The alliance was settled and the Oalipere stayed with Keruaminali one month. Keruaminali was at that time not an old man; he was young.

Five of Keruaminali's children had stayed on the Rio Negro and became soldiers. The children of the Kadapolithana also became soldiers in Barcellos. All of the Hohodene who stayed below became white people; hence there are white people on the lower Rio Negro today. Only one Hohodene remained, Keruaminali, and the Hohodene today are his descendants.

Then after a while Keruaminali's affines invited him to a *pudali*, festival of dance and exchange, at Tucano Point on the Quiary. Many of his affines danced with *ambaúba* dance tubes. They danced and challenged Keruaminali as to whether he could withstand the strong drink. They danced all night long, but Keruaminali met the challenge, and returned home.

Afterward, the Hohodene held a *pudali* with the Oalipere-dakenai at Puatalimam on the Uaraná stream. There the Oalipere asked for land from the Hohodene, since the Oalipere had no more land. The Hohodene land at that time extended from the Quiary headwaters to the Uaraná headwaters. The Oalipere could not survive on their lands any longer because all of their gardens had been exhausted. So, Keruaminali moved to the upper Quiary, where he lived for a long time until his children had all grown up, forming numerous villages on the Quiary. Keruaminali later died, poisoned by the Oalipere-dakenai.

Part 3

Then one day a Baré from the Uaupés went to live in the Oalipere village of Pithiriwali on the Quiary, making canoes. One day he began to tell them, "You have to leave here, you are so sad here." He instructed them to throw away their war-making instruments and to descend downriver with him. He told everyone from the river to go. The Hohodene descended from the Quiary headwaters to its mouth, bringing a lot of farinha with them. The whites went on downriver, but the Hohodene stopped their canoes in a village so that the children could eat. The chief, Malianali, then asked the brothers: "Are we going to go? So it was with our grandfathers. They killed off our grandfathers, we lost all of them, there is no more Hohodene chief. How are your hearts?" One man answered that he was making a new house and garden and did not want to go. Another man answered the same. Some then went downriver with the whites, but the others (three brothers) went to settle at different places on the Aiary and stayed, until today.

Variations

Different Hohodene narrators could elaborate on parts of this story according to their knowledge of details and episodes. In other words, although Keruaminali's version was considered by many as being "certain," I found that—unlike mythic narratives which had to be told in a certain episodic sequence, with a definite beginning and end—the story of Keruaminali had no fixed rules for narrating from a definite beginning to end. Narrators could embellish and add interpretations to any one of the episodes. In fact, at the end of Keruaminali's version, after a slight pause, he remembered another episode which had to do with the Maulieni people, the Maaku of the Hohodene, and their attacks on Aiary settlements.

Another narrator, Marco, began his version of the story with a series of episodes of wars between the Wadzulinai or Wadzuli-dakenai (both of whom belong to the same phratry and are considered enemies of the Hohodene) and various other phratries of the Içana. These "wars" (more exactly, skirmishes) preceded the great war of the whites, allied with the Wadzulinai, against the Mulé-dakenai and Hohodene, which was the point of departure for Keruaminali's version.

Marco's father, Raimundo, was reputed to know a great deal more of the details of the whole story—such as the names of all of Keruaminali's children and grandchildren and the names of all historical Hohodene villages on the Quiary River. Thinking that I might be able to construct some sort of historical genealogy based on this information, when I questioned Raimundo, I found that the importance of such knowledge was relative, and that only certain details could be confirmed—that is, those that were directly related to Raimundo's own ancestors. Raimundo's grandfather had founded one of the three main villages of Hohodene on the Aiary after Keruaminali's children had left the Quiary. But Raimundo could not say with certainty which of Keruaminali's children was his great-grandfather and from which village on the Quiary. In fact, when I interviewed him, already in his late sixties, he had lost much of his memory due to a sickness; hence his lists of names and places did not seem to be really reliable.

In the village of Ucuqui, where I expected to find a complete version of the story—given the thoroughness and accuracy which characterized the elders' knowledge of myths and orations there—I found to the contrary only the most summary recollection, and one which conflicted in various details with Keruaminali's version. Not that the Hohodene narrators of Ucuqui had any less interest or knowledge of local history; on the contrary, they knew intriguing bits of historical detail which no other Hohodene recalled: for example, the names of ancient peoples of the Aiary; the name of the first Portuguese man ("Alistado") to make contact with the Hohodene; and a story about the Manao people of the middle Rio Negro.

The story of Keruaminali, however, was reduced to a minimum, which Laureano, then chief of Ucuqui, summarized for me as follows:

There was a war in Colombia and everyone from the Aiary went. Afterward, they stopped making war, and at the same time, they stopped drinking *kaapi* [*Banisteriopsis caapi*; an interesting indication that the drinking of this hallucinogen and warfare were connected]. The Maku went to the Cauabory River, for they were afraid of their enemies. They said, "We are going to finish off with people, let's stop making war." There was the Wadzulinai; the Mulé-dakenai, our kin; and from São Gabriel, the Baré. Our ancestor and the Oalipere-dakenai killed a Tariana, and they went to complain in São Gabriel. The Baré came from São Gabriel to the Uaraná stream; they came to get our ancestor in the woods. They went by the Içana. At Jandú Cachoeira, on the Içana, the Baré called people but they fled; there were no people. Then they ate all the chickens and came to the Uaraná where the Hohodene

were, in the woods. The Hohodene [chief] was waiting for them
when they came. The Hohodene chief spoke to those Baré soldiers:
"How are we now? We don't want to make war." And he called
them *kamarada* [friend, ally]. They made *ialaki* [cane beer] and
drank. One year later, they took everyone away. The Mulé-dakenai
of Inyaipana, of the Cadanali stream, said, "Let's go kill." They
drank beer; they made war. But they killed all the Mulé-dakenai
and took all the Hohodene downriver for two years. They drank
beer and then went to Manaus. Because of this, there, today, there
is a piece of land for us. Another fled and came back here, but
he had no wife when he got here: it was Keruaminali. He made a
pudali but he danced alone. Then his uncle came. Keruaminali married his uncle's daughter. For that reason, there were children for
us. His grandchildren married again. Thus they grew, until today.

Note that here, the story of Keruaminali is reduced to approximately the last third of the narration, while the theme of the Hohodene's abandonment of warfare is given far greater importance. In
fact, all of the versions emphasize the themes of warfare, the abandonment of warfare, and the reconstruction of society. This seems to be an
important motive for telling the story: as a way of contrasting the past
with the present, as a way of thinking about the past—that it was not
like today, and that what was abandoned in the process of change led
to a "better" condition. In gross form, this can be reduced to the idea
that, for the Hohodene, the past was characterized as a state of war and
their ancestor was a warrior and cannibal; then there occurred a moment of radical change, of rupture, and after that moment, the Hohodene "became civilized." Edu, a shaman of Uapui Cachoeira, made this
vision of history quite clear to me when he said the following:

In the ancient times, the Hohodene did not eat fish, nor hunt—
they only ate other people, like the Maku. Then, at Tucunaré Lake,
on the Içana, there was a big assembly of the Hohodene and Oalipere-dakenai. All the tribes were there—the Tariana, Dessana,
everyone—making war with spears. At midday, the war continued, there was much killing of people and later eating of the dead.
Then the war ended. [How did people stop making war? I asked]
It was the government of Brazil that went there and talked with
them. They had a document and read it: "You have to stop making war and eating people. You have to become civilized and eat
fish. . . ." Then they began to make canoes. Before, they only used
bark, but the government sent machetes and taught them how to
make canoes.

Thus "stopping war" and "becoming civilized" are two associated processes that would seem to reflect Hohodene views of their society in history. Based on this clue, I will now present my interpretation of the story of Keruaminali that seeks to elaborate on this point of view.

Interpretation

In its general outline, the story as told by Keruaminali describes: (1) a "pacification" campaign by the military, in alliance with other Arawak peoples, against the Mulé-dakenai, who were massacred, and the Hohodene, who were taken prisoner; (2) a forced descent to the Rio Negro in which the Hohodene underwent "acculturation," that is, threw away their ornaments, drank and danced in the whites' settlements, and lost their children, who "became whites," specifically soldiers, in Barcellos; (3) a process of ethnic recovery in which the Hohodene fled from Barcellos to the Içana, where after a period of hiding and extreme isolation, they accepted an alliance with the Oalipere-dakenai, consolidating it through marriage, exchange festivals, and the redistribution of land between the two phratries; and (4) a second descent instigated by a Baré *caboclo*, apparently in the service of the whites, but which in large part failed due to the Hohodene's collective decision that their own work and livelihood meant more to them than another descent to the Rio Negro. From their decision to remain, the Hohodene brothers built new villages on the Aiary that are the villages of the grandparents of Hohodene narrators.

Now, for someone interested — as I was at the time I first heard this story and when I wrote my doctoral thesis — in the correlations of this tradition with chronological history from the written sources, there are various clues provided by narrators that allowed me to reconstruct a history of contact. What follows summarizes the methodology I used in my thesis to determine these connections; but as I will show, the very question I raised — of possible correlations to written sources — left more doubts than certainties, although the attempt eventually led to an interpretation that was more consistent with Hohodene socio-cultural patterns.

First, I calculated the age of the narrator for, according to him, the story took place "almost yesterday" — that is, in the time of his grandparents. Other narrators confirmed that their grandparents built the settlements on the Aiary mentioned in part 3 of the Story Summary; that is, in the second half of the nineteenth century, more specifically, in the 1860s and 1870s. Then I compared this part with the written sources for this period, which indicate that, from midcentury on, various Brazilian military, allied with merchants, sought to convince the

Hohodene and Oalipere-dakenai to descend from the Içana River to work in "public service" on the Rio Negro. But the mid-nineteenth century was also a time of messianic movements and indigenous resistance against the entry of the military in the villages of the Içana. The written sources attest that, besides refusing to descend the river, the Hohodene and Oalipere-dakenai of the Içana decided to relocate to the interior of the Aiary River (see Wright 1981b; 1987–1989).

From the 1870s on, merchants began to penetrate the Içana with greater frequency in their exploitation of rubber, taking many Baniwa to work in rubber camps on the lower Rio Negro. In 1903, during the height of the rubber boom, the German ethnologist Theodor Koch-Grünberg visited the Içana and Aiary, noting that there were no more Hohodene villages on the Quiary for "everyone had left" and had built villages on the Aiary—at exactly the places mentioned in the narrative, among others. Thus, it is reasonable to suppose that the process of "leaving the Quiary" described in the last part of the narrative (part 3 of the Story Summary) had begun in the 1860s and 1870s and ended by the beginning of the 1900s.

Based on this initial dating, I estimated the "times" of the second and then the first parts. According to the narrator, they would have taken place various generations prior to the third, or approximately at the end of the eighteenth century, beginning of the nineteenth. Considering the content of the parts, I found it more probable that the events referred to the period of *descimentos* (descents) undertaken by the Portuguese on the upper Rio Negro until the end of the eighteenth century. Another clue intrigued me: the name of the narrator was Keruaminali, the same as the Hohodene chief of the story, which is not strange given that names recycle after various generations. But his name in Portuguese was José Marcellino Cordeiro Capitán. This name I found in the documents of the end of the eighteenth century: Capitão Marcellino José Cordeiro, who was one of the military most responsible for forced descents of Indians of the upper Rio Negro during the 1780s.

The evidence thus suggested the hypothesis that the narrative referred to a sequence of events between the 1780s and the 1870s, a period of approximately one hundred years. Each episode then "made sense" when compared to the history of contact reconstructed from the written sources. In short, working in this manner turned out to be extremely intriguing for it led me to search for other sources and suggested new perceptions on the history of contact. Above all, methodologically, it demanded that I give equal weight to both oral history and written sources, without privileging one over the other as the "true history." The perspective so constructed presented contact as a process that involved the two sides in dialectical relations of conflict and contradiction.

Despite the fascination that this kind of chronological exercise had, however, exactly what I sought to understand—the historical consciousness of the Hohodene—escaped me; for my presupposition was that the events of oral history referred to the events of colonial history as reported in the documents. This proved to be a methodological error, for it ignored the cultural filter through which events are interpreted and reformulated in order to make sense within indigenous sociocultural patterns. Perhaps, I now see, there never was, in fact, a great war of the whites allied with the tribes of the Uaupés against the Mulé-dakenai and Hohodene, as described in the first part of the narrative (part 1 of the Story Summary). Perhaps the "war" is another form of catastrophic relations with "other," socially and geographically distant, groups—hence enemies—in the same sense that cosmic history begins its drama with a catastrophic situation. And perhaps, more than by the memory of the events of colonialism, domination, and oppression, the story of Keruaminali seemed to be motivated by a reaffirmation of Hohodene political power when confronted by the circumstances of contact, a reaffirmation that could serve as a program of action in the present situation of interethnic conflicts. Let us see how in the narrative.

In order to understand the first part, we have to contextualize it with information on the nature of Baniwa war patterns. Narratives of war (see Journet 1995; Wright 1990) indicate that war (*uwi*) had two main objectives: (1) to avenge the death of a kin with the death of an enemy, in accordance with the logic of exchange or "return" (*koada*) in which the end of the conflict coincided with the total, or near total, annihilation of the enemy, even though such vengeance ran the risk of the Baniwa's being exterminated in the process; and (2) to replace the dead with children to be raised or women captured in war, thus ensuring the reproduction of the group, even though this perpetuated hostile relations. Baniwa warfare, then, constituted a system of relations, and not an "accident" of society, through which enemies represented for each other a source of progeny. The search for vengeance, or "return" *koada*, was a means for enemy groups to exchange, to replace their dead and to self-perpetuate. In this system, the relations of alliance by marriage were secondary in importance. War always took place on the frontiers of society, between distant groups unrelated by kinship (e.g., Maaku, the whites). It was situated where the categories that structured social relations had an "other" sense. It could thus be considered an alternative to all other social relations.

In the first part of the narrative, then, the Hohodene and their phratric brothers, the Mulé-dakenai, initiated an attack on the Uaupés in which a child, the son of a white soldier, was killed. In reprisal, following the logic of "return," the indigenous peoples of the Uaupés (Tariana, Baré—"enemies") allied to the whites practically exterminated the Mulé-dakenai and took the Hohodene prisoner to their towns on the Rio Negro. The Hohodene "threw away" all of their cultural adornments, and the sons of the Hohodene were eventually transformed into the whites, or soldiers, thus becoming full members of the enemy groups on the periphery of Baniwa society. From the point of view of the Hohodene, the whites had thus recovered the loss of one of their children. The "period of warfare"—as we may consider the first episode—ends with the annihilation of a group, the Mulé-dakenai, and the virtual inviability of another, the Hohodene. But the warrior-chief of the Hohodene, Keruaminali, decided to flee. Faced by the dilemma of the group being completely annihilated or recovering its viability, the chief affirms the Hohodene's identification with their territory and villages and returns to the Içana.

While the first part of the narrative is marked by the frontier among "enemy" groups, *ipuunda*, the second (corresponding to part 2 of the Story Summary) focuses on the relations among groups who are potential affines, *itenaaki*: the Hohodene and Oalipere-dakenai are two phratries of the same people; hence the frontiers that separate them are open to negotiation and permit as much alliance as conflict. Despite the suspicion on the part of the Hohodene that the Oalipere-dakenai have come in war, they initiate an alliance. They are "abandoning warfare" and offer one of their daughters in marriage to the chief. This act is the first step in the recovery of the Hohodene as a group. The narrator emphasizes that it was like a process of rejuvenation of the chief, almost like a resurrection from the cultural "death" in the towns of the Rio Negro. Another way of saying this is that the alliance with the Oalipere-dakenai propitiated a historical reempowerment of a people that had suffered a near total loss of their capacity for social and cultural reproduction.

Alliance through marriage among phratries is, for the Baniwa, another form of reciprocal exchange, or *koada*, but which excludes warfare. Warfare does not exist among exogamous phratries that mutually exchange women. What marks the relation of affinity is the celebration of *pudali*, the objective of which is to celebrate kin and to drink and dance with affines. We may even consider this second part of the story as the "period of *pudali*."

The result of the change in the sociopolitical situation of the Hohodene is the complete recovery of their phratry. The nature of the chief also changes: a warrior before, now he cultivates his gardens and multiplies the phratry's villages. The same happens with the Oalipere-dakenai: they request lands of their affines, which allows the Oalipere-dakenai to be saved from their desperate situation in view of the exhaustion of their garden lands. There is a return to prosperity, growth, and stability as a result of the definition of social, political and territorial frontiers among the two phratries.

The third part follows the internal progression of the narrative, for it deals with the internal relations among the "brothers" (*namhereri-dam*) of the same phratry, all sons of Keruaminali, each being the head of a local descent group. Relations are also defined between these brothers and the external enemy—the *caboclo* and White Man who attempted to convince the Hohodene that their lands are "poor" and that they should descend to the Rio Negro.

What is remarkable in this episode is the affirmation of historical consciousness as the source of a strategy for action to confront the external enemy. Faced with the choice of either following the White Man or remaining on their lands, the brothers decided to maintain their autonomy because their gardens and houses—in short, their prosperity—stood in contrast with the losses they had suffered. Two diametrically opposed visions are in confrontation: that of the Baré *caboclo* who insists that the Indians are "poor," and that of the Hoho-dene who affirm that their identity with their land, houses, and gardens is superior to living with the whites. The Hohodene are no longer warriors; they are horticulturists who seek to live in peace and at a distance from the whites.

I believe that the vision of history that the Hohodene express complements in various ways their visions of cosmic history as I have discussed in Part I. These are two visions, which are in reality born from the same processes, but which differ among themselves in that the history of the cosmos is, we might say, "macrohistory," while the history of the Hohodene refers to a particular social and geographical context, "microhistory." The two visions are nevertheless comparable in terms of the periods through which the "world" (be it the universe, or the sociopolitical world of the Hohodene phratry) has passed, the qualities of these periods, and the nature of social change in history.

Both visions begin with a state of war (the cannibalistic relations among primordial beings and the animal-tribes of nature; the "war" with groups on the periphery): warfare, in short, is the primordial model that organizes cosmic and social life. It is indeed possible to talk about historical warfare through reference to mythical images. One evangelical pastor, a Maulieni elder of Kepirali-numana, attempted to do as much by explaining warfare as something that was "given by

Iaperikuli" and the abandoning of warfare as something that was prophesied by the shamans. He spoke the following to me:

> In the beginning of night, Iaperikuli began to make war for people, he gave it to them.
> He made war in the night.
> War began there on the Orinoco, in the beginning [there were] many people.
> He got all war—all people—he joined together all the animals.
> He made war in the night, he went to kill, they're called Calipuna, they went to kill.
> Then for a long time, [the Calipuna] came in the night.
> Midday came.
> They didn't kill.
> The dawn came.
> Then, later, he changed, Iaperikuli made [war's] image on the hill, that hill, there at Tunui [a hill on the Içana River].
> Its image.
> So it is, war, in the beginning.
> He made them able to kill, they the Calipuna.
> There it remains this hill, it remains there at Tunui.
> It remains there today, this image, he made its image.
> After that,
> They didn't kill.
> He had shown them how to make war, this Iaperikuli began it among them.
> After that, people made war, only they did.
> It was in their hearts to make war and they killed.
> Fierceness began, he made it among them.
> They killed people there, at the headwaters of the Ucaiali.
> People lived there.
> Arrows, spears, thus Iaperikuli made for them.
> Another came in war to all the villages and took people.
> They went to kill people.
> At the Uaupés headwaters, their enemies.
> Their killing-things: spears, arrows . . .
> Among them those whites—it began for them—the whites killed Another.
> They killed another people.
> At midday, that's all, they abandoned their killing, that's all, the world over.
> He gave them this thought—soon we will finish off [with people].

Then the Padres,
"Stop killing"
They made people stop war.
The old ones made war.
They ate—until they were satisfied.
They killed their grandchildren.
They ate them and they ate them.
They roasted and ate them.
Then . . .
. . .
Long ago, we don't see it anymore, this was in another world.
Before us, they foresaw—"They will no longer kill people."
They foresaw that things would be good. Their exchange.
Their knowledge, the elders.
He's called Iaperikuli's kin, Dzulíferi.
He made them foresee—everything on it.
The sickness—of people.
The headdresses, the dance tubes, and dance instruments.
People
Beat them on the ground.
The dance instruments, drums,
The spears and arrows—Iaperikuli gave them to people and to the
    whites. . . ."

The result of war is catastrophe, where all is drastically reduced to
one single survivor, or where the threat of annihilation is imminent.
Warfare practically ends the world, and the identity of the survivors
is immersed in the formless world of "downriver" (the bone of the
Duemieni is thrown downriver; the ornaments of the Hohodene are
thrown away downriver). But it is the single survivor who is reborn:
either through his decision or through his innate wisdom, he returns
and initiates a process of regeneration.

The regeneration of the new world, postcatastrophe, proceeds by
stages, a series of transformations that end up by re-creating spatio-
temporal order. In this process, the principles of descent and interphratric alliances establish the means by which humanity or sociopolitical units are reproduced and multiply. Both visions affirm that
prosperity is the heritage of the ancestors—whether through the spa-
tiotemporal order created or through the productivity of gardens and
villages—as long as humanity affirms the superiority of *identity* in
contrast with *alterity*.

The two visions complement each other in terms of the nature of
historical agency. Cosmic history elaborates a series of supernatural

mechanisms that permit the intervention of divinity in history, among which I mention here: the prophetic model that secures the cosmos against the threat of destruction; the control of potentially dangerous forces from the external world, through music; and the creation of sanctuaries to revert catastrophe. These are some of the mechanisms that I shall examine in detail in this book. In the historic vision of the Hohodene phratry, agency is shown in the individual or collective decision of the ancestors who affirm the fundamental principles of cultural identity, including the historical transformations through which the phratry has passed.

4. Music of the Ancestors

Perhaps more than any other narrative, the myth of Kuwai and the shamanic chants sung at initiation rites have to do with the production of collective identity and control over various forms of alterity, including the whites. This chapter is thus devoted to an interpretation of the myth and seeks to show how various images of identity and alterity, presented in the figure of Kuwai, are relevant to the themes of catastrophe and regeneration in millenarian consciousness.

I wish to note at the outset that I have deliberately chosen not to present a complete narrative of the Kuwai myth—which I heard on more than twenty different occasions during my fieldwork and to which I have dedicated a greater part of my studies of Hohodene mythology over the past twenty years—for various reasons. The first and most important reason is respect for the explicit wish of the Hohodene with whom I worked that it not be published. The complete version of the myth contains numerous details about the sacred flutes and trumpets, the body of Kuwai, and the music of Kuwai which are secret, taboo to women and the uninitiated for reasons which will become clear later on. As I mentioned in the introduction, I am currently preparing a separate book of Hohodene myths in collaboration with the "Association of Indigenous Communities of the Aiary River," which has given its approval to the publication of all other myths and narratives that I have used in the present book but left it clear that the Kuwai narrative *in its full version*—that is, with details on how the sacred instruments appear or the music they make—should not be published.

It would be impossible, on the other hand, to understand a great deal of Hohodene, and indeed Baniwa, culture and history without at least referring to the myth; as I have shown in previous chapters, shamanism, passage rites, and the whole notion of the spirit world are fundamentally connected to the figure of Kuwai. Indeed all of this book is, since Kuwai has to do with the transmission of culture from ancestors to descendants, i.e., *walimanai*. For that reason, both to respect the cultural norm and yet to be able to refer to some rather fundamental questions of their culture, I have used a greatly summarized version of the story.

A second motive for not including a full version is in consideration of the reader: the full version that I have transcribed, translated, and annotated is more than thirty-five pages in length. Together with the interpretation I shall be making of the myth, this would produce a rather unwieldy chapter; nevertheless, a rudimentary notion of this important myth is necessary.

As I have stated, I was told or heard the myth told on more than twenty occasions during my fieldwork on the Aiary River. Most often, it was narrated in response to my questions in interview situations. Such as the following:

- What does *walimanai* mean? To what does the word refer?
- How did the sickness-giving spirit-darts, *walamas*, begin?
- How do people perform initiation rites today?
- Who, or what, was the mythical "animal" called Wamundana?

Outside of my questions, I heard the myth told, spontaneously, most often in response to questions related to sickness—especially poison, *manhene*. For example, a question asking for clarification of how *manhene* began and whether it was "always with the people" elicited the narrating of the myth as a response.

I recorded narratives of the myth from elders of three villages of the Aiary, mostly of the Hohodene phratry but also Oalipere-dakenai. Most narrators were shamans, dance leaders, chant specialists, or elders with experience in initiation rituals. All of these positions carry with them the tasks of teaching or explaining to others, showing correctly what otherwise might not be clear or well known.

Following my summary of the myth below, I provide a discussion of the contexts in which my or other people's questions elicited the narrating of the myth. I also consider the issue of variability in narration depending on the kind of question to which the myth is being given in answer. Finally, I justify my division of the summary into paragraphs, based on narrators' cues and variability in narration. My interpretation of the myth attempts to stay as close as possible to indigenous exegeses, in terms of the principal questions which elicited narrations. I take the liberty of adding interpretive elements of my own, however, leaving it clear when I am doing so and to what extent my interpretations find support in narrators' statements.

Summary of the Myth of Kuwai

Episode 1. Kuwai is conceived when Iaperikuli sends his thought
to Amaru, his aunt. Iaperikuli eats coca, thinks to where Amaru
is, and his knowledge, *ianheke*, enters her. He chants over his
coca, and she becomes pregnant with Kuwai. But Amaru had
no vagina; Kuwai could not be born. Iaperikuli then took a *pa-
tauá* log and broke a passage in her. She "died" but Kuwai came
out. Iaperikuli revived her and she looked for her son, but the
men took the child away to be nursed by a sloth of the forest. As
Iaperikuli took Kuwai away, he saw that Kuwai was extraordinary, not of This World, for his body began to hum and sing
melodious animal-song as it broke wind, urinated, and cried.
Since there was no way he could stay in This World, Iaperikuli
sent him away to the sky, where Kuwai lived for a long time
before he appeared again.

Episode 2. One day, a long time later, four children were playing
with noise-making instruments, tying up bumblebees and putting them inside earthen pots. As the bees droned inside the
pots, the children danced. Kuwai was watching them from the
sky; he came down to them; and they saw a white man, *ialanawi*, with shoes. They tell him they are making Kuwai music to
which he responds that it is nonsense, for he is the real Kuwai,
and that, if they wish to hear his music, they must undergo ritual seclusion and not eat pepper or cooked food for three dry
seasons. The children accept the condition, and Kuwai sings
to them, whipping them, giving them a fruit to sniff, and then
promises to return later. When Iaperikuli finds out that the children have seen Kuwai, he immediately makes preparations for
his return, sending the children's mothers away and awaiting at
the door of the ritual house. When Kuwai returns, Iaperikuli
takes him to the middle of the house, where Kuwai confirms the
period of fasting and tells them they may eat all types of forest-
fruit, his sweetness, as their ritual diet. He sings for them again,
this time all of his body together in a great roar, and then leaves
them, announcing that he will return at the end of the fast to
whip them.

Episode 3. When the appointed time comes, Kuwai gradually descends from the sky to the ritual house, where he whips the
initiates and sings in an ominous and fearsome way. He stays
with the initiates and Iaperikuli until the conclusion of the fast.
Then, as the seclusion is nearing its end, Kuwai takes the children to Hipana to gather *uacú* nuts. As he sits on top of the *uacú*

tree throwing nuts down to them, three of the children whisper that they will break the fast by roasting and eating the *uacú*. The smoke of their fire blinds Kuwai, causing him to "die." His entire body sings out in a great roar, as streams of saliva pour out of his orifices. He comes down the tree and causes an enormous flood of rains to come. He transforms his mouth and belly into a huge rock cave, and he calls the children inside. Three of the four children enter the cave and are devoured. Only the smallest child stays outside and is safe, for he had seen that Kuwai had transformed into the spirit Inyaime. Kuwai flies back to the ritual house at Enípan, vomits up the remains of the three dead children, and returns to the sky. Iaperikuli knows of the catastrophe, for blood falls from his hand.

Episode 4. A long time later, Iaperikuli wishes to end the fast and to lure Kuwai back down to the ritual house. He makes wooden images of the initiates with their ornaments and sends a wasp carrying white maggots up to the sky to summon Kuwai down. Kuwai gobbles up the maggots and throws the wasp back down. Iaperikuli sends another wasp with maggots who succeeds in squeezing through the door of Kuwai's house and convinces Kuwai to return and end the fast. Preparations are then made for the ritual. Kuwai then comes to chant over the pepper which will be served to the initiates at dawn. Kuwai teaches Iaperikuli and his brothers how to chant *kalidzamai*—pepper shamanism—in an all-night ceremony with dancing and singing. When he finishes the chanting, Kuwai tells Iaperikuli that he knows that Iaperikuli will kill him, but that nothing can kill him for his body is everything—machetes, axes, shotguns, clubs, arrows. Only one thing—fire—can destroy him. As Kuwai continues to dance and sing, Iaperikuli leads him around a huge fire and suddenly pushes him in, throwing the heaviest logs on top. As Kuwai burns, he leaves sickness and poison—his "fever"—in the ashes of the fire, and his spirit ascends to the sky, where he lives immortally.

Episode 5. As Iaperikuli pushes him into the fire, Kuwai tells him to return later to the burning-place at Hipana. Iaperikuli knows that Kuwai will leave, in return for his killing his body, the materials to make the flutes and trumpets for all future initiation rites. When Iaperikuli returns, a giant *paxiuba* tree breaks out of the earth and shoots up to the sky. Iaperikuli gets other plant materials that go along with the flutes. A squirrel then cuts the *paxiuba* tree to the correct lengths of the instruments, in pairs and triplets. A woodpecker breaks the tree, and the logs fall in a heap to the ground. Iaperikuli then takes an eagle feather and adorns the flutes, producing the first music of Kuwai.

Episode 6. A long time later, Iaperikuli is initiating his son with the flutes and tells him to bathe in the river at dawn and to cleanse his penis with suds-making vines. Before the boy arises, Kuwai's mother, Amaru, and the women secretly steal the flutes from Iaperikuli. As he tries to get them back, spirit-darts, *walamas*, shoot out from the mouths of the flutes, turning the men back. The women escape and take the flutes upriver to a hill called Motípan (at the headwaters of the Uaraná, off the upper Aiary), where they made a palisaded settlement. There, their youngest sister had her first menstruation, so the women performed *kalid-zamai* chanting over her food. Iaperikuli secretly watched them in anger; he was their "enemy" and would make war against them to take back the flutes. He went downriver to Tunui (a hill on the mid-Içana) to get arrow poison and magic darts from their owner. He advised the birds that there would be war. Iaperikuli tries out the arrows—one of which pierces the earth, while the other shoots like a lightning bolt to the "sky entrance" and then zigzags back down to earth. Iaperikuli then joins all the animals, his kin, together to go with him back to Motípan. When they arrive, they sing like frogs to warn the women that they have come. When the women finish their chanting and begin to distribute the food, Iaperikuli and the animals charge into the settlement. They grab away the flutes, there is much killing, and Iaperikuli throws the women to the sky. One woman puts a flute in her vagina; Iaperikuli kills her. Another tries to run away with a flute; Iaperikuli kills her. He throws four women to the four directions, one after another, and the war ends. One of the women went in the direction of the west and became the mother of the white people.

Episode 7. Much later, Iaperikuli turns the women's hearts around so that they will not remember Kuwai. He tests them but they have forgotten, and so today they flee at the sound of the music. Satisfied, Iaperikuli completes the instruments, with hair and fur, and then leaves them for all generations of people. Iaperikuli then looks for the ancestors of the phratries and then leaves the world, ascending to his place in the sky.

Ethnographic Notes on Contexts, Variations, and Meaning

The myth of Kuwai is a modular myth, for it is told to explain various critical life concerns:

- The *walimanai* relation, or how cultural institutions are transmitted from generation to generation, from ancestors to descendants. In this regard, I heard the myth told to explain the "beginning of" conception and birth as a process; the growth of the earth from its miniature size in primordial times to its present-day size. In short, for narrators the myth explains reproduction and growth as processes that are transmitted from ancestors to descendants, and in this sense, it is intimately connected to the second main concern.
- Rituals of male and female initiation, called Kuwaipan, which people perform today. In fact, there is a set of very close correspondences which may be established between these rituals and the myth's account of them. Beyond these parallels, however, there is a more important motive: Mandu, who told me the myth on various occasions, made a point of making sure that I understood "why Iaperikuli left Kuwai with us." As he said in response, "to teach Malinaliene," the children of the myth. (Teach them what? The nature of growth, reproduction, and the transmission of culture from ancestors to descendants, as I have said; but also, the nature of sickness and misfortune, and how these began.)
- Kuwai is the "sickness owner"—agent of all serious ailments, and especially those caused by poison, *manhene*. Other sicknesses for which, narrators said, Kuwai is responsible are spirit-darts, *walamas*, that provoke rheumatism, or bone problems; forms of witchcraft called *hiwiathi* that, it is said, are given during Kuwaipan rituals and that are believed to affect women, especially pregnant women, causing problems in pregnancy and birth, i.e., reproductive disorders; and *iupinai*, spirits of the forest who, it is said, were "born from the ashes of Kuwai," and cause various skin ailments to humans.
- Finally, Kuwai is a synthesis of the spirit world, nature, and ancestral human social groups. It is this powerful synthesis, another name for which is Wamundana, that is presented to initiates in rites of passage. In the primordial times, animals were "people" who "walked" with humans, held festivals with them, and taught them their melodious song. They also gave them sickness and "ate" people with poison. Wamundana was such an animal/spirit/person, and not just one animal but all-in-one. The myth thus explains the life of this being and how it came to be reproduced in the flutes and trumpets that people use today in the rituals of initiation. It explains, above all, the relationships of exchange created between humans today and the animal-spirit world.

There may be other questions that could elicit the telling of the myth; yet, as I said, my sample of twenty-odd different occasions represents a good indication of the principal concerns that the myth addresses.

Narrators could tell the story in a variety of ways to explain the same topic or to explain different topics. In my summary of the narration, I have indicated story divisions—that is, places where narrators could begin or end if a question was framed specifically enough to call for only that part of the story to which the question directly referred.

As summarized, I heard the story as an explanation of the beginning of a sickness, *walamas* or spirit-darts, which shot out of the flutes after Amaru took them away from Iaperikuli. At the appropriate point in the narrative when the *walamas* appear, the narrator marked the moment by saying "thus began *walamas*." When people today suffer from rheumatic or arthritic pain, it is diagnosed by shamans as *walamas* and extracted from the patient as thorns of palm trees, especially *paxiuba* palm, the same wood out of which the flutes, Kuwai, were originally made. The source of all *walamas* is Kuwai who, shamans say, has a giant cumare palm, called *dzaui kumale*, in his plantation in the Other World.

What does this explain? That *walamas* are a sickness having to do with gender relations, or relations with other groups? This would seem plausible and would contrast with other ways in which sicknesses appear to be explained in the Kuwai myth.

For example, I heard the story told most frequently to explain the beginning of poison, *manhene*. In the early months of my fieldwork, Keruami's stepson José Felipe had been sent by the missions to a hospital in Manaus because of a severe and near-fatal illness. After months of seemingly ineffective treatment, he returned to Uapui yet the sickness remained. For this, he stayed restricted in diet from eating any animals, fish or pepper, as well as secluded from the village, rarely leaving his house and never participating in communal work projects. The sickness was a great blow to Felipe, for people remembered the past successes of his hunts and the numerous projects to help the community which he had undertaken.

One morning I visited him, and he asked if I had any remedies against the poison which was causing the sickness. It caused intense stomach pain, high fever, and a general drying-out of the body, making it appear thin and pale. Whenever he consumed any animals or fish, the sickness worsened. That night, at the evening communal meal, Mandu, the chief of Uapui and Felipe's wife's father, related to me that such venom was not uncommon, that many people die from it, and that it is generally a very hidden substance—a "leaf" which a sorcerer had mixed in Felipe's food. A youth then asked Keruami, "Has this venom always been with people or how is it?" To this Keruami affirmed, "It is a sickness of the people," and held up both hands in a gesture of starting a narrative (as if to say, "Silence! I will tell you"). So began the story of Kuwai the "poison owner," *manhene iminali*. As the story proceeded, Keruami's voice filled the large communal house, which was then growing dark as night fell. The youth listened in the active mode of hearing an explanation, repeating word phrases and asking one-word questions to clarify actions. The chief, also a shaman, interjected comments, again of a clarifying nature. Both Keruami and Mandu were actively engaged in explaining to the youth the beginning of the sickness. Other elders seated in the room occasionally commented but mostly remained quiet, listening and pondering. The narration, as I remember, involved much more than the story itself, for the elders continued discussing Iaperikuli, the primal shamans, and curing practices for an hour or more afterward.

The next day, Mandu explained the story once again to me and related it directly to a cure which he and Keruami would undertake on Felipe on the following day. The cure would last for three days, for the sickness required prolonged treatment.

How does this explanation differ from that of *walamas*? In the first place, Keruami narrated only to the point of the story when Kuwai was burned, which is the moment he leaves poison, *manhene*, in the form of poisonous plants. This poison is Kuwai's burning "fever" which he gives in return for his own death in the fire. Note here again the importance of the relation of exchange between humans and the animal-spirit world: *humans kill animals and eat them with pepper; in return, animal-spirits kill humans and eat them with poison.* This, I suggest, is the way the myth explains the beginning of poison (I will return to this question in Chapter 5).

Yet there is another sense in which the myth of Kuwai is related to sicknesses—by providing a model for curing rituals. During these curing rituals, the shamans seek Kuwai in the Other World and he shows them where the sources of sicknesses are, on the basis of which the shaman will cure again in This World. During a curing session which I was invited to observe and record, Mandu explained this "showing" as a kind of teaching:

The Other World will show to the shaman. It is not people that make this, it is the Other World that makes this. The first, the ancient world. These other people who are there are in the sky. For this is also in the sky. Where it will end is in the sky. The first that will teach us . . .

The sense of teaching here (i.e., about sickness) recalls what he said was the reason Iaperikuli left Kuwai—to teach the children of the myth; and indeed, shamans refer to themselves as the "universe children."

The myth is also told to explain the notion of *walimanai*, for in it a great many processes are made and given for all future generations. Two examples I present illustrate this quite well: the beginning of menstruation, conception, and birth; and the separation of the spirit world from This World at Kuwai's death.

In the first instance, during an interview, I was discussing with Malewa, an elder of Uapui, the topic of incest and was trying to determine if the "Daughter of the Sun" myth that the Dessana tell had an equivalent in Hohodene mythology. Malewa looked at me with a clouded expression, perturbed by my even raising the question of incest. "People may do this on the Uaupés," he said, "but not here." A moment later, he brightened and asked, "Do you know the story of how, what you say, sexual relations began?" He proceeded to tell first a story of how Iaperikuli made Amaru menstruate, at the end of which Amaru says to Iaperikuli, "Thus it will be henceforth for *walimanai*." Thus menstruation began. Without further thought, he proceeded with a narrative of the Kuwai myth beginning with Kuwai's conception and birth. Malewa remarked after Kuwai's birth, "Kuwai was born right here," and pointed to the falls of Hipana not more than a hundred feet from where we sat. Malewa remarked, after Kuwai was sent to live in the sky, "thus will be for *walimanai*," meaning, it seems, that the birth of Kuwai is directly connected to people's present experience of birth. Malewa then followed with a short myth on how the earth was a small rock at the time of Kuwai's birth and Iaperikuli made it grow to its present large size by blowing the deep, resonant note of a Kuwai trumpet which made the rock open up. Malewa showed how by forming with his two hands an open circle which grew wider each time the note sounded. As proof, perhaps, Malewa pointed to the great rock in the middle of the rapids and said that that was the earth "in the beginning," in "the first world."

As in the case of the Oalipere-dakenai elder whom I cited in Chapter 1, who narrated three stories of the "new order," Malewa, in a piece of creative myth-telling, clearly linked the themes of menstruation, birth and growth. The two short myths are not necessarily part of the narrative—no other narrator included them—but could be tacked on, inserted at the appropriate places to teach more on the topic of sexual relations, reproduction, and growth, primordial processes that came into being with Kuwai. It also shows that episode 1 of the myth is a distinct unit about birth.

The second instance occurred when I simply asked Keruami "What does *walimanai* mean?" for I had heard this phrase so many times in the course of learning Hohodene myths. José Felipe responded with a short answer in Portuguese, and before he had even finished, Keruami began narrating the myth of Kuwai. José Felipe said, "*Walimanai*, this is for the others, how to say, the others that will be born, you know? For the others to be born. Long ago, the ancestors, our ancestors, took care well, and said, 'Well, thus you will stay my child, in the other life like so, after me.' He spoke thus. So—" Then Keruami cut into the dialogue saying:

> *Likenyua ima liuma Kuwai . . .*
> For in the beginning he looks for Kuwai . . .
> *Iaperikuli irikan,*
> Iaperikuli's "son"
> *Hipatuperi.*
> Of coca.
> *Inha lihipatu,*
> He eats his coca,
> *Kenipete Kuwai-apen Iaperikuli*
> To make the child Kuwai, Iaperikuli
> *Likuiro ihriu.*
> His aunt became
> *Kenipena . . .*
> With child . . .

He proceeded with the story until much later when Iaperikuli pushes Kuwai into the fire; then Kuwai speaks to Iaperikuli inside the fire:

> Iaperikuli *pushed . . .*
> *PA! Khhhihh!*
> Kuwai fell in the fire.
> An inferno it made!
> They threw trees . . . *titititi*
> They threw quartz pendants.
> Then it burned the fire . . . *titititi.*
> But it was HHUUGE!
> Not little.

He made an inferno!
"Heyy, you cannot kill me," says Kuwai,
"You cannot kill me,
"You cannot.
"Firewood is my body," this firewood is Kuwai's body.
His body is wood, Kuwai's body is wood.
It does not die.
His body is stone, it does not die.
His body is the quartz pendant, it does not die.
Everything. Iron is his body, it does not die, they can't kill it.
The gun is his body, it does not die.
Clubs, they strike with, it does not die.
Hiwiathi sickness, "My speech, it does not die," he says, "my
    sickness-giving, it will be."
"Poison, my body, poison
"*Hwero* poison plant, my liver," his liver is *hwero*, it does not die.
Then Iaperikuli joins together people around the Great Fire.
They heard how he spoke there, Kuwai.
They heard of *hiwiathi*, of *matikaim* poison,
Eeeeeeevvvverything. . . .
All of them, how *all* the Maaku, *all* the white people die of
    poison . . .
"You come after me, I go *before you*," he says.
He ascended from the Great Fire, *in the fire* he ascends . . .
[singing] *"Heeheehee . . . eeyteyteytete . . . "*
Until today!
Only the shamans see him, they see the body of Kuwai.
Until . . . *there* he is [pointing to the sky] *not dead! There* he is there.
Thus it is.
That's about all I know about Kuwai.

Death by sicknesses is "left" for humanity, yet Kuwai's knowledge,
Kuwai *ianheke*, about sicknesses and their cure is produced and transmitted for future generations. The "Great Fire" in which Kuwai teaches
is a powerful symbol, for it eternalizes this knowledge.

The separation between "before" and *walimanai* which occurred at
this point in the myth signifies an "ending" of the possibility—outside of shamanic voyages to the Other World—that the spirit world
can ever come directly again to This World and mingle with humans.
It is the separation of the spirit world which always remains, is "still
there," into an Other World forever separate from humans. In a larger
sense, all of the primordial beings remain "alive" or immortal in the
Other World of Before, and it is as though the two worlds exist eter-

nally side by side or one above the other, Before and Now. This separation occurred at this point and no other in cosmic history.

Like the moment of Kuwai's birth, the "Great Fire" is clearly understood by narrators as having multiple meanings, depending on the topic being explained, which makes this one of the most dramatic and climactic moments of the myth. Narrators make it clear that these moments are ending-points, which we might call "watershed moments," for they are critical separations, irreversible impasses at which the characters in the drama of the myth have arrived. Narrators frequently used ending-words to emphasize this—"*Pikethem!!*" ("The last, no more return") or "*Khamets'hapeken!*" ("That's truly all!")—and then, "a long time passes" before the action begins again.

The myth of Kuwai or Wamundana also explains, as I have said, the relations among animals, spirits, and people, and it is through the nature of Wamundana as "black sloth-shadow" that we may understand what is being said. In explaining "shadow" relations among animals, spirits, and humans, narrators call attention to the fact that today, animals, fish, and birds each live a separate existence, with ways of life "like real people": they have cooking fires, houses, and so forth and do many of the same things as humans, such as hold dance festivals, practice witchcraft. Humans usually do not see the animals in their "people" form; rather, they see their "shadows," *idanam*. For the fish-people and animal-people, their material bodies are their shadows which humans see, in contrast with humans whose material bodies cast dark, immaterial shadows.

The animal-people generally remain unseen as "people"; however, there are frequent exchanges between them and humans. To give an instance: every year, the fish-people, *kuphenai*, ascend the rivers in March and April to "make their festivals," that is, spawn. Multitudes of them swim upriver, and to someone watching them, their movements appear "crazy," intoxicated with the *caxiri* (manioc beer) they drink. At these times, humans sit and watch their traps or cast their lines. The fish-people meanwhile watch the humans, and when a hook comes, it is said, they put pieces of their firewood on the hooks. As the human hauls it in, the firewood transforms into a fish for people, or as is said, *kuphe ipadama newiki ihriun*. In other words, to get from fish-people to human through a barrier which separates them, a transformation is made. The wood, being a part of the fish-people's "other" existence, transforms into the "body" of a fish, the "shadow" of what it formerly was.

The experience of these unseen "spirit-people" can at times be terrifying. At changes of seasons, for instance, from wet to dry, it is said that the "jaguar-people," "dove-people" and others send great winds,

crashing thunder, leaves and spines flying about in the air. They become "wild," and one must speak an oration "to break their flutes,"
"to cut their noises."

In Chapter 5, I shall discuss the notion of omens, *hinimai*, which is
another instance of the "shadow" relation at work between animal-
spirits and humans. The myth of Kuwai or Wamundana would in
short seem to be the principal explanation for notions of generativ-
ity and reciprocity that define relations among humans and animal-
spirits.

The myth was told most frequently to me to explain rites of initiation,
Kuwaipan. There were actually two ways that narrators could talk
about these rites: through the myth, or through descriptive accounts of
what people today actually do. The two ways differ, though the descriptive accounts may lead into the telling of the myth. When my
questions emphasized contemporary practices—for example, what
the elders of today instruct the initiates on the laws of living; or the
meaning of specific ritual items—narrators answered with descriptive accounts. When I asked in general terms, "How are Kuwaipan
done?" or "Why do people do such-and-such during the ritual?" then
I received an explanation through a narration of the myth. When a
ritual practice has a direct correspondence to the myth, the switch
may also be made.

In fact, narrators frequently said of rituals, "Thus we do, as in the beginning, as it first appeared." Initiation rites, especially, are times when
the "ancient," hidden world of the ancestors and Kuwai, the sacred
flutes, are shown to the initiates, in order "to teach Malinaliene."

When explaining the rituals through the myth, there were various
ways narrators could break up the story into chunks. Usually, narrators began with episode 2 and told the story until very nearly the end,
but within that continuous piece, narrators could make breaks, drop
out pieces, or pick up the story at different points. For example, once
my question to Keruami focused on the songs sung at initiation rites
today. Keruami sang several songs, then immediately led into a part of
the myth when initiation songs are sung, at the final ritual or "coming-
out" festival. He continued with the emergence of the *paxiuba* tree and
ended immediately after the women took away the flutes. I knew that
Keruami in fact never told the rest of the story (episodes 6, 7) and so
chose to conclude it in his own way. Yet it was remarkable that so
small a piece of the story of initiation could form a separable chunk,
constituting a coherent explanation of the songs sung at the coming-
out festival.

In another instance, I asked the elder Makenuli of Ucuqui how people *today* perform initiation rites, hoping for an overall actual description. He responded by telling episodes 3–5 of the myth, which comprise a coherent short story about two critical phases of initiation that occur at Kuwaipan: when the elders first show the flutes to the initiates and whip them, beginning their seclusion; and the coming-out festival when the initiates emerge from seclusion and eat the sacralized pepper.

Thus, as a topic, initiation forms a continuous part of the narrative, but the ways in which narrators could mark different points of the story indicate that *initiation is thought of as a larger process* represented as different phases—some of which correspond directly to rituals that people perform today, others of which correspond to phases of the individual life cycle (e.g., episode 2 would correspond to a phase when boys are considered ready to undergo initiation, but has no direct correspondence to the ritual of Kuwaipan).

Interpretation

In the interpretation I shall now make of the myth, I shall seek specifically to relate these narrative themes to central concerns of the narratives I have examined thus far,—in particular, catastrophe and regeneration in the context of millenarian consciousness, especially relating to the images of Kuwai as the "White Man" and Amaru as the "mother of the whites."

Episode 1

Kuwai is conceived through the union of Iaperikuli with his "aunt" Amaru. While this would seem to be an incestuous relationship, narrators never cited incest as being of importance to the story. In fact, the question makes very little sense in the presexual world described in the beginning of the myth. The proximity of relations among the characters of this episode are, rather, deflected to a level of generality and ambiguity. Amaru could thus be Iaperikuli's father's sister and a kin, but according to the myth of Iaperikuli's beginning, he was orphaned by the animals who had devoured his kin, the Duemieni. The term *likuiro* could also refer to mother's brother's wife and to wife's mother; and in real life, marriage preferences are with mother's brother's daughter/father's sister's daughter. In this case, Amaru would be an affine of another, unrelated group. This would be consistent with other myths in which Iaperikuli and his brothers are married to women of different animal tribes and the *eenunai*, thunders.

Similarly, Kuwai is apparently Iaperikuli's "son," but their relationship is never expressed in kinship terms specific to father/son, nor to "aunt's son," which in real life would be a cross-cousin and potential affine. Kuwai is more generally "Iaperikuli's *child*" in the general and collective sense that is used to express, for example, the notion that all human beings are Iaperikuli's children, or that the Hohodene are the primal sun's children, *Heiri ienipe*. Kuwai is also called "one does not know whose child," *manhekanali ienipe*, which raises doubt about Iaperikuli's paternity. In short, there is an ambiguity which identifies Kuwai as both a child and a close kin—a cross-cousin considered to be like a brother—and yet of an "other people."

The myth further deflects the question of proximity by putting all emphasis into the cognitive, spiritual, and cosmic nature of Iaperikuli's union with Amaru. Thus the elements essential to Kuwai's conception are: Iaperikuli's eating of a cultivated plant food, the coca made potent by his chants (indicated by the suffix *-khai* added to the word for coca); his thinking toward, *iapienta rukhuethe*, Amaru (some narrators render this as a lightning bolt which went from Iaperikuli to Amaru); and his knowledge, *ianheke*, which fertilized her. The creative act is further defined as a vertical penetration from above to below, similar to the way the sun's rays penetrate the lower realms of the cosmos. Thus Kuwai is said to be the sun's soul, *kamui ikaale*, and the sun is Kuwai's father, *Kuwai hlaneri*.

Kuwai's birth is a fundamental event of cosmic proportions, for one reason because it is evident from a consideration of all other Hohodene myths that it marked the transition in primordial time from nonreproductive conditions to a new state of being in which henceforth birth is a process by which humanity perpetuates itself. Thus, narrators emphasized that what is being made in this episode is everything related to birth. In the myths of Iaperikuli's struggles with the animals, the predominant dynamic is the destructiveness of the animals, a never-ending cycle of vengeance and killing. That condition was doomed to extinction, and it is surely symbolic of its nonreproductiveness that Amaru, the first woman, *has no vagina*, no "way" for the child to come out. The break from this condition is aptly portrayed as Iaperikuli's forcibly cutting a passage into Amaru.[1] It is no coincidence either that in real life, when mothers experience extreme difficulties in childbirth, chant specialists seek to "loosen the knots" that "tie up" the child inside the mother's womb, which are said to be produced by the "animal spirits" and *eenunai* and which cause hemorrhaging and the threat of miscarriage. It is as though the animals and *eenunai* continue seeking to prevent the reproduction of—from their point of view of the relation—others (humans). I will return to this point in Chapter 6 in considering the "Spiritualities of Death and Birth."

What is the nature of Kuwai's being? According to the first episode, nothing like him exists in This World. His body is distinct, full of holes which emit sounds as he does his normal bodily functions. His sounds are distinct, like animal-songs but beyond being merely the sounds that animals produce, for they are, to use a metaphor, like the melodious and harmonious "music of the spheres" which is impossible to convey to anyone who has not heard this music, much less through the printed word.

His growth and actions are extraordinary: in an instant, one narrator said, he sucked the tit of the sloth dry, and after a short while living in the forest, he grows into a "little man" whereupon Iaperikuli—convinced of his otherworldliness—sends him off to the sky. His relation to sickness and sickness-giving spirits of the forest make him exceedingly dangerous. In short, Kuwai's being represents an extremely powerful and paradoxical synthesis of creative yet destructive forces incompatible with the ordering of life in This World. This is what Iaperikuli made in order, as Mandu said, "to teach the Malinaliene"—the children of the myth and, in fact, all uninitiated, including the curious anthropologist—about the nature of the world.

Kuwai is an "outsider," an "other" being but one connected in some way to humanity. He is of the cosmos, for the sun is "his father," connected to the Other World of the sky, yet nurtured by forest animals. His relations of kinship are ambiguously situated between kin, affines, and "one does not know whose child." The source of his conception is creative shamanism, yet he embodies and projects destructive sickness. Defying time in his growth, boundaries in his open orifices, and space in his associations, Kuwai's body is liminal par excellence. Kuwai's liminality—*of being-all-things-at-once* and *other-yet-one's-own*—is important for an understanding of how he can become a variety of other beings, including the White Man, throughout the narrative of his life.

Episodes 2–4

Episode 2 of the myth opens with a group of children playing with make-believe instruments (earthen pots and bumblebees) which, by their symbolic associations in other myths, represent spirit-calling instruments. Kuwai, from his position above them and outside their village, responds to their call, descending and traversing space (indicated by narrators through the use of locatives—"there" to "here") where the children see him as a white man. Narrators add various details to his appearance: shoes, watch, hat, beard. The image so created would seem to be a transposition on the thisworldly plane of Kuwai's alterity in the Other World.

The White Man, as a historical image, is a most appropriate form for representing Kuwai's powerfully creative yet potentially dangerous and disruptive figure, a totally other being who has traveled from a distant land to make contact with people. It would not be totally out of keeping with Hohodene historical consciousness of the whites that the Kuwai/White Man in the myth has come to take children away from their natal families and transform them into others.

Kuwai's apparel (shoes, etc.) is consistent with this image of a *wandering intermediary*, and is, at the same time, much like the apparel of shamans in their cosmic travel, which includes shoes, belt, hat, gun, and revolvers—with an additional significant detail of the watch, icon perhaps of temporality. Yet, as appropriate as the images may be, they also serve as a foil which contrasts with the notion of who the children are really to become. At the moment of truth, when Kuwai announces that the children's instruments are "nonsense," he affirms that he is the "real Kuwai," who is known by his music and accompanying restrictions.

From the time the children accept his conditions, they are removed from normal social life, becoming outsiders—they don't eat, they sniff fruits; they don't tell Iaperikuli that they have seen Kuwai—reorienting their spatial movements to outside the village and temporality to the three dry seasons of fasting. Kuwai reveals to them the secrets of his power, *kanupa*, and assumes a position equivalent to elder and ritual "parent" of the children. In fact, the relationship of Iaperikuli to Kuwai at this point in the story is rather like that of a ritual owner to a chief, both of the elder generation in relation to the boys, and both masters of the ritual. Kuwai's full creative power is revealed inside the ritual house, at the center of the house, where he affirms the initiates' food to be exclusively wild forest fruits, and his entire body sings in a great roar.

I translate the notion of *kanupa* roughly as "spiritual power"; it more specifically refers to a dangerous power to open, or to reveal, and transform. Its indissociable complement is interdiction, restriction, the state of being closed, shut (*itakawa*), or secret. Kuwai tells Iaperikuli, for example, "So powerful am I, they must be restricted for three dry seasons, *kanupáde hnua, mandalida hamuli paitakawa*." All of Kuwai's body is *kanupa*. The sacred snuff, *pariká*, as I have mentioned in Chapter 2, which "opens" or reveals for the shaman everything in the cosmos, is "Kuwai's blood," *lirana*, his "power," *kanupa*. In using it, shamans cannot look at women for, they say, they would "see them without clothes," which is to say that female sexuality is perceived as a threat to the shaman's spiritual power. Young girls at first menstruation, however, are also *kanupa*; in general, contact with menstruating women is dangerous only to shamans for it is said that it may cause a "sickness in their blood."

Until episode 3 of the myth, Kuwai's appearances have been momentary and impermanent: he descends from the sky, reveals his power, and returns upward. The complex events of episode 3 begin with his marked and gradual descent at dusk on a cloudy day to the ritual house, where he whips the children and sings in an ominous tone. In fact, Kuwai's nature has changed. While his arrival heralds the conclusion of initiation, his ominous song suggests that things would not turn out that way. Had the children not eaten the roasted *uacú* nuts at Hipana, narrators explicitly say, Kuwai would have returned with them to the ritual house, chanted over their food, and given them to eat, whereupon they would have become adults and Kuwai's task would be complete. What happens in the forest prevents this from taking place and results instead in a catastrophe.

The children and Kuwai are in the forest at Hipana gathering *uacú*, a fruit that ripens during the transition from the dry season to the heavy rains, at the end of the period of seclusion. The children are away from the ritual house at Enípan, downriver from Hipana on the Içana. Kuwai is above them atop a tree; one narrator compared him to a big-bellied monkey breaking open *uacú* nuts and throwing them down to the boys.

By roasting the *uacú* nuts and hence breaking restrictions, the boys put themselves in direct contact with Kuwai's power: the smoke of their fire "blinds" Kuwai, causing him to "die" and streams of his saliva, *liahnuma*, to fall from his orifices. He sings out, "Why do you eat my flesh, the roasted *pacú*, Malinaliene?" (Malinaliene is the name used collectively for the three initiates who ate the roasted *uacú*.) I suggest that we may understand this dramatic moment in the following terms: *pacú* (snapper) fish, like *uacú* nuts, marks the transition of dry to wet seasons, a time of dangerous reproductivity, for enormous runs of *pacú* fish ascend the rivers to spawn at this time. Some narrators mimic Kuwai at this point with a high-pitched hum, like a sloth which, at the beginning of the heavy rains, descends to the ground to eat. In short, I suggest that at this point, Kuwai's power is unleashed as a paradoxical synthesis of a creative yet destructive, spiritualized animal yet demoniacal spirit.

Kuwai transforms into a rock cave, bringing on a great flood and calling the children inside. The three boys who ate, enter Kuwai's mouth— they are "eaten"; the smallest boy perceives what has happened and screams to his companions that Kuwai is Inyaime, a demoniac spirit of the dead. In various myths, Inyaime is characterized as a spirit that persecutes humans, constantly fighting with them, causing fights among them, or bringing on their transformation. At times, Inyaime is cannibalistic, but the most important feature of this spirit is its capacity to transform into an other being. Precisely because of its constant transformations, it is extremely difficult to control. It is said that "only fire destroys it," like Kuwai. Thus, shamans say, Inyaime is an "other Kuwai," which would here mean Kuwai transformed.

The one child who did not eat the roasted *uacú*, who observed restrictions, and who stayed outside watching this transformation, is saved. In his exercise of self-control, autonomy, and knowledge (i.e., he recognized the demoniac spirit)—the prerequisites for growth into adulthood—he escapes the death which his unmediated contact and entry into the mouth of the demon would have entailed. As Mandu stated, "Iaperikuli left Kuwai with people in order to teach Malinaliene." Teach them what? The most fundamental law of exchange between the human, spirit, and animal worlds: the children roasted and "ate" Kuwai's body, "killing him," and in return, he kills and devours them.

It is appropriate at this point to compare briefly the images of Kuwai/White Man and Kuwai/Inyaime, for there seems to be an important progression and intensification of meaning of the notion of alterity underlying the change in image. The White Man image, as I have said, recalls the figure of a wandering intermediary, and the danger it represents is implicit in the historical memory of being one who takes children away and transforms them into "others." Inyaime, by contrast, is an "other Kuwai," shadow of the dead associated with the Other World, who takes away the souls of the deceased who have not respected the "laws," that is, the knowledge and self-control that are the prerequisites of social living. Now, comparing the Kuwai myth with the Hohodene phratric history I have considered in the previous chapter, recall that the whites took away the Hohodene and Keruaminali's children transform into whites, specifically soldiers. Only one Hohodene, Keruaminali, had the self-control and knowledge to escape from the whites' settlements and return to Hohodene ancestral lands on the Içana. Like the one initiate who stayed outside the belly of the monstrous demon Inyaime, I suggest, Keruaminali took control of the situation, and his decision was the indispensable condition for the recovery of the Hohodene phratry from near destruction. Again, as I argued in the previous chapter, historical and mythical consciousness complement each other in the production of collective identity and notions of alterity.

After a long period of the initiate's "suffering," Iaperikuli decides to end the fast and request that Kuwai return to complete the ritual through the chanting of *kalidzamai*, pepper chants, which would permit the remaining initiate to eat. Kuwai is lured back down from the sky: the wasp—which seems to symbolize the initiate's condition itself, with a tiny belly, the result of having passed hunger in fasting—finally reopens a dialogue with Kuwai, who complies with his promise even though he knows it will be his end as initiator.

Kuwai leads the ritual chanting, teaching Iaperikuli and his brothers the sacred chants. At the same time, he teaches the songs and dances of initiation in which he sings of our owner, *waminali*. Indeed, it is Kuwai who is the "owner" of the ritual and *kalidzamai*. The transmission of this knowledge to the pepper and food to be consumed represents at once the full incorporation of Kuwai's knowledge into the ritual society, a process which is to be reproduced by all future generations—*walimanai*—and the completed transformation of children into adults.

No sooner has this creative process been completed, when Kuwai again affirms the "other," indestructible side of his power. His body is "all things" that kill—shotguns, *mukawa*; clubs, *haiko*; machetes, *matseta*; poison arrows, *mawakuli*—against which "only fire, *thidze*" is capable of destroying him. As I have suggested in Chapter 1, fire is, in Hohodene myths, an extremely important element that marks critical moments of transformation when destroyed matter becomes eternal spirit, or that separates matter from spirit. At the risk of being repetitious, I cite again two observations that L. Sullivan has made of the importance of cosmic conflagrations in South American religions. Cosmic conflagrations "demonstrate the absolute spirituality of matter in the primordial world and show that being in all its forms is susceptible to total spiritualization" (1988, 66). Further,

> the conflagration spiritualized the universe. That is, reality proved itself to be transcendent, able to sustain life beyond its primordial appearance. In a sense, universal destruction by fire "creates" the spiritual world by rendering it ethereal and invisible. (69–70)

Remembering that Kuwai is "his father's soul, the sun's soul," and that the Great Fire takes place at noon, when the sun is directly above, I suggest that the Great Fire may be thought of in terms of the descent of the sun to earth—a millenarian image—when the father "kills" the son (i.e., when the son is no longer a child and has become an adult) and when all matter (i.e., the many-things-in-one-being, Kuwai) is consumed and spiritualized. The heaviest and most durable logs that are thrown on top of Kuwai as he burns are used, for example, in the building of houses, for what sustains society in its manifest form are houses, *ipana*, in which the social order is reproduced. Yet Kuwai leaves in the fire *manhene* and sicknesses by which people die, for what most threatens continued existence are sorcery and fatal illness—the negative side of Kuwai's being. *Here again we see the two sides of Kuwai's being—catastrophe and regeneration—which make this figure so important to understanding millenarian consciousness.* Kuwai then ascends to the sky, in a great cloud of smoke, to live eternally in the Other World.

The powerful image of Kuwai's world-burning fire—an "inferno," as the narrator Keruaminali said—has strong parallels in the historical consciousness of at least the Dzauinai and the Hohodene phratries. In the millenarian movements of 1858, for example, the Dzauinai prophet Kamiko evoked the image of a world conflagration and God's descent to earth to be realized on a saint's day (June 24, 1858) as his followers danced and sang the songs of Kuwai's final dance ritual. Kamiko's millenarian ideology explicitly sought to rid the Içana of the corrupting, debilitating, and destructive effects of the whites' political economy represented at that time by the military and merchant alliance in the exploitation of indigenous labor (Wright 1981b; Wright and Hill 1986). Kamiko preached autonomy from the whites and strict observance of ritual fasting, prayer and ceremonies led by him as the way to salvation from "sin" and debt to the whites. In a similar way, the Hohodene children of Keruaminali refused to follow the White Man to the Rio Negro again because their own work—houses and gardens—held greater meaning for them; hence they returned upriver to found the ancestral Hohodene villages of the Aiary today.

Episodes 5–7

In contrast with the sequence of events in episodes 2–4, the final sequence of the myth develops principally on the plane of This World. The connection to the Other World, so prominent before, now assumes a secondary importance after Iaperikuli cuts Kuwai's *paxiuba* tree and it falls, like a heap of bones, to the ground. Consistent with this development on the thisworldly plane, the final sequence is primarily concerned with relations to other peoples and places on the periphery of society. Hence the predominant action is that of a war, *uwi*, between men and women over the control of reproductive powers.

Iaperikuli's son is at the point of becoming a marriageable adult when the women take away the flutes to their settlement. In this loss, the men are vulnerable to sicknesses the women send through the spirit-darts, *walamas*, which shoot out of the flutes' mouths. There occurs a temporary inversion of roles: narrators explained that the men could "do nothing," they "became like women," and "made *caxiri*" in expectation of Kuwai's return. The men's loss triggers a polarization in space as well, as the women assume a horizontally upriver position as "takers" in control over the shamanistic powers of Kuwai, and the men a downriver position as hunters and warriors on the side of nature. The men become animal-others: their kin and allies in the war are the animals; they change into frogs and communicate to the women of their presence through animal-song, an omen to the women of their impending "deaths" in the war. In short, the men become enemy others.

The women take away the flutes in the middle of the night, escaping the wrath of the men by transforming the flutes into spirit weapons, whereupon they bathe with them and go upriver, underwater, until they reach the huge stone hill of Motípan, where they make a large, fenced settlement. There they chant over their younger sister's food for she had already begun to menstruate.

Narrators give a great deal of exegesis on the significance of space and spatial movements in this episode; hence, I will focus on this aspect as well. Motípan is a place noted for its massive rock formations; it is said to be "like a city" with various stone "statues" of Amaru and the women. It is at the source of the Uaraná stream, the principal feeder stream of the upper Aiary and, according to Hohodene narrators, the source of all their water. It is a place where there is, according to some Hohodene narrators, much "gold." Yet it is associated with poison, *manhene*, extremely dangerous and taboo. In the context of this episode, however, Motípan is the ritual house of the women, where *kalidzamai* is done, and thus it is like Enípan of the previous episodes. In contrast, the hilltop of Tunui on the mid-Içana, where Iaperikuli descends, is like Hipana of the previous episodes in being associated with the animals: there is a "house of birds" there, and Iaperikuli seeks arrow-poison from its owner with which to hunt and kill the women. In short, we have the same contrast between ritual house and place of nature expressed here as the context for the events of change as in the previous episode, with the difference that Motípan, the ritual house, is upriver and Tunui, the house of birds, is downriver.

It is my suggestion that the curare poison, used in hunting, and the magical darts that Iaperikuli seeks from their spirit-owner at the hill of Tunui represent perfectly the absolute contrast between male and female temporality in reproduction. Male temporality is characterized by a direct vertical connection to the sky in the form of Kuwai's *paxiuba* palm tree which, although it has been cut into discontinuous pieces, when these are assembled together in Kuwaipan, initiation rites performed today, represents the primordial world in the present. By contrast, the zigzag of the magical dart that Iaperikuli shoots to the "sky door" represents another form of connection of the women to the creative sources of the cosmos. It is a short time, characterized by abrupt but continuous changes, from the primordial past to the present. Again, my interpretation is that this may reflect short female cycles of menstruation, and for that reason, it is significant that in the context of the episode, Iaperikuli gets the magical darts exactly during the girl's first menstruation rite. In Chapter 5, I will continue this argument by showing (1) how the two modalities of time—masculine and feminine—are further contrasted in the myth of how death entered the world, and (2) how shamanic time is absolutely opposed to female temporality, which explains why menstruating women may cause a "sickness" to the shaman's blood.

It is precisely at the point when the women's initiation is complete that the men break into the settlement, take away Kuwai, and "throw" the women to the four directions. While, for the men, the "death of Kuwai" in the great conflagration signified the incorporation of Kuwai's knowledge into a ritual society to be reproduced for all time, for the women "death through war" would seem to signify that, although they have Kuwai's life-giving power within them (e.g., one woman hides a Kuwai flute inside her vagina), they ultimately do not have the power to reproduce it. Thus they do not, and *cannot*, "know the music of Kuwai." They become, as mothers and wives, like the Kuwai/White Man, wandering intermediaries: as they were the mothers of Kuwai, so now they become the "mothers of the whites." Characteristically, it is said, Iaperikuli gave them shoes when he sent them to the four directions.

The association of women with change and otherness in the world of the whites is a theme repeated in other Hohodene myths and in various oral histories of contact. For example, in an important myth of the anaconda *umawali*, Iaperikuli's wife has sex with this figure who is also a White Man. The question of female sexuality and dangerous relations with outsiders which transform into incestuous relations is a central theme here (see Wright 1993–1994), parallel to the questions of control over reproduction in the Kuwai myth. In one oral history referring to early colonial times, the Hohodene recall that a Manao Indian of the middle Rio Negro was taken prisoner to Portugal, where he saw women playing the sacred flutes—clearly an inversion of the way things should be. Another oral history of the nineteenth-century messiah Kamiko tells how his wife disobeyed his instructions to fast and pray in his absence, by dancing and drinking with white soldiers who came in search of the messiah, for which she was condemned by the messiah to dance eternally with Inyaime (Wright and Hill 1986). In all cases, women's associations with otherness—the whites, the spirit world—represent a danger from the outside which is to be controlled.

On the other hand, women's intermediary position has been fundamental to social recovery as, for example, in the case of the Hohodene ancestor Keruaminali, who, as a widower and childless following his return from the Rio Negro, was persuaded by the Oalipere-dakenai women to accept an alliance, which was the basis of the phratry's recovery. And there are the various examples in myths I have cited of female characters who are critical to reverting situations of death and destruction of the animals, such as the elderly "aunt" who nurtures the Iaperikunai back to life. In short, of all the categories of alterity, women would seem to be the most ambivalently valued because they are of two worlds at once—essential to social and biological reproduction, they are most vulnerable to its inversion.

In summary, I have argued that one of the central concerns of the Kuwai myth as a whole is the production of collective self-identity in relation to various forms of "other" beings. Thus Kuwai is represented as an animal, Wamundana, a White Man, *ialanawi*, a demon, Inyaime, but in his final incorporation into the ritual society, as our owner, *waminali*. Kuwai's nature as All-Things-in-One signifies that *one* of his manifestations is the White Man, the most powerful, "other" being of This World. There are two sides to this notion: first, that the destructive external being is ultimately transformed into the collective soul representing ancestral power that remains inside of society; and second, that the women who bore this power are ultimately transformed into wandering intermediaries on the periphery where they become the "mothers of the whites." Without the knowledge of the music of Kuwai, they occupy the same space of alterity as the whites, the dead, and the animal-spirits with no way of reproducing society on their own.

What implications does this interpretation have for understanding the memory of contact history with the whites or the historical events we saw in the documents? What are the relations, in short, of Hohodene history and myth to the themes of millenarian consciousness that I have been exploring in this book?

The myth of Kuwai, I suggest, provides a model for the ritual production of socialized individuals and the reproduction of the social order based on events from the primordial past intimately related to cosmic creation. In this more fundamental sense of history, I see the myth as providing a religious and philosophical understanding of the creation, destruction, and renewal of the world. This model is easily transformed into ritual action; as I have mentioned here and demonstrated in other works, the myth of Kuwai has been at the center of millenarian and messianic movements since the mid-nineteenth century.

In this sense, it is of utmost importance that Kuwai is directly linked to shamanic power and that the myth constitutes one of the bases of shamanism today, for the prophetic movements were almost entirely led by shamans. Through their creative incorporation of the sacred model of individuality in the myth, shamans have done more than re-create Iaperikuli's saving of the world from destruction. Again, to cite Sullivan's perceptive synthesis, Baniwa prophets

> add a new and creative episode to cosmic history, in which the faithful exercise the privilege of playing the role of supernatural or immortal beings. The fact that the hero-prophet is living among his followers is a sure sign that they are living in a totally mythic reality. (1988, 556)

It is worth noting that Tukanoan peoples (Barasana, Dessana) of the Pira-Paraná region in Colombia, distant from the Aiary-Içana region, identify the figure of Warimi, whose name means "He who went away"—and who is equivalent in many respects to Kuwai—as much with the origins of shamanic powers as with the White Man (S. Hugh-Jones 1988; Bidou 1986). As with the Baniwa, Tukanoan history is marked by millenarian and messianic movements led by shamans identified with mythic figures. In the case of the Barasana, Hugh-Jones suggests that this connection be interpreted in the following terms:

> The myth of *Warimi* leaves it clear that the knowledge and power of the White People is conceived as a transformation and concentration of the shamanic power and knowledge responsible for the creation of indigenous society and for its reproduction today. This opens the possibility that contemporary shamans may re-establish contact with *Warimi* and thus redress the balance between Indians and Whites. (1988: 150)

There are important differences between the messianic ideologies of the Tukanoan and Arawakan peoples, as I have previously argued; nevertheless, Kuwai/White Man is equally associated with shamanic and ancestral powers essential to cosmic and social reproduction.

This does not mean, however, that the myth of Kuwai specifically accounts for the existence of the whites, nor does it even raise the question. Indeed, the creation of the White Man, or his wealth, is of relatively minor importance in Hohodene and, I would venture to say, Baniwa myths. The central question of the Kuwai myth, as I have argued, is the construction of collective identity and its relation to alterity. The category of alterity is thus prior to the appearance of the White Man as an image in the myth. Hence, although, according to the majority of narrators, Kuwai first appears to the initiates as a White Man, some narrators say that who appears is the powerful, large, black sloth-shadow Wamundana, the animal-spirit "owner of poison" and harbinger of death, an intermediary between the world of the dead and that of the living. The historic reality of the white man as the most significant other—strange and potentially hostile—certainly led to the identification of Kuwai with him. By radically transforming this powerful outsider, through cosmic conflagration and banishment from the world, the myth provides a millenarian solution to the question of alterity.

Thus, the historical and mythic traditions I have examined so far in this book would seem to indicate two complementary solutions to alterity: oral history provides a model for political strategies constituted by historical precedents and adaptable to the present circumstances. The Hohodene myth of Kuwai, by contrast, presents messianic and millenarian solutions that seek to reconstruct society according to a mythic model that allows the messianists to assume control over cosmic time and to play an active role in the creation of their own destiny. The two solutions are not mutually exclusive either in their philosophical presuppositions or in their political consequences. Rather, history has demonstrated that they work together.

PART III
DEATH AND ESCHATOLOGY

When Theodor Koch-Grünberg lived on the Aiary River in late 1903, one of the things that most impressed him about Baniwa culture was the complex of beliefs and rites related to sickness and death. Besides the masked dance festivals to commemorate the dead which he witnessed among the Maulieni (Kaua, in *língua geral*) of the upper Aiary, he was present at the death of a Hohodene man in the village of Cururuquara, then a large Oalipere-dakenai settlement on the mid-Aiary. What is striking in his description are the numerous references to actions of the dying man and his relatives against "hidden enemies" from the village, or upriver, who were believed to have caused the man's sickness and death. Oalipere-dakenai shamans attempted to cure the man but in vain, for according to them, he had been poisoned through sorcery. They showed the ethnographer a bundle, wrapped in leaves and tied up with string, of what looked like dog's hair, which they had extracted from the victim's body and which, they said, was the visible representation of the "unknown enemy."

At the man's death, various men brandished weapons: the chief of the village took his gun and shot at a tree; one of the village elders was thrashed and accused, "You killed him! You are evil! Your kin killed him! With *manhene*!" The generalized violence, however, soon subsided into a profound silence and a concern to dispatch as quickly as possible the deceased and the "spirit" of the dead from the living. Yet, even later, at the dance festival held five days after the burial, whenever men expounded on the deceased, they were armed with knives, guns, or poison arrows—a "fearsome" sight to the ethnographer (Koch-Grünberg 1967, Vol. 1, Chapter 11).

From what I have said in Part II, the warlike postures of the men against an "invisible, hidden enemy," an "other" who has given poison, are partly intelligible in terms of the myth of Kuwai—specifically, the dynamics having to do with *manhene*, poison, as a focus of conflict or tension among affinal or enemy groups. In the case of the village of

Cururuquara, my Hohodene interlocutors told me that in fact there had been a long history of witchcraft accusations and killings between the Oalipere-dakenai of that village and the Maulieni of the village of Inambú, upriver from Cururuquara—a history of people from each village giving poison to the other, often in the context of beer-drinking festivals. As José Felipe of Uapui explained: "First, someone from Inambú gave *manhene* to someone from Cururuquara. Later someone from Cururuquara gave *manhene* to someone from Inambú. Until the people of Cururuquara were nearly finished off."

This was in the past, and José Felipe contrasted that time to the present, for the survivors of Cururuquara had moved slightly upriver— no doubt abandoning the great longhouse due to an excess of deaths and burials—to form a new village called Kuitchiali-numana, or Canadá as it became known, which eventually recuperated and became the largest evangelical village on the Aiary.

A brief glance at some of the few written sources on Aiary villages in the early twentieth century reveals that José Felipe's story of a reduction in Cururuquara's thriving population had begun about a generation after Koch-Grünberg's visit; Nimuendaju in 1927 noted that the village had about half as many people as in the beginning of the century.

The point I wish to stress here is the centrality of *manhene*, or poison, in the dynamics of witchcraft and sorcery among villages of different sibs and/or phratries. Not only is *manhene* per se important but also significant is the relation that the discourse associated with witchcraft and sorcery has to what I have called the catastrophic vision of the world—that "people were nearly finished off"—and its regeneration—that is, the recovery of prosperity, abundance, and multiplicity.

Chapters 5 and 6 will explore these questions by beginning with an extended case history. Like Koch-Grünberg, I witnessed the death of a Hohodene elder, an important leader in the community of Uapui Cachoeira, and I devoted a significant part of my fieldwork to understanding that event and its historic and symbolic significance. Rather than seeing the death of the elder as an isolated event, however, I will relate it to the eschatological themes which form the central concerns of this book.

The recent discussions in the anthropological literature on "Death and the Beyond" (Cipoletti and Langdon 1992) in South American cultures have opened up new horizons and interpretations to a well-established theme in the discipline. Yet, while these studies have contributed greatly to understanding aspects of dream symbolism, shamanism, warfare, and the person—related to death—few of them have explored the relation of death to eschatology. Sullivan, however, takes this as a central theme in the final chapter, "Death and the End of Time," of *Icanchu's Drum*:

> In death and during the eschaton, symbolic beings confront the primordial sources of new life. Cultures contest the arbitrary limits imposed by death and thereby create terminologies that construe the social world and revitalize cosmic life. Pointing toward the absent but sacred sources of meaning, symbolic life centers itself over death and disappearance. (1988, 609)

The ethnography of the Northwest Amazon has devoted a great deal of attention to certain aspects related to death: masked dances and mourning ceremonies among the Cubeo (Goldman 1963); the sacred flutes and trumpets as representations of the ancestors (S. Hugh-Jones 1979); death in the life cycle (C. Hugh-Jones 1979); shamans' and chanters' relations to the world of the dead (Hill [1989] 1993). The following two chapters are intended as much to contribute to an ethnography of death among the Hohodene of the Aiary River as to examine aspects of the meaning of death and their relation to millenarian consciousness. Specifically, I will concentrate on four themes:

(1) The presence of mythic discourse and processes related to death in the dynamics of a village, Uapui Cachoeira, which in the 1970s lived in the specter of imminent collective death due to the actions and threats of a single sorcerer—most importantly, how poison, *manhene*, and death attributed to enemy sorcerers evoke the specter of the catastrophic destruction of the primordial world, as remembered in the myths, against which shamanic vengeance—particularly shamanism at a distance—is the unique solution.

(2) The primordial construction of death, or "how death entered the world," as the myths explain. Two models of death are examined: reversible, and irreversible, systematically contrasted with one another through different classes of spirits, sacred substances, and notions of time. Death is seen as a process involving the alienation of the individual from the social, and the integration of material and spiritual components of the person into the cosmos. Death is seen as misfortune and evil in the world, a sign of the possibility and imminence of collective catastrophe. Yet death is also seen as a necessary evil for the production of future generations, new life.

(3) The notion of the person and the decomposition of the person at death, as evidenced in the chants and orations spoken or

sung at or after death. The principal concerns of the living
as expressed in this discourse are for protection against the
signs of the dead, particularly their song, and dispatching the
spirit of the recently deceased to various parts of the cosmos.
The "heart-soul," "eye-soul," and spiritual "umbilical cord"
of the deceased become assimilated to the collective ancestral
world of Kuwai, and in this sense, they are the immortal elements of a person, while the body and bones—its material
elements—descend to an inverted existence in the underworld.
The individual shadows of the dead may remain in This World,
as *inyaime*, and be harmful to humans. The "heart-soul" of the
dead lives an alienated existence, imagined as one of eternal
repetition. What returns to life and is reborn in newborn children is the spiritual "umbilical cord." As with death, birth
is imagined as an extremely dangerous "way," a process of
escaping from sickness-giving spirits into life.

(4) The notion of cosmic death present in shamans' songs, as I discussed briefly in Part I, but which the interpretation of myths
and orations here clarifies. Cosmic collapse, conceived as the
rupture of the vertical dimension of the cosmos, is reversible
through the shamans' healing power, which infuses the cosmos
with the sacred powers of the beginning.

5. The Times of Death

Invariably outside observers become caught up in a sequence of events which they understand very little but which is gradually revealed as time passes on, and other events and questioning clarify its meaning. So it was with the death of Seraphim, a Hohodene elder of Uapui, which occurred early in my fieldwork but which, I was to discover, was interpreted as part of a sequence of deaths whose "cause" was the same. Moreover, the history behind Seraphim's death could be, and was, interpreted in eschatological terms—that is, a wider, cosmic meaning related to fundamental processes dramatized in the myths of the primordium. The event itself was shaped not only by cosmological categories but also by cosmological processes relating the real death of a respected elder to the possibility of imminent collective death of the world.[1]

The Specter of Death at Uapui

To understand the dynamic of the events I shall relate, the kin chart below situates the people involved (see Figure 5). The core of the Hohodene population of Uapui in the 1970s consisted of descendants of the founding family which built the first longhouse there in the early 1920s. Of the seven sons of Marcellino and Ricarda, only two remained at Uapui, the others having died or migrated. Keruami, the eldest, had no sons of his own, but was stepfather to two Dessana men, Samuel and José Felipe. Seraphim was thus the only surviving brother with sons, all of whom were married, and whose families formed the largest contingent of the village.

The two sons of Joaquim (Keruami's and Seraphim's younger brother), Edu and Emílio, had an uneasy relation to the rest of the village, for reasons unclear to me since the story may go back to Joaquim's generation. It is curious, however, that when I asked Emílio about the old longhouses of Uapui, he said there was only one and

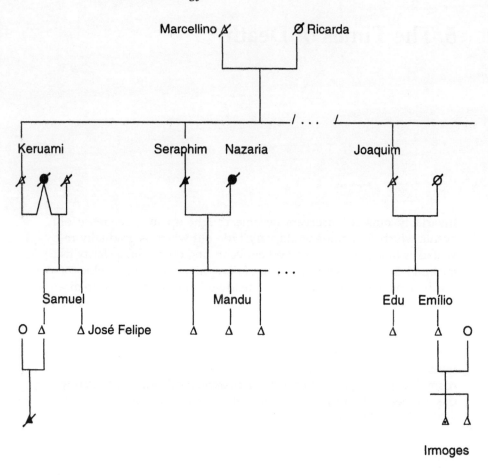

Key: ⚥ / ⌀ = deceased   ⚥ / ⬤ = deaths from *manhene*

△ = sickness diagnosed as *manhene*

Figure 5. Selective Kin Chart of Uapui

that his father was the shaman and "owner of the house," which did not agree with anyone else's statements nor even with the observations of outsiders who passed through Uapui at various times.

In any case, Emílio was considered by the villagers as dangerous, a sorcerer who, it was believed, had poisoned various people. He and his family lived in a house separate from the main village cluster and infrequently participated in communal work projects and other collective activities. He had a long-standing enmity with the chief of the village, Mandu, Seraphim's eldest son. People said that they had "always been enemies," but this was aggravated by a dispute over succession to the position of chief and *capitão* at Uapui. Emílio had taken over the position from the aging chief Keruami, for he was the "oldest brother" in the village at that time, but neither the villagers nor the Salesian missionaries were satisfied with his performance, as "he didn't work for the community," they said. During one of his frequent absences from the village, the missionaries intervened, putting Mandu, then vice-*capitão*, in charge. Although this change solved the community's problem of leadership—for Mandu was one of the most dynamic leaders in the village's history—it only served to deepen the enmity between the two men.

In the early 1970s, one of Emílio's younger sons accidentally drowned while playing near the rapids, but Emílio accused Mandu's children of having pushed him, an accusation which seemed to have little basis in fact. Some time later, Emílio's oldest son, Irmoges—who, the missionaries confirmed, had tuberculosis—was playing in a group when a girl pushed him to the ground, provoking a serious attack in which he coughed up much blood. Emílio was enraged at the sight of his son's being so visibly near death and threatened to kill all the children in the village with poison if Irmoges died. Emílio publicly blamed Mandu for having caused Irmoges' sickness (i.e., having given him poison), and promised vengeance on Mandu's family. Within two years after this incident, three people had died of *manhene*: the girl who had pushed Irmoges, Mandu's mother, and Keruami's wife. Two others were struck with near-fatal illness, both diagnosed as *manhene*: José Felipe and Seraphim.

As people remembered, it was during a Kuwaipan initiation rite that Seraphim's wife saw Emílio put poison in a gourd of beer which he later gave her to drink. Soon after, she showed signs of poisoning—high fever, intense stomach pain, and vomiting. She told Seraphim to put the sacred trumpets away, for she had to return home and it was already dark. They returned and she worsened until morning when she died. She knew it was Emílio and told the people gathered around her as she was dying.

Sometime later, Keruami's wife was poisoned and also died. Mandu and other shamans blamed Emílio, although the evidence was not as clear as in the first case. People said that all through the night of her death, an owl—an omen of death—cried.

José Felipe had been an ambitious and hardworking vice-*animador* of Uapui before his sickness. A successful hunter and a very creative weaver, he had traveled extensively to work, including with his uncle, Antonio Guzmán, Gerardo Reichel-Dolmatoff's principal Dessana informant. He had intended to marry Emílio's eldest daughter, but Emílio prohibited the marriage, so he married Mandu's daughter instead. In early 1976, he suddenly suffered a near-fatal illness, which Mandu and Keruami diagnosed as *manhene*. The Salesian missionary sent him by plane to Manaus for treatment, but neither the FUNAI doctors nor the missionaries were able to cure his ailment. Their treatment enabled him to return to Uapui, but his continued sickness literally ended his career: for a long time afterward, he didn't participate in community work projects and stayed at home, secluded and restricted in diet, periodically seeking treatment from Mandu. Again, the shamans suspected Emílio, but José Felipe, perhaps not wanting to pursue the matter, thought it had happened "just that way, a sickness."

In August of the same year, Seraphim suffered a severe attack of pain in his abdomen while working in his garden. He was flown to Manaus, where the doctors diagnosed the pain as hernia, requiring surgery. After nearly two months in the city, Seraphim sent word to his sons that he still had not been operated on; Mandu at least was relieved to know Seraphim was still alive, for as he said, "Not knowing, we are sad. If he had died, the sadness will pass, because we know he is waiting for us in the sky." After his surgery and recovery, Seraphim finally returned in January 1977, stopping at the mission of Jauareté on the Uaupés. There, by coincidence, he met Emílio and Irmoges. Emílio had taken Irmoges to several Cubeo shamans for treatment; in one village, he met a mission hospital worker who strongly advised him to go to the mission hospital in Jauareté. According to Seraphim, Emílio gave him a bowl of *xibé* (manioc cereal and water) to drink. The next day, Seraphim went on his way upstream to the Uanana village on the island of Jandú, at the entrance to the trail back to Uapui, where he sent word to his sons to come get him. It was there I met him and his sons in the late afternoon of February 2 , 1977.

According to Mandu, on the evening before I arrived, Seraphim had been gathering firewood when suddenly he fell in agonizing pain and took to his hammock, unable to walk. Mandu was most concerned to carry him back by trail to Uapui, where he could at least try to cure him. Since he was without his shaman's apparel, he asked if I had brought any medicine which might alleviate his father's pain. I gave him a pain reliever, which seemed to help sufficiently so that the next day we decided to head over the twenty-kilometer trail, Seraphim's sons carrying him in a hammock, to the village.

In Uapui, Mandu asked for more medicine to continue the treatment together with his cures. But the next day, Seraphim worsened

Figure 6. Uapui—the Chapel and Houses

and the pain reliever ran out. Whatever cures the shamans did proved ineffective, and by that afternoon, convinced that he was going to die and that all that could be done was to relieve the pain but not cure the sickness, Seraphim called his sons together in his house. With the doors and windows closed, he spoke privately with them. This moment, when a dying father speaks with his sons, is a time of advice and settling accounts. I was later told that Seraphim spoke the following: that he had worked and suffered enough in This World; that his sons should continue to live well with others in This World without him, to plant their gardens and to work well; that they should prepare themselves, for the whites are coming (a prophecy that the shaman Kudui had made some years before); and that, in a dream, he had seen two "evil people" in the village whom they should beware of, for they would do harm to others. One of them, Emílio, would kill Keruami, he said.

Seraphim then gave his few possessions (bow and arrow, fishing spear) to his sons and ended his counsel. A short while later, I entered the house and was advised that he would "already go." A shaman came in and inquired of Seraphim's pain, performing brief curative actions to relieve it, but by then it was a matter of waiting.

At dusk, people from the village began congregating in the house which, from then until the next morning, became a focal point for the drama of Seraphim's passage from life to death. As the night drew on, the one-room house literally filled up to a maximum (some fifty to sixty people), all intently watching Seraphim as he lay in his hammock by the fire, his sons sitting closely by his side, weeping, extremely distressed by his constant cries of pain, which they attempted to alleviate. What struck me most was how, at several points, Seraphim, looking upward, gestured with his arm, pointing a way up to a place which he evidently saw, exactly as though he was guiding a canoe through a passage of rocks or rapids. At intervals in this journey, he lay quiet, smoked tobacco, drank tapioca and water, or talked with his sons of what he had seen: Kuwai *dzakale*, the village of Kuwai; Kamathawa, Iaperikuli's pet harpy eagle. Mandu warned him to beware of *inyaime kurara*, the fence of the spirit who calls and takes away many dying people to its village of eternal heat and thirst. The crowd of people listened intently, for it was evident that Seraphim was already making his journey to the houses of the dead, on the periphery of Kuwai's village.

Late in the night, I returned to my quarters in Mandu's son's house next door but noted that, outside the house where Seraphim lay dying, children played and people slung their hammocks, now and then going in to watch, or staying outside to chat of other things. A group of men heatedly discussed what had brought on Seraphim's death. Several times in the night, I heard Mandu vomiting in back of the house, apparently seeking to lessen his father's pain, but all attempts seemed to be futile.

In the morning, I entered the near-empty house to see Seraphim lying quietly, staring off into space. Mandu told me that, in his journey, Seraphim had seen his father and other deceased kin. He had seen Iaperikuli, who had told him that he had to stay on the earth five years more, for the house where he would stay in the Other World was not yet ready.[2] At the end of five years, he could return. I interpreted this to mean that Seraphim had not died, but moments later, Seraphim bent his legs in a fetal position up to his chest and babbled like an infant. Mandu straightened his legs, Seraphim looked around for the last time, and his eyes turned up. Mandu shut his eyes and, with little emotion, said, "He's gone." Alberto, Mandu's thirteen-year-old son, who was sitting to the side with a plastic baby Jesus doll in his hands, wept. Mandu, again with surprisingly contained emotion, arranged a table where Seraphim would lie briefly in wake, took out from his suitcase a set of clean white clothes, and began to dress his deceased father.

The moment for expressing his emotion came shortly after when two women, his wife's sisters, came in and the three squatted in a triangle—one hand resting on the other's shoulder, the other covering the face—and cried, "My [father/elder brother], why have you left us, I am so sad without you." Gaby, Mandu's younger brother, later came in and wept; standing by his father's body on the table, he addressed the corpse promising his father that he would continue to live as he wished them to.

Meanwhile, a coffin had been quickly made ready: two old, sawed-off canoes, one to be placed over the other, and a thick rope for binding. Seraphim was wrapped in his hammock and placed inside the canoe, along with a cigar, a box of matches, a gourd, and some farinha. The coffin was closed, tied with the cord, and quickly carried down to the port. Again, the moment was not one of expressing emotion but of dispatching the dead as quickly as possible. Simple streaks of black carbon marked the faces of those in mourning. For three days, people said, they would mourn, being restricted in diet to *quinhampira*, pepper pot, and manioc bread.

By the time we arrived at the cemetery on the other side of the river from the village, the grave had already been dug in the sandy earth. People no longer buried the dead in their houses, Mandu explained: "The way we bury the dead is not like in the past." A man set fire to the trees surrounding the cemetery, which increased the heat of the noonday sun. I was warned of biting insects in the sand which gave intense pain. Everyone from the village, *except* Emílio and his family, was there. The coffin was lowered into the grave, and at a signal, everyone squatted around the hole and threw in fistsful of sand over the coffin, crying over and over, and hooting "Hoo! Hoo!" for several moments until all fell silent. The cry is the song of the first ancestor of the Hohodene, the partridge Bobole, that Iaperikuli looked for in the holes of the rapids at Hipana at the dawn of creation.

Once the grave was closed, all returned to the village. At the port, everyone bathed in the river. Youths and children, especially, gave momentary relief from the sorrow with their water games, jumping in somersaults into the swift-flowing current of the river, as if to "turn over" the sadness into laughter. As we later sat chatting, Mandu looked to the center of Hipana Falls and remembered the myth of how Iaperikuli had taken the ancestors, one by one, out of the holes in the center of the falls. It was as if he were explaining to me that his father's soul was now part of the collective ancestral body of the primordial times. His body remained in the earth, but his soul would complete the journey to the houses of the dead and there "wait for" his family.

That night, various precautionary measures were taken to prevent the return of the recently deceased's soul into the village: the plaza was swept clean and clumps of debris burned at the edges sending up clouds of smoke. The smoke of burning resin, incenselike, was brushed into the doorways of each house, it was said, to "close the way" of the dead into the houses of the living. Most likely, elders spoke the orations to "open the way" of the soul to the houses of the dead, and to "turn away its gaze" from the living.

In the past, shortly after a burial, a dance festival might be held among villages, but this didn't happen after Seraphim's death. Instead, following another tradition of village dispersion in the summer months to fish on the lower Aiary, most people of Uapui closed their houses and left, which no doubt helped them to forget the dead. Few families remained: Emílio and his brother Edu, and Keruami's son Samuel and his family. Yet a bizarre event not more than two weeks later showed that the specter of death had not yet left Uapui.

Samuel's younger son (some four years old) fell ill with a high fever and stomach pains. Terrified by these signs, Samuel decided to risk a journey to the American New Tribes mission on the Içana River some three days away, to seek what was known to be strong medicine. But the child never recovered and, according to Samuel, he died after his body twisted until his spinal cord broke (most likely spinal meningitis, or—its equivalent name in Baniwa—"the cords of the Anaconda," *umawali iuwepem*).

When Mandu later learned of this death, his immediate reaction was *manhene* and that Emílio was again to blame: "He has given *manhene* to six people already. He is the only one in Uapui who has *manhene*. He wants to kill us all. His only thought is to kill" (*manhekada lima*, a person who gives *manhene*, "who has no other thought but to kill people"). But, if this was true, what was to be done? What mechanisms were there to prevent further deaths? The community believed that Emílio had had a hand in all deaths of Mandu's family since these tragic events had begun. Mandu went so far as to say that it was Emílio himself who had given *manhene* to his own son Irmoges; in short, the epitome of an assassin.

More than this, and most significantly, Emílio symbolized the imminent catastrophic death of the world by poison foretold in primordial times. As Mandu stated explicitly, "He wants to kill us all, one by one, so that *only he* remains alone. He sees the world that way and always has." Mandu's fear was a clear reminder of the treacherous *eenunai* chief, the owner of *manhene*, who sought to kill all of Iaperikuli's kin, to "finish off" with people (see Part I). At the same time that the myth of Iaperikuli can serve as model of a savior, the myths of the *eenunai* provide a profile of witches and sorcerers that can be transposed onto the present—at least, in the understanding of the shamans.

Iupithatem, Shamanic Vengeance

Naturally, such a tense situation demanded constant vigilance. Among long-standing enemies, anger becomes more complicated as time passes and deepened by nearly every incident or word, however seemingly minor. Avoiding the enemy is never simple; it requires a careful observing of the other's actions—for example, "Why has Emílio not eaten with the community these past few days?" people would ask and search their memories for what he had said. On numerous occasions, Mandu discussed "the problem of Emílio" with me, and as I came to know them both more deeply, I found them at various times in increasingly dangerous points of nonresolution. No "talking" between them or in community meetings would ever work.

In another strategy, Mandu used the force of his political weight to heighten community solidarity against Emílio. When, for example, a quantity of money was stolen from my room, Mandu, a skilled orator, spoke strongly several times to the community as a whole reminding them all of the laws of the ancestors, to treat people well: "We don't live this way, we don't treat the *ialanawi* this way." The community's suspicions of Emílio (for he owed a lot of money to Colombian traders) were confirmed when the children saw him secretly return the stolen money, leaving it on the windowsill of my room. But the concern remained: if he had entered the white man's room to steal, what was to prevent him from putting poison in his food?

A more powerful appeal to cosmic sanctions was forthcoming several months later: shamanic vengeance, or *iupithatem*,[3] one of the most effective actions against sorcerers. The hair or "filth" of the deceased is taken by his relatives to powerful Wanhíwa (= Guahibo) and Piaroa shamans of the Meta, Vichada, and Guaviare Rivers in Venezuela, a three-week journey by canoe and foot from the upper Aiary. The relatives pay the Wanhíwa shamans to take vengeance while those who remain in the village "wait to see who is the victim." Cubeo shamans of the Cuduiary in Colombia are also said to be adept at this, and "true" Baniwa shamans may even produce more rapid results, but the Hohodene *prefer* the Wanhíwa shamans.

From what little I was told of this ritual, the hair of the deceased is placed on the ground in front of the Wanhíwa shaman, together with the payment, a bucket of water, and a stone representing the shaman's soul. The shaman sings, looking for the soul of his victim. When a butterfly, or small bird, appears, the shaman uses the stone to snap at it, "bite it," which kills it instantly. The shaman may even hear its death cry. At that time, he sends a great wind to where the intended victim is, and the person goes mad: he begins to eat ashes from the fire, sits on hot coals but doesn't burn, eats his fingernails ("for his hands don't know what they are doing"), runs after women and attempts to rape them, rips off his clothes, and runs about in circles, sometimes into the forest. The madness subsides but, several days later, another great wind comes with thunderclouds and sometimes lightning, all sent by the Wanhíwa shaman. The victim does the same things as before but now he confesses—tells about everyone whom he has killed. He bites his lips and tongue so that he won't tell who has killed him. He rips off his clothes, mutilates his genitals, and finally dies.

Numerous eyewitness accounts of cases of *iupithatem* vengeance confirm its efficacy. Both Protestant and Catholic missionaries had seen (and told me of) instances which made one's hair stand on end: an impressive form of cosmic justice for which reason the Baniwa considered the Wanhíwa shamans as their "police."

Six people from Uapui, including two shamans, made the journey to the Wanhíwa in the early rainy season that year. During their absence, on various occasions the men of the village demonstrated their expectations in conversations about "true shamans," "snuff jaguars" capable of sending their souls above the world, to the highest level of the cosmos. These shamans were said to be permanently "on the edge of This World," but what was fascinating about these discussions was how the Wanhíwa knew and found their victims.

Emílio, for his part, was conspicuously absent from all community activities. Mandu speculated, "Maybe he is afraid of us now, so he doesn't eat with us." Signs of *iupithatem* then appeared in astonishing form: one morning, while we were gathered in the community house for the morning meal, suddenly the sky turned black with thunderclouds and a powerful wind swept through the house. I looked at Mandu, who, by his expression, said what—given the circumstances and following the logic of shamanic vengeance—appeared to be the obvious: the Wanhíwa were looking for their victim.

I recorded no further developments on this case throughout the rest of my fieldwork; shortly after, the Brazilian Air Force began construction of an airfield behind the village of Uapui, occupying the village for months in clearing the ground, and I decided to continue my fieldwork upstream in the village of Ucuqui. Minimally, however, the shamans' actions seemed to have controlled the fear prevalent in the community before then, that Emílio would "kill them all."

A Note on *Manhene*

It would be difficult to find an element more charged with significance in Baniwa culture than *manhene*. Numerous writers since the end of the nineteenth century have noted its importance. In myths of other Arawakan and Tukanoan peoples of the region, Hipana or Uapui Cachoeira is frequently mentioned as both a place of ancestral emergence and a place of poison.[4] An ethnobotanist working among the Baniwa of the mid-Içana in 1985 found that the Indians there were likewise well versed in plant poisons:

> The Baniwa in Tapira Ponta often talk of poisoning and poisoning incidents. It is an important part of their culture. Two renowned shamans live in Tapira Ponta. The seriously ill are canoed more than 100 kilometers from up and downriver by their relatives to be treated there. Most of the cases are alleged poisonings.
>
> Among other plant poisons, the Baniwa are commonly held to possess:
> —the famed piranha poison [or *umai panaitana*] that induces uncontrollable vomiting followed by rapid death;

—the vulture poison that makes the victim's hair fall out;

—various slow-acting poisons that induce headache and fever culminating in the victim's death weeks later.

Specific data about poison plants, however, was not easily obtained in Tapira Ponta. Although I came to conclude that a Baniwa shaman typically knows 15–20 plant poisons, only two were reluctantly pointed out to me. One has already been identified as an extremely strong gastric poison. An alkaloid, riganodine, is the toxic principle in the roots and leaves of the *warecama*. The Baniwa in Tapira Ponta were less reluctant to show their plant poisons' antidotes. (Doyle n.d., 12)

Hohodene shamans added a little information on kinds of poison:

- *Lidzuna*: "the seed of a berry or fruit which appears in the holes of rocks." It is given in the drink of the intended victim, producing intense stomach pain, headaches, high fever, vomiting, followed by death. Shamans, in their cures, extract this poison in the form of black hair, *lidzu*—hence the name—of sloths, *wamu*, of the hills.
- *Likaime*: the same, with the difference that it is extracted as white hair.
- *Mawikuli*: the same, extracted as monkey or rat hair.

Clearly Hohodene shamans know many more plant poisons, but these were perhaps considered the most significant at Uapui. The principal sources of *manhene*, they said, are the tops of some seven hills in southwestern Venezuela and several on the Içana, nearly all of which bear animal names. In the following section, I shall examine in more detail the mythical significance of *manhene* and its symbolic importance for people today.

Mawerikuli, the First Person to Die

The centrality of *manhene* to the notion of death is elaborated in the myth of Mawerikuli, the first person to die in the primordial times and who produced death for all times, "for all those unborn." According to some Hohodene narrators, the figure of Mawerikuli is derived from the Cubeo. A summarized version of the Cubeo myth of Mawerikuli states the following:

It was in the time of the KUWAIWA [first ancestors] that sickness (IJIE) was created. Their older brother, MAWICHICURE, was the first to die and his workers executed the funeral ritual (another myth points out that MAWICHICURE sought death in order to teach the funeral ritual); the ashes of the bones of the deceased were mixed in corn beer which was drunk; the *maloca* [longhouse] burnt like fire. Annoyed at his death, his workers created small predatory animals (scorpions, spiders, etc.) that came out of the *maloca* incarnating sicknesses. The Kuwaiwa, invited to the ritual, came up from the port wearing their masks (JIMAWA) and, carrying bundles of leaves, they set fire to the *maloca*, attacking the predatory animals. Since then, ways of preventing sickness were transmitted from generation to generation. (Correa 1987, 144–145)[5]

The Maulieni of the upper Aiary held the masked-dance festivals of the spirits of the dead, as described by Goldman for the neighboring Cubeo of the Querary and Cuduiary Rivers, until approximately the time of their conversion to Protestant evangelicalism in the 1940s–1950s (see Koch-Grünberg's descriptions, [1909] 1967). Yet, if Mawerikuli is of Cubeo origin, I suggest that it was grafted onto a preexisting mythic and ritual complex, clustering around both the figure of Kuwaikaniri, who is alternately called by Hohodene narrators Mawerikuli, and the spirits of the dead, *kamainiri*, which have great importance in Baniwa culture.

The following version of the myth was told to me by Mandu, Seraphim's eldest son. I have translated the narration directly from the original in Hohodene, and have tried to retain the narrator's style as much as possible, putting brief explanatory notes in brackets.

First, a brief summary of the story: The *eenunai* trick Iaperikuli's younger brother into giving them Iaperikuli's poison. Later they invite Iaperikuli to drink with them at their house. They prepare beer mixed with poison for they wished to kill Iaperikuli. Iaperikuli joins together all the bee-spirits, called *kuwainyāi*, and announces that they would go to take back the poison. Their elderly aunt prepares a special remedy for them to drink, to protect them from the effect of the poison. All the *kuwainyāi* drink this remedy. Mawerikuli, Iaperikuli's younger brother, says he would not go with them. Later he goes, but without having taken the remedy.

Iaperikuli and the *kuwainyāi* drink throughout the night at the *eenunai* house. Then they return home. Halfway back, Iaperikuli could not bear the effects of having drunk so much poison. He lies down unconscious but, before he does, he sets an owl-feather headdress on top of a pole. The *eenunai* come and call out to see if Iaperikuli had died. The owl headdress responds to their call, making them believe that Iaperikuli had not died. Suddenly, Iaperikuli revives and returns home to get more remedies from their aunt. He distributes it to all the *kuwainyãi* who had gone. Mawerikuli arrives and asks for his share but, having said he would not go, there is no more medicine left for him. Mawerikuli dies.

Iaperikuli takes Mawerikuli's body and puts it in a closed-off stone grave. Iaperikuli waited three days and, on the fourth, went to see Mawerikuli. Mawerikuli had revived and would be able to come out of the grave, so Iaperikuli went to prepare a festival to celebrate his return to life.

Iaperikuli went to hunt game and ordered his wife to prepare beer for the festival. But another woman went to see Mawerikuli's grave. She opens it and sees him sit up and speak. Mawerikuli tells her that no one can see him until his festival and that, whoever sees him, has to paint him with red *caraiurú* dye. The woman assures Mawerikuli that she can. She gets the dye and paints his whole body a beautiful red. On the final stroke of her hand, she turns it over, palm-side up, and Mawerikuli falls down, nothing but bones.

Iaperikuli knows that Mawerikuli had "died" again. He returns to the grave, and tries to remake a person. Mawerikuli almost revives but falls down again. Iaperikuli didn't succeed. Thus death entered the world for all times, or until "another end of the world."

So then, Iaperikuli went to where he lived, then, Warukwa. It's called where he lived Warukwa, where Iaperikuli lived. Then they [the *eenunai*] return. They call Iaperikuli. He would go to get back this *eenunai* poison. Three days hence he would go there. "Now, Iaperiko, you go see them there," they said to him. They would kill this Iaperikuli. So Iaperikuli called together those his *kuwain-yãi* [bee-spirits, Iaperikuli's people], his people. They are called *kuwainyãi*, all of those his *kuwainyãi*. "Now we are going to get back this *kurumáhe* [poison]," he said to them. Then he called them, he called them, his *kuwainyãi*, he joined together all of his *kuwain-yãi*. After he had called all of them, he spoke to them, "How many of you are going?" she said, their old aunt. Then they got this, his gourd-fruit remedy, this *mathoaiali* of Jaguar Iaperikuli [powerful remedy against poison]. He gave them a bit of the remedy. For, this is the soul-bringing-back remedy. She distributed it to them. She gave it out to all of those who would go. Then she asked Iaperi-kuli's younger brother, "Are you going, my nephew?" she said to him. Then, he said, "I am not going." He deceived her, but that is what he said. Later, he went after them, he went after Iaperikuli and the *kuwainyãi* had gone.

Iaperikuli arrived at the *eenunai* house. He went to enter and beat on the door, calling out—"Palenaa, where is it, Palenaa, the *eenunai kurumâhe*?" he said like so. "Here it is!" they replied. Then they gave drink to Iaperikuli. But he was doing this, he was getting back this *eenunai* poison, it's called *eenunai* poison. Then after that, they drank with him. He drank with them, the *kuwainyâi* with him. Until midnight, he didn't last until the day. Until he was full of poison. [Mandu explained: "he was poisoned, but when they gave him to drink, Iaperikuli took it out of his body. He took it out. They gave it to him, to Iaperikuli. Another gave him to drink, he took it out. Because they wanted to kill him, but this Iaperikuli does not die."]. When he was full of drink, then he returned. Iaperikuli returned. Midway back, in the middle of the trail, then Iaperikuli fell unconscious. Then his headdress, this owl-feather headdress. He took off his feather headdress and left it on top of a pole and said, "When the *eenunai* call, you have to answer for them to hear." They came and called him—"Iaperikooo!"—"Heeeyyy!" it replied. "It seems he didn't die," the *eenunai* said. Once again, they called out and heard, "Iaperikooo!"—"Heeeyyy!" it answered. "Not dead." But this Iaperikuli had already lost consciousness.

Then, suddenly he got up again and went back to his house. Then she came, their aunt, his aunt. She gave out this, her plant-remedy for them. She gave to one, to another, and to another. To all of those his *kuwainyâi*. She gave it out to all of them. When they had drunk it all, then came Iaperikuli's younger brother. Then Mawerikuli arrived, this Mawerikuli. He saw this Mawerikuli, the unfortunate one. It began with him. In the beginning he made it for us, this misfortune for all of us people, for all of the white men also. Only one did it for us in the beginning, this Mawerikuli. So he saw it for them. Then she said to him . . . he came in and said, "Aunt, where is my share?" Then she said, she the aunt, "This your share?" she said to him. "Yes," he said. "But you said to me, 'I am not going,' you said to me." "There is no share for you," she said to him. So it was then. . . . Dead he was there, this Iaperikuli's younger brother. Dead, that's all, dead he was. So they took him, this Mawerikuli, they took him and laid him down. They laid him down, Iaperikuli made his grave. The grave, they made a grave for him. Then he closed it off well. They began this Mawerikuli. Then he lay for three days, Mawerikuli lay. On the fourth day, Iaperikuli went to see him. "So, my younger brother," he said to him, "you have revived?" "Yes, I have revived," he said to him. "Mawerikuli is better, he is well," he said. "So it is, tomorrow I will raise you," he said to Mawerikuli. Then he went, Iaperikuli went to hunt animals. He would make this, his coming-out festival, it seems.

Then they did a bad thing for him, those women. Iaperikuli's wife said, "now we are going to make manioc beer," she said to them. "Iaperikuli's younger brother will return, he will bring out his younger brother," she said, Iaperikuli's wife. Then she said, "so it is, he is better." Then another woman said, "I am going there to see him, I am going there to see him, quickly, Iaperikuli's younger brother," so she said. After she spoke, she left the house. She approached and entered the grave and saw him. She saw Mawerikuli lying down, she saw Mawerikuli sit up. "Hey," Mawerikuli said well. He had already revived. After he spoke, he turned around and looked, this Mawerikuli. "Pah! It is not right that you come to see me!" he said to the woman. "Who looks at me has to paint me with *caraiurú*," he says to her. Then—"so it is, I have *caraiurú*," she said, this woman. He turns to face her and says, "why did you look at me? No one can look at me. When you look at me, you will kill me again. Thus you do bad for me." She said, "No, you can't die," she said, "it is good, good will it be, for I have *caraiurú*," she said. Then she applied the *caraiurú*, she painted his body. Well! A beautiful red! Then he said, "when he hears [the sound of the *ambaúba* dance tube], then he rises" [i.e., rises from the dead] he said to her. She paints him up with the *caraiurú*. It was done well, for Mawerikuli, she painted all of him well, all of him. Then she, the woman with *caraiurú*, turned over her hand. She said, "You are fierce." Then, quickly he went, that's all, Mawerikuli fell. So she killed him. That's all, he died. Thus was Mawerikuli's falling to the ground: *Khyelulululu*. . . . His bones lay there, Mawerikuli began it. The evil had been done.

Iaperikuli had gone to hunt animals but he knew [that Mawerikuli had died]. Fresh blood fell from the palm of his hand. "Paahhh! They killed my younger brother," Iaperikuli said. Then Iaperikuli returned. He returned and chanted where his younger brother lay. He tried to remake a person; he picked up the bones, he tried to mend them, to remake a person. Until this Mawerikuli wanted no more. Until this Mawerikuli said, "So it is, now it is better, better you leave it like so for me," he said to Iaperikuli. "As I go, so it will be for all those unborn," he said. Which means that thus we live in This World. That's all, in the beginning he saw it for us, this evil. He gave this to us, this misfortune. So it seems he gave it to us.

Then, like so it was done, "now, it stays for them, all those unborn. In the same way, it will stay with them, for all those unborn," he says to him, to Iaperikuli. "So it seems, my younger brother, better it will be like so for them, for all those unborn," he said to him, his younger brother. Mawerikuli had truly done it. Thus he truly gave it to us, misfortune, this Mawerikuli. Like so it became until we have it today. As it was done, then, he made evil. Then Iaperikuli returned and cried in anger, for it was nothing he did. He could have revived him but they did bad for him, for Iaperikuli. Which means that today, other women, do not know the world. All of them like that, for us as they began it for them. But he, the world-master, began it with this Mawerikuli. Iaperikuli gave it to us, thus for us, so he began this Mawerikuli, so it seems long ago. In the beginning he saw it for us.

Interpretation

What in particular interests people about this myth which, in various forms, appears in many religions of the world? One narrator compared it specifically to Genesis and God's banishment of Adam and Eve from Paradise, a fall from grace. It is the sense of impulsive actions and irreversible errors that narrators point to as the cause of the fall: Mawerikuli said he would not go to the festival and later does. The other woman opens Mawerikuli's grave and paints his body; on the final stroke, she turns over her hand, palm-side up, to the "other side," the side of the "shadow of death," as narrators explain. If these things had not happened like so, narrators emphasized, *everyone today would have arisen three days after their deaths, rejuvenated.* Thus what occurs in this myth is a catastrophic fall, when death entered the world—a condition which would remain, as Mandu said, "until another end of the world."

In this myth, and several others besides, there are common themes throughout:

(1) Death inevitably comes from outside one's kin group— "other" tribes, affinally related to Iaperikuli and his kin, who kill or seek to kill, by devouring or consuming, by witchcraft or poisoning.

(2) Death is reversible, through shamanism or the intervention of shamanic beings who, in some form, incorporate the vertical dimensions of the cosmos; irreversible death implies the predominance of unmediated, "horizontal" relations—that is, to affines, "others" over the vertical.

(3) Death initiates a process of exchange, a "return" death inflicted by an "other" group for the loss of one's own.

(4) The primordial beings "left" the vestiges of their deaths in This World as poison, poisonous plants, poisonous places, omens, and above all, songs.

What the myth of Mawerikuli seems to add to this vision is that death is a two-stage process, corresponding to the two rituals in the myth—the *eenunai* drinking fest, and Mawerikuli's coming-out fest. In the first, Mawerikuli alienates himself from his kin group and enters into a direct, unmediated relation with the *eenunai* in which he consumes their poison, and the result is that death is brought into society. The two modes of death—reversible and irreversible—are placed directly in contrast. In the second, the coming-out festival, the possibility of Mawerikuli's rejuvenation from death clashes with the ultimate control over death that lies in the hands of the others, the affines. There was no fest; there was no coming out; irreversible death is the human condition. This is a necessary evil, according to the narrator Mandu, for in order for there to be descendants, or new life, there must be death. It is what the primordials gave to humanity, to "all those unborn." In the following, I will explore these themes in greater detail and demonstrate their relationship to what I have called millenarian consciousness. I will rely as much as possible on narrators' explanations of the myth but will complement these with my own interpretations, making links to related themes that I have explored in this book.

The *Eenunai* Drinking-Fest

The initial situation represents an extreme separation in space (considering that the myth takes place in the miniature world of Iaperikuli in primordial times) between, on the one hand, Warukwa, Iaperikuli's island home on the Uaraná stream, and, on the other hand, the house of the *eenunai*, "on the other side of the river," in the forest—or as some narrators say, on the eastern edge of the world, *eenu táhe*, in a downriver direction, "where the rivers no longer run," *uni diákahle*. This extreme spatial separation, it seems to me, highlights social distance between, on the one hand, Iaperikuli and his kin group—his younger brother, his elderly aunt (or as many narrators say, grandmother), and his "people" or "tribe," the *kuwainyãi*—and on the other, the *eenunai*, affines (*nalimáthana*), a "tribe" of death-dealing thunderspirits, or sorcerers.

The contrast between the *kuwainyãi* and *eenunai* is extremely significant, for it seems to highlight exactly the contrast I suggested above between, respectively, reversible and irreversible death and, more generally, between regeneration and catastrophe, two central themes of millenarian consciousness. The *kuwainyāi* are bee-spirits (in actuality, referring to some eight to ten different species of bees), producers of honey and the nectar of numerous fruits which the Hohodene consider vital to "sweeten" and nourish the souls of victims of witchcraft, bringing them back to life. An important and lengthy set of chants used in curing today tells how the first victim of witchcraft, Kuwaikaniri, was gradually brought back from death during a journey which he and Iaperikuli made from downriver, starting at the edge of the world, to the upper Aiary River. The journey, through what chanters call "a country of fruits," stops in numerous places where Kuwaikaniri is nourished by fruit nectar of the *kuwainyāi* and slowly revives (*liafetawa*) from death. At various points, Kuwaikaniri visits large "cities of bee-spirits" (*mapakwa makakui*), which are considered sources of the most potent honey. As the journey proceeds upriver, Kuwaikaniri's revival is marked by changes in his body posture: from lying down "unconscious" (*maliume*)[6] in a canoe, he gradually sits up, partially revived, regaining his strength until he is eventually able to take a paddle and continue the journey, alone, to the end.

In short, the return and revival of Kuwaikaniri's soul is represented as a "way," departing from an extreme downriver position—outside the territory which the Hohodene consider their homelands, where the victim of witchcraft is "dead," and proceeding upriver by stages until reaching the place of mythic origin, the center of the world at Hipana, where the victim has come back to life and can walk by himself. The journey is like a return to the beginning of life, a sanctuary—or sacred place of protection from the death-dealing external world.[7] In the myth of Mawerikuli, the *kuwainyāi* would thus seem to represent this notion of reversible death through proper relations between individuals and the spirit world; spatial position and body posture are likewise important at various moments for understanding the significance of the hero's death.

By contrast, the *eenunai*—represented in actuality as various species of monkeys, sloths, and other animals (the anteater and tapir)—are, in the primordial times, sorcerers, for they have *manhene*, poison, in their hair or fur. In Part I, I cited the myth of the Dzauikuapa, the chief of the animals, whom Iaperikuli attempted, unsuccessfully, to kill. Dzauikuapa is the "owner of poison," *manhene iminali*, who began *hinimai*, omens of death. Ipeku, the night monkey, is his descendant. Also, according to the Kuwai myth, when Kuwai burned in the great conflagration that marked his death, he left poison in This World as poisonous plants and as his fur which "entered" the fur of the black sloth *wamu* today. Thus, the *wamu* is "the shadow of Kuwai."

With these associations, I would suggest that a plausible interpretation of the symbolic significance of *manhene* and hence of the mechanism of sorcery is that it is believed to represent the "vengeance" (*likoada*) of the animals on humans. "Vengeance" for what? For the fact of human consumption of animals with pepper, as food. In return, the animals consume humans with poison. Poisonous fruits, berries, plants—the food of the animals—are hidden in ritual drink by sorcerers. Once consumed, they transform into venomous hair, *manhene*, in the stomachs of human victims producing burning fever, *kapwamina*, and death. This would be, in short, exactly the opposite process of what occurs at initiation rituals, or Kuwaipan, when young boys and girls consume sacralized pepper; for this is the equivalent of the great conflagration in the myth of Kuwai when the being that represents all-animals-in-one is killed by fire. Furthermore, one Hohodene man told me, somewhat enigmatically, that "burning *wamu* hair is a remedy for pepper," which actually makes perfect sense in the set of mythic and ritual associations to which I have been alluding.

The *eenunai* in the myth of Mawerikuli are sorcerers, embodying within themselves menacing powers. They represent animals driven purely by instinct, without thought, or "whose only thought is to kill," with *manhene*. Various myths and orations which have the *eenunai* as central figures refer to the disastrous effects of sorcery or witchcraft which Iaperikuli, in the role of trickster, succeeds in turning back.

In one oration to "turn back" natural disasters—or *chiakali*—the *eenunai* come from downriver dancing in rounds up to Iaperikuli's house, where they intended to kill and eat him. Unknown to them, Iaperikuli accompanies them and secretly prepares a trap for game which, when the *eenunai* dance to its top, explodes in four directions, immediately killing the *eenunai* and dispersing their danger.

Another myth recounts how the *eenunai* attempted to kill Iaperikuli at night, for typically witches seek to attack their victim's dream-souls at night. Iaperikuli, however, knows of their intention and hides an arrow inside his blowgun while setting aside a quiver with two arrows to later trick his wife, who is an *eenunai* sister. He chants over her to make her sleep, and when the *eenunai* come, his dream-soul leaves his body lying by the fire asleep—a strategy that also appears in the myth of Mawerikuli when, to remain immune from the effects of the *eenunai* poison, Iaperikuli drinks the remedy *mathoaia*, which protects his soul, although his body is consumed by poison.

The *eenunai* chief "spits out a stone" to kill Iaperikuli, but the hero blows the hidden arrow, instantly killing the chief. When his wife awakens, she hears the racket of her kin mourning the dead chief. She cries for Iaperikuli to wake up, but he plays dumb and tells her to go see her dead kin. She attempts to light a torch but is only able to after Iaperikuli puts a special treebark in the torchwood. For the place of the *eenunai* is a dark world, like that of the dead.

Finally, she gets to her kin's house and they cry in anger that Iaperikuli had killed their chief. She returns and questions him but he denies the deed, showing her the quiver of two arrows—a trick which narrators mark by saying "it wasn't him, but it *was* him." The *eenunai* then mourn the loss of their chief and wonder how it will be for them, each in its "house" without a single chief. The death of the *eenunai* chief thus leaves the future completely open for the animals.

Here, the *eenunai* have stolen the primal form of poison—*likuru-máhe*, according to Mandu, which is what shamans invoke today in order to enter the world of the dead; or *kaidali*, according to other narrators, which is white sand usually associated with the beaches of Hipana. In one version of this myth told to me by a Oalipere-dakenai elder, the *eenunai* trick Iaperikuli's younger brother, who is called Eri, into giving them the poison which is Iaperikuli's to begin with. Knowing the catastrophe that this would cause, Iaperikuli calls the *kuwain-yái* together to get back the poison. What is implied here is that if the *eenunai* are left to control the power to inflict death, the world would revert to its initial catastrophic situation of near-total destruction, of cannibalistic animals consuming people without end (see Part I, Chapter 1).

So, Iaperikuli summons two of the most powerful symbols of what I am calling reversible death, or transcendence over death, to assist him: the *kuwainyái* and the "aunt," or "grandmother," who would appear to be similar to the "grandmother" figure who nourished Iaperikuli back to life. Both of these figures seem to represent what I would call a return to a condition of vertical transcendence, a sanctuary of nourishment of the soul, and protection from death-dealing catastrophe originating from the outside. The grandmother here chants over a sweet gourd-fruit—*mathoaia*, one of the same fruits invoked in the chants to cure witchcraft victims, consumed when Kuwaikaniri has nearly completed his journey and recovered his soul.

All but Mawerikuli consume the nectar. Now, in Hohodene myths, the figure of the one-who-remains-outside or separate from a group, usually of four members, is quite common, particularly in myths about life passage, in which the separate figure is the one undergoing transition. The transition itself is usually represented as a moment of consuming or not consuming—that is, abstaining from—powerful substances which pertain to the spirit world or have been spiritualized.[8]

One Oalipere-dakenai narrator from Ucuqui specified that the grandmother chanted over the nectar for three brothers, while Maw-erikuli, the youngest—who said he would not go—received no share. The implication of Mawerikuli's not consuming the spiritualized sub-stance is that, in effect, he alienates himself (i.e., becomes "other")—the first sign of his "death," from the sanctuary which is uniquely ca-pable of reverting death. Worse, by later paradoxically going against his own action—an act which narrators did not try to explain—he places himself in a direct relation to the "other" world of the dead and its death-dealing poison. In other words, Mawerikuli acts indi-vidually and impulsively, "without thought," which—like the three children who acted impulsively in the myth of Kuwai—provokes a catastrophe.

The drinking fest lasts through a long, dark night, during which there occurs a total consumption of poison, but precisely because the spiritual remedy enables Iaperikuli to separate his body, consumed by poison (irreversible death), from his soul, above death (reversible), he succeeds in "taking back the poison," which is his objective. At the end of the fest, Iaperikuli returns, as if from the land of the dead, his body filled with poison, as Mandu says, to the point of "losing con-sciousness," or lying down "dead" on the beach midway back. The image, I would suggest, is that of a shaman's return from the house of the souls of the animals, *iaradate*, on the threshold of the living and the dead—physically consumed by poison but spiritually "not dead" as the owl-feather headdress, which responds to the call of the *eenunai*, indicates.

The Owl-Feather Headdress

In Hohodene and Oalipere-dakenai myths, hawks—which include the owl—are powerful representations of deceased beings who have been transformed (e.g., the harpy Kamathawa who is Iaperikuli's younger brother's heart-soul transformed), whose feathers are the source of shamanic powers and the instruments of vengeance. But the owls, like certain other birds who appear at dawn—the toucan, the brown heron—are considered to be *hinimai*, omens of impending death, and are greatly feared.[9] The songs, *kamaikana*, of these birds and of the animal-spirits forewarn of death. These birds and animals form a class of spirits, or *kamainiri*, specifically associated with the deceased.

In real life, the deceased may appear to the living in two forms: after death, as *inyaime*, soul-less bodies or "shadows of the dead," with their own shadows, *danaime*. These may be experienced by the liv-ing—for example, as a whistling in the air, a gust of wind, a light tapping on the shoulder, in deserted places, in the woods or at the edge of a garden. Or, the deceased may appear in animal or bird form, like an image of the dead, whose song is an omen of impending death. The danger of these *kamainiri* is great, for they bring *manhene* and may provoke sicknesses in their relatives; hence every effort is made to avoid them.

The owl-feather headdress of the myth, then, may be understood as an omen of Mawerikuli's impending death. But there are other aspects of the image which narrators pointed out. Keruami called the owl-feather headdress a "hair/fur cloak," *liidzu maka*. The notion of *-maka* refers to an externalized covering—"like a shirt," shamans said—added to an object or person which empowers the wearer to transcend its physical condition. Shamans and their apparel have numerous *-maka*, like outer skins that cover them with a state or quality of being (e.g., there are "happiness"-*maka*, "sickness"-*maka*).

In the myth, then, the image seems to me to be one of a frontier midway between life and death which the *kamainiri*—here, the owl—represent. This frontier is passable by shamans, who for example, in trance, appear to be "dead" but whose heart-souls are "not dead" and travel to the Other World. Similarly, the image in the myth is that of a middle term between "dead" (Iaperikuli's body lying down on the ground) and "not-dead" (the feather headdress responds to the *eenu-nai*'s call and they say "not dead"); a middle term between reversible and irreversible death: Iaperikuli is "not dead" but the owl's cry is an omen of Mawerikuli's impending death; and a middle term that at once separates and relates the living with the dead.

Mawerikuli's Coming-out Festival

When Iaperikuli and the *kuwainyái* return, they immediately consume the life-giving, shamanized substance prepared for them by the grandmother. In the Oalipere-dakenai version I heard, each of them vomits out the poison they had consumed, but Mawerikuli is unable to vomit; hence death remains inside of him. In Mandu's and Keruami's versions, there is no share for Mawerikuli; that is, as a consequence of his impulsive alienation from his kin, he is excluded from the group and "dies." It is at this point that death is brought into society. More precisely, Mawerikuli is isolated from the rest—in a stone enclosure, inside the earth, or in a closed house—but he is still connected to the group by the promise that, on the fourth day of his seclusion, he would "revive," *liafetawa*.

All passages and transitions require separation, seclusion, and closure in order for there to occur a transformation in the quality of being. What is the nature of Mawerikuli's transformation? The stone enclosure, *padápan*, or "grave," *iriri*, is an image of a container—a common form in Hohodene myths—and, as such, an instrument of passage and transformation of life. Here, it would be like the gourd-fruits shamanized by the old woman, for both revert time, revert death, bring back life. In the case of the grave, this temporal reversal is explicit in Mandu's comparison between Mawerikuli's seclusion and the coming-out festival, *limothuitakaruina*, of newly initiated boys.

In initiation rites, boys "die" to their childhood existence and "come out" of ritual seclusion as thinking, fully cultural beings in control of their impulses, integrated into adult social life. But the transformation of Mawerikuli is the reverse: Mandu stated explicitly that he would *rejuvenate*, become young again, "like a *curumi* [young boy]"—that is, the myth *offers a cyclical model of the passage from death to life-after-death.* On the fourth day of his seclusion—note again, the importance of four as the completion of a cycle—Iaperikuli would raise Mawerikuli up to his new, postmortem life, and the cycle would begin again.

But the myth goes beyond a cyclical model and utopian ideal of eternal return, of death-rejuvenation, by introducing irreversibility into the process. One narrator explicitly stated that if it had not been for what follows in the myth, everyone would go through the same process of "death"—seclusion for four days—and rejuvenation. As things turned out, however, it wasn't so: that is, irreversibility enters the cycle. Once again, the agents responsible for this are men and women (i.e., Mawerikuli and an "other" woman) whose "thought-less," impulsive actions prevent the completion of the ideal cycle of eternal return.

The position of women is critical to this episode. As I observed in Part II, women occupy an ambiguous, in-between state in Hohodene narratives. On the one hand, they carry with them the power of new life (for they give new members to their husbands' descent groups), yet on the other, they are on the side of those who potentially seek to cause death in return (the affines; here, the *eenunai*).

This ambiguity is powerfully represented by the woman's painting of Mawerikuli. In real life-passage rites, women do indeed paint men with red dye, or *kerawidzu* (*caraiurú*, in *língua geral*). This includes the recently deceased who, in the past, were painted entirely red shortly after their deaths. In initiation rites, also, an exchange relation called *kamaratakan* is formed between boys in the final stages of seclusion and girls who paint their partners with *caraiurú*, in exchange for which the girls receive woven baskets and other artwork produced by the boys for their coming-out festival. The Hohodene say it is "like a marriage" although there is no implication of betrothal. The *kamaratakan* relation may occur in other exchange rituals, such as the *pudali*, and involves an array of behavior ranging from joking and sexual relations to mutual weeping for dead kin. I suggest that it is this relation which is being represented at this point in the myth.[10]

Caraiurú has a range of meanings in relation to ritual but principally that of "becoming other" and new. Shamans, for example, invariably paint themselves and their objects in curing rituals with *caraiurú*. They say it is like a "cloak," *maka*, which makes them appear as jaguars. The newly initiated are painted red for their coming-out festival and are said to be like "wildcats," *walidza*; at least one narrator of the Mawerikuli myth stated that the *walidza* is Mawerikuli's "shadow," *idanam*, thus confirming the link that Mandu made between Mawerikuli's coming-out festival and initiation rites.

But Mandu clarified here that *caraiurú* has the sense of "blood" and that the painting of Mawerikuli is to make him "beautiful," consistent with his rejuvenation, his new life which it is the power of women to give. In this, there is, I suspect, a connection between the *caraiurú* "blood" and the danger of "seeing the dead" which may be the critical point where irreversibility is introduced.

For the Hohodene, blood has various associations with temporality and life cycles which I shall attempt to clarify. Shamans say, for example, that their sacred powder, *pariká*, is the "blood of Kuwai," for, by inhaling it, the shaman "dies," becomes "other," and returns to the Other World of the primordium. In curing rituals, the shaman puts the red powder in the palm of his hand, then passes the hollowed-out *pariká*-bone over it, and blows the powder with force into the nostril of his partner shaman. This "blood of Kuwai" is, in short, a vehicle of cyclical time—or better, a vehicle for the transcendence of time, linking the primordial and the present worlds, ancestors and descendants.

It is clear in Mandu's narration that the dead cannot be seen, and I would imagine this is because seclusion and invisibility are necessary to complete the cyclical transformation of anyone undergoing passage. Why, then, does the woman insist on seeing the dead? And why, when she paints Mawerikuli, on the final stroke of *caraiurú*, does she turn over her hand and he fall, nothing but bones? The explanation, I believe, has to do once again with the symbolic position of women in Hohodene myths, for they are invariably linked to the spirit world, especially the spirits of nature: the *eenunai*, the *umawalinai* (aquatic spirits), the Kuwainai (sacred flutes and trumpets which the women stole), and even with *inyaime*, the shadows of the dead.[11]

In short, women, it would seem, "see" the "other" side constantly. Following C. Hugh-Jones' analysis (1979, Chapter 5) of cycles of male and female temporality among the Barasana, I suggest that, beyond women's intermediary social status, it is the short cycle of female fertility that is here opposed to the long cycle of patrilineal descent and the reversibility of time. For that reason, Hohodene shamans explicitly say that contact with menstruating women causes a "sickness of their [the shamans'] blood." That is, female menstruation—and more generally, female sexuality as I have mentioned in Part I—is opposed to the reversible temporality that the shaman represents, and may cut it short.

In the myth of Mawerikuli, then, an "other" woman opens the door and sees the dead before the appointed time, that is, before the completion of a cycle of four days (the number four may refer, I would suggest, to a four-generation cycle of patrilineal descent). I suggest that, by this, she breaks the cycle of eternal return. Mandu, a shaman, has her say, "You will kill me," for Mawerikuli had only partially revived as indicated by his body posture—sitting up. She paints him but, on the final stroke of *caraiurú*, she turns over her hand, as Mandu said, "just a little." Now, the other side of her hand is, as one narrator explained, "the side of *inyaime*," that is, the shadow of death. In other narrators' versions, Mawerikuli attempts to have sex with the woman, causing the disaster, for "he had *manhene* and couldn't have sex with her"—thus relating this event of the myth to real-life experience. In short, I suggest that it is the overdetermination of "otherness" that provokes the catastrophe, the final collapse, introducing irreversibility into the cycle of life.

Mawerikuli falls, a heap of bones, and his body simply disappears. Certainly this image reflects physical decomposition of a corpse, but what is more important to narrators is the falling of the bones and total collapse of the cyclical model with its possibility of rejuvenating ascension. It is interesting that the sound that narrators use to indicate the falling of Mawerikuli's bones to the ground (*"khyelulululululu . . . "*) is the same (perhaps with somewhat less force) as the sound of the falling of the pieces of Kuwai's giant *paxiuba* tree, connecting earth and sky, after Iaperikuli has it cut into determined pieces. While the falling of Kuwai's *paxiuba*, however, is the materialized representation of the life-giving collective ancestral soul in This World for all times, the falling of Mawerikuli's bones represents the materialized reproduction of irreversible death in the world for all times.

In this, the two elements of the person—material and spiritual—are incorporated into the two extremes of time: the end and the beginning of the cosmos. The bones in Wapinakwa continue their existence in permanent, horizontal stasis; in "another end of the world," the beings of Wapinakwa will arise. The spiritual elements of the person are, as I will show in the following chapter, incorporated into the world of the beginning, the beginning of cosmic time, but return to This World in the form of ancestral names, the spiritual umbilical cord that all newborns receive, and the music of the sacred flutes and trumpets that creates new life. This can be represented as shown in Figure 7.

Iaperikuli attempts to remake a person, "putting together" Mawerikuli's bones, but having "died" three times, there is no other way of reverting time. The final dialogue, as spoken by Mandu, between Mawerikuli and Iaperikuli illustrates this well:

> M.: "Now, my brother, I cannot stay any longer. So, leave it like so for me. I go and will wait for you there.
> I.: "No, I don't want it to be so. It's bad for us. Now everything will be bad for people after us." He tried again three times to remake Mawerikuli.
> M.: "My brother, leave it like so for me. I will stay this way. I don't die, my body stays in This World. My soul, I was here, I am waiting for you there.
> I.: "So it will be for all people, for our others who will be born."

The myth of Mawerikuli goes far beyond an explanation of how death entered the world for human beings; its implications are of cosmic proportions, for

(1) Mawerikuli leaves death, misfortune, and evil in the world "for those unborn," for all time. This event signifies the end of the time when the dead could be brought back to life, rejuvenated. All processes by which death entered the world are then left for descendants, the tragic result of the "thoughtless" actions of the primordials who created *maatchíkwe*, the place of evil, to be reproduced until "another end of the world."

(2) Mawerikuli's third death, the falling of his bones, is an image of cosmic collapse, for it not only created Wapinakwa, it signified the possibility of imminent collective death. In the shamans' understanding, this "end of the world" is represented by the rupture in the bone structure which connects lower with upper layers of the cosmos. To revert such a disaster, shamans "mend bones in the sky," re-creating the vertical connection which sustains life (see "Cosmic Death" in the following chapter). Their action may thus revert the disjunction of time and space caused by the primordials.

(3) Historical messiahs among the Baniwa have been those shamans who transcend irreversible time. They "do not die,"

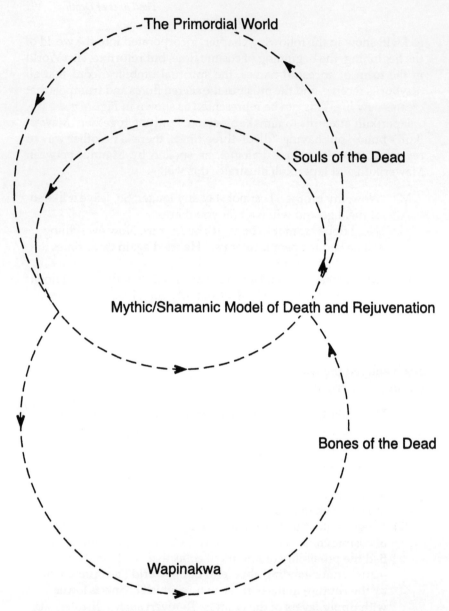

The Primordial World

Souls of the Dead

Mythic/Shamanic Model of Death and Rejuvenation

Bones of the Dead

Wapinakwa

Figure 7. Cycles of Time at Death

for after their physical passage, it is said, they rejuvenate, as Iaperikuli had initially planned for Mawerikuli and everyone else. For example, it is said of the prophet Kudui of the upper Aiary that, after he was buried, his soul reunited with his body beneath the earth and that "his thought is still alive," watching over everyone, counseling those who come to seek his aid.

6. Spiritualities of Death and Birth

Introduction

In this chapter, I will examine in greater detail some of the themes discussed in my interpretation of the myth of Mawerikuli in the contexts of ritual actions and cosmic processes associated with death. It is principally in orations and chants spoken or sung at the moment of, or following, death that we discover the concerns of the living in relation to the dead, what happens to the component elements of the person during his or her journey to the Beyond, and the nature of postmortem existence.

"Death," Sullivan has written in relation to South American funeral rites and beliefs, "when appraised through the symbolic acts, emotions and beliefs attendant upon it, becomes a drama of human life, revealing in an extravagant way the nature of the sacred and the meaning of symbolic life itself" (1988, 488). It is in the language of the orations and chants principally that I suggest we may find these meanings, for the terminology of the end—that is, the "set of signs capable of signifying an appropriate closure to meanings revealed as nearly infinite in number throughout the course of existence" (468)—tests language and its capacity to "reveal and communicate primordial meanings" (469). It is those meanings I seek to elucidate here and their relation to millenarian consciousness, the central theme of this book.

In the first instance, all efforts of the living are directed at repelling the signs of death—above all their songs, *kamaikana*, and omens, *hinimai*—for the two elements of sound and temporality are fundamental to the definition of cosmic order and its reproduction. An omen of death, as I suggested in my interpretation of the myth, is a moment in which the frontier that separates life from death erupts onto the scene, creating an ambivalent situation, in-between past and future. It is the moment in which the animal-spirits, through their images, seek the death of humans "in return." Thus, the act of repelling the signs of death seeks to negate all value attributed to the relation of exchange between animal-spirits and humans.

In the second instance, in the "way of the dead" itself, the elements which make up the person are separated, distributed, and integrated to diverse levels of the vertical cosmos. The bodily elements that endure to the world below, Wapinakwa; the spiritual elements (the heart-soul, *ikaale*; the spiritual umbilical cord, *hliepuhle*; and the eye-soul, *likaalethi*) to the worlds above, passing through a series of separations and transformations until reaching the end of their way.

Each one of these elements is integrated to a modality of cosmic time and a determined finality of eternal existence: the bones in permanent horizontal stasis until "another end of the world"; the heart-soul, spiritual umbilical cord, and eye-soul in the primordial past which nevertheless maintains continuous relations with the living through life-passage rituals, the souls of the dead who "wait for" their kin, and the phratric identities that recycle through naming rites.

The existence of the dead in the Other World is not, as at times has been described, an eternal festival of abundance consuming the purest of honey—at least for the Hohodene. The orations reveal, to the contrary, that the souls of the dead at the end of their journey are enclosed, fenced off, and hidden from sight. In their "houses" they are put to performing eternally repetitive activities—images of their total alienation from the living, their alterity. These images, nevertheless, are consistent with the nature of the primordial world: eternally repetitive and hidden from sight, accessible only to shamans.

But the houses of the dead exist on the periphery of the same level of the cosmos as Kuwai, who stays in the center of the Other World. Consistent with the relation that exists between center and periphery in the world of the living, the alienated and repetitive periphery of the dead highlights the symbolic values of the center: intrinsically ambivalent values, between the enormous cosmic creativity which is the music of Kuwai and the deathly destructiveness that is his sickness and poison.

Kuwai is thus the link between the dead and "those unborn" through the spiritual umbilical cord, *hliepuhlepi* Kuwai, that returns to Kuwai after death, that takes the shaman into the Other World, and that is the first element comprising the newborn, connecting the child to the source of creation. The orations and chants that I shall mention reveal that the "way of the newborn" is the mirror image of the "way of the dead." Both ways are thought of as extremely dangerous journeys: at birth, classes of spirits of nature seek to prevent the entry of the child into life as, at death, classes of spirits of nature call the living to the Other World.

Finally, there is a notion of "cosmic death" or cosmic collapse in certain shamans' songs that I shall cite which refer directly to the myth of Mawerikuli and that relate death to eschatology.

Songs of Death

At Mawerikuli's death, it is said, the bird-spirits and animal-spirits came to mourn, and as he lay in the enclosure, they wept. The spirits wept until they became weak and silent; then they interred Mawerikuli's body.

Keramunhe of Ucuqui explained this story and accompanying orations and chants spoken and sung after an actual burial, in the following way:

> The *kamainiri* [spirits of the recently deceased] oration . . .
> Behold then this Mawerikuli.
> The animals *waki, itchi,* and *dzathe*—three of them cried,
> They were crying a lot it seems.
> They put him in the coffin, they made him lie down, and they
>   cried.
> Throughout the night they wept,
> Throughout the night they wept.
> *Waki* became sad and weak.
> This *itchi* likewise,
> *Dzathe* likewise.
> Then they interred Mawerikuli,
> Dead.
> Then, there was this chestnut, *kuwaida.*
> They were thinking, remembering, silent and sad.
> He threw a chestnut—*tih!*
> He saw it twirl around and around *daahlihlihlihlihlihli . . . tih!*
> It came back
> "You try it"
> He tried—*"he he he he he,"* he is laughing.
> He threw the chestnut, saw it twirl, went to look at it and laughed.
> They came back revived—it brought back their hearts, it brought
>   back their hearts, away from the *kamainiri.*
> They bring back their hearts.
> Their hearts he brings back, those *kuwainyāi.*
>   . . . .
> Their hearts he brings back
> We say, our hearts we have seen the dead *kamainiri,* they say,
> I bring back our hearts from the *kamainiri.*

Thus they bring back their hearts, those *kuwainyāi* away from the
  kamainiri, they say.
That's all,
They chant over pepper pot, *xibé* [manioc cereal and water], they
  chant well, that's all.

Keruami of Uapui added that there is also a "weeping song," *paid-
zaka*, sung at burials in order to "repel" the songs of the recently deceased, recalling when the *eenunai* came to weep for the dead Kuwai-
kaniri/Mawerikuli. The song, however, also refers to the weeping of
the Dzauikuapa, the *eenunai* chief whom Iaperikuli failed to kill. In
short, all of the primordial deaths, the spirits of the dead, *kamainiri*,
and their songs, *kamaikana*, are invoked in this song and "repelled" so
as not to affect the living. A portion of the song goes as follows:

Lidzashuna bda kamainiri
[The weeping of the spirits of the dead]
Lidzashuna bda kamainiri
[The weeping of the spirits of the dead]
Lidzashuna bda Kuwaikaniri
[The weeping of Kuwaikaniri]
Lidzashuna bda
[The weeping]
Ikatsa neramaita eenunai-ia
[Behold the red *guariba*]
neramaita bda eenunai-ia
[the red *guariba*]
Nuaneta waadzawa likamaikana bda, idzashuna bda kamainiri
[I push away from us its song, the weeping of the *kamainiri*]
Pie kono dehre piaka, lidamapale inakemi
[You, I call you, the agouti]
Lidzashuna bda Kuwaikaniri
[The weeping of Kuwaikaniri]
Nuaneta likamaikana waadzawa, lidzashuna bda kamainiri
[I push away its song from us, the weeping of the *kamainiri*.
. . .

The song goes on to name various other *eenunai*, all of them *kamainiri*, whose songs, *kamaikana*, the chanter seeks to expel, get rid of, so
that they do no harm to the living, especially children.
  From these two excerpts, we gather that death is the dangerous
presence of the spirits of the deceased in the world of humans; hence
humans seek to repel their songs and, at the same time, "return the

heart-souls" of those who mourn from their approximation to the spirits of the dead. Specifically, this means reviving the souls of the living, turning their grief and silence into joy and laughter (as, for example, in the somersaults of the youths and children in the rapids at Uapui after Seraphim's burial). It means repelling the smell of the deceased, *hliewekana*, which may enter the respiration of the survivors, and it means tranquilizing the deceased's survivors. Above all, it means avoiding and repelling omens which the deceased may send to the living. If, for example, in interring the dead, earth falls in the deceased's eyes, the deceased may send an omen, in the form of a song, which affects children. Hence the earth, which can only be of two kinds (yellow and white), is carefully prepared before being thrown into the grave. Excerpting a piece from Keruaminali's rendition of this oration:

> For I push away the song of the deceased
> Away from them, our children
> Never does earth fall in their eyes
> The earth, thus they throw it in the grave.
> I will throw it, I push away this white earth
> I push away its song from them
> I push away the yellow earth from them
> . . . .
> They say as they orate over the earth . . .

The signs or omens of the spirits of the dead are numerous. Laureano, of Ucuqui Cachoeira, once told me of a personal experience with an omen which forced him to seek out a shaman for help and also to learn orations to protect himself against these *hinimai*. One day he was walking in the forest and heard a distant whistling; he thought of his deceased brother, and he called out to where the whistling came from. A wind came, and Laureano became afraid. He later asked the shaman Kudui to speak an oration for him, and after Kudui had done so, he told Laureano that he wouldn't get *manhene*. The *kamainiri* are numerous, Laureano said, and may be found in various parts of the woods or old gardens where there are no people. *Danaime*, shades of the dead, are one form of them, while animal omens are another.

The oration that Laureano learned to drive away these omens reveals the nature of the spirits' relation to the living. In it, the *kamainiri* include various bird-spirits (metaphorically called "night children") such as the owls, toucans, and brown herons; the animal-spirits (especially Ipeku, the chief of the *eenunai*); the parrot-spirits and *japú*; the wildcat; and a series of spirits of woven baskets, manioc squeezers, and ceremonial ornaments, such as animal-fur elbow ornaments, feather headdresses, and the dance leader's headdress.[1]

Each of the bird- and animal-spirits can be understood through the corpus of myths related to death, the vestiges of death, and the transformations that occur at death. Somewhat more obscure is the significance of woven baskets and ceremonial ornaments. One suggestion I would make is that these are representations of cultural creations, of humans as creators of culture. Woven baskets are exchanged or given as presents when, for example, initiates come out of seclusion. In various myths, baskets and manioc squeezers are receptacles for the remains of the dead or deadly substances. Headdresses and other ceremonial ornaments are what represent fully cultural beings, the dance leader's headdress being the supreme representation of the art of ceremonial song.

The orator "blows away," *lipia*, these signs of death with the powerful breath of the tobacco-spirits. He "throws them away," *kaduichi pa*, to the east, the end of the world, "where the rivers no longer run," *uni diákahle*. Above all, the orator seeks to *negate the value of the exchange relation* between the *kamainiri* and the living—*makuameka*, no return, no exchange. The (apparently ceremonial) exchange referred to is, I would suggest, *the constant search for return vengeance by the animal-spirits against humans*. The orator thus also protects himself from their omens by "leaving for his body and soul" various animals and predatory birds who repel the *kamainiri*.

Protection from the songs of the dead extends to the food consumed by the mourners. Koch-Grünberg (1967, 1:165–166) mentions that during the period of mourning seclusion (ten days, he says), the souls of the dead remain on earth. During this time, their survivors must fast and empty out all ceramic water pots. At the end of the seclusion, chanters sing a lengthy set of *kalidzamai* chants—as Keramunhe said also—which "repel the songs of the dead," preventing the "manioc-spirits" from harming the living; that is, the chants make safe the first foods, pepper and manioc, consumed by the mourners.

The negation of an exchange relation to the spirits of the dead was also present in ritual treatment of enemies killed in war. According to Hohodene oral histories, decapitation of dead enemies served as a precaution against the omens produced by the gaze of the dead enemy. In the instances when enemies were eaten, chants were sung to avoid vengeance, or the "return" death that the spirits of dead enemies, *inyaime*, could bring. In these chants, the intent is to neutralize the return, *makuada*, associated with the act of eating the enemy (Journet

1995; Wright 1990). The heart-souls of the killers, in this case, were said to be "filled with joy," *huiwi nakaale*, in eating their enemy, in contrast with the heart-souls of those who mourn their dead kin, killed by an enemy, which must be revived, returned to laughter and joy.

If the concern with the recently deceased centers so much on their song, what is the relation of this song to the music of the ancestral flutes and trumpets, Kuwai? The songs of the dead are merely the sounds of death and, as such, they both evoke the primordial past and presage one's own future. Hence they are *hinimai*, omens. In the myth of the beginning of *hinimai* (see Chapter 1), Ipeku, the chief of the *eenunai*, escapes catastrophic death, but his song is a constant reminder of Iaperikuli's failure to kill the "poison owner," who may provoke catastrophic death through consumption by poison. The sounds of the *kamainiri*—the fearsome cry of the hawk and owl, the nonsense chatter and babbling of the parrots, the dreadful calling of the spirits of Wapinakwa—are, like the sound of the falling of Mawerikuli's bones in a heap, the soul-less, symbolically reduced, and alienated remains of life. As such, they contrast fully with the powerful, totalizing, world-opening songs and ceremonial dialogues of Kuwai. What produces this are two elements of life which constitute the person: *ikaale*, heart-soul, and *hliepuhle*, ancestral umbilical cord.

Distribution of the Person in the Cosmos

According to Koch-Grünberg, the spirit of the deceased remains for two days by its grave and then migrates to the "houses of the dead," that is, to ancestral places located in the traditional territories of the phratries (Heemápan, for the Oalipere-dakenai, located on the Paumary stream, mid-Içana; Putúpan, for the Hohodene, located on the upper Aiary). These places, according to Koch-Grünberg, were described as having "many people, large plantations, much game and fish," and "when a new spirit comes, it is greeted, painted, and finds in its honor a large dance festival with *caxiri*" (1967, 166). From what the Hohodene told me, the destiny of the deceased is considerably more complex, and to guide this discussion, the diagram in Figure 8 represents how I understand the process of distribution of components of the person in the cosmos.

Death is the final separation of the spiritual elements of the person from the material body. Unlike the moments in a person's lifetime when his or her heart-soul may get lost or stuck in the spirit world— moments of sickness or "unconsciousness"—death is the irreversible transmigration of these components and their assimilation into the

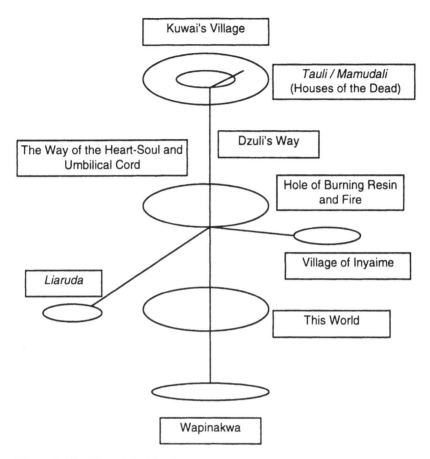

Figure 8. The Way of the Dead

spaces of the dead in diverse planes of the cosmos. This process is represented in terms of a series of radical separations.

Body and bones are put down in the earth, in the hole of interment, where they follow their "way," *iapoa*, *down* to Wapinakwa, Place of Our Bones. The heart-soul, *ikaale*, and spiritual umbilical cord, *hlie-puhle*, leave the body together at the last breath along with the eye-soul *likaalethi* and follow their "way" *up* to the sky worlds and the "houses of the dead"—sometimes referred to as *mamudali*, sometimes as *tauli*—on the periphery of the same plane of the cosmos as Kuwai. The "houses of the dead" in the Other World have equivalents in the localized, *earthly* ancestral "houses of the dead" or *liaruda*, which pertain to each phratry (Heemápan, Putúpan). Thus, the elements of the person are assimilated into the three principal levels of the cosmos: below, This World, and above.

A brief word of explanation on two of the principal spiritual elements which go up: *Ikaale* is the human body-shaped heart-soul which an individual acquires shortly after birth. Its center is the heart which radiates life-energy, or breath, to all points of the body and is the source of passions, action, health, and well-being. *Hliepuhle* is the individual's connection to the collective, ancestral soul, or Kuwai, visibly represented in the navel or umbilical cord. One of the critical elements in the formation of a person at the beginning of life, the *hliepuhle* is also the individual's spiritual connection to the collective, patrilineal ancestral soul which unites all individuals to a common source.

The umbilical cord of Kuwai is represented in material form as the *paxiuba* palm, used in the making of sacred flutes and trumpets to initiate children. This tree, in primordial times, was the vertical connection between earth and sky which shot out of the earth where Kuwai was burned in Hipana, the center of the world. The shape of this palm tree today suggests connectedness, for its multiple, aerial roots evoke the multiple connections of humans to the one, single, vertical source. All people are believed to be connected to the central "umbilical cord" at Hipana, which is at once the place of emergence of all the ancestors, and the spiritual connection to the "umbilical-cord-place-sky," *hliepuhlekwapi eenu*, of Kuwai.

Three other separations at death may be detected in shamanic discourse; these occur on the soul's "way" and appear to represent a progressive deconstruction of the individual and social identity of the person. The first is at a place shamans call the "river mouth," *uni numana*, a place—possibly in Wapinakwa—where the canoes of the souls of the dead come together and where the shaman, as guide, makes them "leave their families behind." The shaman, seated above them, alone, commands a wind to push the canoes on their way up, blowing tobacco smoke over the souls in order to "make them beautiful" and "make them forget their families" ("family" here seems to signify local descent group). It is thus we may understand more fully Seraphim's death as indeed a canoe journey in which his son, the shaman Mandu, was acting as guide.

The second separation is at a fork in the way—again, a place where Mandu warned his dying father of a trap, a fence called *inyaime kurara*—where one trail leads off to the side, down to the village of Inyaime, which, some say, is a place of intense heat and thirst. *Inyaime*, as I have said, is the soul-less human body shape of the deceased, a cadaver that wanders in This World giving sickness to humans. It is a "shadow of Kuwai" (for Kuwai also has his "shadow of death"). As such, *inyaime* manifests itself as destructive, malevolent, and cannibalistic, like the *kamainiri* spirits.

On the other trail, souls continue up until they come to the place where the third separation occurs: the "holes of burning resin, *mainia*, and fire, *mirawaka*," where they "cast off their [bodies]," *lipekuka linewikika*—referring, I believe, to the human body shape of their souls, *ikaale*. It is interesting to note here the symmetry between the "way" down to Wapinakwa, where the body is cast into a "hole" in the earth and where a river of cold water runs, and the "way" up to the Other World, Apakwa Hekwapi, where souls are washed in "holes" of fire and cast off their bodies' shapes. Purified, gleaming white (i.e., substanceless) and formless, the souls finally reach their houses on the outer rim of Kuwai's village where they are to stay.

The bodies which souls "cast off" may include ancestral names and all protective spirit-names of tobacco and pepper associated with the individual's phratric identity. As I have suggested, I believe that this identity is assimilated to the phratry's ancestral houses, *liaruda*, located at diverse points in Baniwa territory.

The way of the dead consists, then, of a progressive disintegration of the person marked by a series of qualitative and moral changes, and a reintegration of the person's components to the three principal levels of the cosmos. Each element consequently becomes part of the temporality implicit in each level. In short, the person is integrated fully, spatially and temporally, into the cosmos and cosmic processes.

Life in the Land of the Dead

In order to send the souls of the dead to their final places in *tauli* or *mamudali*, the Hohodene, according to Keruami, speak the following oration:

> I speak to open its way,
> Dzuli's way.
> It goes into the sky,
> Dzuli's way.
> I open and turn away its face, its sickness.
> There! To where the dead stay.
> I push away its face from us.
> Do not turn around and look at us,
> You, dead one,
> You, you person of this story,
> You, shade of the dead
> Turn your face away from us,

There! To where you stay.
Then,
Then I will raise after you Dzuli's way.
I will make
Dzuli's *paxiuba*
It goes up . . . There, Dzuli's way.
It goes up, his coco palm goes up . . . there, its shadow.
It goes up, his thorny grass goes up . . . there, its shadow.
Do not turn around and look at us there.
In the Vulture's house.
I will put in your hands there,
I will make you
Write on paper there.
You sit in the coffin,
I turn away your face there.
Do not look at us.
I separate you from the living.
Thus I make you go from us, you shade of the dead, woman of the story,
Shade, she the woman.
Man of the story.
I turn away your face from us.
Vulture's house
From them, they, your descendants.
Do not turn around and look at us.
There, you have gone from us.

Following Sullivan's idea that descriptions of the land of the dead evoke "latent but everlasting sources of symbolic existence: alienation, hiddenness and irreversible closure" (1988, 541), we may understand the images created in this oration. The way called "Dzuli's way," Dzuli-apo, is opened for the soul to ascend. The "way" refers specifically, according to the narrator, to a *paxiuba* palm called *mawi*, which is another important symbolic use of the *paxiuba* complementary to the world-opening, soul-giving *paxiuba* of Kuwai. Dzuli-apo, as I shall suggest in the following section, would also be the opposite of the "way" of the newborn, or *keramu iapoawa*, through the birth canal—in the sense that death is the opposite of life—which is a descent that must be opened by chanters with the aid of vine remedies and invocation of a ceremonial cigar holder. Dzuli, or Dzulíferi, as I have said, is the patron of shamans and perhaps the most important symbol of soul-transformation. He is said to live on the same level of the cosmos as Kuwai, and in shamanic discourse, he is a transformation of Kuwai.

His way, then, is the final passage of the souls of the dead to their houses up through the center of the sky and off to the periphery of Kuwai's village.

The final passage is a process of alienation in several senses: "turning away the face" and the "gaze" of the dead from the living, as these may cause sickness to the living; irreversibly enclosing the dead by "raising the way," "fencing off" the enclosure with thatch and thorns; "turning away the face" within the enclosure; and finally—an image of total alienation of memory of the living—putting something such as paper or, another narrator said, a light fruit, in the deceased's hands in order "not to remember anymore."

Why these images, and what do they have in common? Far from being a life of eternal feasting and dancing, or of sunlight and plenty, life in the land of the dead is *one of eternal repetition and of meaningless activity in relation to living cultural production*. With paper in their hands, reading and writing (*idana*, making shadows; *papera*, paper) are images consistent with the *total alterity of the dead*, for the essence of life is oral communication, ceremonial dialogue, and the transmission of culture from ancestors to descendants accomplished by music, the "song," *likaako*, of the collective ancestral soul in ritual.

Another narrator said that the deceased sits with his elbows stuck with gum on a table forever tossing in his hands a light fruit—*maru-dadali*, which is "a kind of *manhene*" for humans—back and forth. Immobilized, eternally at play—versus the "work" of cultural production—with no memory, the dead are reduced to a minimal and harmless condition. Yet they are not totally dead, for in contrast to the body and bones which lie down in permanent horizontal stasis in Wapinakwa, the soul sits up—a position indicating partial revival, a sign that the dead continue their existence, however alienated from the living, "waiting for" their kin to join them.

Birth: Escaping from Death into Life

It would be impossible to speak of the symbolic processes which the Hohodene believe take place at birth without reference to Kuwai, since his conception and birth serve as the mythic explanations for the formation of newborn, *keramu*, today. It is tempting to see in this some sort of "return" of elements of the souls of the dead—*ikaale, hliepuhle*, in particular—to the living. That is, in conception, pregnancy, birth, or naming, there is some sort of reactivation of these elements. Yet, by looking briefly at the orations and chants spoken or sung at these times, I find the process is somewhat more complex. Most of these describe a veritable struggle for a newborn child to enter life, as though primordial spirits—the same which provoke death—seek to prevent childbirth and human reproduction.

Given the length of the chants and orations to which I will refer, I will only provide synopses of those of which various Hohodene specialists informed me:

- *Eenunai* or *itchirinai iakuna*: The *eenunai* or animal-spirits "tie up" the mother's abdomen, producing an intense, "biting" pain. Chanters seek to "break the knots," "loosen" their grip so that birth can take place. These chants are sung in an intense, rapid monotone, each of the more than twenty sets naming (the word *iakuna* means "names") a particular *eenunai* and in sequence. A number of the *eenunai* are explicitly invoked as those who wept at Mawerikuli's death.
- *Iraidalimi iakuna*: A form of witchcraft, *hiwiathi*, which "ties up" the mother's abdomen, "bites" inside, and produces internal bleeding and abortion. It is said that often at Kuwaipan, initiation rituals, witches perform these chants to prevent women from having children. To counteract them, chanters "break" and "throw away" a series of spirit-names associated with the vertical axis of the cosmos, the majority having to do with Kuwai.
- *Madzeekata keramu*: A class of plant-spirits that "bite and cause pain," called *kapíferi*, prevent an infant from being born. Principal among these is the spirit of the *tucum* palm, called *dzaui kumale*, the thorny bark of which is said to "pull the child up," preventing its head from coming out. Specifically, Kuwai, who is the spiritual "owner" of this Tucumá, is said to "close the way" for the child, "like a door that won't open," causing its death if no action is taken.

  Even more specifically, it is Kuwai's umbilical cord, the flutes and trumpets, which "tie up" the way: the bark wrapping and vines which form the outer covering of the flutes have to be "cut" and "loosened" for the child's way to be opened. (The vines themselves may well refer, in reality, to the child's umbilical cord.) The chanters invoke piranha to cut open the way; various fish and rodents with smooth skin to make the passage smooth; sweet *cucura* fruit and the "sweet body" of the piranha to "sweeten the way." In some versions, chanters invoke Iaperikuli's ceremonial cigar-holder, *dthemaapo* (the same instrument that Iaperikuli used to "open the way" for the first ancestors to emerge from the holes of the earth at Hipana) to open the way for the child to come out;

- *Awakarunanai*: Birth generally takes place in the forest, and the predominant concern is to prevent the "gaze" of the forest-spirits, *awakarunanai*, and water-spirits, *umawalinai*, from "giving fever" and killing the newborn. Mother and infant return to the house where a chanter sweetens the earth and hammock. Following a week of seclusion and restriction in diet, mother and infant bathe in the river. The chanter performs pepper-chants, *kalidzamai*, which makes food safe for the natal family to eat. Part of the sacralized pepper is thrown into the river where the mother and infant bathe, to "turn away" the water-spirits. All spirits that might affect the mother are "sent below" to Wapinakwa.
- *Kewakamalinai*: This refers to a class of water and fish spirits which are believed to "enter the bodies" especially of the newborn and its father, "taking out their bones," causing the physical symptoms of weakness and swelling. These spirits appear when, for example, the father goes into the forest, or canoes on the river. The chanter sends them away—up to the sky—at the same time hiding the bodies of the infant and its father from their gazes.
- *Kalidzamai*: These are pepper chants which neutralize the effects of the spirits of the water, forest, and air—from whence food is obtained. *Kalidzamai* for postpartum seclusion are lengthy, sung chants in which all edible species are named and properly "cooked" so that they may then be safely eaten. The most elaborate of the spirit categories included in these chants are the fish, *uleiyãinai*, and water-spirits, but the complete set of chants also includes bird-spirits and animal-spirits (see Wright 1993, 1993–1994 for more on these chants among the Hohodene; and Hill [1989] 1993, for a book-length treatment of this genre of sung narrative among the Wakuenai of Venezuela).
- Procuring a name for a child, in which the chanter recreates the moment of Iaperikuli's looking for the ancestor-spirits at Hipana, and the first Hohodene who were real human beings at the forest rapids of Hwaipan. Tobacco-spirits and the ceremonial cigar holder seek the child's soul/name from the "Center-Place-Sky" at Hipana. The names of the first phratry ancestors are invoked to bestow a name on the child.

The sequence of actions in this entire set of chants and orations may be seen to establish a cluster of thematic movements which center on the birth of children *as an escape from death into life*. In terms of spatial representations, this sequence defines a movement from the periphery to the center (the opposite of the movement of the soul at death); the creation of protective sanctuaries, where the elements comprising the newborn may become fixed; a gradual movement back outward, as the natal family re-integrates into normal life; and finally, an integration, through the sacred center, to the collective, ancestral soul of the phratry, through naming.

In this process, I do not believe there is any sense in which the souls of the dead "return" as in reincarnation. Rather, there is a strong sense of a passage which in many respects is the mirror image of the passage at death. *Both indeed are perilous spiritual journeys or "ways."* Death is a progressive alienation from the living, an absorption into an alien, spiritualized nature; a descent and integration of the material remains to the inverted, predatory underworld; an ascent and/or integration of elements of the soul into the undifferentiated, patrilineal ancestral soul, and a final enclosure of the heart-soul into the eternally repetitive world of the dead. If there is a sense in which we may speak of a return of the souls to life at birth, it is in the form of the souls of the first ancestors, the primal sun, Iaperikuli. At initiation, the collective ancestral soul, Kuwai, completes the construction of the person by turning children into fully cultural beings, reproducers of new generations.

Cosmic Death

As I have discussed throughout this book, Hohodene mythology is marked by a series of images of catastrophic destruction and regeneration of the world. Many of these images have to do with the collective deaths of people, spirit beings, animals, or primordial beings in cataclysmic events. The most compelling of these images—e.g., the devouring of the Duemieni, the devouring of the animals, consumption by poison, etc.—mark separations, ruptures between states "before" and "after" these cataclysmic events, which have disastrous consequences until they are reconstructed in some way: the bone of the Duemieni is recovered and Iaperikuli emerges to remake the world, for example.

Now, one of the powers of the shamans, I was informed, is to "mend bones in the sky." Initially, I thought this might refer to something similar to bone-setting, but I think a more plausible interpretation can be given in terms of the millenarian consciousness which has occupied our attention. For bones, it should be clear by now, are essential to the foundations of the cosmos. Hence the image of a "broken bone" could, I suggest, refer to cosmic collapse. Mending the bone, like the shaman's spiritual healing of the world (see Chapter 2) would then signify restoring unity. As Mandu explained to me when he sang his version of this song—and this, in my view, is a very clear statement of the importance of this song to millenarian eschatology:

> He [the shaman] mends bones in the sky for the world to become beautiful. He cannot let the world fall. When people say This World will end, the shaman looks and says, "No, This World will not end." When the bone is fixed, people become happy. If the shaman doesn't fix it, people will die.

Below, I transcribe my translation of this song as Mandu composed it, seeking to maintain his style as closely as possible:

> *Heeeeey, Yaaaaaaiii,*
> Where will it be, he comes back and walks amongst us,
> Our Transformation Place,
> His Transformation Place,
> Father Dzulíferi.
> Behold he looks for,
> He looks for his bones,
> His bones,
> Mawerikuli.
> Behold he comes back,
> He looks for and sees,
> His body,
> His body, his body,
> Mawerikuli.
> Where will it be,
> His bones, the thoughtless-one.
> For it will be, he looks for,
> He will look for and sees,
> He sees,
> The Eternal Master.
> Thus as it was,
> It began for him,
> The Eternal Master.
> Thus as it was, it began for him,
> The Eternal Master.
> Behold he looked for,
> He opens
> His world,
> Father Dzulíferi.

So he looked for.
He made well his body,
The Eternal Master,
Jaguar Iaperikuli.
Behold he looks for,
He sees his people, the *kuwaikere* [bird-spirits],
Jaguar Iaperikuli.
Behold he will come,
He transforms and sees,
He sees his people, the *kuwaikere*,
Jaguar Iaperikuli.
Behold he comes back,
He transforms and sees,
My grandfather, my grandfather,
My grandfather, my grandfather,
Heiri [the primal sun, Iaperikuli's body].
Behold he will come back,
He transforms and sees,
My grandfather, my grandfather,
Heiri.
Heiri transforms.
Behold he will look for,
Behold he looks for and sees,
The Eternal Master.
He comes back and mends,
The mending-place of his bones,
The thoughtless-one.
Behold he will look for,
The bone of Kamathawa.
This bone,
Behold,
Behold his *pariká*-bone,
Behold it will come back,
That very same,
His eternal bone,
The *pariká*-bone,
Jaguar Iaperikuli.
His *pariká*-bone,
The Eternal Master.
Behold it comes back, that same
His eternal,
His eternal bone.

You have seen it come back.
He makes his people well, the *kuwaikere*,
Jaguar Iaperikuli.
There in the Other Sky,
There in his Other Sky,
The Eternal Master.
Thus he comes and transforms,
He makes his *kuwaikere* well,
Jaguar Iaperikuli.
Behold, it will come back and stay,
There, his Center-Place-Sky,
His Center-Place-Sky.
Behold he will come back and transform
In the Other World Sky,
He comes and mends,
He mends and sees his *kuwaikere*,
His *kuwaikere*.
Thus, as in the beginning for him,
Our ancestor,
Jaguar
Iaperikuli.
Thus as it came back in the beginning for him,
The Eternal Master.
Behold he comes back and looks for,
He sees Jaguar
Iaperikuli.
In the Other Sky.
He comes and stays,
He comes and opens,
The Other World Sky.
You see we come back and stay,
In the Other World Sky.
Behold he will look for and make well,
His *kuwaikere*,
Jaguar Iaperikuli,
Jaguar Iaperikuli.
You have seen the Eternal Master,
The Eternal Master.
His mending-place,
There, in his world,
His world,
Jaguar Iaperikuli.

My grandfather, my grandfather,
We come and stay,
We come and stay, Jaguar Iaperikuli,
We come and stay, we make well his *kuwainyāi*
Kuwaikaniri, Kuwaikaniri.
Behold he comes back,
He makes well his eternal body,
Kuwaikaniri.
Thus it comes, as in the beginning
For him, behold it comes
That same, his eternal bone,
His *parikā*-bone, its image
Jaguar Iaperikuli.
Behold I take his eternal
Bone, his eternal bone.
I look for what he has,
Heiri ienipe [sacred title for the Hohodene],
Heiri ienipe.
We come and transform among them,
Jaguar Iaperikuli,
The Eternal Master.
There, *Heeeeeee*
His world-tip,
His world-tip of long ago,
Behold his hidden place of long ago,
Jaguar Kamathawa's village,
Jaguar Iaperikuli's village,
We go and stay among them,
Jaguar-shaman-others . . .
Haaaaawwww haaaaaaaaawwwwwwww fffff

Mandu explained the song in the following manner:

The shaman walks with Dzulíferi and looks for the bone of Mawe-rikuli. He finds it and looks for the bone of Kuwai. He leaves them both with the broken bone to mend it well. He gets the primordial sun's tobacco—Heiri's tobacco, and blows smoke over the bone, shaping it with his hands, and then he sucks out. He then looks for the bone of Kamathawa, the "eternal bone," the *pariká*-bone. He joins this to the mended bone and makes the bone new. He then looks for where his people, the *kuwaikere*, are and joins them together, to make them better. He ascends to the middle sky, the other sky, and makes the *kuwaikere* better. He takes the bone of Kamathawa from the sky and fixes it again with people. He ascends to the tip of the universe—the ancient, hidden world of Jaguar Iaperikuli and Jaguar Kamathawa. The shaman cannot let people stay sad. When the bone is fixed, they become happy. If the shaman doesn't fix it, people will die.

The bones invoked in the song refer, I believe, to the most fundamental cosmic processes. The bones of Mawerikuli refer to permanent horizontal stasis in Wapinakwa, the lowest layer of the cosmos, which will be opened up in "another end of the world." The bones of Kuwai—Kuwai *iapipemi*—refer to the sacred flutes and trumpets, the connection between This World of humanity and the primordial world, the "umbilical cord of the sky" which represents the continuity of the ancestral world with the present and future. The bone of Iaperikuli, the eternal source of the cosmos, refers to the original rebirth and transcendence of the creator from a condition of dismemberment. The bone of *pariká* is the vehicle of shamanic transformation through which the shaman ascends to the other worlds.

The sequence in which these bones appear in the song thus seems to reproduce a process of ascension along the vertical axis of the cosmos from the lowest to the highest levels, from Wapinakwa to the world of Iaperikuli. This reconstruction of verticality coincides with the "mending" of the universe bone and the reordering of the relations between the worlds above and below and their inhabitants. The *kuwaikere*, bird-spirits and Iaperikuli's people, would seem to be the spiritual components of each level, equivalent to the *kuwainyái* of the myth of Mawerikuli in the sense that both incorporate the reversibility of death, collective or individual.

What the shaman does through his song, in a sense, is to infuse the various levels of the cosmos with the sacred powers of the beginning, transforming its state of collapse into a new form of being. The shaman calls these powers back, in order to mend the bone structure of the cosmos and, at the same time, heal or "make well" the inhabitants of each level, that is, bring them back from death to life and happiness.

With this interpretation, I suggest then that the conclusion of the myth of Mawerikuli is not, after all, final, for cosmic collapse may be reverted by the shaman's recreating the vertical relations to the most powerful sources of rebirth inside the bone. As the *kuwainyái* bring Kuwaikaniri back to life (suggested in the last part of the above song), so shamans, confronted with the threat of permanent rupture and collapse—i.e., collective death—may renew life on all levels through a vertical ascension and shamanic healing up to the most remote levels of the cosmos.

But when does the bone break? When does cosmic collapse threaten humanity? What are the signs of collapse? Recent historical experiences may provide some clues.

In brief summary, Part II had three central objectives. The first was to examine the relations between mythic discourse—particularly that concerning catastrophic destruction of the world—and social action through an extended case history of a sequence of deaths in the village of Uapui which were caused, according to the village's inhabitants, by the actions of a sorcerer. Not an atypical case, as I suggested by citing Koch-Grünberg's observations in a Oalipere-dakenai village at the beginning of the century. Nevertheless, the shamans of Uapui were quite explicit in linking myths about primordial sorcerers and the catastrophic images contained in them to the dynamics of events in the recent history of their village.

The second objective was to examine the relation of mythic discourse to the experience of death—how myths of the "first person to die" shape perceptions of the tragedy, seeking to explain and remedy the loss. This—what we might call—curative aspect of myth links it to a series of ritual actions—orations, chants, and so forth—that administer the experience of death. Of special importance in this mythic discourse are notions of time and mythic models of temporality. On the one hand, I noted the existence of a cyclical model of rejuvenation which the myths suggest as potentially universal but which, given the impulsiveness of men and women as historical agents, becomes restricted to the shamans. This is one strong basis for understanding the messianic powers of shamans; that is, in their very being is incorporated a cyclical model of death and rejuvenation. For other humans, the components of the person become reintegrated into the diverse levels of the cosmos and the temporalities implicit in each.

The third objective was to explore the notion of the person at death and in the afterlife: What happens to the diverse components of the person? In what sense are the elements of the person distributed throughout the cosmos and integrated into cosmic processes, and in what sense do any of these components "return"? Is the "return of the dead" important to millenarian consciousness? What relations do the living have with the dead, and what are the concerns of the living with respect to the dangers these may represent? By examining a series of orations, I focused on some of the critical processes that identify the notion of person with cosmic processes; the notion of the "way" that defines death, birth and initiation; and the concern of the living to differentiate themselves from the dead by negating exchange relations with the spirits of the dead.

In this part I have focused greatly on the experiences of catastrophe—in death, cosmic collapse, poison—one aspect, I have suggested, of millenarian consciousness. The other, regeneration, will be the subject of the following two chapters which explore the relation between history, ritual actions and mythic discourse in the process of conversion to Christianity.

PART IV
WHEN THE MISSIONS CAME

In all the houses we found the "books." Passages of the Evangelists and prayers printed on a "duplicator" translated to Baniwa or to *geral*. Titles in Spanish. They were left by Sophie. Ataide says that some time ago, a Baniwa group led by a Colombian Indian, a disciple of Sophie, descended the river. They came to the mouth of the Aiary where they were stopped by Lino of the SPI. The Protestant New Tribes missionaries were already there and also opposed them. They came downriver bearing flags and singing psalms, taking the inhabitants along with them. They baptized everyone in the river, sang and went on to the next place. The disciple brought a map that was attributed to Sophie locating all the villages, with those of the Padres marked by a circle. The man was taken prisoner to the Uaupés and the rest disbanded. It's a story to be verified. (Eduardo Galvão, Fieldnotes 1954)

In this part, I seek to understand the relation between, on the one hand, millenarian concerns that I have explored up until now primarily through mythology and ritual and, on the other hand, historical religious movements, specifically Baniwa conversion to evangelical Protestantism from the late 1940s on. This was certainly one of the most significant moments in Baniwa religious history, comparable to the messianic movements of the mid-nineteenth century. Yet, the conversion movement was radically different in the sense that it explicitly rejected everything to do with ancient beliefs and practices. The question that I raised at the beginning of this book is worth repeating here: Why and how did so many people—reportedly thousands of converts scattered across the plains and jungles of southeastern Colombia and northwestern Brazil—suddenly decide to cast their lot essentially with a stranger, a white woman who simply ordered them to stop doing what had been familiar to them for generations, centuries?

I propose to explore this question here in two parts: first, in Chapter 7, through an understanding of the historical situations which preceded the evangelical movement and a reconstruction through eyewitness reports of the movement and the conflicts it generated; and second, in Chapter 8, through a consideration of the discourses on, and interpretations of, early conversion by various actors most directly and deeply involved with the movement, and their relation to the themes of catastrophe and regeneration.

7. From Rubber to the Gospel

The description and interpretation of the conversion movement has to be preceded by a consideration of previous historical situations, principally of domination and the hegemony of extractive labor or, as I shall describe, the extractivist regime, as well as by an understanding of the ways Baniwa communities experienced these situations, bearing in mind the specific characteristics of their culture and social organization. The historical record is, in fact, relatively complete from the turn of the century to the 1970s and includes reliable ethnographies produced by, among others, Theodor Koch-Grünberg in 1903, Curt Nimuendaju in 1927, and Eduardo Galvão in 1954. Various scientific travelers, adventurers, and official commissions during this period add to the picture, as do oral histories gathered by Adélia de Oliveira and myself in the 1970s. Finally, unpublished Salesian mission records from 1951 to the 1980s provide extremely valuable and hitherto unused sources which I shall be citing extensively. The Salesian records were only recently made available to researchers of the Instituto Socioambiental in São Paulo from whom I received copies; they were not available even for consultation at the time of my field research.

The selection of a historical baseline according to the existing records is somewhat arbitrary; on the other hand, the turn of the century coincides with the early peak of the rubber boom in the Northwest Amazon, when the extractivist regime was in formation on the Içana. Certain key figures who were to determine the direction of the regime among the Baniwa for decades to come were already in powerful positions. Furthermore, a messianic movement which apparently was a continuation and elaboration of Venancio Kamiko's movement, affords a comparison with the evangelical movement under different circumstances fifty years later. The critical points I discuss throughout this history deal with population movements, the effects of disease, indigenous strategies in relation to the whites, and the changing nature of the extractivist regime over time. Following this discussion, I present my reconstruction, from documents and eyewitness testimonies, of Sophie Muller as missionary, how she implanted evangelical Protestantism in the Northwest Amazon, her and her followers' conflicts with and propaganda campaigns against the Catholic missionaries, from the beginning of the movement until the mid-1970s.

The Extractivist Regime at the Turn of the Century

When Koch-Grünberg traveled on the Içana and Aiary, the contact situation he observed was clearly distinguished by the regime of rubber extraction that had been developing in the Northwest Amazon for nearly thirty years. Local rubber barons vied for control of indigenous labor with virtually free rein to do as they pleased. It is evident from Koch-Grünberg's accounts and other reports of the time that two forms of labor exploitation characterized the relations between rubber patrons and Indians: One was based on the use of terror and violence in which rubber merchants sent their henchmen to gather Indians, often by force and with the help of the local military, into rubber camps for the period of the harvest. The other was based on negotiation and the use of merchandise in which merchants bargained with local chiefs to organize a labor force in exchange for trade goods in advance.

Among the Baniwa, both systems were in effect in the early 1900s. Koch-Grünberg reported that the military "Komandant" at the Fort of Cucuy on the upper Rio Negro was conducting an operation of smuggling goods and forcibly taking Indians of the Içana either to work at the fort or across the border into Venezuela to work rubber. Various Indian villages of the lower Içana were desolate—all the Indians had been so taken. The Katapolitana population (a sib of the Dzauinai phratry) of the large village of Tunui on the mid-Içana Koch-Grünberg found living in a large refuge settlement in the forest near Tunui for "fear of the Komandant." A canoe of Oalipere-dakenai fled at the sight of Koch-Grünberg, mistaking him for the military. And, on the lower Aiary, the Hohodene of the Cará stream had blocked access to their longhouse by felling trees at the entrance of the stream. This was not unlike the situation on the upper Uaupés where the terroristic methods of Colombian merchants and punitive expeditions by frontier military and police had forced the Indians to flee to less accessible regions.

The other, perhaps more predominant, system was under the command of a Spanish-born merchant, Dom Germano Garrido y Otero, based at São Felipe near the mouth of the Içana. Garrido had come to the region in the 1870s, at the beginning of the rubber boom, to make his fortune and, from then until his death in 1921, effectively controlled the traffic of rubber and Indian laborers on the Içana and upper Rio Negro. In 1992, a grandson of Germano Garrido, living in São Gabriel da Cachoeira, recalled to the anthropologist Márcio Meira how his grandfather built his empire at the beginning of the century:

> My grandfather came here when he was 20 years old and liked the village of São Felipe and brought things for the people there and married a woman of Marabitanas. He stayed, earned a lot of money. He was a strong merchant here. It was he who supplied the whole Içana because at that time, the people of the Içana, like the people of the Xié, went around naked, only with g-strings, I have even seen that . . . the women only with those little black skirts, all dirty, and the men with g-strings, boys too, on the Xié and on the Içana River. There were some places . . . there was no trade, there was very little trade with them. So, my grandfather supplied the whole Içana. People came to buy things from him like salt, soap. He was a very rich man. He traveled upriver and sent his sons, because he had many sons. He didn't have just one wife, the old *tuxaua* of the Rio Negro, the old Spaniard had various wives. He came here and here he got rich because merchandise came from his country, to sell. Because he supplied all of it, you know, the whole Içana was his. So, he controlled there and the Albuquerques controlled here on the Uaupés River at that time. But they were cruel, they mistreated the Indians a lot. (in Meira 1993, 82–83)

With numerous Indians living in his house in situations of permanent debt-servitude, Garrido and his sons controlled the instruments of power and force in the region, that is, the police and military at the Fort of São Gabriel at the mouth of the Uaupés River. He maintained local control through several Indian "inspectors"—evidently a title and position which Garrido himself created—on the lower Içana, chiefs (or *tuxauas*) and intermediaries in the organization of labor. While he sent his sons with Indians of the Içana to rubber camps on the upper Rio Negro or lower Uaupés, Garrido controlled traffic and shipment of rubber to export firms in Manaus, the principal one being J. G. Araújo.

In the more distant regions of the Içana, the "inspectors" maintained amicable relations with local *tuxauas* of influence. On the Aiary for example, a Oalipere-dakenai chief named Mandu—Koch-Grünberg's principal informant—of the large village of Cururuquara, had worked for years in rubber camps on the lower Rio Negro, held considerable prestige in the villages of the Aiary, and was held in high regard by the Katapolitana "inspector" Diogo who claimed that Mandu was the "first chief" of the Oalipere-dakenai. Mandu himself claimed that he was the "chief of all dwellers of the Aiary"—evidently, a statement which reveals the exaggerated position of chiefs who acted as inter-mediaries in the rubber trade.

Yet there were places where Garrido's influence stopped for, in the early 1900s, the upper reaches of the Içana and its tributaries had little direct contact with the whites. In such regions, nevertheless, the indi-rect effects of the rubber extraction regime were certainly felt. One was the migration of whole communities to areas of little contact. Such seems to have been the case of the Maulieni Indians who, in Koch-Grünberg's time, made up, according to him, the "chief contingent of people of the Aiary" but who, in the decades immediately before, had migrated in flight from the Querary River to the west. For most of the latter half of the nineteenth century, and most likely well before, the Querary River had been inhabited by Baniwa phratries or portions of phratries: the Kapithi-minanai, or Ipeka; Dzuremen, or Jibóia; and Maulieni, or Kaua (Wallace [1853] 1969; Colini 1885; Stradelli 1890). By the early 1900s, with the intensification of the Colombian mer-chants' presence on the upper Uaupés, the Kapithi-minanai had mi-grated to the upper Içana, and communities of Maulieni to the upper Aiary. The Maulieni were to continue this migration for several de-cades afterward (as did the Dzuremen and Tukanoan Wanano who came to make settlements in the places abandoned by the Maulieni in the late 1920s).

Exogenous diseases increased proportionately with contact. On the Aiary, Koch-Grünberg noted cases of a contagious skin disease called *purupuru* which left white blemishes on the skin. According to the sci-entific traveler José Candido de Carvalho, who canoed up the Içana in the early 1950s, this disease,

> caused by a spirochete of circulating blood (*Treponema carateum* Brumpt, 1939), seems to have been responsible for, among other things, a disequilibrium in the pigmentation of the skin, albino in some points and entirely dark in others, notably around the eyes and nose. (de Carvalho 1952, 61)

There is strong evidence to support the claim that the disease became endemic among the Baniwa during the rubber boom, for none of the written sources before this time mention its existence while sources from Koch-Grünberg on note its increasing prevalence.

In the approximately three months that Koch-Grünberg traveled on the Içana and Aiary, seven people had died, at least one from pneumonia. In fact, much of his ethnographic description of the Aiary is devoted to the mourning ceremonies and masked dances of the Maulieni, shamanism and curing rituals of the Oalipere-dakenai, and direct observations of sickness, death and funeral rites at the Oalipere-dakenai longhouse of Cururuquara. If this can be taken to mean that exogenous diseases were beginning to take a toll on the Aiary, it also suggests that the ritual system for dealing with sickness and death was hard at work to incorporate such changes. The Oalipere-dakenai at least attributed great importance to shamans.

On the Cubate River, tributary of the lower Içana, a shaman and messiah by the name of Anizetto exercised great influence among the Hohodene inhabitants. Most likely, Anizetto had been a disciple and/or relative of Venancio Anizetto Kamiko, the most famous of Baniwa messiahs from the mid-nineteenth century until his death in Venezuela in 1902. According to Garrido, who had no great admiration for Anizetto, for "25 years" he had traveled over the Içana proclaiming himself to be a second Jesus Christu and leading great movements of followers. He healed the sick through protective leaf coverings and visited villages in great ceremonies. He ordered his followers to cease work in plantations for "everything would come from him when he made the sign of the cross on the fields" (Koch-Grünberg 1967, 1:39). People from afar would come to visit and consult with him, bringing him gifts and "dancing day and night in great feasts" (ibid.).

It is not unlikely that Garrido himself—who referred to Anizetto as a "hermaphrodite" and "vagabond," "God knows from which people"—requested that the National Guard in Manaus be sent to take the messiah prisoner. As punishment, he was forced to work for a year on the construction of a cathedral. After being declared "harmless" and set free, he was sent back to the Içana. He nevertheless maintained his influence among the Baniwa "who believe in him firmly and that one can obtain much through him" (ibid.).

During the height of Anizetto's movement, Hohodene disciples of the Cubate reportedly killed and cut up the bodies of a family of seven people—perhaps, Koch-Grünberg speculated, due to an "old family feud." When Koch-Grünberg visited Anizetto at his "retreat" ("Art Retiro") on the Cubate, consisting of six spacious but "negligently kept" houses with half-open walls, he met a "small, ugly, middle-aged man" who would have little to do with the ethnographer, perhaps mistaking him for "an official." The other inhabitants of the village held back from conversation. In fact, the ethnographer's characterization of the settlement as a "retreat" or "*mucambo*" (refuge settlement) fit the character of Anizetto's following who, though they came from the Içana and Uaupés, sought to "flee from public attention."

From Koch-Grünberg's description,[1] the style of Anizetto's movement clearly had much in common with that led by Kamiko in the 1850s: an itinerant, self-proclaimed Christ who healed and advised, an outsider who brought together peoples of different "tribes," who was believed to have the miraculous power, symbolized by the cross, to control growth and produce things, who avoided the whites and sought to create a haven of refuge, a sanctuary. All of these features may be seen in Kamiko's messianism, and what is more remarkable, they also bear a strong resemblance to aspects of the evangelical movement that was to sweep the Içana in the early 1950s. Further, I would suggest that the murder of an entire family by Anizetto's followers may have been related to the movement as, fifty years later, Catholic priests were attacked with knives by the radical followers of the evangelicals on the Içana (Knobloch 1972, 292).

Besides Anizetto's movement, Koch-Grünberg noted several ways that Baniwa communities had assimilated Christian influence. First of all, there seemed to be a pervasive distinction between the Baniwa of the lower Içana, or "Christian" Indians, and those of the upper regions, or "wild" Indians, reflecting the history of mission settlements and descents in the region. Second, considerable importance was attached to certain saints, for example, Saint Anthony. Although Koch-Grünberg's visit didn't coincide with the celebration of saint's days, nevertheless the chief of Cururuquara showed him a figurine of Saint Anthony, carefully kept in a bundle of rags inside an old box, probably handed down from previous generations. Several porcelain dolls which the ethnographer gave to the women and children they called "Tupana," *língua geral* for "God." When Koch-Grünberg inquired about the rock engravings at Camarões Rapids, the chief explained that they were made by "Christu" and that Christu in Oalipere-dakenai was Iaperikuli, or "Tupana," the first Baniwa who made all rock engravings.

No missionaries had been among the Baniwa since the middle of the nineteenth century, yet various Baniwa had grown up in the missions of the Rio Negro. Traders were also seen as "agents of the missions," according to Koch-Grünberg, and frequently were asked to "baptize" Baniwa children. Koch-Grünberg himself was asked to baptize (i.e., give a Christian name to) his principal informant's, Mandu's niece. This attribution of the power to baptize to external agents was perhaps consistent with the kind of interethnic religious identity forged in the context of patron-client relations.

Violence and Terror in Interethnic Relations

The two decades following Koch-Grünberg's visit witnessed the intensification of rubber extraction in the Northwest Amazon, which reached its peak in approximately 1910–1911, followed by the sudden and drastic decline in production, the famous "bust" which led the region and its population to despair. As in other areas of the Amazon at this time, a temporal progression of increasing brutality and genocide of indigenous peoples paralleled the intensification and drastic decline of rubber extraction.

In the Venezuelan Amazon, a rubber merchant named Tomás Funes took over the territorial capital at San Fernando de Atabapo and ruled the Territory of the Rio Negro as an independent fiefdom until his own soldiers mutinied and executed him in 1921. Funes' troops dominated the area as far south as San Carlos del Rio Negro and decimated entire indigenous populations almost overnight (Hill [1989] 1993: 77):

> Wakuenai and Baniwa groups living along the lower Guainía (Negro) fled from the terrorism of the Funes regime up the Guainía and its tributaries. . . . Other Arawakan societies, including the Baré, Mandahuaca, and Yavitero suffered almost total annihilation during this period. (Hill and Wright, in Hill 1988, 95)

Furthermore,

> oral testimonies from indigenous peoples of the upper Rio Negro and Orinoco region recall a pattern of torture, assassination, and genocide that was virtually identical to the atrocities that the Casa Araña had perpetrated a decade earlier among indigenous peoples of the Caquetá-Putumayo region in Peru. (Hill [1989] 1993, 78)

On the Brazilian side, Garrido maintained absolute control over the Içana until his death in 1921, defying anyone who questioned his authority. In 1914 he was publicly accused by the *Jornal do Comercio* in Manaus of "various practices against the Indians of the Içana" and was summoned by the recently formed Delegacy of the Service for the Protection of Indians (SPILTN, Serviço de Proteção aos Índios e Localização de Trabalhadores Nacionais) to respond to the charges. Garrido wrote back that before he would appear, he would demand a retraction of the accusations from the journal.[2]

It may be that the writer of the accusations was a competitor for Indian labor. Within the region, there were many. Koch-Grünberg had met several Colombians who took Indians of the Uaupés by force to work *caucho* (rubber) in Colombia, as well as one Manuel Albuquerque, or "Manduca" as he was called—a Brazilian *mestiço*, who held the position of subprefect of São Gabriel and "Delegate of the Indians of the Uaupés, Içana and Xié" (Koch-Grünberg 1967, 2:13). Like Garrido, he had risen to power during the height of the boom, and his brothers and he had established themselves on the Uaupés, "marrying" Indian women and siring numerous offspring. Oral histories of the Dessana Indians of the Tiquié River leave no doubt that Manduca controlled Indian labor through violence and terror, and that he raped Indian women and girls. In fact, he is probably the same figure described by Gordon MacReigh, who traveled on the Uaupés in 1914, as the "King of the Uaupés" whose nickname among the Indians meant "Man who makes the river bloody" (MacReigh 1926, 320). But MacReigh's description was of a "king" already decadent, awaiting the chance to exploit balata latex, then in greater abundance on the Colombian Vaupés.

The regime of balata extraction was founded on mutual violence: atrocities committed against the Indians were retaliated with murders of Colombian rubber merchants; the families of Garrido and Albuquerques warred among themselves over the spaces of local power. By the 1920s, other Colombian, Brazilian, and Peruvian merchants—too numerous to mention—had entered the scene in a second wave of extractivist invasions. The records of the SPI throughout the 1920s and 1930s are replete with instances of mutual violence and atrocities against the Indians mentioned above.[3] What these documents reveal is a veritable traffic of Indians across the border to Colombia, which the SPI referred to as "enslavement." Indeed, there were many features in common with the system of slavery of the mid-eighteenth century in the region.

Founded in 1910, the SPI had sent its first reconnaissance mission to the Uaupés region as early as 1911[4] and surveyed the population of the Uaupés, Xié, and Içana in 1919; but it only effectively established its presence in the late 1920s, and then only on the Uaupés and its tributaries with the creation of Indigenous Posts at the confluence of the Uaupés and Papury in 1926, on the upper Papury in 1929, and at the mouth of the Querary in 1929, with various watchposts (*postos de vigilância*) and interposts (*entrepostos*). Their presence by no means resolved the "Colombian problem"; what it sought to do was to regulate the traffic of persons, control the more serious abuses, and force the merchants to register the Indians taken from Brazil to work. In terms of creating conditions for alternative markets or local agricultural production, or fixing people in settlements—the agency's declared goals in other areas of Brazil—it met with little success. At most, the agency served as a sort of hiring agency for both the rubber merchants and their own needs, and an occasional outlet for manioc production. The agents' repeated denunciations of labor exploitation and the sale of merchandise at exorbitant prices seemed to have little effect, as both continued for years.

Curt Nimuendaju, who visited the region in 1927, wrote disparagingly about the effects of the SPI's activities:

> The action of the SPI here as in many isolated areas becomes almost illusory due to the lack of funds on the one hand and the lack of sensible personnel on the other. . . . At best, the delegate, in monopolizing the exploitation of the Indians, at least avoids that they be exploited by everyone. With such scandalous and absurd dilemmas, the SPI is obliged to rely on . . . the lack of resources and competent personnel. (Nimuendaju 1950, 127)

Of the two missionary organizations present in the region at this time—the Montfortians on the upper Papury since 1915 and the Salesians (SDB) on the Uaupés (Jauareté and Taraquá) since 1914—the first seems to have had little lasting effect either in controlling labor traffic or in educating and converting the Indians and was even accused by one SPI agent as being "simply rubber merchants." The Salesians, on the other hand, were considered, at least by the agents on the Uaupés, to be the paragons of assistance that the indigenous population needed. According to one agent who wrote in 1932, "All would have been lost if it weren't for the Salesians who continue their wonderful work,"[5] adding that the solution to the problems of the area lay in protection from the uncontrolled traffic of laborers; agricultural development; and the arts and educational establishments which the Salesians offered (for a contrasting view, see Nimuendaju 1950).

Be that as it may, all of this meant little to the Baniwa of the Içana, for neither the SPI nor the Salesians would establish their presence in that region until the late 1940s–early 1950s. After Germano Garrido's death in 1921, and a disastrous fire in 1925 which destroyed his *sitio* (house) in São Felipe along with three tons of balata latex, Garrido's sons were apparently less able to control the entry of Colombian and Venezuelan merchants on the Içana. Nimuendaju and Marechal Boanerges Lopes de Sousa, who surveyed the region a year after Nimuendaju as part of the First Brazilian Border Commission's census, mention two: Natividade Rivas, who frequently took Baniwa to work balata on the Papunaua River in Colombia and who was known for his exploitation in the sale of merchandise; and Antonio Maia, based at the village of Yutica on the upper Uaupés, who was known for his mistreatment of the Indians and who was killed by the Indians themselves in 1927. Valentim Garrido assumed his father's self-appointed role as "Delegate of Indians," designating local chiefs to organize labor, until the SPI set up a post on the Içana in the late 1940s.

The effects on the Baniwa of the extractivist regime during the first three decades of this century were clearly visible in the flight of whole communities seeking refuge, an increase in population movements within the area, increased mortality from diseases and consequent reduction of the population, and a prevailing fear, distrust, and avoidance of contacts with the whites.

Curripaco communities of the Guainía River in Venezuela fled from the persecutions of Tomás Funes. As one Adzanene (Tatú, in *língua geral*; a phratry of the Cuiary and upper Içana) man named Liberato recalled to the anthropologist Adélia de Oliveira in 1971:

> I was about 15 years old when I came to Brazil. At that time [author's note: about 1918], there was a white man who came from San Fernando or below and wanted to take the lands of the Curripaco in Colombia. He took people and tied their hands behind their backs. My uncle, who was a *capitão* [chief of a local community], was taken. They tied his hands and took him for interrogation. They wanted to know if he was hiding people. My aunt, his wife, who reared me, hid in the woods with the children. My mother, who had remarried, came first, when I was small, because of these "revolutions." I was being reared by my aunt and my other two brothers by my grandfather. This Venezuelan white man attacked with armed soldiers. At that time there weren't any whites living on the Guainía River in Colombia. (Cited in de Oliveira 1979, 10)

As Liberato recounts, his family and other Curripaco families relocated predominantly on the Cuiary River, northern tributary of the Içana in Brazil.

The Maulieni migrations, noted by Koch-Grünberg, continued from the upper to the middle and lower Aiary. When Nimuendaju visited these Maulieni, he found their houses small, "poor and decadent" (1950, 139)—this, in contrast with the richly painted and spacious longhouses that Koch-Grünberg had seen twenty-five years before. The Dzuremen (Jibóia) had practically abandoned the Querary, in flight from the Colombians, to occupy eight small settlements on the upper Aiary. Wanano Indians from the Uaupés, also fleeing Colombians, temporarily occupied longhouses of the upper Aiary. Hohodene and Oalipere-dakenai, who in 1903 had occupied the lower Aiary and mid-Içana, had moved to the upper Aiary and its tributary the Uaraná (previously occupied by Maulieni) and to the Quiary stream off the lower Aiary. There also seems to have been some movement of people away from the banks of the main rivers onto the smaller feeder streams, at least on the lower Aiary.

On the Içana, there appear to have been numerous movements of people downstream: as the Adzanene came to occupy the Cuiary, various Mabatsi-dakenai (or Yurupary-tapuya, in *língua geral*) of the Cuiary moved to the lower Içana, as did groups of Kapithi-minanai (Ipeka) from the upper Içana, Oalipere-dakenai from the Aiary, and "Ira-tapuya" (Kutheroeni?) from the mid-Içana (Nimuendaju 1950; Lopes de Sousa 1928).

Most of these movements were the direct result of penetrations by the Colombian rubber merchants and Venezuelan military, but they were also related to deaths from diseases, as the Baniwa traditionally abandoned village sites whenever there was an accumulation of corpses, normally buried inside the longhouses. In 1914, the American traveler Hamilton Rice noted that the Papunaua River, where numerous Baniwa would be taken to work balata in the 1920s, was plagued with malaria, which had decimated at least one entire community (Rice 1914, 158). SPI officials reported two major epidemics in the upper Rio Negro region—one in 1914–1915 of "tertian fevers" (malaria, evidently the same that Rice had reported) and another in 1919–1920 of "Spanish flu," which had "reduced the population to one-half."[6] In 1919, the SPI estimated that the population on the Içana, Aiary, and Cuiary Rivers totaled 1,550 Indians,[7] an extraordinarily low figure if it is based on any accurate surveying. Yet Nimuendaju in 1927 appears to confirm that a drastic depopulation had indeed occurred:

> The entire basin of the Içana and its tributaries has perhaps an indigenous population of 1,055 souls; there are no *"civilisados."* In 1903, Koch-Grünberg calculated the number of Indians in the same area as between 2,000–3,000. They have thus become reduced within the last 24 years to half, or even a third, of their numbers. (1950, 162)[8]

The evidence for an increase in disease is clear in the areas Nimuendaju and Lopes de Sousa visited in 1927–1928. The Katapolitana sib of Tunui on the middle Içana numbered some two hundred people in 1903; in 1927, Nimuendaju believed they were "nearly extinct" (ibid., 130). The Payoalieni (or Pacú) in 1908 lived in three large longhouses on the upper Içana; in 1927, these had been reduced to thirteen people

(133–134). Sant'Ana, a village of Mabatsi-dakenai on the lower Içana, in 1927 comprised these people and the survivors of a recent measles epidemic who had abandoned the nearby village of Carma, as well as the "Arara-tapuya" (Adaro-dakenai?) and "a few survivors of the Urubu-tapuya [Wadzulinai]" of the Piraiuara stream off the lower Içana. Nimuendaju also noted the presence of trachoma and the skin disease *purupuru* in various villages on the Içana and Cuiary and malaria on the Aiary.

In this context, it is not difficult to understand the prevailing climate of fear, distrust, and avoidance of the whites amply evidenced by Nimuendaju and Lopes de Sousa. In village after village on the Içana, Nimuendaju was met—that is, if people had not abandoned the villages immediately prior to his coming—with people fleeing in terror at his approach. When he was able to talk with village leaders, they answered him with distrust, with "terror on their faces": "here there is nothing" (128). He was later informed that this fear was

> due, in part, to the merchant Antonio Maia of Yutica on the Uaupés who had gone up the Içana and Aiary a few days before spreading the word that after him would come a white man who would take note of all the houses and their inhabitants in order to imprison them later, with the young men having to serve in the Army and the women and girls to work for the Whites. (127)

In Tunui the reception was even more "desperate":

> The distrust and fear were never lost. It was enough to walk in the direction of the *tuxaua*'s house, where his family was having a meal, for everyone to jump up terrified, fleeing with their plates out the back. (131)

There were other ways the Baniwa treated both him and Lopes de Sousa which indicated the extreme distortions in interethnic relations produced by the extractivist regime. Both mention various instances of people coming to visit them to trade. At Tunui, however, despite the generous gifts distributed, the people demanded much more, as though they "constantly feared being cheated in each transaction they made" (ibid.).

Certainly there were villages where Nimuendaju felt at ease, was received with hospitality, and given a "natural and innocent" treatment, as among the Hohodene of the Aiary. In these villages he could observe dance festivals, initiation rituals, and the traditional life of the large longhouses. Yet his predominant impression was what led Nimuendaju to conclude at the end of his survey that:

> the Indian sees in any civilized person with whom he deals a cruel and terrible beast. Today it is useless to try to gain the trust of the Indian by means of fraternal and just treatment. Even the most disinterested acts he attributes to base motives, convinced that for whatever convenience the civilized man occasionally hides his beastly nature. For me personally, accustomed to living intimately with Indians of very different tribes and regions, my stay among those of the Içana and Uaupés was often a veritable martyrdom, seeing myself treated as if I were a criminal, perverse and brutish. (173)

More than thirty years of persecution and terror from the military and rubber merchants had left their mark and would continue to do so as the extractivist regime diversified its activities and base. Balata work on the Papunaua, Inirida, and Rio Negro was far too costly and time-consuming to be lucrative by the 1930s; yet numerous other products would serve in the years ahead to reproduce the extractivist regime and its effects among the Baniwa.

It is evident from the life stories of many Baniwa that extractive labor and constant traveling with *patrões* (bosses) in large part defined their lives in the 1930s and 1940s. A life of incessant going and returning, as Keruaminali, Hohodene elder of Uapui described to me:

> We worked balata, four dry seasons of hard work on balata. I returned [to Uapui]. We worked balata, I returned. On the Papunaua, we worked balata, I returned. I went four times to the Guaviare, I returned. Then, on the Guaviare and I returned. Then I went there to work *seringa* [rubber], on the Cassiquiare, the Orinoco, we worked two dry seasons. I went on the Zoa, I returned. Then I returned.

Similar testimony was recorded from several Oalipere-dakenai and Adzanene individuals of the Cuiary and Içana Rivers, by Adélia de Oliveira in 1971 (1979) and Márcio Meira in 1990–1991 (1993). It is evident from this testimony that the products sought diversified considerably during this time: *piaçaba* extraction on the Xié and Padauari Rivers; *castanha* on the Aracá; *ucuquirana* on the lower Rio Negro; *maçaranduba* on the Aiary.

Life stories highlight this period as the "time of the bosses" (Meira

1993), when life trajectories were marked in time and space by relations with merchants. What governed this relation, as it always had, was the "account"—goods obtained on credit and paid off by work— but it was the boss who kept the books and hence control, frequently through a local indigenous chief, or *capitão*.

This itinerant, dependent existence produced numerous hardships such as the separation of children from parents. Often young boys would be taken by a boss to one area but their fathers to another. Years would pass before they saw each other again. Labor migrations resulting in permanent residence in other areas were also quite frequent. Inevitably, this produced distortions in family structure, development cycles, and local descent group organization. At the same time, it solidified the patron-client relation as the principal mode of interethnic contact.

It is difficult to say anything about religious practices or messianic traditions during this time, since the principal sources consist of rapid surveys. Yet it is odd there is no further mention of Anizetto's movement, nor of powerful and prestigious shamans. It may be that the numerous dislocations of individuals and communities and depopulation prevented the development of any sort of leader-organized movement or assembly of people. In that case, the principal strategies for survival would have been either to flee and withdraw, with all the hardships this entailed, or to seek out bosses who would at least pay a decent wage and not terrorize in the process.

Made in America: Rubber, Chicle, and the Gospel

In the early 1940s, the renewed international interest in Amazon rubber, due to the world war, brought an altogether new set of actors to the Northwest Amazon—American companies. The Chicle Development Company opened an office in San Fernando de Atabapo in Venezuela and, later, in São Gabriel da Cachoeira, for the purpose of extracting and commercializing chicle, balata, and rubber. The Rubber Development Corporation (RDC)—one of the principal U.S. companies involved in rubber extraction in the Amazon in this period (see Dean 1989, on the RDC)—established itself in Caracas, Manaus, and Bogotá, with local stations in the Amazon, including Miraflores on the Colombian Vaupés.

The Northwest Amazon was of interest to the U.S. government for another reason: its strategic value as a potential stopover en route to North Africa which avoided the, by then, dangerous North Atlantic. In 1943, the U.S. Army Corps of Engineers, at the request of Nelson Rockefeller—then Coordinator of Inter-American Affairs—was sent to conduct a major survey of the region and its potential for development, evidently to serve war interests and the interests of the three nations with territory in the Northwest for developing their frontiers (U.S. Army Corps of Engineers 1943). The resulting report in fact was a technical evaluation assessing the costs and needs for developing rubber production that complemented the projects of the RDC.

Even with the recent increase in rubber extraction, production was small—roughly 2,500 tons in 1943. "To increase the annual collection of rubber by 100,000 tons," the report concluded, "would require the transportation of approximately 600,000 tons of supplies" (mainly petroleum products) into the region (ibid., 124). It would also require a "force of 80,000 *caucheros* (plus their families, a total of 300,000 people), *practically all of whom would have to be brought into the Amazon basin*" (ibid.; emphasis added). [Similar estimates had already been reached by the RDC in 1941 (Dean 1989, 138).] Access roads and airports would have to be built, as well as a series of locks and dams at the principal rapids of the upper Orinoco and Negro.

> Lesser rubber-production efforts will be able to rely in part on the present limited population and resources, and would not require imports in direct proportion. (U.S. Army Corps of Engineers 1943, 124)

Of the indigenous population of the region, the report had the following to say:

> Many members of the Indian tribes in the region were emigrated during the 1880–1910 rubber boom. Those now remaining, principally of the Guahibo, Baniwa, Maquiritare and Baré tribes, are considered civilized and inhabit for the most part dwellings along and near the waterway. There does not appear to be any substantial number of savage Indians remaining in the region west of the Orinoco, Cassiquiare and Negro. (11)

Outside of a few pockets of agricultural development—the Salesian mission at São Gabriel and a Baptist mission at Iucaby below São Gabriel—the only "productive industry" and source of exchange in the region was extractive. Sickness and disease were one of the reasons why agricultural production was considered low, for

> no physician or surgeon, other than the itinerant Rubber Development Corporation doctor who makes monthly rounds of the Orinoco and Cassiquiare rubber camps, is available to serve the

people living in the thousand miles between Puerto Ayacucho and the lower Rio Negro. (24)

The Army's and the RDC's plans, however, were destined never to materialize, as they foundered on the local power of rubber elites and bosses who were far from willing to give up their power to the war effort (Dean 1989 140); these local leaders eventually forced the RDC to give up its plans altogether for increased productivity, at least in Brazil.

At Miraflores, on the Colombian Vaupés, the RDC maintained a headquarters for several years. While the Indians in their camps were relatively well treated, receiving medical assistance during a measles epidemic in 1943–1944 for example, those of the more remote areas suffered a treatment similar to the boom at the beginning of the century. When I did my fieldwork on the Aiary in the 1970s, Hohodene men recounted vividly their experiences at Miraflores. Most men worked at least three seasons gathering rubber, some as many as a dozen consecutive years. According to them, Colombians came to the Aiary and "took many people,"—up to fifty men and women on any one trip. Their stories are much the same as those of the 1930s, of the extreme difficulties of the work. People who couldn't bear the constant suffering fled and returned by trails at night to their homes. Families were separated, and the economic burdens on wives who stayed at home increased enormously. Bosses were either "good" or "bad": cruel overseers, people said, stood with whips or brandished machetes when people were reluctant to go with them or did not bring in enough latex. Ex-convicts were not uncommon elements in the rubber camps. On the other hand, the earnings could be good, and if one didn't spend them all in the town of Mitú, one could get shotguns, clothes, and other items to bring home.

The constant traffic of Baniwa from the Içana and Aiary to Colombia was undertaken with the complicity and participation of the SPI. Ataide Cardoso, the first SPI delegate on the Içana in the 1940s, is said to have mediated labor contracts between Venezuelan bosses and the Baniwa (see de Oliveira 1979, 72). After a period when the delegacy was suspended, the second delegate, by the name of Alcides, continued his predecessor's role as labor intermediary, this time with the cooperation of a Oalipere-dakenai chief named Leopoldino of the lower Içana. Leopoldino was considered by various outsiders to be a "great friend of the whites, gentle and hospitable" (de Carvalho 1952, 31).

In the late 1940s, the botanist José Candido de Carvalho, of the National Museum (Rio de Janeiro), commented disparagingly on the delegate's work: "We are in need of a reform in the methods and means of treatment of the Indians, at least on the upper Rio Negro" (63). After Alcides' sudden death, Ataide Cardoso returned, and while he initially sought to control the traffic, he ultimately gave in to the merchants. One Baniwa man recalled to the anthropologist Adélia de Oliveira in 1971:

> The Uaupés delegate [i.e., Ataide] had set a time limit and one boss passed the limit which made the delegate get angry and begin to prohibit the transit of these merchants who came to get people. But that didn't work. After that, many merchants came. I think they gave the delegate money. (Cited in de Oliveira 1979, 72)

On various occasions Cardoso assumed a position against the Indians in their conflicts with the bosses and was known to maintain ongoing commerce in *piaçaba* with the Warekena Indians of the Xié River, utilizing

> his position of authority to confer powers on an indigenous leader [of the Xié] who served him and who, in turn, manipulated the status of *capitão* conferred on him to acquire power and prestige in relation to his equals. And all to the benefit of his commerce. (Meira 1993, 91–92)

As the years went on, Cardoso made no pretense of hiding the fact that the SPI sustained itself through the Indians' extractive labor:

> As you know, the *Ajudância* maintains itself through production on lands that legally belong to the Indians; this production is done by the same Indians who are assisted by this agency. (Cited in Meira 1993, 93)

When one reads José de Carvalho's account of his two-week journey up the Içana to the mouth of the Cuiary, it is as though one hears echoes of Nimuendaju's and Lopes de Sousa's observations two decades before: of people fleeing and hiding in the woods when the naturalist's boat approached; of "terror stamped on their faces" (1952, 53); of extreme distrust in trading with the whites; of exploitation by some merchants and others who took children from their parents and mistreated them, or sold *cachaça* at exorbitant prices; of places abandoned as a result of diseases or labor migrations; and of the exaggerated importance of certain chiefs (e.g., Leopoldino). There were changes to be sure: the growth of certain villages such as Sant'Ana; the movements of communities to new locations; the spread of the disease *purupuru*; the loss of certain customs such as body painting. But the structure of the extractivist regime—now dominated by the alliance of the SPI, the merchants and bosses, and local chiefs—had reproduced itself.

To complete the picture, in the late 1940s, the civil war in Colombia that became known as the "Violencia" was just beginning. The ten-year conflict was to have dramatic effects on the indigenous peoples of the Guainía, Vichada, and Guaviare Rivers. Just at this time, the young North American evangelist missionary, Sophie Muller, decided to bring the Gospel to, as she said, "a hitherto unreached Indian tribe in the jungles of South America."

The Adventures of Sophie Muller

Daughter of a German Catholic father and Protestant mother, Sophie Muller was, by all accounts, an extraordinary woman. As I shall show later on when I come to interpret her missionary narrative, *Beyond Civilization*, she had an intrepid pioneering spirit with evident messianic inclinations. In the Foreword to her book, the chairman of the New Tribes Mission (NTM) declares that her principal contribution to the NTM was that she "pioneered the field of Colombia for us as a Mission," bringing the Gospel to various lowland peoples and "working most of the time by herself far beyond civilization" (Kenneth Johnston, foreword in Muller, 1952).

Sophie herself recounts how she "entered the field":

After leaving the United States shores for Colombia, the first rest-less six months were spent, more or less, in trying the patience of a hard-working medical missionary in the city of Pasto, who had welcomed me into her home. Knowing that God had sent me to South America to reach a tribe whose language was unknown and unwritten, I set off by myself—for want of better "visible" com-pany—to find such a tribe.

After months of travel through Colombia by truck, horse, river-boat and canoe, seeking tribal information from various mission-aries, and studying the Spanish language en route, I found myself at the World Evangelization Crusade jungle station among the Cubeo Indians on the Rio Cuduiari. There I learned much about unreached tribes, including the Kuripako, who were located on the rivers northeast of the Cubeo territory.

At the end of three weeks of travel, terrible for a tenderfoot, in dug-out canoes and on jungle trails, I arrived at one of the larger Kuripako settlements known as Sejál, on the Rio Guainía. I was received with great interest by the tribespeople and began to work immediately on their language. The experiences that followed this first contact led, through much trial and error, to a workable plan for reaching these people. (Muller 1952, 7)

After three years on the Guainía, in 1948 Sophie decided to extend her work to the Baniwa in Brazil. She made two journeys, a year apart, the first to the Cuiary and Içana, the second to the Içana and Aiary. Among Eduardo Galvão's unpublished fieldnotes, I found a separate, hand-drawn map (see Map 3) produced by Sophie Muller locating all the villages she visited in these two trips, with names of some of her principal Baniwa and Curripaco interpreters. In 1949, she extended her evangelization to the Cubeo of the Querary River in Brazil.

Her converts, ever increasing in number, took the new religion to neighboring peoples—the Puinave, Guayabero, and Piapoco. The Puinave and Piapoco in turn evangelized the Guahibo, Cuiva, and Saliva. Disciples spread her message in some cases in ways completely unanticipated by her, such as the Colombian Indian, apparently a Curripaco, who in 1950 led a mass movement of Baniwa down the Içana singing psalms and bearing banners (see the introduction to Part IV).

The enthusiasm generated by her following soon attracted the attention of other agents of contact with interests in the region—first of all, from the Salesian missions. In the early 1940s, with the founding of the mission of Tapuruquara, or Santa Isabel, on the Rio Negro, headed by Padre José Schneider, the Salesians had successfully forced the nearby Baptist mission at Iucaby to close. Almost as a sort of demonic vengeance, they believed, the Protestants soon came back to invade the Içana. The Salesians themselves in 1951 described this process in the following manner:

> Engaged in the new Salesian mission of Tapuruquara (S. Isabel) initiated in 1942 in order to neutralize the propaganda of the Baptists at Iucaby, near Uaupés [São Gabriel], the Salesians gained, with the grace of God and visible help of the Celestial Mother, almost total victory. In this interim of more than six years, the Protestants worked secretly, penetrating through the frontiers of Colombia and Brazil, subverting all the territory of the Içana River and its tributaries with the venom of heresy." (*Cronica da Nova Missão Salesiana, de Assunção, Rio Içana, Fundada aos 8 de Fevereiro de 1951*, Salesian Archives, Assunção Mission, Içana River, Prelazia do Rio Negro; hereafter referred to in the text as *Salesian Diaries*)

The Salesians in fact had done extremely little until then in the way of ministering to the Indians of the Içana and its tributaries and, to a

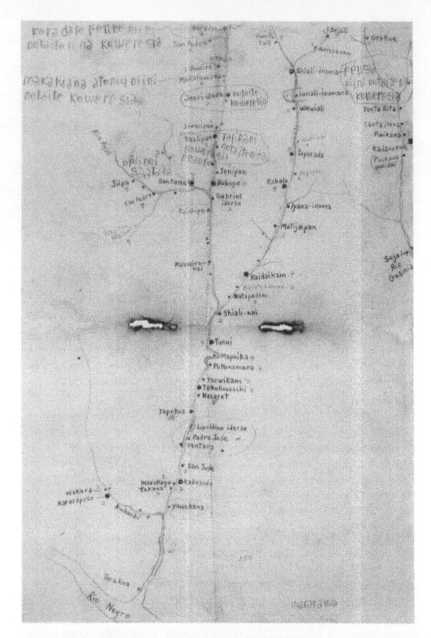

Map 3. Sophie Muller's Map of the Içana and Tributaries
(*Eduardo Galvão Collection, Library, Museu Goeldi, Belém; photo by Janduan Simões*)

certain extent, they felt they had left the way open for Protestant penetration. They recognized the tremendous success with which Sophie Muller had introduced the evangelical doctrine:

> Equipped with the knowledge of indigenous languages, from Colombia and Venezuela, the Protestants, above all the American Miss Sophie Muller, developed great activities, that degenerated into a true religious fanaticism.
>
> Quickly translating the Four Evangelists and almost all the Epistles of the Apostles into the indigenous language, teaching literacy to the quick learners, making them believe that she was sent by God, she had the greatest success. In all the villages, with few exceptions, temples of worship were built and, for long hours at night and in the morning, all the Indians assembled, singing and reading in their own language. (Ibid.)

Besides the obvious loss of a rather substantial population, what most concerned the Salesians was Sophie's explicit anti-Catholic propaganda which, according to the priests, led her to "rip off medals of Our Lady from children's necks while, in other villages, the same medals were found on the necks of dogs" (ibid.).

High Salesian authorities of the Rio Negro Prelacy determined in 1950 that direct combat was in order. As they had done with the Baptist mission of Iucaby, the Salesians sent the veteran Padre José[9] to select a place on the Içana on which to found a new Catholic mission. Early the next year, after consulting with the local Oalipere-dakenai chief Leopoldino, Padre José began setting up the mission of Assunção, or Carara-poço, on the lower Içana.

The Salesians, however, were not the only ones concerned with the Protestant movement; soon the SPI became involved. In fact, the SPI on the national level was increasingly concerned with the growing presence of New Tribes missionaries in the country—not because of its work of evangelization and teaching literacy in the native language, but because of its presence in border areas and the implicit threat to national security that this represented. In response to a request for information about the NTM from the Venezuelan government, SPI director José da Gama Malcher wrote that, given the linguistic diversity of native peoples in Brazil, to teach literacy to them all

> requires the concentration in our country of several thousand missionaries. Now, up until now it has been possible for the SPI to exercise its legal authority over the activities of the New Tribes

Mission, but will it be able to do so when it invades all of our territory, with its ships, planes and the rest that will come, becoming a
dominating organization in our unpopulated backlands?

And further:

> The question of greatest relevance and perfectly clear in our legis-
> lation is our policy of settlement and interiorization that is being
> frontally contested by the New Tribes Mission. The right to evan-
> gelize through preaching and acts of worship does not authorize
> them to enter the country through the most unprotected terri-
> tories of Brazil in order to undertake a type of educative action
> that the Constitution forbids to foreigners. Brazil cannot let go
> of its responsibility to turn into Brazilians its Indians and back-
> woodsmen who, by virtue of their backwardness, are only Brazil-
> ians because they were born in national territory.[10]

On the Içana, the SPI delegate Ataide Cardoso formally registered
several complaints against Sophie's methods of evangelizing. One was
that it was creating intravillage divisions, as on the Cuiary River and
upper Içana, where Cardoso, in his visit there in early 1953, noted the

> disunity that a lady of North American nationality, who answers
> to the name of Sophie and who says she is a Protestant missionary,
> has been causing because she orders Indians who do not accept her
> beliefs to be removed from the village, which is not in accord with
> the regulations of the SPI.[11]

A second complaint, perhaps graver from the point of view of the
SPI, was her outright defiance of government authority in the region.
In early June 1953, the local Police Delegate asked Cardoso to bring
Sophie downriver to São Gabriel for a chat, "in order to investigate
the existing denunciations" made against her (possibly by the Salesians and possibly because she had no documents to evangelize in the
country). Cardoso's story of his encounter with her reveals one more
of her legendary adventures which, even in the 1970s, the Indians remembered vividly and, by the 1990s, had taken on mythic qualities:

> Finding her in Limão-rupitá, an indigenous village located on the
> right bank of the Içana River, near Tunui Rapids ... I presented
> her with notice of the summons by the police authority, request-
> ing that she await my return there, to be taken to the Delegate
> who required her presence to defend herself from the denuncia-
> tions of which she was accused. Sophie Muller bluffed in accepting

the summons and shortly after I left, she fled in a canoe with five Indian rowers, passing by me late at night as we stayed the night at Tunui Cachoeira where, on the other side of the rapids, she got another canoe and went on to the village of Tajuba (at the mouth of the Cuiary, tributary of the Içana), where she got new rowers and went on, day and night, up the Cuiary until getting into Colombian territory, thus repeating the same itinerary as when, surprised by the Inspector Carlos Corrêa, she was also able to flee.[12]

I shall have occasion in the next chapter to show how these incidents have been transformed into Baniwa mythic discourse turning Sophie Muller's escape adventures into a messianic flight similar to that in the mid-nineteenth century of Kamiko, who likewise had fled from the authorities several times to a refuge settlement in the forest north of the Içana. Also remarkable is the Baniwa's allegiance to Sophie, to the point of rejecting SPI authority. Cardoso in fact recommended that it would be better for the SPI not to allow her back on the Içana for a period of at least two years, for the agency was being

held in contempt by the Indians due to the erroneous interpretation that they make of the teachings of the Protestant missionary. One may take as an example what happened recently at Tunui Cachoeira, where I—needing people to carry *sorva* below the rapids, as well as the motor and canoe—asked the *tuxaua* to bring me five men to help me. To my surprise, the Indians refused to obey my request and the *tuxaua*'s order (something that never happened before). Seeking to find out the reason for their refusal and disobedience of the *tuxaua*, I was informed that it was for fear of displeasing Dona Sophie (when she would come to find out about it), as well as the [North American Protestant pastors] that were present.[13]

At this refusal, Cardoso acted "with energy," using the authority of the SPI to round up a sufficient number of Indians to help in the transport, although admitting that it turned out to be more expensive since he had to pay the Indians for the service.

Again, I believe, there is a parallel that may be drawn with other moments of messianic movements in Baniwa history. The followers of Kamiko, according to oral histories and written documents, likewise had refused to submit to government and military authority, for the messiah had urged his followers to give their allegiance to him and there were severe consequences of breaking this pact. Sophie Muller seemed to repeat this pattern, or at least so her followers initially thought.

In any case, she had aroused formidable expectations among her disciples, creating a difficult-to-control situation that other evangelical missionaries who came afterward were forced to deal with and control. These sought to collaborate with the SPI and the Catholics—at least so they said—and requested to set up a permanent residence on the Içana.

After her escape in 1953, Sophie Muller never again returned to evangelize the Baniwa in Brazil. She settled in Colombia where, despite persecutions suffered by her NTM and SIL (Summer Institute of Linguistics) colleagues from the Catholic Church and government authorities, she worked on the Guaviare and Vichada Rivers, where the priests and police never reached.

David Stoll's superb research on evangelical missionaries in Latin America (1982), which led him to interview Sophie Muller in Bogotá in 1975, suggests that her politics of creating separatist "believer" communities in fact may have helped Indians to withstand frontier violence during the ten-year Colombian civil war, or "Violencia":

> According to the Matallana Commission, an official Colombia Commission which investigated the Summer Institute of Linguistics and New Tribes Mission in 1974, a fundamental point of her indoctrination was "to convince Indians that any contact with the 'whites' leads to the damnation of their souls. . . . [arguing] that the highly communal Indian life is what God wants. . . . She always struggles to prevent the Indians from acquiring . . . the most common vices among the settlers." Unlike the traditional hacienda-style Catholic missions, Muller trained Indian pastors and never created stations which exploited Indian labor. (Stoll 1982, 170–171)

During the Planas affair of the 1960s and '70s, when cattle ranchers surrounded and confined the Guahibo Indians of the savanna, perpetrating brutal repression of Guahibo resistance movements, Muller aligned herself with the Guahibo against the ranchers:

> In 1967, a man claiming 8000 hectares in Vichada territory told a court that she had arrived on his property with 200 persons armed with bows and arrows and shotguns. Under her orders, the Indians worked day and night to erect a 500-meter fence, which deprived the rancher of most of his claim. (Ibid.)

Not that she sided either with the Guahibo cooperativist movement nor with reformed Catholic missionaries who sought to help the Indians. As she explained to Stoll, the cooperative's organizer was a "communist" and the Catholics his "successors":

> In the Book of Revelations there are two beasts, she explained, one red and the other white. One is to rule the world and the other is the false church. "The first must be the Communists," she said, "they're the only ones who want to dominate the whole world, and the other must be ecumenism." (Ibid.)

Nevertheless, the strategies she offered for confronting the corruption and violence of the world of the whites were certainly one important reason for her success in this area. In relation to the Baniwa, at least, "avoiding the whites for it would lead to the damnation of their souls" was also a fundamental tenet of Kamiko's ideology in the mid-nineteenth century and perhaps of Anizetto's in the early twentieth.

Not long after the initial millenarian enthusiasm on the Içana had subsided, various Baniwa communities of the lower Içana, around the new Catholic mission especially, began to reevaluate the new religion and, dissatisfied, return to the old ways. In fact, her erratic and eccentric ways had alienated many "believers" from the beginning, as I shall have occasion to show in Baniwa testimonies cited in the next chapter. This "backsliding" occurred not only on the Içana but in many other places where she had planted churches; as Stoll reports, by the mid-1970s,

> Muller's empire was crumbling. . . . Converts were in rebellion against her authoritarian ways. There was also more effective competition than before. "Influence?" Muller responded, "Not anymore. That's a thing of the past when I could tell them what to do and they'd follow me. [Other outsiders] are coming in from all sides now, whole bands are going back to their old ways." She was especially disgusted with the Guahibo and Cuiva. . . . When Muller returned to a Guahibo village near Planas in 1974, only three families were still faithful. The others had painted themselves up and were dancing the dances. They would not allow her to stay in the village, and a spokesman told her that she had deceived them. (Ibid.)

Revivalist movements among the Cubeo of the upper Vaupés, according to anthropologist Irving Goldman, similarly weakened NTM's position by the 1970s, although they still retain a small following today (Goldman 1981, 8).

Despite her loss of popularity, Muller was still well-received on the Guaviare, where she remained until her death in the early 1990s. In the course of more than forty years of evangelizing in the Northwest Amazon, she had translated the New Testament in three languages and portions into eight others, teaching many of her followers to read and write in their own languages. She had trained hundreds of Indian pastors and, directly or indirectly, planted evangelical churches in scores of communities throughout the region. Even in areas which she never again visited—such as the Içana, Cuiary, and Aiary—the Indians still today guard a well-lit place in their memory of the early days of the millenarian enthusiasm which she had helped to revive.

Catholics versus Protestants

The Catholics, meanwhile, had set up a base on the lower Içana, the mission of Assunção at Carara-poço, headed initially by Padre José Schneider and later Padre Carlos Galli, with various other priests relieving them for brief periods. Over the years the Catholics attempted, albeit unsuccessfully, to make inroads into the Protestant-dominated areas of Baniwa villages. A close reading of the Salesian mission diaries over the past forty years reveals a sequence of strategies to bring the Baniwa into the Catholic fold—in essence by attempting to create a new set of alliances with the Brazilian military which would in effect oust the Protestants from their privileged position. In this struggle for Baniwa souls, Salesians and Protestants from the early 1950s to the mid-1960s waged propaganda wars, which forced the SPI to intervene and finally the military to remove the Protestant pastors from the area.[14]

Protestant propaganda throughout the decade of the 1950s caused the greatest consternation on the part of Catholic Church authorities. In light of the constant provocations, the bishop of the Rio Negro appealed to state and municipal authorities to "react," because what the "Protestant movement" represented above all was a "real and true threat to peace, public tranquillity and the normal work of the frontiers." Hence, the Salesian missionaries recommended that the Protestants be removed from national territory, "as had already been done in relation to the initiator of the movement, Sophie, who was expelled from Brazil" (*Visitas Pastorais da Missão Salesiana do Rio Içana, 1956,* Bishop of the Rio Negro, 12-01-56). Even violence was legitimate in view of the gravity of the situation, according to the bishop:

Brazilian national sentiment and patriotism should serve as powerful levers in the extremely urgent work of reaction—even, at times, the threat of violence if the circumstances call for it: what is at stake is the defense of all our work . . . that requires drastic remedies to confront the seriousness of the sect's permanence and depth, its boldness and audacity, its propaganda and its violence on this river, as well as the imminent threat of its penetration into other rivers and the collapse of the fruits of nearly forty years of missionary labor and the presence of the Christian and religious life in these villages. (Ibid.)

So serious an accusation and appeal to national consciousness as this brought action from the military several years later. In 1961, the same year that the Brazilian Air Force inaugurated an airstrip at the Carara-poço mission, military officials from Cucuy on the upper Rio Negro visited the Içana "to find out about the propaganda of the Protestants in the region and take due measures." They removed from the area Henry Loewen—one of the pastors most responsible for the propaganda wars and provocations—who, along with other Protestant pastors, was presented to army officials in Manaus. Apparently the pastors were prohibited from returning to the Içana, which was a reason for celebration for the Catholics: "It seems that Divine Providence wishes to facilitate the conversion of these Içana people, who have been dragged away by heresy" (*Salesian Diaries*).

"Divine Providence" in the form of the Trinity FAB (Força Aerea Brasileira)–Salesian missions–SPI, to be precise, initiated their alliance by vaccinating some five hundred Baniwa in April 1961. In the same year, the Salesians inaugurated the first boarding school on the Içana with some forty Baniwa schoolchildren. The priests believed that "removed from the Protestants, these will be the propagandists of the true religion" (ibid.). In short, the way was open, according to the bishop, "to intensify an apostolate in order to see if, little by little, we recover what has been lost "(ibid.).

Confident in the possibilities, Salesian inspector João Marchesi in 1963 recommended a series of measures to advance the work up the Içana, among which were to set up a permanent residence in exactly the same village where the Protestants had had their base; to learn the Baniwa language in order to evangelize, as the Protestants had done so successfully; to treat the *crentes* well, seeking to attract them to the Catholic faith; and "as far as the *crentes* who ask to become Catholic, they will be rebaptized and before baptism, they will have to confess publicly to the errors of the sect and hand over all of the books of the same" (ibid.).

Despite these energetic measures and high hopes for expansion, from then until the end of the decade, things seemed to happen the opposite of what the priests expected. One missionary wrote in 1964, for example, that only by a "miracle" would it be possible to "regain a field that has been lost." The mission at Assunção seemed to suffer chronically from a lack of supplies, food, and electricity. Fewer people turned up to masses; various cases of witchcraft were reported, in which the victims, near death, refused to receive the sacraments. A number of what might be called "disciplinary problems" (e.g., involving a group of boys who fled from the mission school) created situations of tension between the Baniwa and the director of the Mission, Padre Carlos, who used repressive and punitive measures to control them. And there are few indications from the *Diaries* that the Baniwa reconverted to Catholicism.

The records leave a distinct impression that by the end of the decade the mission was barely functioning, with few priests and nuns in residence. The 1969 visit of the Salesian inspectorate laments the state of the mission:

> With the nuns' leaving at the end of 1967 and the permanence of a single priest, the mission was practically closed. This is lamentable! Where there used to flourish two boarding schools with numerous schoolchildren, today we find a small group of day students. Where there used to grow abundant plantations, today there are now weeds and the fruit trees are now being overrun by the fury of the *sauva* ants. A river infested by Protestant heresy needs support and not destruction. . . .
>
> It's a shame to see so much effort of the brothers reduced to a handful of abandoned buildings and plantations. And the souls? (Ibid.)

Desperate appeals for help were made to the highest authorities of the Catholic Church on the Rio Negro, "to comprehend the lamentable situation in which they have left this reduced people of God" (ibid.).

Perhaps, as one inspector thought, the immensity of the work which they had taken on among Tukanoans on the Uaupés and its tributaries prevented a more effective presence on the Içana. As usual in the long history of Catholic missions on the upper Rio Negro, the people of the Içana and its tributaries remained relatively neglected. Consequently, few inroads were made into the evangelical communities, thus allowing them to continue developing the new religion into a form that was distinctly theirs. The most the Catholic missionaries could do was respond to signs of interest from ex-Protestant communities or communities wishing to leave the evangelical faith.[15] The New Tribes Mission, for its part, held its own with bases at the mouth of the Içana and in São Gabriel and occasionally visited around Jandú near the mouth of the Aiary. From these bases, North American pastors maintained contact through training courses and contacts with the faithful who came to visit them. Yet the conflicts and propaganda wars, as I have described them, had in a sense implanted and marked differences of religious identity between Catholics and *crentes* which have lasted until the present day.

Conclusion

At least four points are worth highlighting from the preceding historical analysis. The first is the importance of a messianic and millenarian tradition among the Baniwa dating from at least the mid-nineteenth century through the early twentieth. Far from being "sporadic outbursts" (Brown 1991) of enthusiasm, the movements affirm common historical patterns at different moments: self-proclaimed Christs, or messengers of Christ, who heal and advise, who bring together different peoples, who are believed to have the miraculous power, often symbolized by the cross, to control growth and to produce goods, who avoid the whites and seek to create havens of refuge, or sanctuaries, from political and economic oppression. The movements led by Kamiko and Anizetto appropriated Christian symbols within the framework of Baniwa belief while offering a solution to domination by the whites. There are various indications, which I shall explore further in the next chapter, that the enthusiasm generated by Sophie Muller's evangelizing was consistent with this millenarian tradition and that her peculiarly solitary and eccentric ways, defiant of authorities, led to her being identified with previous messianic figures.

Second, the predominance of the extractivist regime from the end of the nineteenth century until the decline of rubber, and its aftermath in the 1920s and 1930s, had grave consequences for the Baniwa, producing situations of extreme dependence on the rubber bosses, instability and social disorganization, exploitation by the merchants and military—in short, a regime of terror and violence. Disease and population decline contributed to the overall climate of fear. Under these circumstances, the prevalent strategy of the Baniwa, given the impossibility of sustaining a multicommunity movement, was flight and refuge and, minimally, an extreme distrust of commercial relations with the whites.

Third, with the diversification of extractive industries on the upper Rio Negro from the 1930s on, and the renewal of rubber-gathering during the Second World War, labor migration intensified, producing a cycle of constant journeys to distant labor camps and returns for

Figure 9. Protestant "Temples"
(photo by E. Galvão, Eduardo Galvão Collection, Library, Museu Goeldi)

brief stays in home villages. This itinerant existence, dependent on the bosses and their accounts, contributed to the disorganization of families, communities, and other levels of social and political groupings.

Fourth, although the Baniwa never stated so explicitly, I suggest that one of the repercussions of the evangelical movement was that it provided the basis for a solution to such situations of dependence, instability, disorganization, and exploitation under the extractivist regime. In this sense, I agree with Galvão's perception that the conversion movement represented in part a revolt against economic and social oppression. While many Baniwa continued to work for "bosses," it was of their own choosing and not because they were forced to do so. Working for bosses became secondary to the more fundamental, communitarian way of life of the *crentes*. Evangelicalism brought Baniwa back home after years of constant traveling to distant and hostile lands. It affirmed the possibility of the Baniwa's improving their material position without giving up their communitarian way of life—God would provide if one observed the rules. It enabled them to overcome their fear of the whites and gave them a way of dealing with the merchants. To be sure, evangelicalism accentuated internal divisions, particularly in the early, chaotic years of introduction of the new religion. Once grounded, however, it assumed the identity of a "Church of the United Tribes"—the name written on a signpost in front of the chapel at Tunui Cachoeira on the Içana River in the early 1970s—an impressive two-thirds of the Baniwa population claiming allegiance to the *crente* faith in 1980. Despite the turmoil created by Protestant and Catholic propaganda wars, and the Catholic campaign, supported by the military, to eradicate and replace the Protestant influence, vicissitudes of the Catholic mission and a silent resistance from the Baniwa against reconversion solidified evangelicalism as a predominant religious form on a greater part of the Içana and its tributaries.

8. *Deo iako*: The Creation of a New Generation of Believers

The complexity of early conversions to Muller's evangelism demands that it be understood from multiple points of view. To this end I present in this chapter the testimonies of several key sources: Sophie Muller, whose observations are recorded in her book *Beyond Civilization* (1952), which refer to her two trips to the Içana, Cuiary, and Aiary; the Salesian priests—interviewed by E. Galvão and myself—who began working among the Baniwa a few years after Muller's first conversion campaign, no doubt because of its tremendous success; and the Baniwa, whom I interviewed and who remember vividly the time of her coming. What my interpretation of these discourses seeks to emphasize are the cultural "filters" through which these actors understood the process of conversion. For the missionaries—Protestant and Catholic—Baniwa "paganism," beliefs in witchcraft, and an "innate fanaticism" predisposed them to convert to the new faith. The statements of various Baniwa—*crentes*, pastors, ex-*crentes*—reveal that the turmoil and transformations produced by evangelism were understood as related to the dynamics of ritual and political processes, specifically rites of passage, alliances and hostilities among phratries, and shamanism. What the converted Baniwa expected to realize was a sort of concrete utopia, in which evangelical teachings were molded to pre-existing processes (especially, the production of new generations of adults)—in some cases substituting for them, but in others, introducing new dimensions and sources of conflict that produced a dynamic of their own.

Sophie's Mission

Throughout her book, Muller gives clues as to how she understood her mission among the Baniwa. She thought of herself as

—a mediator between them and the Divine:

A thirsty people wanted to drink. They didn't know that that
which could satisfy was close at hand. They needed a human
mediator—one to whom God had revealed it—to bring it forth.
(1952, 14)

—a pilgrim sentinel who had come to warn of the imminent end:

The one thing you know is that you are one of the souls on this
earthly pilgrimage who knows the Way of Life. There are pilgrims
further on who do not know. . . . They must be overtaken and
shown the Way before night comes, when no man can work. (17)

—one moved by faith alone into the unknown:

If we had the faith of a grain of mustard seed, we too would move
in the program of God, responsive to His will, unresponsive to
the world around us. We would live as an ambassador on business
for His King, as a pilgrim and a wanderer in a strange land; as an
exile from Home whose heart is filled with the glory of his heav-
enly Country and whose voice is sounding for the message of
His King. (41)

—one constantly reminded through the powers of nature of the imminence of the Second Coming:

If the sight of things created can be so awesome and frightening, I
wonder what it will be like at the coming of the Creator. I wonder
what He will say to us about all those hearts who have been prepared to receive His Word, but who have never been told? Will He
say, "Well done, thou good and faithful servant"? (21)

—one whose mission was to release the Indians from Satan's bond:

I prayed aloud that the Lord would release them from the Devil's
grip so they could pray, and then some of them came through to
the Lord, it seemed. (23)

—one sent to cleanse them in order to be "possessed":

These people seem like "empty houses, swept and garnished,"
waiting to be occupied. I pray that the Lord will be allowed to take

possession of each one, so that the Devil doesn't return in power and "the last state of [that] man be worse than the first." (24)

—one sent to bring them "light":

They needed the light of the sun in their homes and they needed the Light of the Word in their hearts. (27)

—one sent to teach them detachment from worldly suffering and pain:

Earlier in the morning I had wished to get their minds off physical things and onto glorious things to come. . . . For it is a strange thing how detached one can be from physical aches while the Holy Spirit is using you as a channel for the Lord. (31)

—and one sent to prepare them for the Second Coming:

The most important lessons I taught in all the villages were on the Second Coming and the end of the world. It was just what they needed to give them an upward look and to break their love for this world. (48)

Demonology

By far the most striking aspect of Muller's text is its preoccupation— indeed, obsession—with demons. In the first village where she set foot on the Cuiary, she was confronted with people whose faces were streaked with charcoal, a traditional sign of mourning. Muller says she was told that these were "bad people, they're born like that" (5). Of course, the word for "bad, evil"—*maatchi*—could just as well refer to the misfortune people suffer at the death of a relative, but her inter- pretation of the word fit her preconceived notions of the omnipres- ence of evil.

According to her, Satan was everywhere among the Indians: "All the Rio Içana is still Satan's undisputed territory"; the Devil was manifest

—in their dances:

Moving along in a slow, funeral-like procession, they blew on long, tube-like poles, swaying slowly from side to side in time with the hollow notes that issued forth and re-echoed throughout the jungle.

One could easily associate these weird strains with witchcraft and demon worship, especially on a moonlit night in the heart of the jungle. (12)

—in invisible forces, called *"manjne-nai* (evil spirits)" that forced people to abandon their villages:

These people used to live at the mouth of the *canyo*, but fear of the *manjne-nai* (evil spirits) caused them to desert it. (13)

—and in the engravings on the boulders of the rapids at Uapui, marked on her map as *"oopinoi Satana"*—that is, "old-times Satan":

"They are from old times, they say; from the beginning of the race. I told them it was the Devil that made himself look like a shining angel who taught the first witch doctor" (55).

The shamans' stones, she told them, were "handed down" from the Devil, and she ordered doubtful "witch doctors" to throw them in the river. In village after village, she found Satan's most dreadful manifestations in the "demons and evil spirits" (variously written as *maneeti, manemna-nai, manemnali*—all apparently referring to the same concept of *manhene*, poison) which inflicted disease and death: "they all looked encased in witchcraft and fear"; "last night we seemed to be surrounded by demons" (23).

I never saw people like this before who felt so keenly that they were in the grip of the evil spirits. Probably it is because so many of them are in the grip of death in various stages. (24)

Muller came to the Baniwa with the idea that the Devil was Inyaakaim, evidently the Curripaco version of Inyaime, which refers to a spirit of the dead, an "other Kuwai" according to Hohodene shamans, whose village is located on the periphery of the Other World. As I have discussed in Part II, the village of Inyaime is opposed to the collective, patrilineal phratric soul houses, *tauli*, in the village of Iaperikuli, or "Jesus Christu." In her own way, Sophie made meaningful connections in terms of Baniwa cosmology when, for example, she warned them:

If you go to *Inyaakaim's* village, you'll see Judas Iscariot there; but if you go to Jesus' village, you'll see all these others who love Him. (9)

To Muller, Inyaime and Kuwai were one and the same. In one village on the Guainía, she nearly caught a glimpse of "Kuwai (the Devil)" when, on hearing "a strange, muffled, minor wail," she rushed down the path to see. The Indians told her,

> They're coming—the *manemnanai*! . . . They're coming to kill us! They're black; they look like animals, but they are people, bad people. (45)

As I discussed in Part II, the body of Kuwai, as represented by the sacred instruments, is indeed exceedingly dangerous for its associations with *manhene*, poison. In the myth of Kuwai, at the end of the first initiation rite, Kuwai is burned in an enormous fire and his liver becomes the first poisonous plants. At initiation rites today, the men who play the Kuwai instruments do indeed paint themselves black and are said to look like "forest-spirits," *awakarunanai*, but are "people," *newiki*. The combination of forest-spirit/person/body of the collective patrilineal ancestral soul is, as I have argued, a powerful synthesis of cosmology to which young people are introduced in initiation.

There is no reason to believe that the incidence of death from disease was any greater at the time of Sophie's visit to the Içana than it had been before. What most impressed her was the skin disease *purupuru*: "These Karom [sic] seem like an entirely different tribe than the Kuripako, as they are all spotted with light and dark purplish blotches" (9). One village, Gialinai (or Shialinai)—probably Vista Alegre—at the mouth of the Cuiary, was notable, for "half of them seem to be dying of a disease that makes them yellowish, bloodless and thin. Their legs start swelling above the knee, and their stomachs too, and death is near" (23). Outside of this one village, however, she mentions not more than three cases of tuberculosis on the Içana. By contrast, the Curripaco of the Guainía in Colombia, among whom she had worked for more than a year, seemed to be worse off, with some kind of "deadly fever" which made them turn to their shamans for help.

On her second trip to the Içana, she claimed that "many had died from pneumonia, fevers, parasites, etc.," concluding that "no doubt, a medical missionary could put the witch doctors out of business in a hurry in these tribes. Even the medicine I brought along had saved many lives and won lifelong friends" (48). Such claims nevertheless should be read with caution; after all, her evangelism had as a central tenet "Christ's triumph over Satan and the tomb" (10). She frequently expressed her own horror, fear, and anxiety over death (10, 16, 55), and warned the Baniwa to "set your eyes on things above, not on things of the earth; for you are dead, and your life is hid with Christ in God" (23).

If the actual incidence of disease was not as great as she made it out to be, the prevailing fear and distrust of whites were quite real, as evidenced by all sources since the beginning of the century. It is not unlikely that, by midcentury, many Baniwa had concluded that whites in general were harbingers of death, sorcerers and witches who brought disease and destruction, on a par with the animal- and water-spirits associated with the downriver, peripheral world outside of Baniwa territory.

When Sophie Muller came from the upper Içana with a message that appealed to vertical connections with divine sources of cosmic and social regeneration, she in effect presented a possible solution to the imminence of catastrophic destruction at the hands of the peripheral world of the whites. Her message of the imminence of the Second Coming surely resonated with the ideologies of earlier Baniwa prophets whose influence, as I have shown, lasted well into the twentieth century. It is not unlikely that the memory of their messages assumed a new importance at the time of her coming.

"Something New in the Realm of Their Experience"

There is strong evidence from Muller's account that she was received as someone with extraordinary powers, far different from the way Baniwa had received white people before. In the village of Iarakaim on the lower Içana, the chief thought she had "come from heaven":

> He kept asking me to keep them all from getting sick, chase the "evil spirits" away, rid his clearing of ants, etc., etc. "Is it all right to talk with the Devil?" they asked. "What do you want to talk with him for?" I replied, "Ask the Lord Jesus to keep him away." (52)

A year later, the botanist José de Carvalho passed through the same village, but the Indians fled at his approach. Six years later, the same village, no longer *crente*, had built a Catholic chapel with prominent figures of the saints. Evidently, at the time Sophie came, the Baniwa of Iarakaim were on the lookout for shamanic intermediation to solve their problems.

There is also no doubt that Sophie's concept of herself as divine messenger and her own inner motivations, which conformed to biblical, Protestant understandings, shaped the manner in which she translated Baniwa concepts to fit her conversion project.[1] In another village downriver, she confirmed their expectation of a divine messenger:

My village was called New York, but that isn't my village anymore. My village is Jesus' village in Heaven. He is the Capitán
there. Now I'm an *eeno-rikodaru* [resident of Heaven]. There's a
beautiful house waiting for me there in Jesus' village. (14)

To which the Baniwa agreed: "Our house is in heaven too," referring to their belief in the existence of collective ancestral soul houses,
tauli, in the Other World.

Following the logic that she was "from Heaven," however, her Baniwa converts, according to *their* expectations of divine emissaries, attributed to her the power to produce things—for example, "trousers
from Heaven" (24)—and to make their gardens grow well (28), powers which she admitted made her feel uneasy:

I'm scared of these people. They look at me as if I were something
supernatural. I'm afraid they'll turn and think I'm a devil one of
these days. (24)

This, coupled with their evident enthusiasm for literacy and the
printed word, explain why, by her second trip to the Içana, flotillas of
canoes followed her from one village to the next and why, in eighteen
different villages, they had made shelters or cabins to receive her:
"some were just palm-leaf shelters; some were finished white-clay
cabins with all kinds of weird decorations in red clay on the walls"
(53).[2] She estimated by then that she had about one thousand pupils
and about two thousand evangelized. She claims to have received
"dozens of notes" from pupils affirming their faith and rejecting the
ways of the past (50–53). An unprecedented triumph for her, "nothing ever before opened up like that on the Guainía" (104).

In her first trip, it was evident that her followers saw her in ways
that made sense to them—as a curer. The manner in which they prac-
ticed the orations and reading lessons seemed to her like their own
curing chants: "They were chanting forth the syllables in unison with
the monotones of a witchcraft rhythm, with a slight drop at the end"
(10). They made every effort to understand her messages about *"hwa-
niri Dios"* (Our Father God) in terms of Iaperikuli. As she perceived,

Something new has come into the realm of their experience. Strange
thought-patterns loom in the twilight fringe of consciousness, and
so they try to bring it down into the realm of their understanding. (14)

By the second trip, a year later, many believed that she was of divine origin and that what she taught was the key to the knowledge of the whites. Her translators and interpreters were clearly pathbreakers in reinforcing this belief—Felicia of the upper Içana, "a most brilliant and unusual Indian girl," who helped to explain Sophie's talks in the dialect; Alberto, "real leader material and could be a power for God" (37); chief Leopoldino, of the lower Içana, who translated and interpreted for her; and others. The opposition to her project came from the shamans of the Guainía and upper Aiary, and from certain "prophetesses" (unfortunately, she does not go into more detail) of the same regions. The Catholic missionaries, then still in São Gabriel, had not yet begun to work on the Içana:

They say that a priest from São Gabriel had them make my shelter about a year ago. He only stayed a few days, they said, and never came back. If he taught them anything, they evidently did not understand, because they know nothing about the Lord Jesus— or Catholicism. Hope the priest stays away until the Indians are rooted in the Word of God at least. (21)

In the context of her faith mission, then, Sophie saw the Baniwa as, literally, in the grip of Satan—"surrounded by demons," as she said, or "encased in witchcraft and fear," which she attributed to their culture. Her task, as she saw it, was to liberate them—that is, destroy their culture, which she openly admitted (see Stoll 1982, 170), so that they could assimilate the evangelical faith. Early in her work, she recognized what she thought to be Baniwa enthusiasm with her presence. At least on the lower Içana, she was received in ways that indicated their perception of her as a divine emissary. She reinforced this image, but as it became apparent that she was treading on delicate grounds, she found she had to set them straight that she was not from heaven. As did the priests (see next section), Sophie perceived that many Baniwa sought to understand the new religion by making meaningful connections to their own beliefs and practices.

According to the Priests

On Sophie's map, three places on the lower Içana are circled, indicating the influence of the priests: Lipoldino-iderse, or the village of the Oalipere-dakenai chief Leopoldino on the island of Hekoari; "Padre José," or the village of Carara-poço; and Sant'Ana. These three villages, along with several other *geral*-speaking communities, became the principal base from which the priests sought to extend their influence. It was a region which, at least since Koch-Grünberg's time, was notable for its complex interweaving of popular Catholicism and Baniwa traditions. In a sense, this predisposed these communities to follow the Padres and not the *crentes*.

Before presenting the Padres' views on Baniwa conversion, I will briefly characterize this allegiance to the Padres and its basis both in the sorts of patron-client relations that characterized interethnic relations at that time and in traditions of popular Catholicism.

At least in the early years of the Padres' presence, Baniwa communities of the lower Içana seemed to welcome them. Padre José was held in high esteem because, according to Mandu of Uapui, "he was a worker," who helped people return from the rubber camps and build new houses, and for whatever services he received, he paid the Indians well. Eduardo Galvão observed the following on Padre José's relations to the Indians:

> The expectation of the Indian in relation to the Padre is that he be a friend and give them presents. Also—and this in general for all the whites—never refuse what is offered to him in trade. . . . Even if it's a cup of tapioca, Padre José paid something in return. When it wasn't possible to pay for the product, the Indians remained in debt. (Galvão, Fieldnotes 1954)

Quite different was their relation with Padre Carlos, about whom Galvão observed:

> He's the type that expects the faithful to seek him out, when the opposite should be the case. On the other hand, he lets his competition with Padre José become clear in his attitudes. In his sermons he declares that the Padre is not a merchant who gives cloth or presents. To him, he is owed respect and the obligation to go to Mass. It is God who speaks through him. (Ibid.)

Various incidents in which, for example, Padre Carlos underpaid Indians for services led them to conclude that, despite his sermons, he was little different from the merchants:

> "Doesn't he sell merchandise to us?" one man asked. "If he sells, he cheats people, for all *cariua* (whites) steal and cheat." . . . This is their greatest concern, that of being cheated. . . . This is the basis of relations between Indians and traders, the eternal certainty that they're being cheated. (Ibid.)

Beyond these economic relations, it is interesting that both Padres seem to have been attributed powers that went beyond simple patron-client relations. According to Padre Wilhelm Saake, a Salesian who undertook on the Içana a month's research of myths and rituals (which produced the first published collection of Baniwa narratives; see references in bibliography), Padre José was considered by the Baniwa of the lower Içana to be a "very powerful shaman" (1959–1960a, 435) who had the ability to cure *marecaimbara*, or poison. Several Hohodene of Uapui told me that Padre Carlos was a "saint" who had the power to "order the devil away." (Wright, Fieldnotes)

Such statements indicate that, as in the case of Sophie Muller, Baniwa sought to interpret the Padres in terms of their traditions and expectations, in this case by building on an already existing historical association between shamans, chanters, and Padres. The number of shamans on the lower Içana in the early 1950s was in fact small, being outnumbered by chanters (Galvão gives three names for these: *dzuri*, in Baniwa; *mutawari*, in *língua geral*; and *benzedores*, in Portuguese). While only shamans could cure poison, the chanters "blessed" or, as it was said, "baptized." Now, "baptizing" or the bestowing of names is an apt description for what Baniwa chanters in fact do: they invoke classes of spirit-names in order to protect people undergoing rites of passage. According to Galvão, rituals of initiation were indeed referred to as "baptism." At the same time, the Baniwa affirmed to Galvão that "baptism is only by the Padre and a Christian name." Saint's day festivals on the Içana, as elsewhere on the Rio Negro, furthermore, were officiated by a native "padre" or "Paí" who sang the litanies of the saints in Latin; these litanies—like the lengthy *kalidzamai* chants sung at initiation rites—consist of ordered sequences of sacred names.

How, then, did the Padres explain the phenomena of Sophie Muller and the mass conversion movement to evangelicalism? Galvão's interview with Padre José in 1954 and my interview with Padre Carlos in 1976 indicate that both attributed the movement to an "innate fanaticism" of the Indians that resonated with Sophie's personality. Padre José said she was

a lady of a little over 30 years of age, quite polite, who spoke German, but of a tremendous fanaticism. Her appearance dates to a few years ago when news got to Uaupés [São Gabriel da Cachoeira] of a "saint Sofia." He [Padre José] confirmed the leadership that she exercised on the upper Içana and its consequences. In only one case was there depredation of the Catholic chapel. In Tunui, he was forced to take away the images of the saints because they were covered by mud that the *crentes* had thrown. According to the Padres, the problem of the Indians is their fanaticism which leads them to excesses. Tacitly, he admits the advances of Protestantism, consoling himself with the affirmation that "they will return" to the Church. (Galvão, Fieldnotes 1954)

Padre Carlos' explanations and descriptions of the movement were rather more complete. In response to my inquiries, he first spoke of the Baniwa situation in the 1950s, of how "they lived in slavery to the rubber bosses; they hardly had any gardens; many villages were abandoned; and people looked miserable, sad and hungry" (Wright, Fieldnotes). Then he went on,

Sophie came to the Içana because she had made a promise to herself to evangelize in an area where no-one before had. She came to Brazil from Colombia but she had no papers. So, when the SPI heard of her evangelizing and that it was causing fights in the villages, she was ordered to leave.

She told the Indians that she was sent by God and had received orders from God to evangelize them. She told her disciples to destroy fruit trees because, she said, Adam was tempted by the fruit. She told them not to buy merchandise from the whites, because all goods that people needed would come from Heaven. So she didn't trade with them or give them material goods.

She would have people sing and pray for days without a break and with no food. She prohibited tobacco and *caxiri* because, she said, they made the body and spirit weak and besides, caused fighting. Catholics were weak because they did both. (Wright, Fieldnotes)

On the anti-Catholicism of the *crentes*, Padre Carlos said,

The *crentes* would have nothing to do with the Catholics. The Catholics were told they couldn't share meals with the *crentes* and couldn't even enter their houses. Even if a Catholic stayed for a night in a *crente* village, no food or refreshment would be offered to them. The Padres' lives were threatened several times. Some *crentes* even made a coffin for the next time the Padre would visit them. At the least, when a Padre would visit, they would cross their arms over their chests, bow their heads, and call the Padre Inyaime. For years, they refused to have a reconciliation with the Catholics. (Ibid.)

Padre Carlos recounted, with some indignation, how he had received the North American pastors with hospitality and they returned
it by calling the Salesians "fools." Indeed, from the Salesian mission
diaries, we learn that in January 1957, Protestant pastors visited the
Catholic mission and left some "books" [perhaps their translations
of the New Testament?] with Padre Carlos. The priest "perceiv[ed]
the malice of the visitors [and] burned the books on the beach in the
presence of the Indians. The pastors left the mission laughing" (Salesian Diaries). No sooner had they left, however, when there occurred a
disaster: the pastors stopped to heat up some food, but the fire caused
an explosion in their boat which destroyed all of their equipment. Padre Carlos rescued them and the pastors went back home embarrassed
by the confusion they had caused.

According to both him and Padre José, they were attacked with
knives by crentes in villages of the upper Içana, and Padre José suffered
various attempts to poison him (Knobloch 1972, 292). The chiefs of
various Catholic villages of the lower Içana (e.g., Leopoldino, who had
become an ally of the priests) likewise suffered poisoning attempts
and sought the protection of the Salesians.

To what did Padre Carlos attribute these actions? "Fanaticism," he
responded, "it's in their blood." But why would they believe what Sophie said? I asked. Padre Carlos offered three reasons, evidently attributing their conversion to a sort of simplistic syncretism with Baniwa
mythical figures: Iaperikuli is "the one who gives food, like God";
Kaali, the Master of the Earth, is the "first man, made from earth, like
Adam"; and Amaru, "the mother of everyone, like Eve."

There was yet another reason which Padre Carlos mentioned in
passing, but it was Padre Wilhelm Saake who suggested it as an important motive for conversion to evangelicalism: disgust with marecaimbara or poison, manhene, and the failure of shamans to cure it. Sophie Muller repeatedly noted this motive in her book. Citing the case
of a shaman named Benedito, Saake reported:

After the death of his mother, which he couldn't prevent, he
became so disgusted with shamanism that he never again prac-
ticed it, throwing his apparel into the river. Another shaman told
me the same, that after his conversion to Protestantism, he didn't
want to know anything more about shamanism and marecaimbara.
(1959–1960a, 435–436)[3]

If this rejection was seen as a solution to witchcraft, however, it was
only partially successful, according to the Padres, for one of the

contradictions in the new faith was the fact that people continued to practice witchcraft, indeed even in the context of evangelical rituals. Padre Carlos cited instances which, he said, occurred during the monthly "Santa Céia" rituals, when the baptized drink a fruit juice made from *assaí*, a winelike mixture which the evangelicals call "the blood of Christ." This ritual is supposed to be "a time to await Jesus." The faithful shut their eyes and cover their faces in prayer. In the midst of this most fervent moment, according to Padre Carlos (and several Hohodene), witches have slipped poison into the drink, killing several people in any one ritual. If this is true, then it is one more indication that the evangelical rituals were shaped by and substituted for the *pudali* and Kuwaipan rituals, both being occasions when witches also put sickness and even poison in their victims' *caxiri*.

The priests thus explained Baniwa conversion in terms of their own notions of native religion and fundamentalist faith: Sophie Muller and the Baniwa were equally given to "fanaticism"; according to the priests, this was part of the Indians' nature. Besides, the priests recognized by 1960 that, with the removal of the Protestant pastors from the area, the "fanatic spirit had diminished and they [the *crentes*] are seeking to get closer in order to know the truth better" (*Salesian Diaries*).

Sophie Muller's literalistic teaching of the Bible was quickly accepted, according to the Padres, because the Baniwa understood it in terms of their mythological heroes. As did Muller, the Padres pointed to sorcery and witchcraft as one of the compelling reasons for conversion. Both no doubt emphasized the issue of witchcraft because it was the most challenging to any conversion effort, but the Padres used the fact of the continued existence of elements of witchcraft among the *crentes* as proof of the weakness of the new faith.

But how do Baniwa *crentes*, Catholics, ex-*crentes*, shamans, and others remember and interpret the evangelical movement, the phenomenon of Sophie Muller, and the conflicts generated by Protestant and Catholic missionaries? To what extent did *they* attribute their conversion to an antiwitchcraft movement?

According to the Baniwa

Here I present a series of Baniwa statements to anthropologists on Sophie Muller and their experiences with the new religion. These were obtained from the following sources: Eduardo Galvão's interview with a Dzauinai man of the Içana in 1954; Adélia de Oliveira's interview with an Adzanene man of the Içana in 1971; and my interviews and observations among Hohodene, Oalipere-dakenai, and Maulieni *crentes*, ex-*crentes*, and Catholics of the Aiary in the late 1970s.[4] Evidently, there are qualitative differences between Galvão's interview, representing early views on evangelicalism, and my material which represents over a generation of reflection on the changes it produced.

This material offers ample opportunity to make comparisons and contrasts of Baniwa statements with Sophie Muller's and the Padres' views that reveal aspects of the conversion process which utterly escaped the missionaries' understandings. Their statements first of all have to do with her prohibitions and orders to change their ways: the longhouses, dance festivals and musical instruments, *caxiri*, shamanism, tobacco, and everything of the ancestors were to be "left behind."[5] The enormous rupture which this represented would have irreversible consequences which were no doubt difficult to foresee at the time, particularly if the enthusiasm over her presence was as great as she claimed. It was nothing less than a radical and violent break with tradition with concrete manifestations: shamans' instruments were thrown into the river, the sacred flutes and trumpets were exposed in public, the longhouses and beer troughs were put to the ax, the music was forgotten.

Yet, as I shall show, the shape of the transformation as it is remembered was in large part defined by the dynamics of political and ritual processes. When I conducted fieldwork on the Aiary, more than a generation had passed since this transformation had begun, and my initial impressions were that the divisions between *crentes* and Catholics had solidified into two distinct ways of life. The *crentes* in short had forged a sort of concrete utopia in which evangelical teachings were molded to preexisting processes, particularly related to the production of new generations of adult *crentes*.

I shall also examine in detail, through a case history, the confrontations between pastors and a powerful prophet of the upper Aiary, Kudui—to whom I have already referred several times in this book—as an especially illuminating instance where "millenarian consciousness" came into focus in the movement. Finally, I highlight the motives which the Baniwa cited for converting—the positive aspects of being *crente*—and the reasons for leaving the faith—the flaws, as it were, in the utopia which the evangelicals sought to create.

Perhaps the first glimpse I got of the distinct lifeways forged by the *crentes* came during a canoe trip I made early in my fieldwork to survey the Aiary settlements. At Loiro-poço, near the mouth of the Aiary, I and my guides stayed for a weekend, during which time two native evangelical pastors visited from the Quiary River, a tributary of the lower Aiary entirely populated by *crentes*. They had come to evangelize, or teach *"Deo iako,"* the "word of God," to the people of Loiro-poço.

The village had a grade school, maintained by the Salesians, and a young Oalipere-dakenai teacher from the Catholic mission of the Içana would lead the community in daily prayers and weekly masses. A curious situation—and, from what I knew of the history of religious conflicts, I waited anxiously to see what would develop.

The pastors, both well mannered and soft-spoken, made a point of finding out what my purpose was in coming and staying. I explained my project, my interest in history—"how people lived in the past and today." In turn, they told me of their mission. They frequently traveled to evangelize. Both pastors had known "Dona Sofia" and both had learned to chant with her and her successor "Henrique."[6] Indeed, I noted in the Protestant service that they conducted later on that both pastors had an impressive knowledge and literacy in the New Testament and could answer questions from the congregation with facility. The people of Loiro-poço listened to their sermons attentively and responded (the Baniwa *crentes* in fact refer to themselves as *hliepaka-peri*, "responders") to their questions on passages from the New Testament.

One of the pastors, however, was visibly troubled by my presence and, following the service, sincerely tried to find out how it was that I didn't personally know the American pastors on the Içana, why wasn't I a *crente*, and wouldn't I take some literature (berating alcohol and smoking) to study? When he realized that I was uncommitted, he dropped the matter, concluding that I was someone "of the *governo*," a representative of FUNAI.

The next day began with the pastors singing in the early morning waking hours, followed by a Protestant service. Then the Catholic schoolteacher conducted weekly "mass" (i.e., a reading from the missal). I asked the schoolteacher what he thought of this dual situation—did it make any difference? To which he responded that he thought that the only differences between Catholics and *crentes* was in the former's use of signs such as the cross and medals representing the saints, but "there is only one God for both, so there is no reason to fight over which is better or more the truth."

The situation seemed then to be marked by tolerance, at least in Loiro-poço, and even among *crentes* it was said that there were several different modes of "being *crente*": learning but as yet unbaptized; baptized but "half-*crente*" (i.e., occasionally participating in dance festivals and smoking tobacco); studying with a missionary to become a pastor or elder. Yet to take Loiro-poço as typical of the religious situation would be an error, for it would ignore the innumerable memories of the radical transformation and its ensuing conflicts which, now and then, flared up in uncomfortable ways. *Crentes* had, after all, forged a distinct identity from the Catholics, with visible marks of that identity which they sought to maintain. These will become evident in the statements I shall now introduce.

The first is from an informant of Eduardo Galvão, a Dzauinai man named Ernesto of the village of Sant'Ana on the lower Içana, where Galvão conducted fieldwork in 1954. Sant'Ana had a rather peculiar history and composition, according to Galvão. Since the time of Nimuendaju, the village was divided into two sibs (Maracajaí and Jurupary-tapuya, in *língua geral*), a division which had crystallized into their spatial separation—each living in a separate part of the village—by the 1940s (which even led Galvão to suspect the existence of moieties). Besides that, the population of the village was then quite large, having grown from forty to fifty people in 1927–1928, to some twenty houses (perhaps one hundred fifty to two hundred people) by 1948–1949—the largest village on the Içana in the early 1950s—which further emphasized the socio-spatial separation of the two sibs. Galvão's informants gave differing versions of the nature of the rivalry: one said that what was at stake was a dispute over chiefly succession; Ernesto and the then chief, however, agreed that the two sibs were "brothers" (i.e., agnatic siblings, belonging to the same phratry) but disputed over rank (i.e., which was the elder brother).[7]

It is interesting in this context, then, that religious divisions between Catholics and Protestants also occurred along the same lines as the social divisions. The sib called "Jurupary," which claimed to be the "elder brother" and which had previously held the position of chief of the village, was known as the "group of Sofia," while the other sib, which had recently assumed chieftainship, the "younger brothers," was identified as the "group of the Padres." Ernesto who was of the "group of Sofia," had left the evangelical fold and sought to ally with the "other side." Galvão explains:

He was a *crente* for a month under the influence of a visit from Sophie. He received a Bible and, every night, would learn with João [his brother-in-law]. He didn't learn to read; he learned to listen. Sophie was in Sant'Ana two or three times, a few days each. At nightfall, she would go into the woods saying that she went to pray, and returned in the middle of the night. Ernesto began to dislike her. One day his son was playing and Sophie came and asked who was his father. She warned him [Ernesto] that he ought to

teach the boy that he wasn't worth anything, that he wasn't thinking holy. She thought the boy was doing something indecent, but
he was a child, he was only playing.

She said that boys were worthless because they didn't think holy
like the old people. When Christ would come from below the
earth, he wouldn't want boys because they were worthless. It was
best to tie a rope around their necks and throw them in the river.
Ernesto pondered on what the Padre had taught, that one must not
kill people, for they wouldn't go to heaven. She kept on saying that
children were worthless, and he didn't think it right to order them
to kill children. He went to talk with the Padre who told him to
forget Sophie, that she was lying.

Another thing she would say was that people should only "think
holy." After baptism, men were brothers to women and couldn't
have children, because children were worthless, and only the old
people thought holy. He also didn't like that part about not having
children, and he wasn't sure about the business of husbands
being like brothers to their wives. These ideas probably weren't
explained this way. She must have been referring to the Last Judgment, and the need to teach a puritan line to the boys, and about
luxury or something similar. But Ernesto is more than convinced
that she really wanted to order the children to be killed and prohibit sexual relations among married couples.

Padre José got the better, for only two *crentes* are left, Inocêncio
and his son-in-law. Even so, the latter asked the priest to baptize
his son, which I attended. To give an idea of the understanding of
the doctrine by the people here, it's enough to say that Ernesto is
the most intelligent informant that I have, who has assimilated
with ease my objectives in areas such as kinship, the origin and
division of groups. (Galvão, Fieldnotes 1954)

We might speculate on the meaning of these affirmations, without
ever having the certainty of why they were strong enough motives for
the people of Sant'Ana to leave evangelicalism. Galvão gives us some
clues in referring to obvious contradictions between Sophie's puritan
morality[8] and Baniwa social norms: for example, sexual abstinence
among married couples and fraternal relations among spouses would
suggest violation of traditions of incest among "brothers," people of
the same sib, and rules of exogamous marriage.

Yet how are we to understand the apparently dubious point about
killing young boys? Admittedly, Sophie Muller said and did many eccentric things; nevertheless, this statement seems to misinterpret her

prophecy of an imminent inversion in the existing cosmic order. Christu has always been associated with Iaperikuli and the upper realms of the cosmos, not the underworld which is the place of the bones of the dead and a host of cannibalistic spirits who will appear at the end of the world. Killing children is an act attributable to sorcerers and witches—the very opposite of the enormous value the Baniwa attribute to the young, the sources of future generations. In short, what mattered to Sophie, according to Ernesto, was the elders who "thought holy," but not the reproduction of their knowledge in the young or through family relations.

Another detail may be noted in Ernesto's observations: Sophie's nocturnal wanderings, which were real (she mentions them several times in her book). Hohodene Catholics whom I interviewed in the late 1970s interpreted these wanderings, again, as moments of inversion typical of witches; that is, they said that in the forest, she would transform into the "demon-without-a-head," Inyaime-hmewidane, and that her arms, legs, and head would fall off and she would fly away.

Thus, at least for the disaffected evangelicals of Sant'Ana in the 1950s, there were readily apparent and unresolved cosmological contradictions in the new religion: what Sophie seemed to preach was Apocalypse, not Paradise.[9]

The second set of statements is from the Hohodene of the village of Ucuqui Cachoeira (or Kuliriápan) of the Uaraná stream off the upper Aiary, who recounted to me on numerous occasions stories of Sophie, Henrique, and the *crente* elders of the Quiary, as well as conflicts between *crentes* and the shaman and prophet Kudui, who was their "uncle" (sib brother).

The first citations come from my conversations with Laureano, then chief of Ucuqui, a Catholic who, at the time of Sophie Muller's visit to the Aiary, became a disciple of the new religion. One of his daughters in fact is named "Sofia." He spoke of various aspects of the conversion movement and the conflicts it generated:

> Sophie taught in Uapui in one of the *malocas*. She sent messengers to call us to hear *Deo iako*. At Uapui there was a big gathering ["congresso"] of people from the Uaraná and Aiary. She spoke in Curripaco. Before this, people had told us, "Sophie is coming, Sophie is coming!" So we said, "Let's go see." She spoke a lot in Uapui—that people had to become half-civilized, wear clothes, stop the festivals—a lot of things.
>
> She baptized, taking many people to the river to do it. She taught *Deo iako*. She had many followers. But if you were not baptized, the

crentes would not allow you into the chapel to pray. Then, many people wanted to become *crentes*. Today, there is only one or two left here.

Later, I went to hear her speak at a large gathering on the Querary, in a Cubeo village. She greeted me and right away wanted me to hear more *Deo iako*. She didn't even let me eat before. She talked and talked, but I couldn't understand anything because it was all in Cubeo.

There was a man named Correa who accompanied her. He wanted to marry her but she wouldn't let him near her, and she threatened him with the authorities if he didn't stop.

Henrique told people to stop drinking *caxiri* and smoking tobacco. He said that the dances and festivals had to stop and that people had to become civilized like the whites. He said that people couldn't enter the chapel if they hadn't been baptized. (Wright, Fieldnotes)

In referring to his own disagreements with the *crentes*, Laureano said that he once told the *crentes* of Canadá that "tobacco was given to us by God, as our stories say," and that the *crentes* could not prohibit it. God also "gave us all animals to eat, for our food." He remembered that *crente* elders from the Quiary River would go around telling women of various villages about Kuwai and "the bark wrapping, what it looked like." Once they went to the upper Uaraná to the village of Seringa Rupitá (where the people of Ucuqui used to live), and one elder was going to tell, but "he became afraid and kept quiet." Some *crente* songs, Laureano recalled, had the refrain "When do you want to leave Kuwai?"

Finally, Laureano recalled incidents of *crentes* leaving the faith; for example, there was a *crente* elder who knew well the songs, but as a result of some people putting poison, *manhene*, in the "blood of Christ" *assaí* drink that the *crentes* take at "Santa Céia," the man decided to leave being *crente* and to go back to dancing *pudali*.

Laureano's statements emphasize three aspects of conversion: the millenarian enthusiasm at the time of Sophie's visits; her and other pastors' messages to transform and to mark the transformation ritually through baptism in the river; and the conflicts and contradictions between the new ways and rituals and the old.

Laureano's descriptions certainly provide strong grounds to believe that the large gatherings at the Uapui *maloca* and the Querary *maloca*, announced beforehand by messengers who summoned people from distant villages, were millenarian assemblies. More remarkable is the admiration of her capacity to speak *Deo iako* in several languages, transcending the specificity of local dialects, often a characteristic of messianic figures.

The very place of the first major gathering, Uapui, is also of great significance to the Hohodene, for its connection to the sacred "center of the world." Sophie understood some of the mythical significance of the place (and drew it in her book) and understood that by striking at the center—demonizing it, as in the expression she put on her map, referring to Uapui as "*oopinoi Satana*," or "the old-times Satan"—this would be a key strategy for conversion.

The ritual and ideology that Laureano (and others) remembered would accomplish this transformation included, essentially, baptism in the river, a sort of initiation which produced the hiatus between *crentes* and non-*crentes*, initiated and noninitiated, insiders and outsiders; *Deo iako*, or "the word of God"; and "becoming half-civilized" by renouncing cultural practices.[10]

But renunciation encountered powerful resistance principally in relation to shamanism and ritual. Laureano mentions the incapacity of the evangelicals to "prohibit" or even repress belief and practice—the divine sources of food and tobacco and their mythical legitimation; the secrecy of the sacred flutes and trumpets, Kuwai, which was strong enough to force the *crente* elders to remain silent; and the secrecy of poison which was strong enough to undermine evangelical drinking of "the blood of Christ." In relation to the last mentioned, Laureano seemed to be saying that, while the evangelicals prohibited *caxiri*, the weakness of their own ritual drinking as a mechanism for generating "happiness," or social solidarity, proved to be a way back to the drinking fests.

Laureano's reference to the case of the *crente* elder who left the faith because of *manhene* is important and highlights one of the most frequently cited motives for abandoning evangelicalism. The missionaries' campaigns against shamanism and their prohibition of tobacco left the converted in a vulnerable position in relation to witchcraft and sorcery. Many in fact had converted because of *manhene*, but just as many left the faith because *manhene* continued to exist. "Without shamans or tobacco," one Catholic man said, "if a *crente* got *manhene*, he could only pray or die."

It was the strength of the shamans and, in particular, of the Hohodene prophet Kudui, of the village of Ucuqui—"uncle" of the descent group to which Laureano belonged—that deterred the advance and consolidation of Sophie's conversion movement on the upper Aiary, as she herself recognized in *Beyond Civilization*.

In the mid-1950s, Kudui (or Guilherme Garcia, his Portuguese name) already had considerable fame. Padre Wilhelm Saake, who met him in 1956, said, in almost exactly the same words as the Hohodene described to me in the late 1970s, that Kudui was considered a "true shaman":

> He knew of events that took place far from his house, he knew who was coming to visit, he understood sicknesses and had the force to overcome *marecaimbara*. His house was full of things highly valued by the Indians which were given him in payment for his cures. (1959–1960a, 435)

The Hohodene of Ucuqui and Uapui Cachoeiras added numerous stories of his miraculous cures and powers. According to them, he had gained this power as a result of a sickness which had nearly killed him. In his sleep, his soul had gone to the house of the dead, where he was advised by Iaperikuli that he wouldn't die. Another shaman, Kumadeiyon of the Dzauinai phratry, reputed to "know even more than Kudui," cured him. Ever since then, Kudui's dream-soul would, whenever he slept, talk with Iaperikuli who advised him about events to come. Hence his power to prophesy and divine, to advise people about sickness. According to Mandu, a former apprentice to Kudui, he was able to "say there will be no more sickness, and that all would become better." For these reasons, the Hohodene considered him to be "like Iaperikuli, our salvation." Indians from all over the region— the Uaupés and Içana—would come to consult with him.

He was also considered to be one of the only legitimate interpreters of Baniwa religion. He told people, for example, that the true "center of the world" was a stone island slightly above the rapids of Hipana. The rock, he said, was "Dzulíferi's body" and "whoever stepped on it would get *manhene*."

Kudui died in late 1975 at Warukwa, an island on the Uaraná stream, which is also, according to myth, the place of Iaperikuli's house. According to Mandu, however, "he didn't die, he still lives and people pray to him through God." As with the mid-nineteenth-century prophet Kamiko, people would bring offerings to his grave and ask for his protection.

That Kudui was identified with Iaperikuli signifies that he was also identified with Jesus Christu, and many of people's memories of Kudui are expressed in Christian terms. It is said that whenever people entered his house, they would make the sign of the cross first. According to João, Laureano's brother, Kudui's dream-soul would sing "Gloria! Gloria!" as he slept, and he told people that "the city of God is like the city of the whites but more beautiful."

These statements are intelligible in the context of the evangelical

and Catholic movements of the 1950s and '6os. Many of Kudui's closest relatives were early followers of the evangelicals. Undoubtedly,
they turned to Kudui for advice on the new religion, and he unfail-
ingly defended Baniwa belief and ritual against *crente* attacks while,
at the same time, interpreting Christianity in terms that made sense to
his followers. It was for this reason that the upper Aiary was able to
withstand the radical change sought by the *crentes*.

Once, João recalled, *crente* elders from the upper Içana came by trail
to the upper Uaraná and told people that "the world would come to
an end, everything would become dark at midday, and that people
should close their houses and leave their dogs out on the appointed
day." To this, Kudui advised his kin that the *crentes* were talking "nonsense" for the world was not about to come to an end. He added that
the Bible itself was a "good book" but that the *crente* elders spoke nonsense. With the strength of Hohodene conviction in Kudui's powers to
cure, to know and communicate with Iaperikuli, the *crentes* were
discredited.

The *crente* elders attempted to go a step further: four of them, again
from the upper Içana, returned to Kudui's house with the intent of
killing him but, according to João, Kudui knew that they wanted to
"give him poison, *manhene*." He told them he knew, for "God had
advised him, and they became afraid and left." For João and many
others, this convinced them that Kudui held greater powers over the
truth (Wright, Fieldnotes).

Fortunately for the Hohodene of the upper Aiary, they had Kudui
to defend their traditions against the attacks of the *crentes*. In other
communities, Sophie and her converts introduced serious dissension
over the shamans, which led many of them to abandon their practice
and convert. Of Uapui, Sophie said:

> The Indians told me that some of the witch doctors would not
> come to see me, but three of them have adopted the Lord, I believe.
> One was terribly in earnest. He wanted to know what to do with
> his stone that is supposed to have been handed from Zooli [Dzulí-
> feri] and gives them authority to practice witchcraft.
> "Throw it in the deep part of the river," I said.
> "Yes," said another, "and give it back to the Devil." (1952,
> 111–112)

When I visited *crente* communities of the Aiary a generation later,
people remembered this moment of "abandoning" shamanism by
throwing their instruments into the river. In one community, Graciliano, a former *crente*, declared to me, with some bitterness, that

there used to be many shamans on the Aiary. It was Sophie who ordered them to take their rattles and stones and throw them into the river. *Rudzeekateka maatchi*—she did a terrible thing.

Graciliano referred me to various of his kin of nearby communities who were converted ex-shamans. I interviewed several of them who revealed that their knowledge of mythical and curing traditions had not been totally suppressed, although one elder excused himself for not being able to narrate exactly, because a "sickness" had made him forget.

Verbal and printed abuse was another frequently used tactic in the *crentes'* declared war against shamanism. Early in my fieldwork, I was shocked to read the following songtext in a *crente* pamphlet printed in Portuguese:

> Brazil is against alcohol
> Tobacco is a sin,
> The *pajé* is a liar
> The *pajé* is of the devil.

Several people at Uapui confirmed that *crente* songs were used as propaganda against the shamans. José Felipe told me of a kin from a downriver community—a former resident of Uapui, who had left to make his own community due to the "fights" caused by evangelical propaganda—who berated the shamans, his kinsmen, calling them "frauds": "They only put rocks or thorns in their mouths to vomit them up later. They deceive people." He would reinforce his accusations by citing a passage of the New Testament in which Simon Peter belittles the healers as frauds. Ironically, in this case, according to José Felipe, the man remained a *crente* for only a short time but "left it" because his daughter had married a *crente* from the village of Canadá, the largest *crente* village on the Aiary, who later abandoned her. In disgust, her father left the faith.

Interesting, too, is the way people spoke of "leaving" evangelicalism, as they spoke of "leaving" shamanism and Kuwai behind. In village after village on the Aiary, a little probing into the recent history of religious changes reveals that people had a range of possible options of religious affiliation in sequence, such as the following:

> From shamanism, etc.—to *crente*—to Catholic (or)
> From shamanism, etc.—to "half-*crente*" (or)
> From shamanism, etc.—to uncommitted.

To return to Hohodene statements, I introduce now a third testimony: that of a Hohodene shaman of Uapui, Edu, who remembered the conflicts vividly, as he was directly involved in expelling the Protestant pastor Henry Loewen from the village, and was never a follower of the evangelicals:

> They took the statues from the chapel and threw them in the river. They said they were idols. They said material things would come from heaven. They gave out books, Bibles, and paper. That's all, no clothes or anything else. They wouldn't speak with José [then chief of Uapui]. They wouldn't greet the Padres and said the Padres are liars. They would cross their arms over their chests and call the Padres Inyaime. When I didn't want to be baptized, and I refused to throw the statues in the river, Henrique got angry with me and said, "When you die, your soul will go to Hell." I told him, "No, when I die, my body will stay in the earth, and my soul will go to Iaperikuli."
> Once Sophie was taken to prison in São Gabriel but she escaped by night and went to a stream on the upper Uaupés in Colombia. The police looked for her, they searched three or four times. In Tunui, they said they didn't know where she was. So they gave up looking for her, she'd escaped.

Note that Edu's reference to throwing statues from the chapel into the river may in fact refer to throwing shamans' rattles and sacred objects, as there was no chapel at Uapui until much later. Note also that Edu's rendition of Sophie's escape from the police coincides quite well with the version presented by the SPI, but with a touch of legendizing that hints of the stories about Kamiko's escape from the military in the last century.

But the predominant theme of his discourse is the *crentes'* radical exclusivism—absolutely asocial beings, in Edu's view, in their refusal to observe the most basic social rules of greeting, speaking with the chief, and treating people well, besides being full of promises but incapable of delivering. Consistent with Sophie's condemnation of Baniwa religion, Loewen radicalized the separation of *crentes* from non-*crentes*. The unbaptized were prohibited access to Protestant chapels and even to heaven; *crentes* were induced to desecrate images of Catholic saints, and to refuse to greet or share meals with non-*crentes*; the Padres and shamans were demonized and their lives threatened.

All of this produced a state of internal conflict among Baniwa communities that went far beyond a question of religious differences,

articulating with ancient hostilities, witchcraft, and vengeance killings. I suggest that the *crentes'* violent break with the past projected
them into a state of society prior to the formation of social alliances,
when violence and the logic of return killings predominate. In this
context, I suggest that we may understand more fully the impact of
the evangelicals' repression of the *pudali* dance festivals. The loss of
the *pudali* seemed to create a temporary vacuum—a "black hole," as
it were—in the organization and management of intercommunity relations. The *pudali* were one of the principal means by which relations
of antagonism and potential hostility were administered and transformed into alliance and solidarity (Journet 1995; Wright 1990).
Hence, the Hohodene said that *pudali* "made people's hearts happy."
Without this mechanism of social solidarity, hostilities became a predominant pattern until the new system of *crente*-introduced rituals
took hold.

The final statement from the non-*crentes* is by Mandu, shaman and
chief of Uapui and one of my principal interlocutors in the village.
Mandu's discourses on the evangelicals demonstrated his understanding of, on the one hand, the positive moral changes that they had introduced and with which he was in agreement and, on the other hand, the
limitations or inviability of the social changes they proposed.

On various occasions, he went into long discussions of New Tribes
missionaries he knew, who had taught *Deo iako*, and how he was a
friend of Sophie Muller and others. He spoke of how Sophie traveled
all over the region, stopping in Uapui and Tunui Cachoeiras, and how
she decided to stay in Venezuela with the Curripaco and Puinave. He
recalled that she had a "friend" Correa, who went with her; and that
she went to San Fernando de Atabapo and he to Colombia on the
Querary. She only taught *Deo iako* and told people of Uapui to "stop
drinking because when you drink, it causes fighting among brothers."
Mandu was particularly emphatic on this point.

In describing how the *crente* "conferences" were conducted, Mandu
spoke in detail of their being occasions of much food and trading for
food through the *"capitão"*; of how there are "soldiers" that guard the
doors of the house and that when one wants to go out, one has to ask
permission; of the singing that begins at dusk and lasts well into the
night; and of how the elders teach *Deo iako*, baptize in the river and
give names, and make marriages.

Of these marriages, however, Mandu cited cases in three Aiary villages of very young *"curumis"* (boys) marrying older girls at the Conferences, when the father of the boy asks for the bride. In one village,
a *curumi* married an older girl but the boy was too young to do any
heavy work, like cutting trees to make gardens, so the girl left him.

Finally, Mandu noted that Sophie ordered people to make other houses, to stop living in the longhouses, but "people didn't obey her, she wasn't a worker, she didn't help to make new houses."

Mandu thus recognized positive aspects of Sophie's prohibitions, as a way of recovering unity among brothers, which alcohol so often destroyed. On various occasions during my stay in the field, Mandu hammered on the issue of how, "in the old days," there was much fighting because of excessive drinking. Mandu and his brothers also admired to a certain extent the ritual organization of *crente* Conferences, occasions of abundance, like the *pudali* festivals, and with a ritual structure of authority controlled by them—a Christian gathering thoroughly transformed and accommodated to Baniwa ritual organization.

The failures of evangelicalism, according to Mandu, centered first on the incapacity of its policy of exclusivism to sustain viable social and economic units. *Crentes* could only marry other *crentes*, which disorganized the structure of marital exchange patterns among communities and produced distortions in age differences among spouses. It is interesting to observe how various informants referred to problems in marital relations among evangelicals. Recall how Galvão's informant, Ernesto, referred to exogamy and incest, and the issue of marital infidelity appears in various people's statements.

Mandu also criticized Sophie's lack of political leadership: she ordered people to make new houses, but unlike leaders among the Hohodene, she didn't take the initiative to produce the change. Once again, it was the incapacity of the *crentes* to produce viable social and economic units—in this case, houses—which put the evangelical project, at least among the people of Uapui, in doubt.

The statements I shall now present of the *crentes'* points of view reflect several things: that there were strong moral grounds for conversion, and that the conflicts between the *crentes* and Catholics were as much produced by the Padres as by the evangelical pastors. It is admitted that a great deal was lost of the traditions as a result of conversion; on the other hand, the *crentes* over time forged a way of life relatively compatible with their religious expectations. Today, many recognize that there is no longer the enthusiasm as in the "time of Sophie," but it is a relatively stable way of life which many *crentes* do not want to give up, for it provides satisfaction as a tradition. The present situation is also relatively more tolerant; besides permitting gradations in faith, and the possibility of leaving the faith, it is also more open to the Catholics.

In the early 1970s, anthropologist Adélia de Oliveira gathered a series of life histories from Baniwa of the Cuiary and lower Içana Rivers.

Various of these refer to contacts with the priests and Sophie Muller in the decades of the 1950s and '60s, and the conflicts generated by the religious situation. One man related these conflicts to conversion, and is worth citing: named Eduardo, he was of the Adzanene phratry, born in Maçarico on the lower Içana around 1935 but resident at Nazaré at the time of the interview. According to him, around 1940 a measles epidemic killed half the population of Maçarico, and the rest moved to Tapecua, slightly upriver. Roughly at the end of the '40s, Eduardo's family moved to Carara-poço, where the priests were building the new mission, and Eduardo was one of Padre José's first pupils. Later he worked for Padre Carlos. As he then relates:

> I cut wood to make a house and cut thatch to cover the houses. The Padre taught me religion. I confessed and took communion. I stayed with the Padre some two years.
> After that I went to Nazaré. I returned to Carara-poço. Here in Nazaré, I heard for the first time the "word of God" as spoken by Mário. When I went back to Carara-poço, Padre Carlos began to get angry with me. So I decided to come live here. I came down and stayed in the house of Guilherme. My family stayed in Carara-poço. Then I went to sell boards to Padre José, and Padre José paid less because he was angry with me. After that, I went again to Nazaré, to attend the Santa Céia. After the gathering, I returned to Carara-poço and Padre Carlos got very angry with me. I went back to Nazaré to live here because Padre Carlos and Padre José did not want *crentes* to live there and I was becoming *crente*. I preferred to be *crente* because people there drank, despite what the Padre said, and because the Padre quarreled with me and here we *crentes* did not fight. I was baptized in the *crentes* by Mário, and after I began to make a house and garden. (Cited in de Oliveira 1979, 25–26)

In Santarém, a *crente* community of about twenty people, two to three hours downriver by canoe from Uapui, I interviewed the pastor Nocêncio and his brother Marco, who said he was a "half-*crente*." Santarém was a community that surprised me, as I have said, because for all of the criticism that the Catholics of Uapui made of the *crentes'* "transformation into whites," Santarém appeared to me to be one of the most traditional (in the sense of having the least influence of non-indigenous society) that I had seen on the Aiary. The aged grandparents of the village, for example, lived in an open-thatched shelter and wore traditional attire (a long skirt for the woman, a loincloth for the man). Marco and his two brothers were exceptionally well versed

in curing chants and myths—the only thing that was lacking was tobacco and *caxiri*. But they were *crentes*: when Padre Carlos passed
through the village, Nocêncio and his brother Erminio did not go
down to the port to greet them. And it was clearly not bad for the men
to talk about Kuwai and the sacred flutes in public (i.e., to women and
children): "In the past," Marco said, "it was bad, but now it does no
harm for the women and girls to know."

I asked Marco to talk about Sophie and he responded:

Sophie didn't stay in any one place. She traveled from village to
village on the Içana and Aiary. She told people in Uapui, "Leave
everything of your ancestors behind. Then obey the following
rules—no smoking or drinking, for they weaken the body. No killing other people, or stealing their things. And no having sex, for it
is better to remain single." But I am a half-*crente*, I smoke a little
and drink *caxiri*. These are my only two sins.

Sophie's ability to communicate in various dialects of Baniwa, as
well as other languages, and her production of written material in
these languages were certainly crucial elements in differentiating her
from all other whites who had preceded her. Even more so was her
literacy campaign, which laid the groundwork for reproducing *Deo
iako* among her converts. For by this, I think it is plausible to suggest
that she unwittingly embodied one of the critical functions of the
ritual specialist whose "speech" (e.g., *Kuwai iako*, the words of Kuwai)
transmits the knowledge necessary for producing generations of
young adults in initiation. This, I suggest, may be important to understanding the conversion process as a historical rite of passage modeled
on initiation.

I base this suggestion on the following similarities between what
Marco remembered Sophie as saying, her "orders" for them to change,
and Kuwai's instructions to the children at the time of their initiation
in the myth of Kuwai. "Leave everything of your ancestors behind,"
she said, in a way that recalls Kuwai's instructions to the initiates to
leave their families behind in order to ear his words, the "true" music
of Kuwai. "Then obey the following rules . . . ," she said, in a way
that recalls Kuwai's instructions to the initiates to fast and observe
restrictions for three dry seasons, at which time they would complete initiation. Sophie's "rules" are in fact remembered as restrictions—no drinking, no smoking, no sex, no festivals. Or they are
remembered as referring to the types of behavior which elders commonly emphasize to all initiates during Kuwaipan: do not kill other

people, do not steal other people's things. By observing these rules, the final transformation—"become civilized, like the whites"—would complete the process of producing new generations of society that, through *Deo iako* and its attendant structure of ritual authority, would be self-reproducing, as the Kuwaipan initiation rituals did.

This interpretation—which, I emphasize, I never proposed to the *crentes*, but which was suggested to me by the tone of Marco's discourse—also provides a way of understanding the importance of Sophie's map and the mass baptisms to the early movement (see opening citation, this part). For in initiation rituals, chant specialists name all places in the world where Kuwai music was played by the women, after they had stolen the sacred flutes and trumpets from the men. This sacred geography creates the world for the initiates in rituals performed today. In a similar way, Sophie's map, I suggest, showed all the places where she had taught *Deo iako*. It was an icon—and significantly, a woman produced the map—of the new world created by and for the evangelicals.

To follow this line of thinking for the moment, it may be useful here to evaluate the question of whether and to what extent Baniwa elders perceived Sophie as a divine emissary. In fact, there is very little in Hohodene statements to me which would indicate the sort of extraordinary powers they attribute to messianic figures, that is, powerful shamans such as Kamiko or Kudui. There is a vague similarity between the memory of her flight from the authorities and stories of Kamiko's repeated escapes from military prison. Kamiko's escapes, however, were interpreted as instances of his miraculous shamanic power to transform, to rejuvenate, and to turn back the violence of his persecutors against them (see Wright and Hill 1986). In other words, they are demonstrations of his messianic power to overcome the political and economic oppression of the whites. In Edu's rendition of Sophie's escape, cited above, there is no larger context which would render her "escape" meaningful as a messianic triumph.

Recent information I have obtained, however, indicates that at least some Baniwa *crente* communities of the Içana remember Sophie in terms similar to oral histories of the messianic figure of Kamiko. According to Geraldo Andrello, researcher for the Instituto Socioambiental, currently working on the Içana, "They [Baniwa *crentes* of the lower Içana] say that she was thrown into the river inside a closed wooden box. They say it was the Baniwa who tried to kill her. She survived all of these attempts, however. On the other hand, they declare that the arrival of the missionary had been previously announced by the shamans" (personal communication, 1996).

Here is a transposition of the image of Kamiko (see Wright and Hill 1986) onto the figure of Sophie with one important difference, however: "it was the Baniwa who tried to kill her," but she survived all attempts, indicating that she, a white woman, was attributed superior shamanic powers. Nevertheless, this does not confirm any messianic qualities on a par with Kamiko.

The attribution of supernatural qualities to Sophie is, rather, ambiguous: "saint" or "demon," the opinions varied. Hohodene Catholics, as I mentioned above, associated her nocturnal wanderings to pray, for example, with Inyaime, a totally transformed and inverted being, decapitated and dismembered, who may persecute and fight with people. Curripaco crentes of the upper Içana in Colombia, on the other hand, seem to associate her with the mythic model of Amaru. French anthropologist Nicolas Journet writes that:

> her legend is that she was not really a woman like any one: she was considered as absolutely chaste, she had no menses, she would not eat but very small quantities of powdered milk. I met a man who told me that he refused to follow Sophie Muller's teaching because he was convinced that she had a lover, a Venezuelan merchant. (Personal communication, 1996)

Coupled with the images of Amaru as a wandering outsider, who leaves the music of Kuwai in the world, I suggest that there may be some grounds for the identification of Sophie with this mythic figure, but as a transformation of this model not as its reproduction. More appropriately, from the "legend" cited above, she had the attributes of a woman shaman: the details that she "had no menses," that she fasted, and that she was virtually an asexual being would all be consistent with what a woman would have to be in order to be a shaman, according to shamanic discourse.

The final statement is from Marco's brother, Nocêncio, pastor of Santarém, who had much to say about crente rituals and the traditional Hohodene dance festivals he had seen in his youth.

Now, in the early years of the evangelical movement, Protestant rituals seem to have been limited to daily orations and readings from the Gospels. With time, these were supplemented by a calendar of evangelical meetings: monthly "Holy Suppers" (Santa Céias), held the first week of every month, lasting a day and night, according to a rotating system of host villages; and "Conferences" (Conferencias) every two to three months in selected villages, lasting four days. Both events are occasions of massive gatherings: at one Holy Supper, I counted eighty to ninety people from five villages on the Aiary; Conferences are larger, with upward of several hundred, and involve villages spread over a wider region; some are so large, *crentes* say, police from the municipal capital have to be called to help.

Both occasions are much anticipated, for they are times of meeting friends and engaging in common activity: besides the prayers, there is much feasting and later, games of volleyball or tug-of-war, and so on. In effect, these events replaced the *pudali* exchange festivals, channeling the enthusiasm which people had for ritual production and exchange into a new form of relationship with the Divine and with other human communities. Holy Suppers and Conferences were also probably organized along many of the same community circuits as the *pudali*. It is thus certainly the case that the Holy Suppers and Conferences produced an alternative, one which provided *crentes* with satisfaction, anticipation, and internal order, in a way that the *pudali* had done. Nocêncio's descriptions of *crente* rituals—naming rites and Conferences in particular—it seemed to me, were similar in various ways to Hohodene naming ceremonies and *pudali*.

On naming ceremonies, Nocêncio said "the elders give Portuguese names, invoking Christ, God, and the Holy Spirit, and look for the growth and good health of the child." In Hohodene naming ceremonies, an elder likewise invokes the ancestors and seeks the good health of the child.

On the Conferences, Nocêncio said people

"do the same things as at Santa Céias but there are many more people. Usually it lasts four days and, on the fourth, everyone leaves for home, making a grand exit. There is always a lot of food and, by the second day, one can hardly eat anymore. There are at least two tables full of food. There are guards. The men sit in the front row, the children behind them, and the women behind them. Each one recites a verse and sings, in Portuguese or Baniwa. Sometimes there's an American pastor at the Conference."

Abundance of food, order, and a grand exit—these were also attributes of the *pudali*.

Nocêncio and his brothers would comment on the Conferences and Holy Suppers with fondness—on a person's style of doing prayers, or on the people who were present. The *crentes* prepared weeks in advance for these occasions, gathering produce, processing manioc, hunting and fishing far at the headwaters of the Aiary where the best game and fish were to be found.

By the same token, Nocêncio and his brothers were also quite fond of listening to my tape recordings of Hohodene *pudali* songs which I had taped from elders of Ucuqui, and they sincerely lamented the loss of *pudali* rituals among the *crentes*. As Nocêncio said,

> When I was young and lived at Itewiali-numana [on the Quiary], I saw the dances with the masks of the Maulieni. But my children don't know how these are, nor the *waana* [*ambaúba* dance tubes], nor the *surubí* flutes. They don't know what these are like. We don't see them anymore. There are people from the Quiary who don't even know the music of the panpipes or the *iapurutu* flutes.

It should be noted that lamenting the loss of past ways and, especially, the enthusiasm of the past was as characteristic of Hohodene discourse about dance festivals and dance instruments as it was about the "time of Sophie." Various *crente* elders complained to me how the *crentes* were "not like they once were," that it was "*desanimado*" (dispirited), that people didn't know the songs well, nor did they pray as well as they used to.

The *crentes* nevertheless have successfully forged an identity in opposition to the non-*crentes*. In 1970, Father Franz Knobloch, on his visit to the Içana, observed that "on the Baptist chapel of Tunui, there was written 'Church of the United Tribes,'" which Knobloch took to mean that "consciously or unconsciously, the Baniwa appear to be seeking a church of their own" (1972, 90). I suggest that this observation can be taken a bit further: it was fundamentally a new identity Baniwa *crentes* sought to forge, and this became evident in numerous ways. The *crentes'* differences from the Catholics included not only house styles,[11] but also village names and the system of religious authority and ritual organization;[12] literacy in the New Testament and evangelical literature;[13] the use of money, as opposed to trade, for buying food or goods; and the preference for Western remedies and rejection of traditional and Catholic medicines. I was told by several non-*crentes* that all of this made sense because the *crentes* "only want to become like white people," and this meant adopting and teaching the ways of the whites by the two models that were most often visible: the evangelical missionaries and the river merchants. The two models were related, for one of Sophie's early teachings was that the Baniwa should detach themselves from material goods for these would "come from heaven." Evidently, with time, *crentes* understood by this that the river merchants brought and sold, as one *crente* elder told me, "things from God who helps us."

Yet, it is a curious situation for, consistent with their exclusivism and anti-Catholicism, the *crentes* criticized the Catholics for their posture of contact with the national society. Before the prophet Kudui died, he warned the Hohodene that "many whites would come" to the Aiary and that they should be prepared—a message remembered by his followers in the late 1970s when the Brazilian Air Force constructed airstrips on the Aiary and upper Içana. The contrast in strategy between the *crentes* of the upper Içana and the Catholics of the Aiary at that moment could not have been more dramatic.

The Catholics of Uapui, led by the chief and shaman Mandu, participated fully in the airstrip clearing. The *crentes* of the upper Içana, who were holding a Conference at the very moment the air force initiated construction, sent word to the Hohodene that all people at Uapui were *"inyaime,"* that the air force had come to "take away" the women and should be avoided. Many *crentes*, believing this to be the case, "became afraid" to work on the airfield.

According to Mandu, who accompanied the air force officers to the upper Içana to explain the airstrip project to the Kumada-minanai of the village of São Joaquim, all the villagers immediately fled to the forest when the helicopter landed, and only after considerable persuasion on the part of Mandu (who was given a revolver to bring them back), did they return. After hearing the air force officer explain the project, the *crentes* made only one request: that they not be asked to change from being *crente*; "they wanted to remain *crente*" (Wright, Fieldnotes).

Conclusion

In the course of time, evangelicalism has become one among several alternative approaches to the sacred which the Baniwa in Brazil have available to them. Its stronghold remained in the communities from the mid- to upper Içana, the Cuiary and parts of the Aiary. On the lower Içana, and scattered along the Aiary, were the Catholic communities that cultivated the saint's day festivals and secular drinking parties. The more "traditionalist" communities—who guarded the knowledge of shamanism, the initiation rituals, and large-scale dance festivals, and who were guided now and then by prophets—were concentrated on the upper Aiary, at Uapui and on the Uaraná stream. These are alternatives because each in its own way cultivated an inter-community structure of rituals, defined by a calendar and organization of production, a set of specialists, a corpus of religious knowledge, and expectations of moral behavior. While one could argue whether these alternatives are truly interchangeable, the important point is that the Baniwa have lived with alternatives such as these for a long time.

I began this part with a series of questions that I considered crucial to understanding Baniwa conversion to evangelicalism. Why and how did the Baniwa suddenly decide to cast their lot with a total stranger who ordered them simply to stop doing what had been familiar to them for centuries? Given Sophie's radical opposition to native religion, which led her and her followers to violate some of the most sacred taboos, why didn't the Baniwa simply expel her from their communities—as the Arawakan Tariana of the Uaupés had expelled in the 1880s Franciscan missionaries who defiled their sacred flutes and masks? Since she was all by herself for years, waging her campaign against shamans and sorcerers, why didn't they simply eliminate her? What was at stake for the Indians at that time? What did they hope to accomplish through their conversion?

I approached these questions first through an analysis of the historical situations prior to the conversion movement, and second through interpretations of the discourses of the main actors involved in the drama. By confronting discourses, I did not expect to arrive at "the truth" or "what really happened," but how each actor understood and "filtered" through his or her own cultural perceptions the events of this complex time. For the Hohodene with whom I spoke, conversion went far beyond simple associations with traditional beliefs—or "syncretism"; nor was it seen exclusively as an antiwitchcraft movement. I emphasize this point because missionary explanations, formed by preconceived notions of "paganism," tend to go in this direction. By contrast, I suggest that Baniwa conversion must be understood in terms of millenarian and messianic traditions and expectations.

In the first place, it is more than likely that the Baniwa in general sought change from the increasingly intolerable situation which, for generations, had left its mark, as all outside observers since the beginning of the century had noted. It was not unlike their situation in the mid-nineteenth century when Kamiko emerged to preach a new "song of the cross." Far from being a "fear of demons," it was a fear of the whites, "stamped on their faces," demonstrated by their immediate flight at the whites' appearance and their "eternal certainty that they're being cheated" (Galvão, Fieldnotes 1954).

Out of the blue, a divine emissary proclaiming the Second Coming of Christ appears speaking (after a fashion) their language, who healed and advised—like a shaman—who promised that material goods would "come from heaven" and that great changes were about to occur. The Baniwa would be saved from catastrophe but on the condition that they "leave behind" their ancestors' ways of life.

It should be noted that in none of the previous millenarian movements in the Northwest Amazon—so far as I am aware—was this last
aspect a part of the messianic message. In historical narratives, however, at various times institutions are "abandoned" in order to produce a desired change. Thus the Hohodene recount how they and the
Oalipere-dakenai abandoned warfare because it was leading to the
end of their society. In order to reconstruct social alliances and to
guarantee a prosperous future, all war instruments were "thrown
away" into the river and forgotten. Similar themes appear in myths in
which, in order to attain a new state of order and prosperity, something from the old had to be thrown away.

As shown in Chapter 3, the Hohodene understand the history of
their phratry in terms of a succession of periods beginning with warfare and leading up to their settlement on the Aiary River. Transformations in their society are thought of in terms of a process of becoming sedentary horticulturalists or, as many say, "civilized." Their
conversion to evangelicalism may thus be consistent with this process;
that is, it represents a continuation of these historical transformations.
In the same way that "becoming civilized" meant throwing away war
instruments, "becoming white" meant throwing away shamans' rattles and the Kuwai flutes and trumpets in order to adopt the new way
of life to meet their needs.

There are parallels I have tried to draw—supported by indications
in Hohodene statements about Sophie Muller and the evangelical
movement, as well as in certain observations that Galvão made of the
relations between Catholic rituals and initiation—between conversion as a historical process and rites of passage, specifically initiation.
Both obviously involve three phases: separation from a previous "unbaptized," or uninitiated state; a marginal period of restrictions and
prohibitions; and a transformation into a new state of society. Crucial
to this comparison is the explicit attribution of Sophie's role as shamanic specialist like, I suggest, the *kalidzamai* chanters who in essence
re-create the world though shamanistic journeys sung at the height of
initiation rites.

The knowledge which Sophie transmitted (in the chants, orations,
lessons, translation—in short, *Deo iako*—and above all, her map of
evangelical communities) formed the basis for the production of a
new generation of converts who would henceforth reproduce this process in much the same way that the initiation speeches and chants had
done. Thus "becoming like whites" meant that it was the knowledge
of the whites which would be incorporated into the mold by which
society is reproduced.

This didn't mean necessarily that the cosmos, as religious and nonreligious specialists understood it, was altered in any fundamental way, although aspects of it were, no doubt, rethought. Thus, for example, the importance that *crentes* attribute to Inyaime who, they say, "exists in all parts of the world," is evidently a modification of its previous importance. Clearly, this rethinking was not a process which occurred overnight, and involved a complex negotiation between what could or could not be sustained or transformed from the old and what was to be learned from the new. This is a question, however, which I shall leave for future research.

The marginal period of the transition was marked by conflicts, first of all because the ways being left behind (the *pudali* rituals especially) were instrumental to the management of intercommunity relations, and second because the new order imposed an opposition between *crentes* and non-*crentes*, that is, a realignment of cleavages along predominantly religious lines, but without the mechanism for managing or overcoming this opposition. Thus, intergroup hostilities and witchcraft, I suggest, increased as a result of the changes produced (see, for example, the case I described of the *crente* pastors' attacks on the prophet Kudui) and not, as the missionaries claimed, because of Baniwa culture.

From the beginning, the Baniwa detected contradictions and flaws in the utopia they expected (i.e., that all would become brothers, that witchcraft would be controlled, that there would be no more sicknesses) which led many to suspect that what they had gotten into was not the ideal society they hoped to create. For example, neither the explanation for death offered by the evangelicals nor the means for coping with serious ailments proved to be adequate. Given that *manhene* explains the most lethal sickness, it required a fundamental rethinking of beliefs in sickness, death, and eschatology to change. To say, as *crentes* did, that sickness and death were "punishment from God" (*castigo*) or that "God called the deceased away from life" implies a fundamentally different notion of the nature of divine action in the world from what is given in mythology. It is the understanding of Iaperikuli's nature as Provider-of-all (animals, fruits, fish, tobacco, etc.), as Advisor and Counselor (whose actions are transparent in myth, or through the revelations of the shamans), but not as Punisher (who acts on the Baniwa but whose motives cannot be known) which separated the beliefs of non-*crentes* from *crentes*. Hence what the missionaries assumed could simply be imposed, the *crentes* needed to rethink—from the destruction of their longhouses to the role of the divine in human affairs.

Conclusion

The ethnology of the Northwest Amazon has dedicated considerable attention to indigenous cosmologies, myths, and rituals. Stephen and Christine Hugh-Jones' classic monographs (1979, 1979) provide rich studies of the cosmic symbolism in the mythic thought of the Tukanoan Barasana of the Pira-Paraná River region in Colombia. Jonathan Hill's study of chant specialists ([1989] 1993) among the Wakuenai in Venezuela extends the Hugh-Jones' analyses to the domain of music and mythic speech. Nicolas Journet's monograph of the Curripaco in Colombia (1995) presents an analysis of the indigenous vision of society as a "continuation of the myths of clan origin, initiation rites and agriculture," contrasting this vision with another, also expressed in myth, of life in nature as represented through narratives of warfare, hunting, and a forest-dwelling existence.

One of the interesting parallels between the Tukanoan- and Arawak-speaking peoples of the Northwest Amazon has to do with what various of the authors mentioned above call vertical and horizontal space-times, and their uses in myth, ritual, and social life. Christine Hugh-Jones, the first to analyze these features, argues that space-time systems that delimit the universe in myth are transposed to ritual systems, and it is through this process that concrete changes can occur:

> In order to contact the ancestral past described in myth, people must transpose the system of the universe onto the systems which they are able to change through concrete action. This is what they do during ritual and thus, although it refers to all kinds of metaphysical powers and "impossible" processes, such as death and rebirth, resuscitation of the ancestors, transfer of souls and so on, ritual is essentially the art of the possible. (1979, 280)

The complex system of space-time concepts which she synthesizes in her monograph leads C. Hugh-Jones to conclude:

These concepts set the Pira-Paraná individual with his or her internal bodily processes on the one hand, and the socially imposed descent group identity on the other, at the centre of a system which expands outwards to embrace the whole universe, past and present. (ibid., 281)

Hill's study of similar rituals among the Wakuenai elaborates on the speech forms through which the process of transposition is realized, specifically through a double movement of "mythification"—or the transformation of "powerful sounds of language music into mythic speech" ([1989] 1993, 274) and of "musicalization"—or the transformation of "taxonomies of mythic speech into dynamic language music" (276). The processes complement each other: the first is a "miniaturizing process, an inscription of the macrocosmic creation of natural species onto the microcosm of individual human bodies" (274).

Giving birth, fasting and eating are the processual matter through which the macrocosmic opening up of a vertical structure of worlds, generations, and human developmental stages is engraved into the geography of microcosmic, bodily space. What sets the macrocosmic creation in motion is the raw, unsocialized, musical naming power of Kuwai, or the "powerful sound that opened up the world." (275)

The second is nearly the inverse of the first: "a process of expanding, opening and augmenting the miniaturized, vertical creation into a horizontal dimension of exchange relations among a plurality of peoples from different places" (276).

Musicalization produces and mediates between collective, social categories of Others through placing both "us" and "them" into the framework of naturalized, or animalized, social being. To control musicalization is to be a custodian of Amaru's chthonian powers to open up a horizontal world of distant peoples, to travel from here to there and back again, to become Other to one's own people and yet return to one's own social being. (277)

In both the Hugh-Jones' studies, the structures of space-time are analyzed principally in terms of ideal conceptual models and their properties. Christine Hugh-Jones dedicates considerable attention to the dynamic characteristics of these models in practice, and both studies raise important historical questions that confirm the utility of their structural analyses. The relations between structural processes and history, however, are more fully examined in Hill's discussions of mythic images as metaphors of historical relations, and of ritual chanting as a dynamic process of filtering historical events. Similarly, Hill argues that narratives about the messiah Kamiko contain "historical metaphors" of Wakuenai experience of power relations in the interethnic context ([1989] 1993, 312).

While recognizing the contributions of these studies, I have sought to develop some of the same themes but in different directions. As I have stated at various moments, this book takes as one of its models the pioneering interpretations of native South American religions elaborated by Lawrence Sullivan in *Icanchu's Drum*. In constructing an "argument of images" based in Baniwa—and specifically Hohodene—narratives and religious practices (i.e., what Sullivan sought to do for the entire South American continent), I have tried to show the coherence of meaning in religious symbols that permeate a wide variety of forms: cosmogonic myths, cosmology, shamanism, cosmic history, phratric history, passages in the life cycle, eschatology, and the experience of conversion. My effort was not to discover or synthesize underlying structures common to all of these forms, but to clarify how narrators and religious specialists and, to a certain extent, nonreligious specialists understand the meanings of these religious symbols in their contexts.

This book takes as its title one of the key phrases of myths that link human beings today to their sacred origins and one of the key expressions of indigenous religiosity: "thus it will be for our others who will be born," a phrase that refers to a notion of temporality that, I argue, defines the conditions of human existence in time. "Until another end of the world," as some narrators say, signifies the possibility that the great cosmic cycle begun in the ancient times and, in principle, eternal and omnipresent may come to an end, reach closure.

In order to understand this "millenarian consciousness," as I have called it, and its implications for human existence in time, I was led to examine a variety of mythic narratives and discourse about the "ancient times" (the primordial world) and their significance for people who seek answers to their questions about the world through them. Themes of catastrophe and regeneration that characterize so many of the narratives and indeed seem to be a predominant pattern in cosmic history are, I hope to have shown, transposable to present-day experience. In the same way that *oopídali*, ancient times, become the present, *pandza*, in rites of passage, for example, or curing rites, or even in the narrating of a myth, so people may interpret or transpose their understandings of mythical figures such as Iaperikuli—who saves the world from total destruction—or the *eenunai*—witches who forever seek to destroy it—onto the present or historical experience.

In order to understand more fully how this may happen, I suggested that one way is through the qualities and senses of the various modalities of time, their associations with vertical and horizontal space-times, and with the notions of identity and alterity. One theme that has pervaded my interpretations in this book is the multiple meanings narrators attribute to the vertical and horizontal dimensions of the cosmos, which I believe are critical to understanding "millenarian consciousness." Mythic and sung narratives associate the vertical dimension of the cosmos ("vertical" in the literal sense that all narrators, shamans, and nonshamans with whom I conversed understood; see Figures 2 and 3 in Part I) with creation, curing and reversible death, the ancestral world, hierarchy, and so on. Narratives associate the horizontal dimension, on the other hand, most clearly with other peoples and places, potentially dangerous enemies, witches, and sorcerers. It is also associated with ritual exchange relations, egalitarian relations, and the organization of society through warfare and alliance. In order to control, or at least live with, these alien and potentially death-dealing powers, chanters and specialists through their orations, chants, and ritual actions attempt to neutralize or incorporate them in some way into the vertical dimension.

The vertical and horizontal dimensions coincide, I suggest, with two complementary aspects of "millenarian consciousness"—utopic and catastrophic. Utopic in the sense used here is temporal and spatial; that is, the vertical dimension is the ultimate source of creative power that is capable of transcending the chaos and destruction of time and matter. According to the shamans, *kathimákwe*, Iaperikuli's place of happiness, harmony, beauty, and order, stands in contrast with *maatchíkwe*, place of evil, *kaiwíkwe*, place of pain, and *ekúkwe*, place of rot, This World where people suffer and die. Mythic narratives mark the horizontal dimension with catastrophic images, when all is drastically reduced to one single survivor, a time of night and darkness, when multiplicity and magnitude are reduced to singularity and the miniature. Time and space are reduced from their complexity and differentiation to an undifferentiated, unique state. As I have shown, such is the vision through which many Baniwa narratives depict the beginning of the cosmos and through which Hohodene narrators at least interpret their history of contact with the outside and local events.

According to the narratives, it is through processes that take place along the vertical dimension that total catastrophes are averted and multiplicity regenerated. More specifically, the narratives represent such processes as a return or bringing-back to the "center of the world" and hence vertical source of all life (in the sense of Hipana being the "world navel," the "sky umbilical cord" that eternally connects This World with the Other World above). Various narratives cited in this book describe a movement from this center to the outside world on the periphery downriver, where characters experience loss, followed by a return back and upriver to the center which, like a sanctuary, permits the regeneration of life and return to order. The return back to the center is often represented as a gradual process, through which subjects pass through metamorphoses or concrete changes until, when fully integrated with the vertical dimension, they become autonomous, cultural beings.

Shamans and chant specialists, in their practice and in the nature of their being, most clearly embody mastery over both dimensions. First, the shamans undergo a process of metamorphosis ("becoming other," or *padamawa*) which, in the highest instance, identifies them with the creative sources of life in the beginning; their dream-souls may be in constant communication with Iaperikuli. These prophetic figures are the living testimony of the omniscient and omnificent power of creation. They are also the messengers of utopia. In "knowing everything," they are "like Iaperikuli." Second, shamans and chant specialists utilize the vertical dimension of the cosmos to revert the potentially catastrophic destruction of the horizontal—sorcerers, false prophets, and enemies. Third, the chant specialists, especially, control, through the music of their chants, the alien and dangerous powers of the spirit world—thereby, as Jonathan Hill has aptly stated, "musicalizing the universe," a kind of socializing process that empowers the universe with the central symbols of growth and reproduction.

Under what circumstances and in what forms have messianic, millenarian, or prophetic movements arisen among the Baniwa? The complexity both of their religious situation which has permitted several alternatives to exist at any one time (e.g., the "song of the cross" prophets, Catholic saint's days, evangelical pastors) and of the contact situation at various moments in time does not permit any simplifications in terms of "*longue durée*" cycles of hierarchy and egalitarianism. Rather, from my summary of contact history in Part I, and microanalysis of recent history in Part IV, it seems plausible to suggest that the histories of at least some phratries (Hohodene, Oalipere-dakenai, for example) have been characterized by movements of dispersion and concentration. Both Hohodene oral history and evidence from the documents indicate periods when the Indians were taken away from their homelands to work on the Rio Negro, in Venezuela and Colombia, and often were assimilated into ethnically mixed populations. Yet the Hohodene also describe a return to their territory and a renewal and consolidation of their ties among themselves and with other phratries. These periods of return have sometimes coincided with concentrations in large villages, in defined territories, and have been accompanied or followed by an explicit desire to remain autonomous from the whites. Even when the whites have appeared again, the Indians may or may not have gone—it has been a voluntary decision. The important point is that prophetic or messianic figures have often been instrumental to these times of return and concentration and decisions of autonomy from the whites. Even more, it would seem to be the case that these prophets and messiahs have appealed to the vertical dimensions of the cosmos in order to reinforce their messages of utopia and/or salvation.

A brief review of the cases will show this to be so:

Venancio Kamiko in the 1850s prophesied a world conflagration that recalled the fiery transformation of Kuwai at the moment of his ascent to the sky. Oral histories of the Dzauinai phratry of the Guainía and of the Dessana Indians of the Uaupés (see Wright 1992c; Wright and Hill 1986) recount Kamiko's miraculous powers to produce things, to avert the death plotted for him by white soldiers, and to resurrect, rejuvenated, from the dead. Kamiko urged his followers to avoid the whites and, instead, to give their full allegiance to him. The utopia that he promised was one free of "sin" and "debt" to the white merchants and military.

While the evidence is slim, the messiah Anizetto of the Cubate River was also seen to have the creative power to produce things, for example, to make gardens grow with the sign of the cross. Likewise he was known as a miraculous healer and was identified with "Jesus Christu" and Iaperikuli. He established a sort of sanctuary on the Cubate River where he and his followers sought to avoid contact with the white rubber-gatherers and military.

Kudui, half a century later, more clearly than the others (perhaps because I was able to interview his followers and sons), shows the transcendence of the vertical dimension over the horizontal. A shaman of enormous prestige, known for his miraculous cures and powers of prescience, Kudui promised a utopia in which "there would be no more sicknesses" (which again may be understood as a sanctuary in the vertical sense for, in the cosmos, this may refer to the place shamans call *litalewapi riku Dzuli*, where, they say, "there is no sickness," in the "Other Sky"). He spoke of Iaperikuli's place of happiness, *kathimákwe*, or as he said, "the city of God—like the city of the whites but much more beautiful." Like other prophets, Kudui was identified with Iaperikuli, with whom his dream-soul communicated constantly, and Jesus Christu, "our salvation." His village, an island on the Uaraná stream, was the mythical home of Iaperikuli. He didn't so much defend autonomy from the whites as prophesy their coming and that, through respect for the instructions of the elders in Kuwai-pan, the Hohodene would be able to withstand inevitable contact.

Initially, Sophie Muller seemed to fit the sort of expectations that at least some Baniwa communities had for prophets. Her demonology, eschatology, and translation of Christianity in terms that made sense to the Baniwa produced, in effect, a quickening of messianic and mil-lenarian expectations. Her and her followers' attacks on the shamans and Kuwai, however, provoked a crisis of belief in the viability of the vertical dimension for in effect these attacks ushered in the closing of the cosmic cycle, the "end of the world" as many Baniwa understood it. This left the horizontal dimension with all of its contradictions and difficulties. Paradoxically, while Sophie defended avoidance of con-tact with the whites—in line with some of the earlier prophets, and with a demonological (*inyaime*) view of contact—her followers under-stood that they would "become white, half-civilized."

Today, after half a century of experience with evangelical Protes-tantism, *crentes* understand that conversion produced a moral reform among their communities. Since access to the primordial sources of creative power along the vertical dimension, as they had previously known it, had been severed or at least weakened, the most they could expect of a utopia would be that people would live a fully moral life within a temporal community of believers. Yet, without an eschatology that could offer a solution or satisfactory explanation for sorcery and witchcraft, evangelicalism often foundered against the powers of the prophets, whose continuous access to the vertical dimension proved to be more effective than the *crentes'* apocalyptic and dismal prophe-cies and attempts to show that their sorcery was stronger.

It may well be that the evangelicals' militant rejection of the vertical cosmos represented, as Michael Brown has suggested, a "critique of the failure of indigenous models in the face of a vastly changed world, an assertion of subjecthood . . . and a vital moment in a long-term, underlying cycle within which native peoples actively explore alter-natives to their own structures of power" (1991, 408). Nevertheless, there are reasons for raising doubts concerning Brown's hypothesis in relation to "utopian renewal," as I suggested in the introduction.

In the first place, and with regard to his suggestion of the "cyclicity" of such movements, patterns in Baniwa histories do not support his hypothesis. Kamiko's movement, for example, was far from being a "self-limiting experiment" or "flirtation with chiefly politics" for, as I have shown in various studies, his influence spanned the latter half of the nineteenth century and generated a series of movements among Tukanoan-speaking and Warekena peoples that, likewise, were marked by a continuous series of prophetic figures, lasting until the early twentieth century. Obviously, this was more than a mere "flirtation" for it produced what came to be known as the "song" or "religion of the cross"—a prophetic tradition which has its adherents even today.

Second, regarding the question of whether Kamiko's movement "did much to change native reality" (404), which Brown doubts, a more careful reading of the sources indicates that it did, for the provincial government of Amazonas was forced to intervene in the area and, as a result of its *investigation* (and not merely repression), removed the military officials and missionaries who had exacerbated the unrest or had suppressed the movement's ritual dances. Obviously, when confronted with threats of military reprisal from these same missionaries, Kamiko and other leaders preferred refuge in inaccessible areas where they could continue their activities (Wright 1981b). It is rather remarkable, in fact, that despite the intensification of exploitation which the Baniwa suffered during the immediately ensuing rubber boom, prophets such as Anizetto continued their activities on the Içana, seeking to maintain sanctuaries, or pockets of resistance, in an increasingly hostile world. The forces that shaped the rubber boom and its aftermath went, after all, far beyond what a handful of prophets and their followers could control. Even so, what they preached and did remained in the consciousness of their followers for generations.

The movements, it goes without saying, were never universal among the Baniwa; they affected segments of the population, while other segments pursued different strategies for dealing with the situation of contact: influential chiefs emerged, promoted by the rubber patrons, for example, who acted as labor intermediaries for the whites; whole groups, apparently not influenced by prophets, sought refuge in inaccessible areas, refusing to follow the whites. In short, the complexity and variety of Baniwa strategies in relation to contact prevent any generalizations correlating these with "cycles" of internal political change.

Third, with regard to the "militant appropriation of Christianity," what I have shown in relation to Baniwa conversion to evangelicalism (and what Jonathan Hill and I have argued in relation to Kamiko's "religion of the cross"; Wright and Hill 1986) is precisely the central importance of indigenous religious practices and beliefs to the realization of the changes produced. In other words, such movements were transformative but at the same time fundamentally conservative: radical changes were sought in order to preserve what was most essential to Baniwa identity, that is, the reproduction of their identity through

ceremonial speech. Whatever "critique" that occurred was not in relation to native models but to the utopia that evangelicalism promised
but failed to deliver. Once Baniwa pastors had negotiated the new
faith—that is, adapted it to local realities—changes resulted which
have lasted nearly half a century.

Fourth, Brown's political reading of native millenarian movements
falls short of an adequate comprehension of these phenomena because
it ignores their symbolic dimension, or what Sullivan has termed
"spiritualities of the end of time" (1988, 550). As I have tried to show
through repeated references to myth and ritual, such spirituality has
to do with the imagery of catastrophe, or cataclysmic destruction, in
which all is reduced to one single survivor, and regeneration, in which
a savior emerges to restore the order of the world through a series of
transformations, most importantly through the shamanic reconstruction of the vertical dimension of the cosmos. Such images inform
mythic narratives, implying far more than the partial, political dynamic of hierarchy and equality.

Finally, if the movements had chiefly politics as their central concern, then how are we to explain the emergence of female prophets
(something that has never been investigated in these traditions)? I
have suggested at various moments in this book the importance of the
mythical figure of Iaperikuli's old "aunt," who recovers Duemieni's
bone and revives the heroes; who guards the remedy that reverts
death by poison; and who closes the hole in the earth to save humanity
from the fire that burned the world. And I suggested that Sophie
Muller herself may initially have been associated with such figures
and the space-time of Amaru, through, among other things, the map
she produced of her travels on the Içana and tributaries, which served
as a centerpiece in the early conversion movement.

A key point, it seems to me, is the long-term exploration of alternatives, for this book has demonstrated that Baniwa communities have
long lived with varying interpretations of their own religion (variant
myths and interpretations of Iaperikuli, Kuwai, and Amaru, for example), as well as varying relationships to Christianity, from the selective assimilation of the Christian pantheon into Baniwa myths to a
preference for the calendrical rites of the saint's days. Such an exploration is also far from being a closed question—Baniwa convert and
leave the faith, return to the *pudali* and other festivals in new contexts,
giving them new meanings and interpretations. What is constant and
continuous, however, is the quest and the expectation of a "place of
happiness" as it was made in the beginning "for those unborn."

Notes

Preface

1. My translation. Unless otherwise noted, all translations are mine.

Introduction

1. This book is not merely a revised version of my doctoral thesis, approved in 1981. The greater part of it consists of material which did not enter the thesis or which received little attention. My thesis in fact turned out to be far different from what I had anticipated. Instead of a description and interpretation of Baniwa religion and history, my focus broadened to a history of contact in the Northwest Amazon from the eighteenth century to the twentieth, with special concentration on the messianic movements of the mid-nineteenth century. My consideration of religion focused on the interpretation of a single myth, Kuwai, which I considered to be fundamental to understanding messianism. As will become apparent in the pages to follow, I believe that a deeper understanding requires extended treatments of cosmology, shamanism, and eschatology.

Part I. Cosmogony, Cosmology, and Shamanism

1. "Cosmogonies provide the terms with which to recognize and reflect upon the passage from nothingness (or chaos, prime matter, indistinction, the indiscernible) to the multiple beings, times, and spaces characterizing the present world" (Sullivan 1988, 26).

1. Cosmogony: Perspectives on the Beginning and Its Legacy

1. It is noteworthy that the principal transformations and spatial movements occur in the gardens. Nicolas Journet, who has studied among the Curripaco of Colombia, suggests that Iaperikuli is associated with a wild manioc plant:
"The association is based on a story with common structures: in the same way that the hero is the last scion of his village, the "orphan" plant [wild

manioc] is the sole survivor of an abandoned garden, and both are taken in by women." (1995)

In Journet's view, one way of interpreting the myths of Iaperikuli is as the "vengeance of the plants" against the predator animals who constantly attempt to subdue or kill Iaperikuli but who, in the end, are transformed into game animals or wild and poisonous plants.

2. The "owner of sickness," Kuwai, whom the shamans seek in their cures is said to have hair all over its body like the *wamu*. Kuwai "embraces," as the sloth does, the souls of sick people, suffocating them if no action is taken, but he also allows the shaman to recover and return souls to the living. More serious ailments are seen as processes of entrapment of human souls by this collective animal soul and recovery, their separation.

3. The story of how Iaperikuli obtained fire for humanity repeats this pattern. As narrated by Keruaminali of Uapui, the story is as follows:

"Yawalíferi first had fire. Iaperikuli went to where he lived to get fire. Then he took it to Warukwa, his house. There was a caiman there that stole the fire and ate it. The caiman went inside its house underwater, beneath a rock. Iaperikuli was left in the dark. He made frogs that called the caiman outside its house. They called, 'Father, father, give us light!' Caiman came out a bit but didn't open its mouth. The frogs hopped about, 'Father, father, give us more light!' The caiman came out more. The frogs hopped about, 'More! more!' It came out. Then Iaperikuli stuck a forked stick on its chest, trapped it, and opened its mouth—'Aaaaghh!' Iaperikuli took the fire away from it. He put it on torchwood. He had taken it away from the caiman. The caiman stayed without fire. Then he showed all people, all people in the world."

2. Guardians of the Cosmos

1. The relations of "owners" and "masters" have parallels in social and political organization in this world. Ownership relations refer to places or objects that have been made or worked to be given to posterity. Thus a family owns a garden, a man or woman owns a house, a phratry collectively owns a part of the river frontage and land where its members make their gardens and villages. Rituals and ritual objects have their phratric owners.

The system of Baniwa phratric names—with its tripartite classification into "-owners" (*-minanai*; e.g., Dzaui-minanai, Jaguar Owners, a phratry of the Içana River), "-children" (*-ene*; e.g., Hohodene, Partridge Children), and "-grandchildren" (*-dakenai*; e.g., Oalipere-dakenai, Grandchildren of the Pleiades)— would seem to follow along these lines, although there has been no evidence yet found that this classification represents a system of interphratric organization, or of hierarchical relations among phratries. Nor is there any evidence that nonindigenous peoples, or other indigenous peoples outside the system, could be considered "owners."

Phratric chiefs of the past were given the title of "master" (e.g., Hohodene *thayri*, Hohodene chief; Dzauinai *thayri*). Phratries of the past were probably organized into groups of four to five sibs ranked according to a model of agnatic siblings and assigned the ritual statuses of chiefs, warriors, shamans, and *maaku*, or servants. Chiefly sibs, called *enawinai, newiki thalikana,* usually the highest-ranking of the phratry, played key roles in its internal matters. While there seem to be few chiefly sibs remaining, they are remembered as the "good people," *newiki matchiaperi.* In at least one narrator's interpretation, chiefly sibs were like the "governor" of the whites—those to whom one listens and follows advice, or obeys orders.

The relation between chiefs and their followers—whether it be chiefly and junior sibs, war chiefs and their warriors, or peacetime leaders and their communities—is also defined by "work," *ideihi.* Traditionally, elder sibs could order "their *maaku*" to work for them and they were expected to obey. Peacetime chiefs advise their communities of work parties and organize them to completion.

2. A brief note, to be taken up again in Chapter 8, on the influence of Christianity on shamanism: Since missionaries have taught for more than a generation among the Baniwa, it is to be expected that shamans have incorporated some of their ideas into statements about their practices. Yet such statements are often made in the form of comparison between two ways of knowing and representing the sacred. Thus, shamans say that Iaperikuli is "how we know whom the white man knows as Jesus Christu." Iaperikuli has a house as Christu has a chapel, and a pet harpy eagle as Christu has the "Holy Ghost," a tribe of people as Christu had the disciples. Shamans' souls are "like angels" that fly to the heavens—and so on. Shamans are indeed the principal interpreters of missionary teachings, which they explain to the people. On Catholic saints' days, for example, when Catholic missionaries visited Uapui to show films of Christ's life, the shamans and elders would sit together as a group in the audience and make comparisons between what they saw on the films and the myths of Iaperikuli. The really influential shamans of the past were adept at this kind of interpretation, such that in times of the rapid influx of Christian ideas they not only could make meaningful statements on the interconnections but also guide their followers in making decisions about them.

3. Indians and Whites in Baniwa History

1. "Descents" refer to the supposedly voluntary and nonviolent removals of indigenous communities of the "backlands" to villages administered by missionaries; in practice, they were almost impossible to distinguish from the transportation of people by the official slave trade (Sweet 1974, 810).

2. At the end of the seventeenth century, beginning of the eighteenth, the Manao were the most numerous, powerful, and enterprising people of the middle Rio Negro. They were known for their role in long-distance commerce and quickly assumed an important role in the slave trade with the Dutch on the northern coast of the continent, until their defeat in a war waged against them by the Portuguese in the 1720s.

3. Kamiko's influence lasted until his death at the beginning of the twentieth century. In the 1920s, the Baniwa of the Cubate River, one of the areas of

Kamiko's influence, still demonstrated a disdain for contact with the whites (Nimuendaju 1950, 126), but the forms of white penetration had grown considerably by this time, along with the violence of the rubber boom.

4. Music of the Ancestors

1. A variety of means are cited by different narrators: pointed objects such as treetops; various fish with sharp, pointed teeth; and in one remarkable image, Iaperikuli encircles the crown of his head—where knowledge is centered—with his hands and puts the shape onto the place of Amaru's vagina creating the passage.

5. The Times of Death

1. In my thesis and later writings, I avoided writing of the events I will now recount, owing to my concern that doing so would provoke intervention by outside agencies of contact (the missionaries and FUNAI) in the internal affairs of the community. Nearly two decades have passed since then; Uapui is a very different place. Hence I bring them to light now, in a sense as history to which I was witness.

2. Reflecting on this statement today, I understand that he meant that Seraphim's "shade," *danaime*, would remain on the earth until, at the end of this period, it would disappear.

3. The word is apparently related to *iupinai*, sickness-giving spirits of the forest that, shamans say, were "born from the ashes of Kuwai's fire." They come like a wind, when people walk in the forest, surrounding their victims and making them "go crazy" (*napikaka*).

4. The scientific traveler Ettore Biocca in the 1950s recorded a tradition of the Tariana Indians of the Uaupés concerning the poison of Uapui Cachoeira:

"In the place where Jurupari was burned, near the waterfall on the Aiari, a beautiful place, there is lots of charcoal. The smell of the charcoal is poisonous. There are lots of poisonous plants there. Fruits cannot be taken from there. If Indians go there, they die. Only the children of the Tariana and Baniwa can go there. They know what to do to stop being killed. This is why the Baniwa possess lots of poison; they get it from there; it is for killing their enemies. When they walk on that ground, a noise like a drum is made. They sing, 'I'm coming to ask for poison, I want poison to kill my enemies.' They can take it." (E. Biocca, cited in S. Hugh-Jones 1979, 308)

5. Irving Goldman makes little mention of Mawerikuli, only that "the *habókü* [ceremonial leader] of the dead is *Mavitcikori* [sic], grandson of *Dzurédo*, an Ancient of the *Órobavo* and of other high-ranking sibs such as the *Hehénawa*, who was the first headman at Uaracapori. However, the Cubeo have no great interest in speculating about the life of the spirits of the dead since, except for the Ancients, they have no formal relationship with them" (1963, 261).

6. The word for "dead," *maliume*, can be rendered literally as "without will" (*ma-*, neg. part.; *liume*, will). It would be the complement of *manhene*, literally, "unconscious," without knowing. *Maliume* implies the absence of the

heart-soul; *manhene* signifies the absence of thought. The two elements—thought, and control over one's will—define fully cultural human beings.

7. The notion of a vertical sanctuary is found in various orations; for example, to protect a house against the attacks of witches, *malinyãi*, a chanter creates through the oration a protective fence around the house and sends the collective soul of its inhabitants up to the sky, to a place "where there is no sickness," called *litalewapi riku Dzuli*—under the protection of the primal shaman, Dzulíferi.

8. Recall that in the myth of Kuwai, three initiates undergoing seclusion eat roasted uacú nuts, the "flesh of Kuwai," and are devoured by him. One initiate who does not eat, who exercises control over his hunger, escapes death and completes initiation. In the second phase of the initiation, Kuwai teaches three elders the sacred chants of initiation and gives them pepper to eat, completing the initiation.

Without seeking to press the question, I think that a plausible interpretation of this three-plus-one combination would be that it represents relations among generations within a descent group and, more broadly, relations between ancestors and descendants.

9. The Cubeo name for Mawerikuli, "Mawichicure," is evidently an Arawak word, *-chicure* meaning "hair." It may be translated as "heron feathers," again a reference to *hinimai*, for the heron is one of the birds classified as *kamainiri*.

Both Koch-Grünberg and I. Goldman mention the owl figure among the dance masks worn at Maulieni and Cubeo mourning rituals. Goldman noted that the owl "has a mask covering only the head. Holds a torch in one hand and a stick in the other and jumps up and down in imitation of the owl jumping from branch to branch. Regarded as an evil devourer of people" (1963, 251).

10. Among the neighboring Cubeo, I. Goldman mentions a relation of "ceremonial friendship" between men and women, like a substitute sibling tie, in which partners paint one another with red pigment which they refer to as "blood."

11. One Hohodene myth of Inyaime relates that, following a *pudali*, a group of people roasted and ate fish in Inyaime's house, then danced with *ambaúba* dance tubes from the longhouse to the port and disappeared into the river. A young girl, in menstruation, wept for the death of her kin, and Inyaime, sitting atop a tree, threw a kiss in her direction telling her that they had not died. She went into the water and there saw her kin alive but transformed into fishpeople, *kuphenai*.

6. Spiritualities of Death and Birth

1. The *kamainiri* have a considerably more fearsome aspect than this apparently harmless list would suggest. There is a myth of the monstrous two-headed *kamainiri* called *hiwidamitha*, replete with images of the horrors of death: whose hands come out entirely, who gives deathly poison, who has an insatiable hunger for fish and thirst for water, but who is eventually devoured

by piranha and the anaconda. Had this spirit not been devoured, Keruami, the narrator, warned, "people would have two heads on their shoulders and not one." The myth of *hiwidamitha* is lengthy, and I was only able to obtain a portion of it.

7. From Rubber to the Gospel

1. I have as yet found no further information in any of the documents before or after this time on Anizetto. When Nimuendaju visited the Içana in 1927, he mentions in passing the reputation of the Cubate River Hohodene who were known in São Felipe for treating whites "with arrogance and grossness," but he makes no reference to the messiah.

2. S.P.I., *Correspondência*, 1914, in Archives of the Museu do Índio, Rio de Janeiro.

3. *Relatório do Inspetor do SPI*, 1930–1931; *Relatório da Iª Inspetoria Regional, Manaus*, 1926; *Ofícios Recebidos dos Postos Indígenas do Alto Rio Negro*, 1932; *Ofícios Recebidos dos Postos Indígenas do Alto Rio Negro*, 1931; *Ofícios Recebidos dos Postos indígenas do alto Uaupés*, 1928; *Relatório do Inspetor referente aos trabalhos realizados nos exercícios de 1930–31, Iª Inspetoria Regional* (in Archives of the Museu do Índio, Rio de Janeiro).

4. *Relatório do Inspetor, Iª Inspetoria Regional, 1930–31*: doc. 165; *Ofícios de Delegados de Índios Diversos, 1919*.

5. *Ofícios Recebidos dos Postos Indígenas do Alto Rio Negro, 1932*.

6. *Relatório do Inspetor, Iª Inspetoria Regional, 1930–31*.

7. *Ofícios de Delegados de Índios Diversos, 1919*.

8. It is difficult to confide in any of these figures, however, as neither Nimuendaju nor Koch-Grünberg nor probably the S.P.I. agent ever visited the upper Içana. Nimuendaju considered that all of the Içana above Jandú Cachoeira, at the mouth of the Aiary River, was Colombian territory. The First Brazilian Border Commission in the 1930s was the first to actually have surveyed the upper Içana region thoroughly.

9. Padre José Schneider, a Czech, had by 1950 lived some twenty years on the Rio Negro, during which time he founded three missions: Tapuruquara, or Santa Isabel; Taraquá, at the mouth of the Tiquié; and Carara-poço, or Assunção, on the Içana.

10. Gama Malcher—Diretor do C.N.P.I., *Ofício 962*, 01-10-52, Ministério de Agricultura, C.N.P.I., Archive No. 276, film 355, phot. 1484 (in Archives of the Museu do Índio, Rio de Janeiro).

11. Ataide Cardoso—Chefe da Inspetoria Regional 1 do S.P.I.—Manaus, no. 4, 02-05-53, film 379, phot. 238–240 (in Archives of the Museu do Índio, Rio de Janeiro).

12. Ibid.

13. Ibid.

14. On the side of the Protestants, the pastor who apparently was most involved was one "Henrique," or Henry Ronald Loewen, who, with his wife, Anita, a linguist, began evangelizing on the Içana around the time of Sophie's expulsion. Eduardo Galvão described Loewen in 1954 as a "tall, blond fellow

of German origin. A bit raw in speaking and even more so in Baniwa organization, ignoring clan division and dialect. He intends to speak, or better, to make his first sermon in Baniwa in six months. It took 10 to make one in Portuguese" (Fieldnotes 1954).

15. In the early 1970s, a lay Catholic missionary was sent to Uapui Cachoeira to start a grade school for the children of the upper Aiary. Uapui, a strategic location for its direct connection by trail to the upper Uaupés, would at least prevent the Protestants from venturing into that region. It would also serve as a base for the Salesians to expand their influence on the Aiary, with the help of the FAB, in the mid-'70s. For a more detailed discussion of Salesian activities in Uapui Cachoeira and their articulation with social, political, economic, and religious organization, see my thesis, Chapter 1 (1981b).

8. *Deo iako:* The Creation of a New Generation of Believers

1. I am grateful to Bob Fullilove, editor for the University of Texas Press, for this helpful perception of Muller's mission.

2. The cabins or shelters became the famous chapels or temples of Sophie that Galvão observed in 1954 scattered along the Içana. The chapel at Embaywa, Galvão wrote, had a sign posted on the door, "Evangelical Church," and "nailed to the wall a great cross with the following words written in *geral*: 'He gave His blood for us' on the vertical beam and the name of Jesus on the horizontal. Also, a sheet of paper with a prayer in Spanish" (Fieldnotes).

The shelters and cabins they built for her were in some ways like the small houses or shelters built for the "owner [feminine] of the dance festival," *pudali iminaro*, an important figure in the celebration of traditional exchange rituals who assured an abundance of the harvest. Similarly, Sophie was asked by several village leaders to make their gardens grow well.

3. It was perhaps for similar motives that Baniwa converts accelerated their abandonment of the initiation rituals, given, as I have discussed, the intimate association between Kuwai, or Jurupary in *língua geral*, and poison. Galvão reported that one Baniwa man told him, "Today they don't use masks and for many years have not held a festival of the moon with Jurupary because people don't like it anymore, people are afraid. The abandonment is due to the pressures of the missionaries and the *'civilisados'*" (Fieldnotes).

4. My information on *crente* villages on the Aiary is not as complete as it might be, partly because of my long association with the Catholic village of Uapui and the ex-*crente* village of Kuliriana, or Ucuqui. My stays in *crente* villages were brief—passing through, attending a *crente* assembly, visiting for several weeks in Santarém, Dakatali kudzua, and São Joaquim. The ex-*crentes* and Catholics of Uapui and Kuliriana, however, provided considerable information on the early movement and on reasons for leaving the faith.

5. Or, as one *crente* elder of the village of Canadá told me, "Step on it. Our grandfathers lived in sin." Everything of the past—"*ialaki* [fermented fruit drink], *dabukuri, Jurupary, pajé*"—went.

6. This must have been in the village of Paichipe on the Içana. In fact, Sophie Muller wrote of the meetings she held during her visit to this village:

"A big crowd comes to the meetings every night; about 100, I guess. Several canoe loads came down from the Rio Ayarí. They brought their wives, babies, grandmothers, chickens and dogs. I'm afraid of such large groups; it seems the Devil can divert them too easily. . . .

"Even the big, impressive-looking *capitán* came and asked me to let his clearing grow well. You have to keep telling them all the time that no person on earth can do such things, only God." (Muller 1952, 60)

7. Galvão suggested that "there had been a scission [between two brothers] reinforced by succession. In order to assume leadership, the chief identified himself with one group [Marakaiaui, or "little Jurupary"], the place and his kin coming to form the nucleus of the new group. The chief also affirmed the identity of the two groups, but uses preferentially the denomination of Marakaiaui" (Fieldnotes, 1954).

8. According to Stoll, her campaign against drinking *caxiri* and dancing was predicated on the idea that "dancing leads to immorality" (cited in Stoll 1982, 170).

9. There were other motives expressed by Galvão's informants. The Oalipere-dakenai chief Leopoldino of Hekoari—the same whom José de Carvalho called "a great friend of the whites," an ally of the S.P.I. and rubber merchants, a *tuxaua* appointed by Valentim Garrido in the 1940s, and one of Galvão's and Saake's principal informants in Baniwa myth and ritual—seems to have been an early follower of Sophie, for in her memoir, she praises his great help in translating and interpreting (1952, 50). Yet, no more than a few years later, in 1954, he expressed to Galvão his bitterness and remarked on the irony of the *crentes*: "those people who only know how to sing the prayers of Sophie and are against *caxiri* and *cajuba*." When his life was later threatened by the *crentes* of the upper Içana, he sought protection from the Padres at the mission.

10. The figure of "Correa" to whom Laureano refers seems to have been important in the production of the new religion. He was supposed to have introduced the ritual of communion, or drinking the "blood of Christ" at Santa Céias. Most likely, this self-made "John the Baptist" was also responsible for attributing the title of "saint" to Sophie. And it was most likely Correa who led a mass movement of Baniwa down the Içana bearing banners and singing psalms (the incident to which Galvão refers in the opening quotation of Part IV). My impression, however, is that his understanding of Sophie's evangelicalism moved in a different direction from that which she actually preached—more like the historical saint-cults of popular Catholicism or a renewal of Kamiko's "song of the cross." Correa was eventually forced by the S.P.I. to leave the country and sought refuge on the Querary in Colombia.

11. Sometimes the houses are open-air shelters without walls or with simply poles for walls without mud coverings. Sometimes they have plaited thatch roofs or walls of bark, like the styles of the old longhouses, except they are single-family units. Moreover, they may be houses with finely painted mud walls with many tiny individual rooms inside, or houses with old and decaying, crumbling walls. These different styles are striking to someone coming from Catholic villages where houses are generally uniform earth, painted

white with red and blue trim, usually with one large room or two (a receiving and visiting room, and a sleeping compartment with kitchen).

At times I heard that *crente* house styles reflect the millenarianism of the '50s and '60s, for at that time they were told by the missionaries to make their houses airy and light so that when a person died, it would be easier for the soul to ascend up to heaven. Also at the "end of the world," the celestial ascension of the saved would be easier. If this characterized the thinking at that time, in the '70s it mattered very little to people. Rather, house styles were one among many distinguishing features of the *crente* way of life that differentiated them from Catholics.

12. *Crente* leadership consists of the following positions: *ancianos*, or "elders," who have been baptized by the missions and who act as daily prayer leaders and organizers in any of the assemblies; *diakonos*, or "deacons," who specifically act as prayer leaders in the Conferences, and who enforce order in their proceedings; and *pastores*, "pastors," who are the proselytizers, usually one per community, who organize and lead all prayer activities and preparations for Conferences and who make periodic visits to other *crente* communities to instruct *Deo iako*. Pastors are often the preachers at the Conferences and have the power to baptize and officiate at naming ceremonies, marriages, and so on.

13. Hence the omnipresent thick black books (New Testaments) lying about on benches in *crente* villages. These are translated in two dialects. Besides these, there are innumerable mission tracts and hymnals, many in Portuguese, distributed by the missionaries, mostly dealing with the high morality expected. New Testaments and hymnals are used daily.

The New Testaments seem to symbolize the newly acquired knowledge of the whites, a sort of key to the reproduction of the new world the *crentes* sought to create. Whereas before, elders were seen as masters of an esoteric knowledge which reproduced society through initiation rites, there emerged a counterpart in elderly pastors who, it is said, always carry around one or two big Bibles under their arms.

Anyone who wishes to may receive instruction in literacy at the American evangelical mission at the mouth of the Içana or in São Gabriel da Cachoeira.

Bibliography

Archives

Coleção Eduardo Galvão. Biblioteca do Museu Paraense Emílio Goeldi, Seção de Arquivo. Belém do Pará. Four boxes of field notebooks and reports, 1951–1954. Referred to in text citations as Fieldnotes.

Museu do Índio, Seção de Arquivo. Fundação Nacional do Índio. Rio de Janeiro. Reports and official correspondence from indigenous posts on the Upper Rio Negro, from 1911 to 1959.

Primeira Comissão Brasileira Demarcadora de Limites. Ministério das Relações Exteriores. Belém do Pará. Technical reports of expeditions undertaken in the years 1934, 1936.

Publications and Papers

Abreu, Stela Azevedo de. 1995. Aleluia: O banco de luz. Master's thesis. Departamento de Antropologia, Universidade Estadual de Campinas.

Agüero, Oscar. 1992. *The millennium among the Tupi-Cocama*. Uppsala: Uppsala Research Reports in Cultural Anthropology.

Albert, Bruce. 1988. La fumée du metal: Histoire et représentations du contact chez les Yanomami du Brésil. *L'Homme* 28, nos. 106–107 (Apr.–Dec.): 87–119.

Andrello, Geraldo. 1993. Os Taurepang: Memoria e profetismo no século XX. Master's thesis. Departamento de Antropologia, Universidade Estadual de Campinas.

Barabas, Alícia. 1989. *Utopias indias: Movimentos socioreligiosos en México*. Mexico City: Colección Enlace.

———, ed. 1994. *Religiosidad y resistencia indígenas hacia el fin del milenio*. Colección Biblioteca Abya-Yala, No. 11. Quito: Ediciones Abya-Yala.

Basso, Ellen, ed. 1990. *Native Latin American cultures through their discourse*. Bloomington: Folklore Institute, Indiana University.

Bidou, Patrice. 1986. Le mythe: Une machine à traiter l'histoire. *L'Homme* 26, no. 100 (Oct.–Dec.): 65–98.

Biocca, Ettore. 1965. *Viaggi tra gli Indi: Alto Rio Negro–Alto Orinoco; Appunti di un biólogo*. Vol. 1, *Tukano-Tariana-Baniwa-Maku*. Rome.

Brandão de Amorim, Antonio. 1987. *Lendas em nheengatu e em português*. Manaus: Fundo Editorial–ACA.

Brown, Michael. 1991. Beyond resistance: A comparative study of utopian renewal in Amazonia. *Ethnohistory* 38 (4): 388–413.

Carneiro da Cunha, Manuela. 1973. Logique du mythe et de l'action: Le mouvement messianique Canela de 1963. *L'Homme* 13, no. 4: 5–37.

———. 1978. *Os mortos e os outros*. São Paulo: Hucitec.

Carvalho, José Candido M. de. 1952. *Notas de viagem ao Rio Negro*. Publicações Avulsas do Museu Nacional. Rio de Janeiro: Universidade do Brasil.

Cipoletti, M. S., and E. Jean Langdon, eds. 1992. *La muerte y el más allá en las culturas indígenas latinoamericanas*. Colección 500 Años, No. 58. Quito: Ediciones Abya-Yala.

Clastres, Hélène. 1978. *Terra sem mal: O profetismo Tupi-Guarani*. São Paulo: Brasiliense.

Clastres, Pierre. 1987. *Society against the state*. New York: Zone Books.

Colini, G. A. 1885. La provincia delle Amazoni. *Bollettino della Società Geografica Italiana* (Rome) 22: 136–141, 193–204.

Colson, Audrey Butt. [1960] 1967. The birth of a religion: The origins of a semi-Christian religion among the Akawaio. In *Gods and rituals: Readings in religious belief and practice*, ed. J. Middleton. New York: Natural History Press. Originally published in *Journal of the Royal Anthropological Institute of Great Britain and Ireland* 90 (1960): 66–106.

Correa, François. 1987. Medicina tradicional Cubeo. *Boletín de Antropología, Universidad de Antioquia* 6 (21): 141–159.

Dean, Warren. 1989. *A luta pela borracha no Brasil*. São Paulo: Nobel.

Doyle, Michael. n.d. Aspects of Baniwa medicinal flora and ethnoecology. Manaus: Fundação Universidade do Amazonas, unpublished ms.

Galvão, Eduardo. 1959. Aculturação indígena no Rio Negro. *Boletim do Museu Paraense Emílio Goeldi*, n.s., *Antropologia* 7: 1–60.

Geertz, Clifford. 1983. *Local knowledge: Further essays in interpretive anthropology*. New York: Basic.

Goldman, Irving. 1963. *The Cubeo: Indians of the Northwest Amazon*. Illinois Studies in Anthropology 2. Urbana: University of Illinois Press.

———. 1981. The New Tribes Mission among Cubeo. *ARC Bulletin* (Boston) 9: 7–8.

Graham, Laura. 1995. *Performing dreams: The discourse of immortality among the Xavante of central Brazil*. Austin: University of Texas Press.

Hill, Jonathan. 1984a. Los misioneros y las fronteras. *América Indígena* 44 (1): 183–190.

———. 1984b. Social equality and ritual hierarchy: The Arawakan Wakuenai of Venezuela. *American Ethnologist* 11: 528–544.

———. 1985a. Agnatic sibling relations and rank in northern Arawakan myth and social life. In *Working papers on South American Indians*, ed. Judith Shapiro, 25–33. Bennington, Vt.: Bennington College.

———. 1985b. Myth, spirit-naming, and the art of microtonal rising: Childbirth rituals of the Arawakan Wakuenai. *Latin American Music Review* 6 (1): 1–30.

———. 1987a. Representaciones musicales como estructuras adaptativas. *Montalban* 17: 67–101.

———. 1987b. Wakuenai ceremonial exchange in the Northwest Amazon. *Journal of Latin American Lore* 13 (2): 183–224.

———, ed. 1988. *Rethinking history and myth: Indigenous South American perspectives on the past.* Urbana: University of Illinois Press.

———. [1989] 1993. *Keepers of the sacred chants: The poetics of ritual power in an Amazonian society.* Tucson: University of Arizona Press. (The manuscript version, used in this book, has the earlier date of 1989.)

———, ed. 1993. Discourses and the expression of personhood in South American inter-ethnic relations. *South American Indian Studies*, no. 3 (October). Bennington, Vt.: Bennington College.

Hill, Jonathan, and Emilio Moran. 1983. Adaptive strategies of Wakuenai people to the oligotrophic rain forest of the Rio Negro basin. In *Adaptive responses of native Amazonians*, ed. William Vickers and Raymond Hames, 113–135. New York: Academic Press.

Hill, Jonathan, and Robin M. Wright. 1988. Time, narrative and ritual: Historical interpretations from an Amazonian society. In Hill 1988, 78–105.

Hinnells, John R., ed. 1984. *The Penguin dictionary of religions.* London: Penguin Books.

Hugh-Jones, Christine. 1979. *From the Milk River: Spatial and temporal processes in Northwest Amazonia.* Cambridge: Cambridge University Press.

Hugh-Jones, Stephen. 1979. *The palm and the Pleiades.* Cambridge: Cambridge University Press.

———. 1988. The gun and the bow: Myths of white men and Indians. *L'Homme* 128, nos. 106–107 (Apr.–Dec.): 138–156.

———. 1989. Shamans, prophets, priests, and pastors. Paper presented in the workshop on "Shamanism, colonialism, and the state." King's College, October 3.

Humboldt, Alexander von. 1907. *Personal narratives of travels to the equinoctial regions of South America during the years 1799–1804.* 3 vols. Translated and edited by Thomasina Ross. London.

Journet, Nicolas. 1980–1981. Los Curripaco del Río Isana: Economía y sociedad. *Revista Colombiana de Antropología* (Bogotá) 23: 125–181.

———. 1993. Hommes et femmes dans la terminologie de parenté curripaco. *Amerindia: Revue d'Ethnolinguistique Amérindiennne* (Paris), no. 18: 41–74.

———. 1995. *La paix des jardins: Structures sociales des indiens Curripaco du haut Rio Negro (Colombie).* Paris: Institut d'Ethnologie, Musée de l'Homme.

Knobloch, Franz. 1972. *Geschichte der Missionen unter den Indianer-Stämmen des Rio Negro-tales. Zeitschrift für Missioneswissenschaft und Religioneswissenschaft.* Nos. 2–4. Münster: Verlag Aschendorff.

———. 1974. The Baniwa Indians and their reaction against integration. *Mankind* 15 (2): 83–91.

Koch-Grünberg, Theodor. 1907. *Südamerikanische Felszeichnungen.* Berlin.

———. 1911. Aruak-sprachen Nordwestbrasiliens . . . *Mitteilungen der Anthropologischen Gesellschaften* 41: 33–267.

————. 1967. *Zwei Jahre unter den Indianern: Reisen in Nordwest Brasilien, 1903–1905*. Stuttgart: Strecher und Shroder.

Langdon, E. Jean. 1996. *Xamanismo no Brasil: Novas perspectivas*. Florianópolis, S.C., Brazil: UFSC Editora.

Lopes de Sousa, Marechal Boanerges. 1928. *Do Rio Negro ao Orenoco: A terra—o homem*. Rio de Janeiro: CNPI.

MacReigh, Gordon. 1926. *White waters and black*. New York: Century.

Matos Arvelo, Martin. 1912. *Vida indiana*. Barcelona: Casa Editorial Mauci.

Meira, Márcio. 1993. O tempo dos patrões: Extrativismo de piaçava entre os índios do rio Xié (Alto Rio Negro). Master's thesis, Departamento de Antropologia, Universidade Estadual de Campinas.

Melatti, Julio César. 1972. *O messianismo Krahó*. São Paulo: Herder.

Meliá, Bartomeu. 1986. *El Guaraní—conquistado y reducido*. Biblioteca Paraguaya de Antropología 5. Asunción: CEADUC.

Muller, Sophie. 1952. *Beyond civilization*. Chico, Calif.: Brown Gold Publications.

Nimuendaju, Curt. 1950. Reconhecimento dos rios Içana, Ayari e Uaupés. *Journal de la Société des Américanistes de Paris* 39: 125–183, 44: 149–178.

Oliveira, Adélia de. 1975. A terminologia de parentesco Baniwa—1971. *Boletim do Museu Paraense Emílio Goeldi*, n.s., *Antropologia* 56: 1–36.

————. 1979. Depoimentos Baniwa sobre as relações entre índios e "civilisados" no Rio Negro. *Boletim do Museu Paraense Emílio Goeldi*, n.s., *Antropologia* 72: 1–31.

Oliveira, Adélia de, and Eduardo Galvão. 1973. A situação atual dos Baniwa (Alto Rio Negro)—1971. *O Museu Goeldi no Ano do Sesquicentenário* 20: 27–40.

Oliveira Filho, João Pacheco de. 1988. *"O nosso governo": Os Ticuna e o regime tutelar*. São Paulo/Brasília: Editora Marca Zero/MCT-CNPq.

Oro, Ari. 1989. *Na Amazonia um messias de índios e brancos: Traços para uma antropologia do messianismo*. Petrópolis: Editora Vozes/PUC-RS.

Porro, Antonio. 1987–1989. Mitologia heróica e messianismo na Amazônia seiscentista. *Revista de Antropologia* (São Paulo) 30–32: 383–389.

Ramos, Alcida R. 1990. *Memórias sanumá: Espaço e tempo em uma sociedade Yanomami*. São Paulo: Editora Marca Zero/Editora Universidade de Brasília.

Regan, Jaime. 1993. *Hacia la tierra sin mal: La religión del pueblo en la Amazonia*. 2d ed. Iquitos: CETA.

Reichel-Dolmatoff, Gerardo. 1975. *The shaman and the jaguar*. Philadelphia: Temple University Press.

————. 1985. Tapir avoidance in the Colombian Northwest Amazon. In *Animal myths and metaphors in South America*, ed. G. Urton, 107–143. Salt Lake City: University of Utah Press.

Ribeiro, Berta. 1980. A civilização da palha: A arte do trançado dos índios do Brasil. Doctoral dissertation, Universidade de São Paulo.

Rice, Hamilton. 1914. Further explorations in the Northwest Amazon basin. *Geographical Journal* 44: 140–168.

Rosaldo, Renato I. 1980. *Ilongot Headhunting, 1883–1974: A Study in society and history*. Stanford: Stanford University Press.

Saake, Wilhelm. 1958a. Aus der Uberlieferungen der Baniwa. *Staden-Jahrbuch* 6: 83–91.

———. 1958b. Die Juruparilegende bei den Baniwa des Rio Issana. *Proceedings of the 32nd International Congress of Americanists.* Copenhagen.

———. 1958c. Mythen über Inapirikuli, des Kulturheros der Baniwa. *Zeitschrift für Ethnologie* 93: 260–273.

———. 1959–1960a. Iniciação de um pajé entre os Baniwa e a cura de marecaimbara. *Sociologia* 6: 424–442.

———. 1959–1960b. Kari, der Kulturheros, feiert mit den Baniwa-Indianern das erste Dabukurifest. *Staden-Jahrbuch* 7–8: 193–201.

Santos Granero, Fernando. 1993. From prisoner of the group to darling of the gods: An approach to the issue of power in lowland South America. *L'Homme* 33, nos. 126–128 (Apr.–Dec.): 213–230.

Schaden, Egon. 1976. Le messianisme en Amérique de Sud. In *Histoire des religions*, Vol. 3. of *Encyclopédie de la Pléiade*, ed. Henri-Charles Peuch Paris: Gallimard.

Sherzer, Joel. 1983. *Kuna ways of speaking: An ethnographic perspective.* Austin: University of Texas Press.

Stoll, David. 1982. *Fishers of men or founders of empire: The Wycliffe Bible Translators in Latin America.* London: Zed Press.

Stradelli, Ermanno. 1890. L'Uaupés e gli Uaupés. *Bollettino della Società Geografica Italiana.* Série 3, 3: 425–453.

Sullivan, Lawrence. 1988. *Icanchu's drum: An orientation to meaning in South American religions.* New York: Macmillan Press.

Sweet, David G. 1974. A rich realm of nature destroyed: The Amazon valley, 1640–1750. Dissertation, University of Wisconsin–Madison. Ann Arbor: University Microfilms.

Taylor, Gerald. 1991. *Introdução à língua Baniwa do Içana.* Campinas: Editora UNICAMP.

———. 1993. Breve léxico da língua Baniwa do Içana: Document du travail. URA 1026 du CNRS Ethnolinguistique Amérindiennes. Paris, working paper.

Turner, Terence. 1988. Ethno-ethnohistory: Myth and history in native South American representations of contact with Western society. In Hill, ed., 1988, 235–281.

———, ed. 1993. Cosmology, values, and inter-ethnic contact in South America. *South American Indian Studies*, no. 2 (September). Bennington: Bennington College.

U.S. Army Corps of Engineers. 1943. Report on the Orinoco-Cassiquiare-Negro Waterway, Venezuela-Colombia-Brazil, prepared for the Coordinator of Inter-American Affairs. Washington, D.C.

Vidal O., Silvia M. 1987. El modelo del proceso migratorio pre-hispánico de los Piapoco: Hipótesis y evidencias. Master's thesis, Instituto Venezolano de Investigaciones Científicas, Caracas.

Viveiros de Castro, E., and M. Carneiro da Cunha. 1985. Vingança e temporalidade: Os Tupinambá. *Journal de la Société des Américanistes* 71: 191–208.

Wallace, Alfred R. [1853] 1969. *A narrative of travels on the Amazon and Rio Negro*. New York.

Wright, Robin M. 1981a. Demons with no heads: NTM and the Baniwa of Brazil. *ARC Bulletin*, special issue on "The New Tribes Mission in Amazonia." Boston: ARC.

———. 1981b. The history and religion of the Baniwa peoples of the upper Rio Negro valley. Ph. D. dissertation, Stanford University. Ann Arbor: University Microfilms.

———. 1983. Lucha y supervivencia en el noroeste de la Amazonia. *América Indígena* 43 (3): 537–554.

———. 1986. As guerras do Ouro no Alto Rio Negro. In *Povos indígenas no Brasil—85/86*, ed. C. A. Ricardo, 85–87. São Paulo: CEDI.

———. 1987–1989. Uma história de resistência: Os heróis Baniwa e suas lutas. *Revista de Antropologia*, 30–32: 355–381.

———. 1990. Guerras e alianças nas histórias dos Baniwa do Alto Rio Negro. *Ciências Sociais Hoje* (São Paulo), 217–236.

———. 1992a. Guardians of the cosmos: Baniwa shamans and prophets, pt. 1. *History of Religions* (University of Chicago), August, 32–58.

———. 1992b. Guardians of the cosmos: Baniwa shamans and prophets, pt. 2. *History of Religions* (University of Chicago), November, 126–145.

———. 1992c."Uma conspiração contra os civilisados": História, política e ideologias dos movimentos milenaristas dos Arawak e Tukano do noroeste da Amazonia. *Anuário Antropológico* 89: 191–234.

———. 1993. Pursuing the spirit: Semantic construction in Hohodene Kalidzimai chants for initiation. *Amerindia: Revue d'Ethnolinguistique Amérindiennne* (Paris), no. 18: 1–40.

———. 1993–1994. Umawali: Hohodene myths of the anaconda, father of the fish. *Bulletin Suisse des Américanistes* (Geneva), nos. 57–58: 37–48.

———. n.d. Uma política de dividir-e-conquistar: Os Baniwa, a mineração e o Projeto Calha Norte. Unpublished ms.

Wright, Robin M., and Jonathan D. Hill. 1986. History, ritual, and myth: Nineteenth century millenarian movements in the Northwest Amazon. *Ethnohistory* 33 (1): 31–54.

Index

Abreu, Stela Azevedo de, 11
Agüero, Oscar, 10
Albert, Bruce, 99
Andrello, Geraldo, 11, 278
animal myths, 40
Anizetto (Baniwa messiah), 223–224, 232, 243, 247, 291, 293, 300n1
Apakwa Hekwapi (Other World), 43, 66, 67, 69–72, 203

Barabas, Alícia, 1
Basso, Ellen, 26
Bidou, Patrice, 99
Biocca, Ettore, 298n4
birth chants and orations, 148, 195, 204–208
bone symbolism, 37, 208–209, 213–214
Brazilian Air Force (FAB), 24, 83, 175, 245, 282, 301n15
Brotherhood of the Holy Cross Movement, 9, 10
Brown, Michael, 6–7, 247, 292–294

caraiurú (red paint), 178, 180, 188–189, 190
Carneiro da Cunha, Manuela, 2, 3, 9, 104
Carvalho, José Candido M. de, 222, 234, 235, 255, 302n9
catastrophes and regeneration, 12, 25, 45, 100, 104, 105, 134, 147, 154, 183, 218, 288, 289, 294
Chicle Development Company, 232

chiefs, 109, 112, 220, 221, 222, 228, 235, 236, 261, 293
Clastres, Hélène and Pierre, 2, 3, 6, 7
Colson, Audrey Butt, 10
conflagrations, 4, 30, 39–40, 43, 47, 68, 153–154, 156, 159, 183, 184, 291
conversion, 217–285
"Correa," 268, 274, 302n10
cosmogony, 25, 295n1
curing chants and orations, 67, 86, 88–89, 90–94, 183, 256, 277

danaime (shades of the dead), 186, 198, 298n2
death, reversible and irreversible, 163, 165–193, 200–201, 204, 289
death chants and orations, 194–200, 203–205
demonology, 242–255
descents to the Rio Negro, 103, 108
disease, 108, 222–223, 228–236 passim, 247, 254–255
Dzulíferi, 58, 69–93 passim

eenunai (thunders), 40–44, 147, 148, 173, 177–179, 182–189, 197–198, 200, 206
ethnopoetics, 25–26
evil omens (hinimai), 41, 44, 45, 146, 183, 186, 195, 198, 200, 299n9
exchange, 87, 139, 141, 145, 152, 181, 195, 199, 215, 275, 287, 289, 301n2. See also kamaratakan; koada; pudali

www.ingramcontent.com/pod-product-compliance
Ingram Content Group UK Ltd.
Pitfield, Milton Keynes, MK11 3LW, UK
UKHW010305240525
458861UK00002B/255